Teaching 3: Evaluation of Instruction

Wesley C. Becker

Professor of Special Education University of Oregon

Siegfried Engelmann

Professor of Special Education University of Oregon

SCIENCE RESEARCH ASSOCIATES, INC.
Chicago, Palo Alto, Toronto, Henley-on-Thames, Sydney, Paris, Stuttgart

A Subsidiary of IBM

To Julie

ISBN 0-574-23035-1

Library of Congress Cataloging in Publication Data

Becker, Wesley C   1928–
   Teaching—a modular revision of Teaching, a
course in applied psychology.

   Includes bibliographical references and indexes.
   CONTENTS: 1. Classroom management.—2. Cognitive learning and instruction.—3. Evaluation of
instruction.
   1. Educational psychology. I. Engelmann,
Siegfried, joint author. II. Thomas, Donald R.,
joint author. III. Title.
LB1051.B2985   1975   371.1'02   74-31012
ISBN 0-574-18025-7 (v. 1)

contents

iii

preface

This three-part series is basically a psychology of teaching. It attempts to cover the knowledge and skills important to the classroom teacher arising from the scientific study of behavior. *Teaching 1* concentrated on classroom management; *Teaching 2* focused on instruction and the learning process; *Teaching 3* is concerned with decision making by the teacher, or what is commonly called the evaluation of instruction.

Decision making for the teacher falls into three main areas: the initial adoption of programs and procedures, on-going evaluation of students and programs, and longer-term evaluation of students and programs. Usually, the teacher has help, in the form of curriculum specialists and research directors, in making decisions on program adoptions and outcome evaluation. In fact, these decisions often are made for teachers, whether they like it or not. However, as often as not, the teacher is on his or her own when it comes to these decisions. In any case, it is important for every teacher to be informed about basic evaluation processes in order to intelligently defend good practices and criticize poor ones.

In this text, we attempt to build from simpler concepts and procedures to more complex ones. We begin with a detailed look at testing geared to the on-going evaluation of a program (process evaluation) and move toward a concern with outcome evaluation with criterion-referenced and then norm-referenced tests. Statistical concepts essential to understanding issues in testing and evaluation are introduced as they are needed. Issues in the design of research studies are examined for their relevance in outcome evaluation as well as their relevance in evaluating claims relating to program effectiveness and effective teaching procedures.

The skills needed for evaluating programs for adoption consist of a knowledge of the essential requirements for learning to occur as covered in *Teaching 2*, and a critical understanding of good research methods in program evaluation.

We close *Teaching 3* by revisiting the issue of the role of intelligence in learning (see *Teaching 2*, unit 12), sometimes called the aptitude-achievement issue. This is probably the social issue of our time as far as teachers are concerned. Is it really okay not to teach some kids because they are presumed not to have the aptitude? Or, is this a phony issue? We hope you have a fuller understanding of this issue and take a strong position on it by the time you complete this text.

We wish to thank Kathy Kjosness and Dorothy Mellin for their help in preparing the manuscript.

to the instructor: course organization

This course is designed to operate with minimal lectures. The *Instructor's Manual* that accompanies this text makes it possible for the instructor to use a variety of procedures. The following suggestions represent teaching formats that have been found to be effective:

Self-Paced Progress

Each student reads a unit, does the exercises, checks his own exercises, goes over the discussion questions, and then is checked out by another student who has already passed that unit. In conducting the checkout, the examining student uses the Instructor's Manual as a source of questions and criteria for acceptable responses. Tests are taken as scheduled.

Leader-Paced Progress, Students as Group Leaders

In this course format, each student reads the assigned unit, completes his exercises and checks them, and prepares for the group session, being sure he can answer each of the discussion questions. At the group session, each student is asked to write out answers to two of the questions selected by the instructor. Papers are turned in for credit. Then the instructor appoints one-fourth of the class to be group leaders for that session. Small groups of four are formed. Each group leader then uses the Instructor's Manual to take the other three students through the objects of the unit. The leader asks questions from the manual and the students take turns answering. The leader and the group members help when there are mistakes or omissions.

Leader-Paced Progress, Former Students as Group Leaders

In this format there is an instructor and group leader for each ten students. The students do a lesson, complete the exercises, and check their answers prior to the group discussion session. The group leaders have the only available Instructor's Manuals. At the group sessions, group members are asked in turn to respond to questions. The whole group writes answers to two questions each session, or takes a ten-minute quiz at each lecture session. Remedial assignments are made when performance is not adequate.

Each of these course organization formats attempts to provide appropriate consequences for appropriate study behavior and thereby increase the chances of each student being successful in mastering the objectives of the course. Whatever procedures are used in your course, keep in mind that *knowing* is not *doing*. Aim for changes in what students do as well as what they say.

to the student: how to use this text

Our experience suggests that you will gain the most from this text if you follow these steps.

1 Read a unit.
2 Do the self-test. If you miss 0 or 1 item, skip the programed practice exercise and do the other exercises and discussion questions. If you make more than one error, do the section called programed practice.
3 When an item gives you trouble, return to the text to study the problem in context.
4 Calculate the percentage of items correct and record it for each programed practice exercise.
5 If a score on a programed practice exercise is above 90 percent, go on to the discussion questions and other exercises. If a score is much below 90 percent, review the unit before going on to the discussion questions.
6 In answering the discussion questions, be prepared to give your answers orally or in writing. The questions serve as a basis for discussion in the group sessions.

Acknowledgments

P. 8: From *Distar® Reading I, Teacher Presentation Book A,* Second Edition by Siegfried Engelmann and Elaine C. Bruner. © 1974, 1969, Science Research Associates, Inc. Used by permission of the publisher.

Pp. 43-44: From *Distar® Reading I, Teacher's Guide,* Second Edition by Siegfried Engelmann and Elaine C. Bruner. © 1974, 1969, Science Research Associates, Inc. Used by permission of the publisher.

P. 50: Reprinted by permission from S. Engelmann, *Survival Skills Reading Test,* published by E-B Press, Eugene, Oregon.

P. 66: Reprinted by permission from Reading I Continuous Progress Test, to be published by Science Research Associates, Inc.

P. 82: Reprinted by permission from Don Bushell, Jr., U. of Kansas, and Josephine E. Thex, Labre Indian School, Ashland, Montana 59003.

Pp. 90, 91, 92: From Don Bushell, Jr., *Classroom Behavior: A Little Book for Teachers,* © 1973, pp. 40, 44, 46. Reprinted by permission of Prentice-Hall, Inc., Englewood Cliffs, New Jersey.

P. 93: Reprinted by permission from R. Tony Eichelberger, Learning Research and Development Center, U. of Pittsburgh.

P. 124: Reprinted by permission of A.M. Hofmeister from a text in preparation.

P. 129: Reprinted by permission from S. Engelmann, *Survival Skills Reading Test,* published by E-B Press, Eugene, Oregon.

Pp. 130, 131: From *Prescriptive Reading Inventory.* Copyright © 1972 by McGraw-Hill, Inc. Reprinted by permission of the publisher, CTB/McGraw-Hill, Del Monte Research Park, Monterey, CA 93940. All rights reserved. Printed in the U.S.A.

Pp. 154-155: Reproduced by special permission from the *Gilmore Oral Reading Test,* copyright © 1968, by Harcourt Brace Jovanovich, Inc.

P. 159: From *California Achievement Tests, 1-A* devised by Ernest W. Tiegs and Willis W. Clark. Copyright © 1957, 1963, 1970 by McGraw-Hill, Inc. Reprinted by permission of the publisher, CTB/McGraw-Hill, Del Monte Research Park, Monterey, CA 93940. All rights reserved. Printed in the U.S.A.

P. 160: Reproduced by special permission from the *Metropolitan Achievement Tests,* copyright © 1970, by Harcourt Brace Jovanovich, Inc.

P. 161: Reproduced by special permission from the *Stanford Achievement Test,* copyright © 1952, by Harcourt Brace Jovanovich, Inc.

Pp. 162-163: From *SRA Achievement Series, Multilevel Edition, Form D* prepared by Louis P. Thorpe, D. Welty Lefever, and Robert A. Naslund. © 1963, Science Research Associates, Inc. Used by permission of the publisher.

Pp. 187-189: From *Manual California Achievement Tests, 1-A* devised by Ernest W. Tiegs and Willis W. Clark. Copyright © 1957, 1963, 1970 by McGraw-Hill, Inc. Reprinted by permission of the publisher, CTB/McGraw-Hill, Del Monte Research Park, Monterey, CA 93940. All rights reserved. Printed in the U.S.A.

P. 191: Reproduced by special permission from the *Metropolitan Achievement Tests, Primary II Teacher's Handbook,* copyright © 1971, by Harcourt Brace Jovanovich, Inc.

P. 226: Reproduced by special permission from the *Metropolitan Achievement Tests, Primary II Teacher's Handbook,* copyright © 1971, by Harcourt Brace Jovanovich, Inc.

P. 227: From Harold Gulliksen, *Theory of Mental Tests,* © 1950 by John Wiley & Sons, New York.

P. 263: From C.H. Bishop, "Transfer of Effects of Word and Letter Training in Reading," in *Journal of Verbal Learning & Verbal Behavior,* vol. 3, 1964.

P. 264: From E. J. Gibson, "Learning to Read," in *Science,* vol. 148, 1965.

P. 285: Reprinted by permission of the *Phi Delta Kappan* and Emery P. Bliesmer.

Pp. 300, 301, 302: From pp. 292-294 in *Essentials of Psychological Testing,* 3rd ed., by Lee J. Cronbach. Copyright © 1970 by Lee J. Cronbach. By permission of Harper & Row, Publishers, Inc.

unit 1

Kinds of Tests: Norm-Referenced and Criterion-Referenced Tests

objectives

When you complete this unit you should be able to—

1 State the major differences between norm-referenced and criterion-referenced tests and give examples of each.
2 Describe and evaluate two major approaches to developing criterion-referenced tests to evaluate instruction.
3 List the four steps for planning instruction recommended by Popham.
4 Describe how tests are used in monitoring IPI and Distar instruction.
5 Indicate where norm-referenced, objectives-referenced, and instructional-program-referenced tests are especially useful.

lesson

This text is concerned with evaluation procedures which can help teachers *improve instruction.* Our goal is to provide the teacher-to-be with an understanding of the problems and issues in the evaluation of instruction and to provide some potentially useful procedures for making decisions relating to instruction. There is another major function of evaluation in education. Tests are often used to measure student achievements, aptitudes, and interests to provide information for future educational and career decisions. This text *is not* concerned with evaluation for *student guidance.*

Technologies for evaluating instruction are currently unsettled. The methods that have been in common use for the past 40 to 50 years are being questioned, and better methods have not necessarily been established. Because of the unsettled nature of the field, it is extremely important for the teacher to be aware of the issues. We will begin an examination of the issues by looking at the general properties of two kinds of tests commonly used to evaluate instruction.

1

Defining Norm-Referenced and Criterion-Referenced Tests

A test is a systematic procedure for assessing some behavior. The systematic procedure specifies the stimulus conditions under which the behavior occurs and gives the response requirements. Once a person performs the tasks specified by a test, it is necessary to interpret the result. Interpreting a test score involves making comparisons. When the comparison made is to the distribution of scores obtained by other persons taking the same test, the interpretation is called *norm-referenced*. When the comparison is made to some specified standard of performance, the interpretation is called *criterion-referenced*.[1] Figure 1.1 illustrates that norm-referenced interpretations involve comparisons of individuals. Mildred has the highest score in the group. Angie has the lowest. Ziggy and Julie are in the middle. When we say a student is in the top 10 percent, we are making a norm-referenced comparison. When we say John's grade level in reading is 4.2, we are making a norm-referenced comparison. John obtajned the same score that is obtained by the average student at grade level 4.2. Most traditional tests of achievement and ability are norm-referenced.

With a criterion-referenced test, the score of an individual is compared to some standard or criterion. For example, to pass a test for a driver's license, it is necessary to score *above 85 percent* on the written test of driving rules and to score *pass* on each performance objective on the road test. This standard must be met by everyone. What other people score makes no difference in determining pass or fail. On the performance tests, each component is graded *pass* or *fail* according to whether the defined performances are present. Does your performance in controlling the vehicle in traffic, parking, use of signals, and following the rules of safety meet the criteria established to define a good driver? When the teacher builds a test based on a given instructional goal and then requires each student to perform at 90 percent mastery before going on to a new goal, he or she is using a criterion-referenced test.

Norm-referenced tests are useful in selecting *relatively high-* or *relatively low-scoring* groups. Colleges look for students who score high on the Scho-

| Angie | Susan | Ziggy | Julie | John | Mildred |

Low ⟵——————————————— Scale ———————————————⟶ High

Figure 1.1 Norm-Referenced Test Compares People to Each Other

lastic Aptitude Test. Special Education classes are set up for students who score low on intelligence tests. Criterion-referenced tests are useful when one is concerned with specified standards of performance. For example, the state of Oregon has mandated that schools establish performance requirements specifying the minimum basic skills a student must demonstrate to receive a high school diploma. When *instruction* is concerned with the development of skills that meet specifiable standards, criterion-referenced tests are especially useful for evaluating that instruction.

It is possible that all students going through a given instructional program could pass the criterion and show mastery of the objectives tested. Such an outcome would be very unlikely with a norm-referenced test because of the way items are selected. Items that everyone passes (or fails) are eliminated from norm-referenced tests because the goal is to make each item useful in contributing to a spread of test scores. An item that everyone passed would make no contribution to measuring individual differences. If the goal is to evaluate instruction, items that everyone passes after instruction, but not before, might be very valuable in showing the effects of instruction. There are other problems associated with norm-referenced tests. For example, because norm-referenced tests are not related to specific instructional objectives, they are difficult to use for evaluating instruction. We will return to the problems and potentials of norm-referenced tests in unit 9.

Criterion-Referenced Tests

The main use of criterion-referenced tests in education today is to demonstrate where instruction has occurred and where it has not. There are essentially two approaches to the developing of criterion-referenced tests. One approach begins with a set of behavioral objectives or statements of what a student should be able to do after instruction and builds a test to measure each objective as stated. We will call a test built with this approach an objectives-based test. The second approach begins with an instructional program and sets out to build a test(s) of what is taught in the program. We will call a test built with this approach an instructional-program-based test.

Driving Test (a hypothetical example)

X		X	X		Pass
	X			X	Fail
Rules of the Road	Vehicle Control in Traffic	Backing-Parking Road Test	Signals	Follows Safety Rules	

(Passed 3 of 5 criteria)

Figure 1.2 Criterion-Referenced Test—Compares a Person to a Standard of Performance

Objectives-Based Tests

The use of criterion-referenced tests is one key to the popularity of the behavioral objectives movement.[2] Tests are written for each objective so that the teacher will know when the objective has been reached. Popham has gone so far as to rename the teaching-by-objectives movement *criterion-referenced instruction*. He recommends that teachers use the following strategy in planning for instruction.[3]

1 *Statement of objectives.*   What will the students be able to do when instruction is completed? The objectives must be stated in terms of observable performance. For example: The student will be able to spell with a 90% accuracy any sample of 25 words taken from a specified list of 1,000 common irregular words.
2 *Preassessment.*   This involves a test for preskills assumed by the objectives and a test to see that the student cannot already perform the objectives.
3 *Instruction.*   General guidelines are provided to the teacher for teaching an objective, but the teacher is expected to work out his/her own lesson plan. The teacher is advised to inform the students of the objective, to show why the objective is personally important, to provide practice in performing the requirements of the objective, and to give the student feedback on correct and incorrect responses.
4 *Evaluation.*   Test items which sample the behavioral requirements of the objective are given. The teacher can then determine how many students met the criterion and how many did not. The goal is to evaluate the quality of the teaching and provide a basis for improvement in teaching, not to grade the students.

This four-point strategy is potentially very valuable. It requires the teacher to specify what he or she is trying to teach. It provides for finding out how the students perform initially and for feedback after the instruction. In the hands of a capable teacher, these procedures make possible the continual improvement of instruction.

According to Popham, however, problems did arise in implementing this strategy.[4] The task of writing and selecting possible objectives is an arduous one, as is the building of tests for them. Why should each teacher have to re-invent the wheel? In an attempt to respond to this problem, Popham has been building a depository of objectives and test items at UCLA.[5] Teachers can ask for materials in their area of concern. Others have tried to solve the objectives-writing problem by publishing books of objectives or inventories.[6] Bloom put out one of the earliest lists of educational objectives. Flanagan, Shanner, and Mager[7] have published a listing for language arts, mathematics, social science, and science. CTB McGraw-Hill has elaborate inventories of objectives with tests for them in reading and math.[8,9]

In addition to the problem of objectives design, there is a problem in designing procedures for evaluating test items for an objective. If criterion-referenced testing is to contribute to instruction, it should show where *instruction* has succeeded or failed. A good test item is one that is failed if the instruction did not succeed and is passed if the instruction did succeed.[10,11] However, if items are written *in the absence of an instructional program*, they may be failed for many reasons. This possibility arises from the fact that: (1) *given an instructional program, we can build any number of valid tests of that program; but* (2) *given a criterion-referenced test (of some objective), it may be consistent with no instructional program.* Consider the following diagrams:

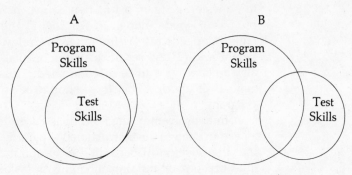

The goal of criterion-referenced testing is to test what is taught. However, if the tests are designed independently of the instructional program, there is no guarantee that they will adequately cover a given teaching program. Figure A shows the test skills as a subset of the program skills. This is the main goal when developing criterion-referenced tests. In figure B, there is only a small overlap between program skills and test skills. This is likely to occur if the test is written in the absence of a specified program. When this is the case, students may fail items for any of the following four reasons:

1 *The test may cover skills not taught in a particular program* (or level of a program). For example, the test may require "identification of vowels," but this skill may not be taught in a particular beginning reading program.
2 *The examples used to test a skill go beyond the range taught in the program.* For example, the test might require discrimination between the letters a and d when the program requires only the discrimination between a and d.
3 *The sequence of skills assumed by the test may not parallel that covered in the program.* Thus, although the test skills and program skills may overlap, the wrong skills may be tested at the wrong time. For example, a test of logical inferences (part of reading comprehension) may use vocabulary that has not been taught. Even though the students could pass the test with a known vocabulary, they fail because they lack an assumed subskill.
4 *The instructions and response conventions assumed by the test may not be of the same form as those used in the program.* For example, the test may require "plussing" of two numbers, and the program requires "adding." The instructions from test to program are not parallel. Similarly, the test may require a multiple choice (circling) response, whereas the program uses an oral identification response. The response requirements from test to program are not parallel.

Thus, if test items designed to measure a behavioral objective can be failed for many reasons, it becomes difficult to tell a good test item from a bad test item. These problems are more readily overcome when the test is built around a given instructional program.

Another major problem in building criterion-referenced tests from behavioral objectives concerns the generality/specificity of the objectives. Popham found that some teachers wrote objectives that amounted to specific test items; others wrote a few general objectives. But the generality of an objective to be tested is again a function of the instructional program (or levels of a program). As developed in *Teaching 2*, the nature of a general case that is taught depends on: (1) the range of irrelevant characterictics that have been taught and (2) the set of related concepts, operations, or skills from which a given concept is to be discriminated. Thus, it is not possible to decide how general or specific objectives should be in the absence of an instructional program.

A final problem of the objectives-based test is that test failures may imply a need to change the instructional program. The teacher can easily be trapped into the position of becoming a "program modifier" when the teacher has little practice or training in doing this skillfully. Furthermore, there is no clear evidence that program modifications are necessary, since the test objectives may be no better than the program objectives. For the evaluation of instruction, tests based on objectives rather than an instructional program clearly have limitations.

Instructional-Program-Based Tests

Baker has pointed out that to be maximally useful "tests must be specifically referenced to defined instructional materials."[12] More and more educational teaching systems are being sold with testing programs built into them. McGraw-Hill's *Programmed Reading, Individually Prescribed Instruction* (IPI), distributed by Research for Better Schools, and the *Distar*® programs published by SRA are examples of instructional programs with tests geared directly to them. When tests are directly geared to an instructional program, it is easier to write test items that are logically valid measures of what is taught, to show that the test items are sensitive to instruction, and to use the tests to carefully monitor the process of instruction. The potential advantages of tests geared to instructional-programs will be discussed with illustrations from IPI and Distar.

Testing in IPI. Individually Prescribed Instruction (IPI) was developed by Robert Glaser, John Bolvin, and C. M. Lindvall at the University of Pittsburgh Learning Research and Development Center. Programs were initially developed for kindergarten through sixth grade in language arts and math. IPI was conceived by Glaser to be a program centered around a *sequenced set of behavioral objectives* (which he called a learning continuum). Progress through the continuum of behavioral objectives is controlled by a set of criterion-referenced tests (placement tests, pretests, posttests, and curriculum-embedded tests). Placement tests locate the general level at which the student is performing satisfactorily. Pretests for each objective check in detail what the student needs to learn on that objective. The curriculum-embedded tests let the student and teacher know the student is ready for the posttest. The posttest checks mastery of the objective.

As Glaser conceived of IPI, the sequence of behavioral objectives and the tests geared to each objective were the key. These were built first, and then materials were created or borrowed from available programs to provide a teaching mechanism for each objective. The test data then provided the feedback needed to build or select better teaching mechanisms. This use of criterion-referenced tests started out very similar to Popham's use. There are two important differences, however. First, the objectives were sequenced in the IPI (from simpler to more complex skills). Second, the instructional program was systematically geared to the objectives. Thus, it was possible to see if test items were sensitive to instruction, that is, to see if they were failed before and passed after instruction. If they were, both the test items and the instruction could be accepted as adequate (but not necessarily efficient). If they were not, test items, instructional procedures, and the sequence of objectives were examined for possible deficiencies, and revisions were made. As revisions were made, the tests, instructional program, and objectives came closer together. As a result the tests in IPI shifted from being not only *objectives-based,* but also *instructional-program-based.*

Glaser's approach in IPI adds to the behavioral objectives approach an instructional system and an empirical evaluation of the instruction and tests. This is a long step forward.

Testing in Distar. Currently, the Distar programs designed by Siegfried Engelmann and colleagues provide the most explicit examples of instructional-program-based tests. The Distar programs provide three years of daily lessons for the teacher to present. The lessons are sequenced using advanced programing principles to teach generalized skills in basic reading, language, and arithmetic. The programs were designed by using the strategies for teaching concepts, operations, and problem-solving skills described in *Teaching 2* and were field tested for effectiveness prior to publication. As with IPI, they went through several cycles of revision to improve effectiveness before publication.

In the Distar programs, the tests are designed to:

1 Test the process of instruction *throughout the program,* not just at the end, and provide for *corrective action* where needed
2 Impose no new response requirements through changing of response requirements and directions
3 Use a range of examples that has been covered or implied by program procedures
4 Make sure the testing sequence follows the teaching sequence

The interlocking of instruction and criterion-referenced testing can be illustrated by looking at *Distar Reading Level I.* As noted previously, explicit daily programed lessons are provided in the form of scripts to be followed by the teacher in small group instruction. Figure 1.3 gives an example of a script page from Lesson 44.[13]

What the teacher says is underlined, what the teacher does is in plain type, and what the children should say is in italics. Inspection of the tasks will show that the children need the following skills to do such tasks:

1 Identify letters by sounds.
2 Follow the arrow left to right.
3 Say the sounds without pausing between sounds.
4 "Say it fast" after sounding out the word.

44

Get ready to read all the words on this page without making a mistake.

TASK 15 Children sound out the word and say it fast

a. Touch the ball for **mē. Sound it out.**
b. **Get ready.** Touch m, ē as the children say *mmmēēē* without
   pausing between the sounds.

c. Return to the ball. **Again.** Repeat *b* until firm.
d. **Say it fast.** (Signal.) *Me.* **Yes, what word?** (Signal.) *Me.*

TASK 16 Children sound out the word and say it fast

a. Touch the ball for **is. Sound it out.**
b. **Get ready.** Touch i, s as the children say *iiisss* without pausing
                between the sounds.

c. Return to the ball. **Again.** Repeat *b* until firm.
d. **Say it fast.** (Signal.) *is.* **Yes, what word?** (Signal.) *Is.*
                    Yes, is. We say is. That dog is fat.

TASK 17 Children sound out the word and say it fast

a. Touch the ball for **thē. Sound it out.**
b. **Get ready.** Touch th, ē as the children say *thththēēē* without
   pausing between the sounds.

c. Return to the ball. **Again.** Repeat *b* until firm.
d. **Say it fast.** (Signal.) *Thē.* **Yes, what word?** (Signal.) *Thē.*

TASK 18 Individual test

Call on different children to sound out one word and tell what word.

Figure 1.3 Lesson 44 from *Distar Reading I*

mē

is

thē

By Lesson 44, the children have had 44 lessons in which they have been taught sound identification, 14 lessons in sounding out words without pausing between sounds, 20 lessons in following the arrow, and 34 lessons involving "say it fast." The test for children who are on Lessons 41-50 involves:

1   Identifying by sounds the letters f, th, and i (These are sounds most recently taught, but introduced at least three days before they appear in a test.)
2   Saying sounds without pausing (ma) *mmmmmmmmmaaaaaaaa*
3   Sounding out words (am, sad) and saying the words fast

In the latter two tasks, the children follow an arrow left to right. At this level there is also a test for rhyming, since this skill also has been taught and will be used in word reading.

Tests of this sort allow for a precise diagnosis of which skills have been adequately taught, where the deficiencies are, and what the remedial tasks should be. Remedial lessons can be specified by referring the teacher to earlier forms of the tasks involving the deficient component skills. In actual practice, in the Engelmann-Becker Follow Through Model, these instructional-program-based tests are given each six weeks, but they can be given more often when there is a need for precise information.

One further characteristic of instructional-program-based tests should be noted. If we can establish that a program works under specified conditions and if the test requires only skills covered in the program, then failure of test items can be clearly attributed to the fact that some students were not taught the skills covered. Furthermore, we can determine whether the problem is with a particular student or a teacher by looking at the pattern of scores for a set of skills taught to a group of students. For example, a test of four skills shows this pattern of scores for a group of students given the same instruction:

Students	Skills				Percent
	A	*B*	*C*	*D*	Pass
1	+	+	−	+	75
2	+	+	−	+	75
3	+	+	−	+	75
4	−	−	−	−	0
Percent Pass	75	75	0	75	

It is readily apparent that skill C is not being taught and that child 4 is in need of reteaching on all skills.

From a logical point of view, instructional-program-based tests are what the criterion-referenced testing movement is all about. From the start, the goal of the movement has been to develop test procedures tied more directly to the goals of instruction so that test performance can be used as a precise basis for evaluation of instruction and the remediation of problems. Ways to achieve this goal are now clearly in sight.

A Comparison of the Information Provided by Three Kinds of Tests

In evaluating norm-referenced and two kinds of criterion-referenced tests, it is helpful to summarize their usefulness for various purposes. Such a summary is provided in table 1.2.

TABLE 1.2 INFORMATIONAL USES OF THE VARIOUS KINDS OF TESTS

Information Provided	Norm-Referenced Tests	Criterion-Referenced Tests	
		Objectives-Based	Instructional-Program Based
1. Pre-program to post-program gains	Depends on the fit of the specific test and program	Yes, on the objectives tested	Yes, on program skills
2. Process evaluation	No	Depends on fit of test and the specific instruction used.	Yes
3. Comparison of programs	Yes. To the extent the tests are acceptable as criteria	Depends on fit of test with the programs to be compared.	No
4. Identifying weaknesses for specific children and teachers	No. Most errors can occur for many reasons	Unlikely. No basis for telling why items were failed	Yes, for program skills
5. Implying specific remedies for weaknesses	No	No	Yes, earlier tasks in the program
6. Showing continuity in skill development from grade to grade	Only in the sense of grade-norm progress. The skills tested change from grade to grade and fail to show sequenced mastery	No	Yes, if same program (or program series) is used
7. Identification of extremely high or low performances	Yes. Especially useful here	Possibly useful as a screening device, but not especially sensitive to extreme performances	Possibly useful as a screening device, but not especially sensitive to extreme performances

Norm-referenced tests are not useful in process evaluation, that is, in evaluating progress through an instructional sequence. They also have little use in analyzing specific weaknesses and specifying remedies. They can be useful in selecting the most skillful and least skillful persons in a particular area of competency. Norm-referenced tests may also be useful in comparing the effectiveness of different programs to the extent the tests meet the logical requirements of being measures of the goals of two or more programs. Similarly, where there is a logical fit of objectives, norm-referenced tests can be useful in showing pre-program to post-program gains.

Objectives-based criterion-referenced tests are especially useful in showing pre-to-post gains for the specific objectives being tested. Their usefulness for other purposes depends on the fit of the objectives to the instructional programs being used.

Instructional-program-based tests are most generally useful in showing progress through a program, in showing pre-to-post gains, and in analyzing and remediating weaknesses. They are usually not appropriate for comparing different programs.

summary

Tests are systematic procedures for assessing behavior under specified stimulus conditions. Norm-referenced tests compare people to each other. Criterion-referenced tests compare a person's performance to some standard. Norm-referenced tests are especially useful in selecting relatively high and low members of a group. Criterion-referenced tests are useful for showing who meets or fails to meet a standard of performance. A good item on a norm-referenced test is one that some pass and some fail. An item that everybody (or most) passed would be eliminated from a norm-referenced test. For a criterion-referenced test used to evaluate instruction, such an item might be very valuable.

One of the main uses of criterion-referenced tests in education is to evaluate the process of instruction to show where it has occurred and where it has not. There are two approaches to developing criterion-referenced tests. One bases the tests on a set of instructional objectives, the other ties the tests to a specified instructional program. Objectives-based tests have had considerable popularity in the past ten years. They require the teacher to specify what he is trying to teach, to pretest the students, and to get feedback after instruction through posttesting. Such procedures can assist in improving programs.

The difficulties with objectives-based tests are:

1 It is a lot of work to write objectives and build tests. If every teacher had to do it, the waste of effort would be considerable.
2 It is difficult to evaluate good and bad test items without an instructional program. The test might be failed because of poor teaching, use of dif-

ferent directions and response requirements from those taught the students, use of examples beyond the range of those taught, and so forth.

3   It is not possible to say how specific or how general an objective should be in the absence of an instructional program.

4   The tests tend to dictate program change. Such change may not be justified.

As Baker noted, to be maximally useful "tests must be specifically referenced to define instructional materials." When this is done, it is possible to monitor the process of instruction throughout the program and provide for corrective action when it is needed. Precise diagnosis of problems and their remediation is possible with such tests. Also, when working with a program that has been previously demonstrated to work, it is possible to analyze the test results to determine if failures are due to poor teaching (most students fail items which have been "taught"), or to student difficulties (one or more students fail many tasks on the test which are not failed by most students).

Many of the problems inherent in objectives-based tests are avoided by instructional-program-based tests, which do not go beyond a specific instructional program. They do not purport to dictate the form, manner, or level of skills to be taught. They merely test program sequences designed to cause new learning. The form of the tasks in these tests is the same used in the program. They therefore provide a precise basis for identifying whether or not each child is meeting each instructional objective. They also imply why adequate learning is not taking place in specific cases.

self-test

This section provides you with a check of your understanding of the material in this unit. Cover the answers on the left with a marker. Read each item and write your answer. Then check it by moving your marker down one step. If you get nine or ten answers right, we suggest you skip the Programed Practice and go on to the next exercise. If you make more than one error, do the Programed Practice, go back to the text to correct any mistakes, then do the next exercise.

1   When the comparison made is to the distribution of scores obtained by other persons taking the test, the interpretation is called _____- _____ .

2   When the comparison is made to some specified standard of performance, the interpretation is called _____-_____ .

1 norm-referenced

2 criterion-referenced

3 high

3 Norm-referenced tests are useful in selecting relatively _____ or relatively low scoring groups.

4 Criterion-referenced tests are especially useful for evaluating instruction concerned with the development of skills that meet specifiable _____.

4 standards

5 A goal of criterion-referenced testing is to test what is taught. However, if the tests are designed _____ of the instructional program, there is no guarantee that the test will adequately cover a given teaching program.

6 IPI was conceived by Glaser to be a program centered around a _____ _____ of behavioral objectives (which he called a learning continuum).

5 independently

6 sequenced set

7 Since the instruction was systematically geared to the objectives, it was possible to see if test items were _____ to instruction.

7 sensitive

8 The tests in the Distar programs are designed to test the process of instruction _____ the program.

9 Properly designed, program-based tests allow for a precise _____ of which skills have been adequately taught, where the deficiencies are, and what the _____ tasks should be.

8 throughout

9 diagnosis; remedial

NUMBER RIGHT _____

exercise 1 programed practice

Cover the answers on the left with your marker. Read each item and write in your answer. Then check the answer by moving your marker down one step. Accept your answers if the meaning is the same as that given. If you are not sure about the material covered, return to the text.

1 A test is a systematic procedure for assessing some _____ .

1 behavior

2 Interpreting a test score involves making _____ .

3 When the comparison made is to the distribution of scores obtained by other persons taking the test, the interpretation is called _____-_____ .

2 comparisons

3 norm-referenced

4 When the comparison is made to some specified standard of performance, the interpretation is called _____-_____ .

5 When the teacher builds a test based on a given instructional goal and then requires each student to perform at 90 percent mastery before going on to a new goal, he is using a _____-_____ test.

6 Norm-referenced tests are useful in selecting relatively _____ or relatively _____ scoring groups.

7 Criterion-referenced tests are especially useful for evaluating instruction concerned with the development of skills that meet specifiable _____.

8 Items that everyone passes (or fails) are eliminated from norm-referenced tests because the goal is to make each item useful in contributing to a _____ of test scores.

9 If the goal is to evaluate instruction, items that everyone passes _____ instruction, but not _____ , might be very valuable in showing the effects of instruction.

10 One approach to the use of criterion-referenced tests begins with a set of _____ _____ or statements of what a student should be able to do after instruction and builds tests to measure them.

11 A second approach begins with an _____ program and sets out to build a test(s) of what is taught in the program.

12 Popham recommends that teachers:

a. State their objectives in terms of _____ performance

b. Test for _____ assumed by the objectives and test to see that the student cannot already perform the objectives

c. Work out a lesson _____

d. Test to determine how many students met the _____ and how many did not

13 A goal of criterion-referenced testing is to test what is taught. However, if the tests are designed _____ of the instructional program, as Popham proposes, there is no guarantee that the test will adequately cover a given teaching program.

---

4 criterion-referenced

5 criterion-referenced

6 high; low

7 standards

8 spread

9 after; before

10 behavioral objectives

11 instructional

12a. observable

b. preskills

c. plan

d. criterion

13 independently

---

14 When the test is written in the absence of specific knowledge of the teaching program, items can be failed because:

a. The test includes skills not _____ in a particular program

b. The examples used to test a skill go beyond the _____ taught in the program

c. The _____ of skills assumed by the test may not parallel that covered in the program

d. The instructions and _____ _____ assumed by the test may not be of the same form as those used in the program

15 If test items designed to measure a behavioral objective can be failed for many reasons, it becomes difficult to tell a _____ test item from a _____ test item.

16 These problems are more readily overcome when the test is built around a given _____ program.

17 IPI was conceived by Glaser to be a program centered around a _____ _____ of behavioral objectives (which he called a learning continuum).

18 Progress through the continuum of behavioral objectives was controlled by a set of _____-_____ tests.

19 The sequence of behavioral objectives was built, tests geared to each _____ were constructed, and then materials were created or borrowed from _____ programs to provide a teaching mechanism for each objective.

20 The test data then provided the feedback needed to build or select _____ teaching mechanisms.

21 Since the instruction was systematically geared to the objectives, it was possible to see if test items were _____ to instruction.

22 The Distar programs designed by Siegfried Engelmann and colleagues provide an explicit example of _____-_____-_____ tests.

14a. taught

b. range

c. sequence

d. response conventions

15 good; bad

16 instructional

17 sequenced set

18 criterion-referenced

19 objective; available

20 better

21 sensitive

22 instructional-program-based

23 The tests in the Distar programs are designed to test the process of instruction _____ the program, not just at the end, and provide for _____ action where needed.

24 They are constructed to test only the skills which are _____ or assumed by the program.

25 Properly designed, program-based tests allow for a precise _____ of which skills have been adequately taught, where the deficiencies are, and what the _____ tasks should be.

26 With a program which has been demonstrated to work, one can determine whether the problem is with a particular student or the teacher by looking at the _____ of scores for a set of skills taught to a group of students.

27 Norm-referenced tests are especially useful in selecting the _____ _____ and _____ persons in a particular area of competency.

28 Norm-referenced tests may also be useful in comparing the effectiveness of _____ programs to the extent the tests meet the logical requirements of being measures of the goals of the programs.

29 Objectives-based criterion-referenced tests are especially useful in showing _____-_____ gains for the specific objectives being tested.

30 Instructional-program-based tests are most generally useful in showing _____ through a program, in showing pre-post _____, and in analyzing and remediating _____ .

23 throughout;
   corrective

24 taught

25 diagnosis;
   remedial

26 pattern

27 most skillful;
   least skillful

28 different

29 pre-post

30 progress;
   gains;
   weaknesses

discussion questions

1   What is a test?
2   How do the comparison standards differ for criterion-referenced and norm-referenced tests?
3   Give examples of criterion-referenced and norm-referenced tests.
4   Describe two approaches to developing criterion-referenced tests to evaluate instruction.
5   What are the four steps for teachers to follow in planning for instruction as recommended by Popham?
6   Why is Popham's strategy potentially valuable to the teacher?
7   Give three common problems with objectives-based test approach.
8   What are some possible solutions to these problems?
9   What advantages do instructional-program-based tests have over objectives-based tests?
10 What are the essential features of IPI?
11 What are the essential features of Distar?
12 Explain how the results of testing a group in a Distar program can be used to identify teacher problems and student problems.
13 When are norm-referenced tests especially useful?
14 When are objectives-based tests especially useful?
15 When are instructional-program-based tests especially useful?

unit 2

Understanding Test Scores

objectives

When you complete this unit you should be able to—
1 Define these terms: frequency distribution
                     mean
                     standard deviation
                     standard score
                     percent right score
2 Given a set of scores, build a frequency distribution.
3 Compute the mean and the standard deviation for a set of scores.
4 Compute standard scores, given the raw scores, mean, and standard deviation.
5 Compute raw scores, given the standard scores, mean, and standard deviation.
6 Compute percent right scores.
7 Interpret standard scores in terms of relative positions in a frequency distribution.
8 State why percent right scores are often preferred in evaluating instruction.

lesson

Tests are used to measure behavior. Measurement is a process of making comparisons. When we measure distances, weights, or volumes, we make comparisons to some standard measure, such as a yard, a meter, a pound, or a liter. The comparison standard is a measurement unit, and we use it to answer the question, "How much do you have?" To measure behavior, it is also necessary to make comparisons. As noted in the last unit, norm-referenced tests compare a person's score to the performance of other people. Criterion-referenced tests compare a score to some performance standard.

18

To see how these different standards give different answers to the "how much" question, it is necessary to introduce a few concepts involving descriptive statistics. Our objective in teaching these concepts is to develop a basis for analyzing fundamental properties of test scores.

An Introduction to Descriptive Statistics— or Who Did Better in What?

Assume that you have just given two tests to your class. One involves spelling 40 irregular words that the children have been learning for the past month. The other consists of 50 problems covering multiplication of two-digit numbers. The number of right answers (the test score) obtained by each student is given in table 2.1.

TABLE 2.1 TEST SCORES FOR A CLASS IN SPELLING AND ARITHMETIC

Name	Spelling	Arithmetic
Joe	25	45
Ned	28	42
Julie	25	49
Aaron	22	50
Sharon	32	40
Carlos	23	48
Jessie	25	49
Brenda	28	49
Donna	29	50
Rodney	27	48
Kathy	24	48
Milly	26	50
David	20	50
Gary	26	49
Joanna	27	50
Felix	27	48
Kerry	24	49
Vonda	26	47
Tom	30	49
Helen	26	50

Did Joe do better in spelling or arithmetic? Which subject matter requires more teaching? To answer these questions, we need to understand the following concepts and the operations required to produce examples of them:

1 The *frequency distribution* of a set of test scores
2 The *mean* of a set of test scores
3 The *standard deviation* of a set of test scores
4 How to express test scores as *standard scores*
5 How to express test scores as *percent-right scores*

Making a Frequency Distribution

A frequency distribution shows graphically how many people received what scores. The vertical dimension on the graph shows frequency (how many) and the horizontal dimension shows the scores (in this case, number right). For spelling, the frequency distribution of the scores in table 2.1 would look like this:

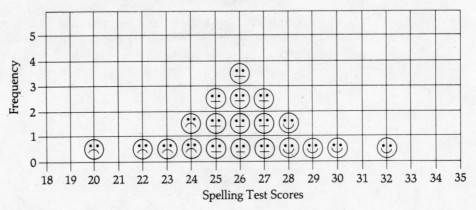

Figure 2.1   Spelling Test Scores

If three students got a score of 25, then three circles, boxes, or other marks would be placed on the 25 for each student. If one student got a score of 30, one mark would be placed on the 30.

Use the arithmetic data in table 2.1 to make a frequency distribution for the students in arithmetic on figure 2.2. Check your frequency distribution by comparing it to the one given on page 33.

A frequency distribution gives a graphic picture of the relative position of scores on a test. It provides a norm-referenced comparison of people. We can now see that Joe is near the middle of the distribution in spelling (25) and on the low side in arithmetic (45). Ned's 28 in spelling now looks like a pretty good score compared to the rest of the class, but his 42 in arithmetic looks like a poor performance compared to the rest of the class.

Computing the Mean of a Distribution

In talking about scores in a frequency distribution, two measures are particularly useful, especially when you are comparing a large number of children with each other. These are the *mean* of the distribution and the *standard deviation* of the distribution. The mean (M) is the same as an average. All of the scores (Xs) are summed and then divided by the number of scores (N).

$$\text{Mean} = \frac{\text{Sum of scores}}{\text{Number of scores}}$$

$$M = \frac{\text{Sum Xs}}{N}$$

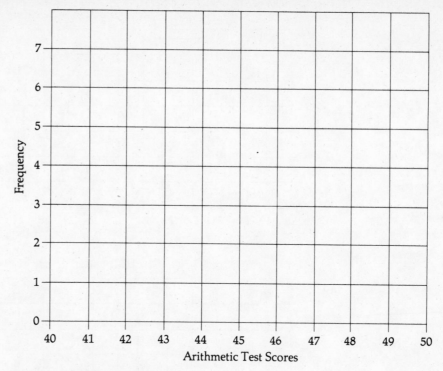

Figure 2.2 Arithmetic Test Scores

For spelling, the sum of the scores is 520. The number of scores equals 20. So, the mean of the distribution is 26. Find the mean for the distribution of arithmetic scores.

$$\text{Arithmetic Mean} = \frac{\text{Sum of scores}}{\text{Number of scores}} = \underline{\hspace{3cm}}$$

Check your answer by turning to page 33.

By computing the means, we can see that the average raw score in spelling was lower than that in arithmetic. To find out whether Joe and Ned did better in spelling than arithmetic, we need to place both distributions on the *same scale*. This can provide us with a basis for comparison. One way to do this is to use the standard deviation as the unit of measurement. Another way is to convert both sets of scores to percent-right scores.

Computing the Standard Deviation of a Distribution

To describe a distribution of scores (frequency distribution), we first find the mean. Then we find the *standard deviation*, which tells us how far the average score deviates from the mean. For example, in figure 2.3, distribution A has a larger standard deviation than distribution B because the scores spread further from the mean. The standard deviation for distribution A is 2.9 and that for B is 1.9

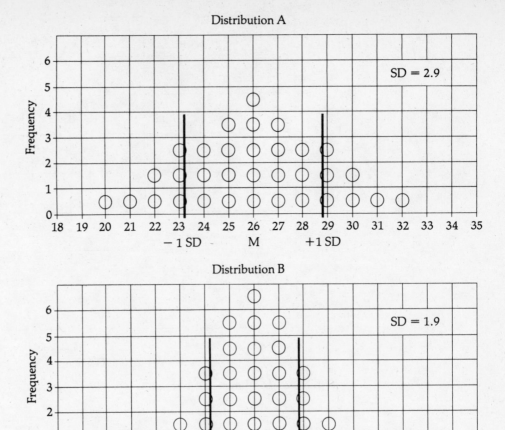

Figure 2.3 Illustration of Standard Deviations for Two Distributions

If we smooth out the frequency distributions and draw them as curves, we can readily illustrate the standard deviation for a number of distributions (see figure 2.4). To make the comparisons easier, we have kept the mean of each distribution the same. Distribution A has a standard deviation of 7. It is smaller than the standard deviation for distributions B and C because there are more scores near the mean and fewer scores away from the mean. Distribution B has a large standard deviation relative to A and C because there are more extremely high and low scores and relatively fewer scores near the mean. The standard deviation for distribution C is in between that of A and B. Each of these figures illustrates that the standard deviation depends on the average spread of the scores from the mean of the distribution. To compute a standard deviation, follow these steps:

Step 1   Subtract the mean from each score $(X-M)$

Step 2   Square the deviations obtained in step 1 $(X-M)^2$

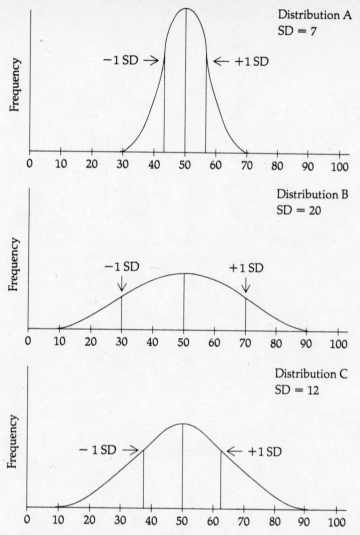

Figure 2.4 Illustration of Standard Deviation for Three Smoothed Distributions

Step 3   Sum the squared deviations   Sum $(X-M)^2$

Step 4   Divide by N (the number of students) $\dfrac{\text{Sum } (X-M)^2}{N}$

Step 5   Take the square root of the result $SD = \sqrt{\dfrac{\text{Sum } (X-M)^2}{N}}$

The deviations from the mean are squared to eliminate the problems of dealing with negative numbers. Squares and square roots can be found by using Appendix A or a calculator. The standard deviation for the spelling scores can be calculated as follows:

TABLE 2.2   CALCULATION OF THE STANDARD
DEVIATION FOR THE SCORES ON THE
SPELLING TEST

Name	Step 1			Step 2
	X	− M	= (X − M)	(X − M)²
Joe	25	−26 =	−1	1
Ned	28	−26 =	+2	4
Julie	25	−26 =	−1	1
Aaron	22	−26 =	−4	16
Sharon	32	−26 =	+6	36
Carlos	23	−26 =	−3	9
Jessie	25	−26 =	−1	1
Brenda	28	−26 =	+2	4
Donna	29	−26 =	+3	9
Rodney	27	−26 =	+1	1
Kathy	24	−26 =	−2	4
Milly	26	−26 =	0	0
David	20	−26 =	−6	36
Gary	26	−26 =	0	0
Joanna	27	−26 =	+1	1
Felix	27	−26 =	+1	1
Kerry	24	−26 =	−2	4
Vonda	26	−26 =	0	0
Tom	30	−26 =	+4	16
Helen	26	−26 =	0	0

Step 3: Sum $(X − M)^2 = 144$

Step 4: Sum $\dfrac{(X − M)^2}{N} = \dfrac{144}{20} = 7.2$

Step 5: SD $= \sqrt{\dfrac{\text{Sum }(X − M)^2}{N}} = \sqrt{7.2} = 2.68$

This calculation was relatively easy because the mean was a whole number (26). Usually this is not the case. For example, if the mean in spelling had been 25.6, then Joe's deviation score (X − M) would have been −.6, Ned's +2.4, Julie's −.6, and Aaron's −3.6. Squaring and adding these numbers would take a little more work. Usually, it is easier to compute the standard deviation directly from raw scores (Xs) using a calculator. The raw score formula* is:

$$ SD = \frac{1}{N} \sqrt{N \cdot \text{Sum } X^2 − (\text{Sum } X)^2} $$

An outline of steps and a computing example using this formula are given at the end of this unit (page 31).

---

*The expression N · Sum X² is read "number of scores *times* the sum of the squared scores." The · is used for a times sign (×) in most statistical work so that it is not confused with X or x which are used to refer to scores.

With a mean and a standard deviation, we have two kinds of averages for describing a distribution: the average score in the distribution (M) and a kind of "average deviation" or average spread of scores from the mean of the distribution (SD). These two scores can be used to change the scale of any distribution to a standard score scale which more readily permits comparison of scores from different distributions.

Standard Scores

Let us return to the distributions of scores from the spelling and arithmetic tests. On the spelling test, the mean was 26 and the standard deviation was 2.68. On the arithmetic test, the mean was 48 and the standard deviation is 2.65. To convert a raw score (X) to a standard score (SS), subtract the mean (M) from the raw score and divide by the standard deviation (SD).

$$\text{Standard Score (SS)} = \frac{X - M}{SD}$$

Thus, the standard score for a raw score of 26 in spelling is 0, since $X - M = 0$.

Raw scores higher than 26 have positive values, while those lower than 26 have negative values. A raw score of 29 has a standard score equivalent of $\frac{29 - 26}{2.68} = +1.12$. A raw score of 22 has a standard score equivalent of $\frac{22 - 26}{2.68} = -1.49$. Most standard scores will fall in the range between +3 and −3. (More information on interpreting standard scores will be presented in Unit 9.)

To change a standard score back to a raw score, use the following:

$$X = SS \cdot SD + M$$

For spelling the raw score equivalent for a standard score of 2 is: $X = 2 \times 2.68 + 26 = 31.36$. The raw score equivalent for a standard score of −1 is: $X = -1 \times 2.68 + 26 = 23.32$. With calculations of this latter sort, we can rescale the distribution of spelling scores as follows:

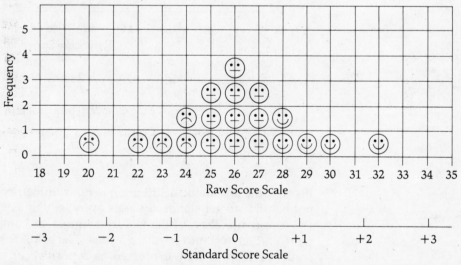

Figure 2.5 Spelling Score Distribution on a Standard Score Scale and a Raw Score Scale

Note that all of the scores fall between +3 and −3 on the standard score scale, or between +3 and −3 standard deviations (between 17.96 and 34.04) on the raw score distribution. This is usually the case. Note also that the *standard deviation becomes the unit of measurement* (the yardstick). On the standard score scale, plus one unit (+1) is 2.68 above the mean (28.68), plus two units (+2) is 2 × 2.68 above the mean (31.36), and plus three units (+3) is 3 × 2.68 above the mean (34.04). Similar properties can be shown for scores below the mean. *Standard scores are scores expressed in terms of the number of standard deviations they are from the mean.* The standard deviation is used as the unit of measurement. For arithmetic scores, the rescaling is as follows:

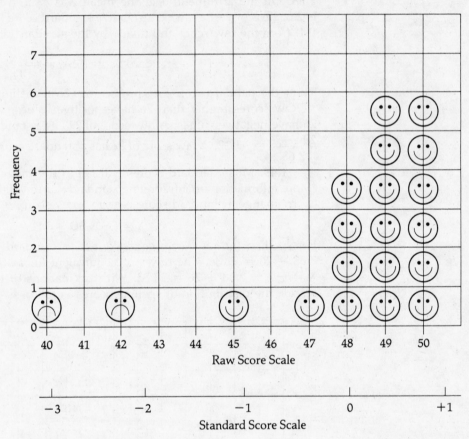

Figure 2.6 Arithmetic Score Distribution on a Standard Score Scale and a Raw Score Scale

Because the arithmetic distribution is not symmetrical around the mean, it is not possible to get standard scores even as high as 1.0.

We can use the standard score formula to convert each student's raw score on each test into standard scores. The result is shown in table 2.3. Each student's score is now expressed as a positive or negative deviation from the mean, and the yardstick for asking "How much is much?" is based on the standard deviation of the distribution rather than on the raw scores. The student's scores are expressed in a form which compares each score *to the distribution of the scores in the group.* The scores are expressed in relative terms, rather than in absolute raw score units. That is, they are positive or negative relative to the mean, and their size depends on the size of the standard deviation. From table 2.3, we can now see that Joe did do better in spelling (−.37) than arithmetic (−1.13) relative to the group, Ned did much better in spelling (+.75) than arithmetic (−2.26), and Julie did better in arithmetic (+.38) than spelling (−.37) relative to the group.

TABLE 2.3   STANDARD SCORES ON THE SPELLING AND ARITHMETIC TESTS FOR EACH STUDENT

Name	Spelling		Arithmetic	
	Raw Score X	Standard Score $\dfrac{X-M}{SD}$	Raw Score X	Standard Score $\dfrac{X-M}{SD}$
Joe	25	− .37	45	−1.13
Ned	28	+ .75	42	−2.26
Julie	25	− .37	49	+ .38
Aaron	22	−1.49	50	+ .75
Sharon	32	+2.24	40	−3.02
Carlos	23	−1.12	48	0
Jessie	25	− .37	49	+ .38
Brenda	28	+ .75	49	+ .38
Donna	29	+1.12	50	+ .75
Rodney	27	+ .37	48	0
Kathy	24	− .75	48	0
Milly	26	0	50	+ .75
David	20	−2.24	50	+ .75
Gary	26	0	49	+ .38
Joanna	27	+ .37	50	+ .75
Felix	27	+ .37	48	0
Kerry	24	− .75	49	+ .38
Vonda	26	0	47	− .38
Tom	30	+1.49	49	+ .38
Helen	26	0	50	+ .75

Percent Right Scores

Another approach to comparing the performance of the group (or individual students) in spelling and arithmetic is to use *percent right scores.* This approach is commonly used in criterion-referenced evaluation. If both tests had been constructed to test the teaching objectives for the past four weeks, quite different conclusions about the students' performances and instruction would follow from comparing percent right scores than were derived from the standard score analysis. To compute the percent right, the raw score (number right) is simply divided by the number of items in the test and the result is multiplied by 100. Examine the scores in table 2.4 carefully.

TABLE 2.4   A COMPARISON OF RAW SCORES, STANDARD SCORES AND PERCENT RIGHT SCORES ON A SPELLING AND ARITHMETIC TEST

	Spelling			Arithmetic		
	Raw Score	Standard Score	Percent Right	Raw Score	Standard Score	Percent Right
Name	X	$\dfrac{X-M}{SD}$	$\dfrac{X}{40}\cdot 100$	X	$\dfrac{X-M}{SD}$	$\dfrac{X}{50}\cdot 100$
Joe	25	− .37	62.5	45	−1.13	90
Ned	28	+ .75	70	42	−2.26	84
Julie	25	− .37	62.5	49	+ .38	98
Aaron	22	−1.49	55	50	+ .76	100
Sharon	32	+2.24	80	40	−3.02	80
Carlos	23	−1.12	57.5	48	0	96
Jessie	25	− .37	62.5	49	+ .38	98
Brenda	28	+ .75	70	49	+ .38	98
Donna	29	+1.12	72.5	50	+ .76	100
Rodney	27	+ .37	67.5	48	0	96
Kathy	24	− .75	60	48	0	96
Milly	26	0	65	50	+ .76	100
David	20	−2.24	50	50	+ .76	100
Gary	26	0	65	49	+ .38	98
Joanna	27	+ .37	67.5	50	+ .76	100
Felix	27	+ .37	67.5	48	0	96
Kerry	24	− .75	60	49	+ .38	98
Vonda	26	0	65	47	− .38	94
Tom	30	+1.49	75	49	+ .38	98
Helen	26	0	65	50	+ .76	100
Means	26	0	65	48	0	96

Recap

We can summarize the relations between the statistical concepts we have been discussing and types of test scores as follows:

Norm Referenced

Given a set of scores, a *mean and standard deviation* can be computed to describe the *frequency distribution* for those scores. The mean and standard deviation can then be used to express raw scores in *standard score* form. Standard scores readily tell where a score falls in a frequency distribution relative to other scores.

Criterion Referenced

Given a set of scores, we can compute a mean and standard deviation, but it is unlikely that the latter would be used if computed. A frequency distribution can be plotted if desired. Standard scores would not be used. Instead, *percent right scores* would be computed to see how many students met a criterion of say 85 or 90 percent right.

How Much Is Much?

Now, let us return to our earlier questions: "Did Joe do better in spelling or arithmetic?" and "Which subject matter requires more teaching?" Using a norm-referenced standard based on group performance, we concluded that Joe did better in spelling. Looking at the tests as criterion standards of what he should have learned, we now see that Joe did better in arithmetic. Joe scored 90 percent in arithmetic and 62.5 percent in spelling. The criterion-referenced approach leads to a remarkably different conclusion! For the total class, we are now also able to ask how many met a 90 percent standard of mastery in each subject. For spelling the answer is *none*. For arithmetic, it is 18 out of 20 or 90 percent. On the average, the percent right was 65 percent for spelling and 96 percent for arithmetic. Referencing the scores to the group distribution, threw away vital information about *level of mastery* of spelling versus arithmetic. In fact, the means of both distributions were made the same (zero). When we use the information on the mean level of performance, we see that all but two students are above a 90 percent mastery level in arithmetic. The teacher can safely go on to new instruction with most of the class in arithmetic. On the other hand, the mean level of performance in spelling indicates a need to reteach the unit.

To develop an understanding of test scores, we have initially looked at the difference in conclusions to be drawn from using the standard deviation from a mean as a measuring stick, and using the percent of test items right to measure by. This analysis provides a beginning in answering the "How much?" question. Later, when we examine normative testing in more detail, we will see that the "How much?" question can be answered in a variety of ways, depending on the group used as the reference for comparison and the method of comparison. We will be examining standard scores in more detail as they relate to ranks, percentile ranks, age norms, and grade norms. At that time, we will make further use of the concepts of the mean, standard deviation, and a frequency distribution, so be sure to spend enough time on the exercises in this unit to learn the operations which produce examples of these concepts.

Other questions and problems also remain in finding "How much?" with criterion-referenced testing. Does it make a difference how items are chosen or written? Are there ways to weight items differently depending on their "importance?" We must also be able to deal with two additional questions if we are to understand test scores:

How reliable are the scores?
How valid are the scores?

We will examine these issues in later units.

Supplementary Statistical Concepts and Procedures

Other Measures of Central Tendency

The mean is the most important and widely used descriptor for the central tendency of a score distribution. Two other less frequently used descriptors are the median and mode. The *median* is found by starting with the highest (or lowest) score and counting until you find the middle score in a distribution. An equal number of persons fall above and below the median. In figure 2.1 where there are 20 scores, the median score is 26. Count the scores in one direction until you find the score falling between person 10 and 11. This happens to be the same as the mean score in this case, but this will only happen in a distribution that is balanced around the mean. For figure 2.2, the median score is 49, while the mean is 48. Note that if there are 20 scores in a distribution, and person 10 has a score of 31 and person 11 has a score of 32, the median score would be 31.5, the score that puts an equal number of persons on each side of the median.

The *mode* is the score obtained by the most students. For figure 2.1, the mode is 26 and for figure 2.2 the mode is 49-50. It is possible for a distribution to have more than one mode.

Another Measure of Dispersion

The *range* is an easy way to compute a measure of dispersion and it can sometimes be used instead of the standard deviation. The range is determined by subtracting the highest score from the lowest score. For figure 2.1, the range is 12. For figure 2.2, the range is 10. The scores in arithmetic have a slightly smaller range than the scores in spelling, just as was found for their standard deviations.

Computing Standard Deviations from Raw Scores

The formula for the direct calculation of a standard deviation from raw scores is:

$$ SD = \frac{1}{N} \sqrt{N \cdot \text{Sum } X^2 - (\text{Sum } X)^2} $$

Follow these steps:

Step 1 *Sum* all raw scores to get Sum X.
Step 2 *Square* each X and sum the squares to get Sum X^2.
Step 3 *Multiply* Sum X^2 by N to get N · Sum X^2.
Step 4 *Square* Sum X to get (Sum X)^2.
Step 5 *Subtract* the result in step 4 from the result in 3 to get N · Sum X^2 − (Sum X)^2
Step 6 *Take the square root* of the result from 5 to get
$$ \sqrt{N \cdot \text{Sum } X^2 - (\text{Sum } X)^2}. $$
Step 7 *Divide* the result of 6 by N to get SD.

Note: With most calculators, Sum X and Sum X^2 can be computed at the same time. If you are working with a calculator, find out how to do this.

Let us follow these steps through to see if we get the same SD in spelling using this raw score formula as we did using deviation scores.

TABLE 2.5   COMPUTING THE STANDARD DEVIATION FOR SPELLING SCORES WITH RAW SCORE FORMULA

Name	X	X²	$SD = \frac{1}{N} \sqrt{N \cdot Sum\ X^2 - (Sum\ X)^2}$	
Joe	25	625	Step 1:	Sum X = 520
Ned	28	784		
Julie	25	625	Step 2:	Sum X² = 13,664
Aaron	22	484		
Sharon	32	1024	Step 3:	N · Sum X² = 273,280
Carlos	23	529		
Jessie	25	625	Step 4:	(Sum X)² = 270,400
Brenda	28	784		
Donna	29	841	Step 5:	273,280 − 270,400 = 2,880
Rodney	27	729		
Kathy	24	576	Step 6:	$\sqrt{2,880} = 53.67$
Milly	26	676		
David	20	400	Step 7:	$\frac{53.67}{20} = 2.68$
Gary	26	676		
Joanna	27	729		
Felix	27	729		
Kerry	24	576		
Vonda	26	676		
Tom	30	900		
Helen	26	676		

N = 20   Sum X = 520   Sum X² = 13,664

summary

Tests are used to measure behavior. Measurement is a comparison procedure. In norm-reference testing, comparisons are made with the performances of other people. In criterion-referenced testing, comparisons are made with some standard of performance. Five statistical concepts were introduced to permit examination of the nature of norm-referenced and criterion-referenced scores.

A *frequency distribution* graphically depicts how many people received what scores on a test. The vertical axis on the graph shows "how many" people, the horizontal axis shows "what scores." Two important statistics for describing the set of scores that make up a frequency distribution are the mean and the standard deviation. The *mean* (M) is an average. All of the scores (Xs) are summed and then divided by the number of scores (N).

$$M = \frac{Sum\ Xs}{N}$$

The *standard deviation* (SD) is a measure of the degree to which scores in a distribution deviate from the mean. It can be thought of as the average of the deviations from the mean, except that the deviations are squared and then the average is later "unsquared" by taking the square root. The standard deviation tells us how far the scores in a distribution spread from the mean on the average.

$$SD = \sqrt{\frac{Sum\ (X - M)^2}{N}}$$

$\leftarrow$ unsquaring
$\leftarrow$ squared deviations from mean
$\leftarrow$ taking the average

The mean and the standard deviation of a distribution can be used to convert each score in the distribution to *standard scores* (SS). The raw scores are expressed as a deviation from the mean, and then they are divided by the standard deviation.

$$SS = \frac{X - M}{SD}$$

The sign of a standard score tells you immediately whether the score is above or below the mean. Most raw scores will fall between +3 and −3 on a standard score scale. Standard scores provide one frame of reference for comparing scores of individuals within a distribution, and between distributions involving different measurements. We will learn more about standard scores in unit 9.

The most common approach to comparing scores in criterion-referenced testing is to compute the *percent right*. These scores tell how close one comes to meeting the objective the test was designed to measure.

An example involving spelling and arithmetic was presented to show how widely different conclusions could be drawn from the test scores using standard scores rather than percent right scores. "How much is much?" depends on the comparison standard. Standard scores discard the absolute level of performance in looking at score distributions. Percent right scores retain this information and are generally more informative when one is concerned with teaching mastery or competency.

This unit is only the first step in understanding test scores. In future units, we will be examining both criterion-referenced and norm-referenced scores in more detail with respect to the questions:

How much is much?
How reliable are the scores?
How valid are the scores?

In-Lesson Exercise Answers
Arithmetic Test Scores for Figure 2.2

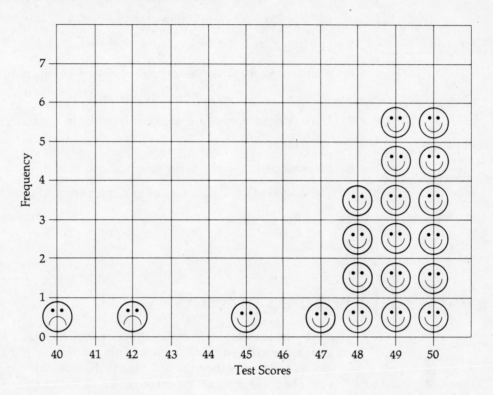

Mean of distribution = 48.0

self-test

If you get nine or ten right, skip the Programed Practice and go on to the next exercise. If you make more than one error, do the Programed Practice, go back to the text to correct mistakes, and then do the next exercise.

1 The vertical dimension on a graph of a frequency distribution shows _____ (how many) and the horizontal dimension shows the _____ .

2 The mean (M) is the same as an _____ . All of the scores are summed and then divided by the _____ of scores.

3 The standard deviation tells us how far the scores _____ _____ from the mean on the average.

1 frequency;
  scores

2 average;
  number

3 spread out

4 The mean and standard deviation can be used to change the scale of any distribution to a _____ score scale which more readily permits comparison of scores from different distributions.

4 standard

5 Using symbols, the formula for a standard score (SS) = _____ .

5 $\dfrac{X-M}{SD}$

6 Standard scores are scores expressed in terms of the number of _____ _____ they are from the mean.

6 standard deviations

7 Percent right scores are commonly used in _____-_____ evaluation.

7 criterion-referenced

8 Referencing the scores to the group distribution threw away vital information about level of _____ of spelling versus arithmetic.

8 mastery

NUMBER RIGHT _____

exercise 1 programed practice

Cover the answers on the left with your marker. Read each item, and write in your answer. Then check the answer by moving your marker down one step. Accept your answers if the meaning is the same as that given. If you are not sure about the material covered, return to the text.

1 A _____ _____ shows graphically how many people received what scores.

1 frequency distribution

2 The vertical dimension on a graph of a frequency distribution shows _____ (how many) and the horizontal dimension shows the _____.

2 frequency; scores

3 A frequency distribution gives a graphic picture of the _____ position of scores on a test.

3 relative

4 In talking about scores in a frequency distribution, two measures are particularly useful. These are the _____ of the distribution and the _____ _____ of the distribution.

4 mean; standard deviation

5 The mean (M) is the same as an _____ . All of the scores are summed and then divided by the _____ of scores.

5 average; number

6 The symbol X is used to refer to the _____ obtained by the individuals.

6 scores

7 The symbol N is used to refer to the _____ of individuals.

7 number

8 The standard deviation tells us how far the scores _____ _____ from the mean on the average.

9 To compute a standard deviation, follow these steps:

Step 1 Subtract the _____ from each score.

Step 2 _____ the deviations obtained in step 1.

Step 3 _____ the squared deviations.

Step 4 Divide by _____ .

Step 5 Take the square _____ of the result.

8 spread out

10 The mean and standard deviation give us two kinds of _____ for describing a distribution, the average score in the distribution (_____) and the average _____ of scores from the mean of the distribution (_____ _____).

9 mean; square; sum; N; root

10 averages; mean, M; spread; standard deviation, SD

11 These two scores can be used to change the scale of any distribution to a _____ score scale which more readily permits comparison of scores from different distributions.

12 (Put the symbols in the blanks) To convert a raw score (_____) to a standard score (_____), subtract the mean (_____) from the raw score and divide by the standard deviation (_____).

11 standard

12 X; SS; M; SD

13 Using symbols, the formula for a standard score (SS) = _____ .

14 To change a standard score back to a _____ score, the following formula is used: X = SS · SD + M. If the standard score is 2.0, the mean 5, and the standard deviation is 2.5, what is the raw score? _____

13 $\dfrac{X - M}{SD}$

15 If the standard score is 3, the mean 5, and the standard deviation is 3, what is the raw score? _____

14 raw; 10

16 Standard scores are scores expressed in terms of the number of _____ _____ they are from the mean. The standard deviation is used as the _____ of measurement.

15 14

16 standard deviations; unit

17 divided; 100

17 To compute the percent right, the raw score (number right) is simply _____ by the number of items in the test and the result is multiplied by _____ .

18 norm

18 Standard scores are commonly used in _____-referenced evaluations.

19 Percent-right scores are commonly used in _____-referenced evaluations.

19 criterion

20 Standard scores and percent right scores can lead to quite _____ conclusions when comparing scores on different tests. For example, using standard scores, Joe did better in _____ . Using percent-right scores, Joe did better in _____ .

20 different;
spelling;
arithmetic

21 Referencing the scores to the group distribution, threw away vital information about level of _____ of spelling versus arithmetic. The means of both distributions were made the _____ (_____).

21 mastery;
same; zero

exercise 2 computational practice

1 Make a frequency distribution for the following scores: 99, 95, 93, 96, 89, 99, 89, 98, 96, 95, 95, 97, 94, 93, 92, 94, 95, 96, 97, 94.

2 Compute the mean and the standard deviation of the distribution given in 1 above.

3 Convert each raw score to its standard score equivalent. (Note that if the raw scores are the same, the standard scores are the same.)

4 Plot the distribution of the deviation scores and raw scores (one above the other) for spelling. Use data in table 2.2.

5 The sum of the deviation scores for any distribution is equal to what? Why?

6 Given that the mean is 25 and the standard deviation is 10, what is the raw score for each of the following standard scores: 2.5, 1.5, −2, −1

7 If on a 12-item test, a student passes 7 items, what is his percent right score?

Answers for Exercise 2

1

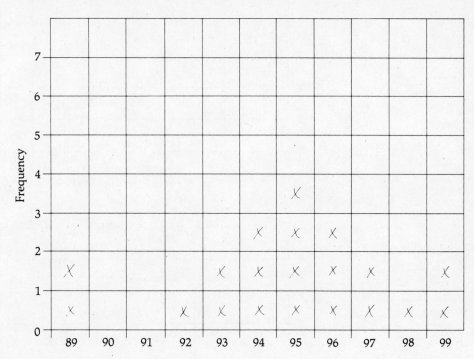

2   Mean = 94.8   Standard Deviation = 2.68

3   Raw Score   Standard Score
        89   −2.16
        92   −1.04
        93   − .67
        94   − .30
        95   .08
        96   .45
        97   .82
        98   1.19
        99   1.57

4

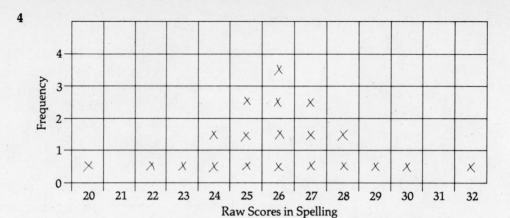

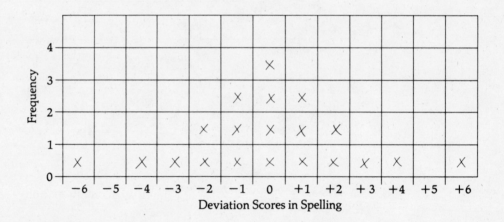

5 a. Zero.
   b. Because the deviations from the mean in one direction are exactly equal to those in the other direction.

6
Standard Score	Raw Score
2.5	50
1.5	40
−2.0	5
−1.0	15

7 7/12 = 58%

discussion questions

1. What does it mean *to measure* something?
2. How are the mean and the standard deviation related to a frequency distribution of test scores?
3. How many standard deviations would include most scores in most frequency distributions?
4. Give the formula for computing a mean of a set of scores.
5. Give the formula for the standard deviation of a set of scores.
6. Explain the five steps you would follow to compute a standard deviation from the formula in 5 above.
7. Draw a smoothed frequency distribution. Then draw on the same scale a distribution with a standard deviation that is half as large as the one first drawn.
8. Give the formula for computing a standard score.
9. Suppose you have a raw score frequency distribution and you wish to rescale the distribution to show where the various standard scores fall. You know the mean and standard deviation. What would you do?
10. What does it tell you to know that a person's standard score is +3, 0, or −2?
11. How are standard scores useful?
12. Why are percent right scores often preferred in evaluating instruction?
13. What determines the answer to a "How much?" question?

unit 3

Constructing Instructional-Program-Based Tests

objectives

When you complete this unit you should be able to—

1 Define and give examples of general-case sets and linear-additive sets.
2 State seven steps to follow in building a test based on an instructional program.
3 Describe in detail the procedures to follow in analyzing an instructional program with the goal of building a series of tests for that program.
4 Explain how to decide what should be tested and when.
5 Give five rules for constructing test items.
6 Given a curriculum segment, analyze its objectives and construct a test for those objectives. (Achievement of this last goal will depend in part on the amount of practice in analysis required by your instructor.)

lesson

To be most useful criterion-referenced tests should provide the teacher with information for remediation or for evaluating teaching procedures; that is, they should be referenced to an instructional program. Ideally, every educational program on the market would be pretested for effectiveness under specified conditions, and tests would be provided by the publisher to monitor progress throughout the program. The classroom teacher could then efficiently devote time to teaching, rather than to building tests or modifying programs. Presently, educational materials and tests are not designed in this way, so the teacher needs to know how to build and use tests.

The Prerequisite: An Instructional Program

It makes no sense to build an instruction-referenced testing program, if no particular instructional program is followed. If the teacher operates on moment-to-moment impulse, rather than following some planned procedures (that can be followed again if they work), a testing program will be of no value. Test results cannot be interpreted if they are not geared to an instructional program. In presenting and illustrating procedures for constructing instructional-referenced tests, we will rely heavily on illustrations from Distar programs because their structure more readily permits analysis. However, with diligence and time, it is possible to construct a framework for progress testing with any program that specifies the *student response requirements* at points in the program where testing is appropriate.

Defining Skills to be Tested

In defining skills for testing, it is most desirable to define a set of tasks any one of which the student should be able to perform. This then permits an economy in testing by drawing a sample from the set, rather than testing each member. Two kinds of skill sets can be defined. One involves a general case, the other does not. How to teach a general case was the main topic of *Teaching 2: Cognitive Learning and Instruction.*[1] A general case has been taught when, after instruction on some tasks in a particular class, any task in that class can be performed correctly. When we teach the general case about a concept, an operation, or a problem-solving rule, all possible examples or applications of the skills taught can be tested, even though the particular examples were not presented during the teaching. For example, when students have been taught sounds and blending skills, they should be able to decode *any* regular-sound word using these skills. General case sets assume that there are essential characteristics (S+ or R+) that hold for any members of the set. Thus, the teaching of *some* members of the set imply the teaching of *any*.

Note however, that *how an objective is taught determines whether or not it forms a general case.* One could teach reading by a sight-word method and have no general case. One could teach addition as number facts to be learned by rote, instead of as a set of problem-solving operations to handle any problem of a given type. This means that the definition of classes of skills depends in part on the teaching method. Thus, you have to analyze the teaching sequence to be able to define skill classes that can be tested for a given program of instruction.

We will call the opposite of a class involving a general case a linear-additive set. For skill classes involving linear-additive sets, each new member of the class must be taught explicitly. Having taught the sounds *m, s,* and *t* has no implications for being able to identify *particular* other sounds. It is true that if the same teaching format is used, members of the set taught later may often be learned with fewer trials, but each new member must still be taught. Language concepts usually form a linear-additive set. The learning of one concept does not teach you another. For example, if you teach the concept "on," you cannot assume you have taught "under." However, each member of a linear-additive set may involve a general-case (sub) set. (When the student has learned to identify the sound m, any m can be identified.) In general each new concept, each new operation, and each new rule is a member of a linear-additive set and should be specifically identified in defining a skill objective. With a linear-additive set, the teaching of one member of the set has no *specific* implications for the learning of other members.*

In sum, when classes of skills to be tested involve a general-case set, it is sufficient to describe the characteristics of the set in defining the class. When a linear-additive set is involved, the specific members of the set must be identified.

With this background, we are now in a better position to discuss the steps involved in constructing an instructional-program-based test.

Step 1. Identify Main Terminal Skills

Terminal skills should be defined as sets of tasks, any one of which the student can perform at the end of a program level. In beginning reading, the main terminal skills involve decoding and comprehension. But most first level programs would not define a terminal skill as "Read any English word," or "Demonstrate comprehension of any paragraph or set of paragraphs in English." More precise statements of the decoding and comprehension skills taught are required. Very often the scope and sequence chart in the teacher's manual, or a test of terminal skills provided with a program will help to determine the main terminal skills. When these are not provided, start with activities specified near the end of the program. These usually represent the skills the program has been building towards.

Figure 3.1 presents the Scope and Sequence Chart from *Distar Reading 1* (second edition).[2] From this chart, terminal level 1 skills are indicated by the tracks that continue to Lesson 160. In decoding, the skills could be defined as:

1 *Sounds* Say any one of forty sounds using Distar orthography. (See figure 3.2 for a definition of the set of sounds and the orthography.[3] This is a linear-additive set.)
2 *Reading words*
  a. Read by sounds any regular sound word (including nonsense words) using Distar orthography. This is a general-case set.
  b. Read irregular words from this list: was, is, said, do, to, of, car, you, your, etc. This is a linear-additive set. (Note that there are some families of irregular words such as not-note, rot-rote, mat-mate, that form a general-case subset. However, these are not covered in *Distar Reading 1.*)
  c. Read the fast way, any word introduced in Distar 1 (about 450). This is a linear-additive set.

---

*If language concepts are taught in terms of morphographs (roots, prefixes, suffixes), general-case sets may be generated.

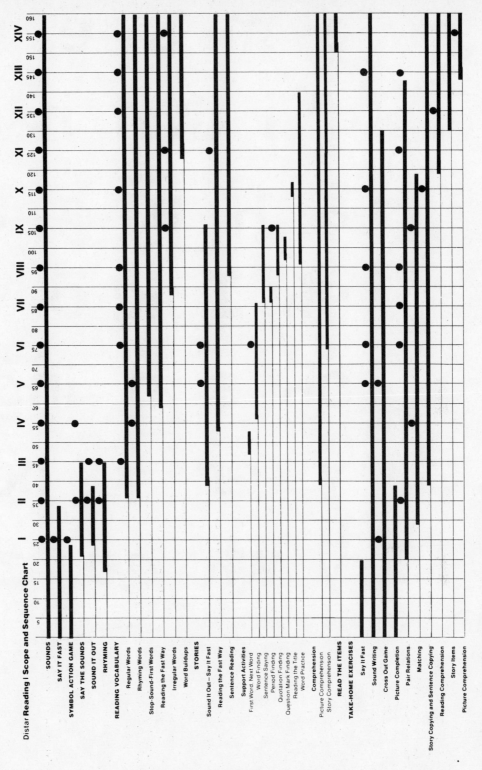

Figure 3.1 A chart showing main terminal skills

Figure 3.2 Sounds and orthography from Distar Reading I

3 *Story reading* Read stories containing words following the rules in number two above, sentence by sentence, and stopping at periods. This is a general-case set.

In comprehension, the terminal skills for level 1 could be defined as:

1 *Picture comprehension* The student correctly answers factual questions about a picture related to a story. ("Who did something?" "What did someone do?") The questions are initially presented orally, later they are in writing. This is a general-case set.
2 *Story comprehension* The student will answer informational questions about something she or he has read. The questions may be oral or written. This is a general-case set.
3 *Following directions* The student will follow the directions given in "Read the Item" tasks. This is a general-case set.

A series of reading-related skills are also taught:

1 *Writing sounds and words* The student will copy any of the 40 Distar sounds. This is a linear-additive set.
2 *Spelling by sounds* The student will write regular sound words said by the teacher. This is a general-case set. (Note that spelling of irregular words often involves a linear-additive set except as noted in 2b above.)
3 *Workbook skills* A variety of workbook skills are also taught, such as matching pictures and words, and matching phrases that say the same thing.

The product of step 1 should be a series of statements, such as those given for reading above, which specify what the students should be able to do under what conditions when the program is completed.

Step 2. Identify the Specific Directions and Response Requirements

What form is used to demonstrate mastery of an objective? What vocabulary is used for directions? How are responses to be made? The vocabulary used in the program should be used for the test. If *adding* is called *plussing*, then *plussing* should be used in the test directions. Are the students required to *write* the answer in showing they know what a car is, or can they just *point* to a car? The response requirements taught are the response requirements that should be tested.

Suppose the terminal skill in "addition of numbers with sums of 20 or less" are taught using the column addition format. Testing with row formats such as $13 + 6 = \boxed{}$ or $13 + \boxed{} = 19$ would be inappropriate. Conversely, if the beginning program focuses on row addition formats (as it might, in order to lay a strong basis for later work with equations), then testing with column formats would be inappropriate. Test items should test what the program teaches and not impose new requirements. If you are not satisfied, change the program before changing the test.

Since the Distar programs give detailed procedures for each teaching activity, there is little problem in determining directions and response requirements. The test items can just follow the procedures used by the teacher when requiring student responses in the program. With other programs, this information can usually be found by examining the teacher's manual or the student workbooks.

The product of step 2 should be a list of test directions and sample test items appropriate for each terminal skill.

Step 3. Find If and Where Each Skill is Taught

Work backward through the program and try to locate the first appearance of new skills. Find the directions, discussion, and exercises associated with them. In working back, you may find new concepts and operations not encountered near the end of this program. These will usually be *subskills* important in terminal skills. If they are, list them and trace their introduction into the program also. For more advanced texts, the index may be helpful in charting skill sequences. For others, a teacher's guide may contain a usable analysis of scope and sequence. The key to the search is to locate where instruction occurs on each subskill and terminal skill, and where and how the children make responses using the skill.

The product of this analysis should be a listing of the lessons and page numbers where the subskills and terminal skills are introduced and taught. Figures 3.1 and 3.2 show some of this kind of information for *Distar Reading 1.* In figure 3.1, the bars start where the teaching begins and stop where the teaching ends. Note that some skills are taught for short periods and then made a part of more complex skills. In figure 3.2, the numbers under each sound indicate the day of introduction.

Step 4. Divide the Skills into Tracks

In this step, we are looking for an organization of "what is being taught when." Tracks may be defined as a set of skills taught with a common format *or* as a sequence of skills using different formats that build to a terminal objective. In arithmetic, we might have a number-identification track (a set of skills taught with a common format) or an addition track (a sequence of formats such as regular addition with lines, algebra addition with lines, addition facts, and addition story problems). In reading, saying sounds might be one track defined by a common format, but comprehension skills might involve a sequence of formats which build on one another. Figure 3.1 shows the track structure for *Distar Reading 1.* In this example, most of the tracks are defined by a common teaching format.

The product of step 4 is a chart showing the temporal relations among the main subskills and terminal skills in a program.

Step 5. Divide the Tracks into Testing Units

The number of testing units selected depends on the instruction that is carried out. If all teaching is done in large groups and the students are kept together, a test for each six-weeks of the program might be adequate.

If the program is individualized by student or groups of students, then it should be possible to test a given student at any point in the program. The Continuous Progress Test for *Distar Reading 1* was designed to provide a test for each two weeks of the program after the first 20 days. Normally, students are tested each six weeks, but they can be tested more often if needed. The structure of the test components can be seen in figure 3.1. The roman numerals across the top indicate sections of the test. The dark circles on the tracks indicate the point where skills in a given track are tested.

Section I is used to test students who are at Lesson Day 21 to 30. It covers only skills introduced in the program by day 18. Section II is given to students who are at Lesson Day 31-40, and so on through Section XIV.

The product of step 5 is a statement of how many tests are needed and at what points in the program they will occur.

Step 6. Determine the Skills to Be Tested at Each Cycle

It is usually not possible to provide an independent test of each skill taught. Choices have to be made. Key building blocks and their consolidation into complex skills are given priority. Also, when testing related sets of concepts, the testing should emphasize the members which are likely to be confused with each other (like *d* and *b* in the sounds track).

In the *Reading 1* Continuous Progress Test, three to six tracks are tested in each ten-day section of the test. As noted above, a given track is tested where indicated by the dark circles on the track lines in figure 3.1. Sounds are the basic building blocks for the program, so new sounds and review sounds are tested for every section of the program. Word Reading is also tested in every section in one form or another (regular words, extrapolation words, rhyming words, or irregular words). After this, the testing *samples* skills in tracks that are about to be integrated into more complex skills, or that have not been tested for some time. Many of the skills related to the Take-Home Exercises involve combinations of reading, writing, and comprehension skills.

By carefully testing key building blocks, it is possible to analyze why a more complex skill is failed. For example, at day 45, by testing Sounds and Sound It Out (blending), it is possible to analyze why Reading Regular Words is failed. Thus, a basis for remedial action is provided.

The product of step 6 will be a statement of which tracks are to be tested at each test cycle.

Step 7. Construct Test Items

If the first six steps are carried out well, this final step should be routine. However, there are a number of basic rules to be followed in designing test items.

Rule 1. Test What Has Been Taught

First, *make the range of items used in the test consistent with what was taught.* If you are dealing with a general-case set, you *can* test with examples not used in teaching. For example, in arithmetic the children are taught to solve problems of this form $13 + 7 = \boxed{}$ by putting 7 lines under the 7 and counting from 13 until they reach the number represented by adding seven more (that is, by counting 7 lines). There are 171 problems of this type with sums of 20 or under (excluding zero and negative numbers). Assume that the teaching program uses only 10 examples from this set to teach the rule. The test items could draw on any of 171 examples, including the 161 that the children had not seen before. However, if you have taught regular addition problems with sums of 20 or under, you *cannot* test with examples of algebra addition problems such as $13 + \boxed{} = 20$.

If you are dealing with a linear-additive set, only the set members taught may be used in testing. Let's say that you have taught these concepts: hot-cold, heavy-light, long-short. All are polars (opposites), but they form a linear-additive set, which means that you should test the students on only the concepts taught. You could not test them on light-dark, tall-short, or any other concept not taught. However, the students have been taught long-short, which means they have learned a general case. So you can test long-short by presenting any pair of objects, one of which is longer than the other. You would not have to restrict the selection of long-short examples to those taught in the program.

Finally, *use only directions and response requirements taught in the program.* If the program teaches decoding by showing letters and asking the children to "say the sound this makes," then the test cannot ask the children to "look at the pictures on this page and circle the letter for the first sound in the word the picture stands for." The directions and the response requirements have to be consistent with what has been taught. A more extreme example might help the reader to better understand this point. Suppose you were taught to identify and name pictures of the first five presidents of the United States. Then, on the test, the teacher asks you to "draw a picture of John Adams." The test would be obviously unfair, having response requirements not taught. A final example focuses on unfair directions. Suppose the children are taught in the teaching program to refer to these signs (> , <) as "more" and "less" signs. On the test, they are given this problem: "Is 9 *greater than* or *less than* 6? Draw the sign which shows which is greater." Without being taught that "greater than" means the same as "more," this is an unfair test item.

By carefully identifying the specific directions and response requirements used in a teaching program (as detailed in step 2), and identifying general-case sets and linear-additive sets, test items can be made fair—they will test what was taught.

Rule 2. Give Preference to Most Recently Taught Items and Highly Similar Items Taught Earlier

In good programing, the items within a track build cumulatively. Thus, there will usually be more practice on items taught earlier in the program than those taught most recently. Since errors are most likely to occur on least practiced items and testing is looking for weakness, preference is given to most recently taught items. The other main source of errors is the confusion that can arise when concepts or tasks share many identical characteristics (Sc) and differ in few or small ways (S+ vs S−). (See *Teaching 2*, unit 9.) Thus, testing also focuses on items taught earlier that are most similar to recently taught items.

Suppose in a corrective reading program, we are teaching decoding skills focusing on long-short vowel confusion. Long-o and short-o sounds were emphasized first (mod-mode, bon-bone, con-cone). Then, long-a and short-a sounds were introduced (mad-made, ban-bane, can-cane). It would be important in testing long-a and short-a words to also test long-o and short-o words that differ only in the vowel. For example, one test item might be:

Say: *Read these words.* Point to each word in order by row.

can	con	cane	cone
bane	bone	ban	bon
mad	mode	made	mod

The only way the student can discriminate words in a given row is to show mastery of the long-o and short-o sounds *and* the long-a and short-a sounds. If the test focused only on long-a and short-a words, it is possible that confusions with long-o and short-o words would still exist and be missed.

Consider another example. In the *Distar Reading 1* Continuous Progress Test for days 51-61, only five sounds are tested, although 12 sounds have been taught by day 48. The three sounds taught in the past ten days (days 39-48) are tested (*t, n,* and *c*) along with two taught earlier (*m, th*). The *m* sound was included because of its possible confusion with *n*. The *th* sound was included because of its possible confusion with *t*. For days 111-120, four sounds are tested. At this point 25 sounds have been taught, two of them in the past ten days (*v* and *g*). The two recent sounds are tested along with *p* and *d*. These were added because of their possible confusion with *g*. Inspection of figure 3.2 showing the Distar Reading orthography, shows that *d* and *g* have the same kind of oval shape, and that a rotation of *p* makes a *d*. Thus, the testing attempts to make sure that the most critical discriminations in the set being taught have been mastered. If these are mastered, it is very likely (but not sure) that easier discriminations have also been mastered.

Rule 3. Do Not Test a Skill Until It Has Been Taught for Three Days

This is a crude rule-of-thumb. It is followed simply because experience in teaching basic skills shows that three teaching days are needed to solidify most new skills. This rule does not necessarily hold in teaching the advanced learner, although it would do little harm to follow it even there.

Rule 4. Do Not Test Trivial Skills

A trivial skill is one that is taught but never again used in the program. For example, in one reading program, the children are put through exercises where they are asked to indicate whether a particular sound occurs at the beginning, middle, or end of a word. This skill has no relationship to skills taught later and certainly not to reading. We are concerned with whether a child can *read words* when a given sound occurs at any location in a word. We are not concerned with whether the child can describe the position of a sound in a word he hears. The activity is not a reading subskill.

Rule 5. Avoid Ambiguous Instructions

A test instruction should not be subject to more than one interpretation. In writing instructional-program-based tests, ambiguities are most likely to arise from oversights that can be detected by analyzing tryout data. The following example is taken from the tryout of the Engelmann and Hanner *Survival Skills Reading Test.* [4]

Here is an item as it appeared in the original test:

Read these sentences:
  The old woman ran after the robber. When the robber fell, the old woman grabbed him.
  45. Circle the words that tell when the old woman caught the robber.
  46. Underline the words that tell who ran after the robber.

In the original test, for item 46 the student was expected to underline *the old woman* both times it occurred (as specified in the scoring key). That this should be done is not clear from the item. The revised item was written as follows:

Read these sentences:
  The old woman ran after the robber. When the robber fell, she grabbed him.
  45. Circle the words that tell when the old woman caught the robber.
  46. Underline the words that tell who ran after the robber.

Adapting Procedures to Less Structured Programs

In dealing with materials that are less structured than the Distar examples given, some modification of procedures may be necessary. First, in many "spiral curriculum" programs, some skills are not used again (that year) beyond the section in which they are first taught. For such programs, skills should be tested for the units in which they are taught. Only with additional reviews would good performance be expected on such skills at a later point in time.

Second, very often analysis may show that activities assumed to teach new skills are weak. Your choice at this point is between rejecting the program and testing the adequacy of the program. If the second choice is taken, test the skill about three days after its introduction. In this way decisions, based on facts, can be made about use or revision of the program.

A Note on Procedures for Selecting Instructional Programs

Some of the procedures for analyzing an instructional program to build a test are also useful in selecting instructional programs. Consider the following questions in evaluating possible programs:

1 Are the objectives of the program consistent with district goals?
2 Are the preskills for entry to the program specified at each level and commensurate with the capabilities of your students?
3 Is there evidence that the program can achieve the stated goals? Is the evidence based on students like yours?
4 What is the internal evidence that the program can do the job? This requires an analysis similar to that required to construct instructional-program-based tests:
   a. Begin with the objectives and find out where they are taught and how.
   b. Evaluate the adequacy of the teaching examples. See if essential prerequisite skills are taught.
   c. Determine the effort involved in correcting errors and so on.
5 What are the provisions for individualization (or grouping) of instruction for students at different levels in the same class?
6 What are the training requirements for effective use of the program?
7 What is the cost in relation to potential effectiveness?

summary

It makes no sense to try to build a test based on an instructional program if in fact no consistent program is followed. So be sure first that the program can be used with consistency before spending time building tests to use with it.

It is also important in building tests to be able to tell the difference between sets of skills that define a general case and those that do not. A general case has been taught when after teaching some members of a defined set, all members can be performed correctly. Examples or applications of concepts, operations, or problem-solving rules form general-case sets. Linear-additive sets involve skill sets where each new member has to be taught. This can occur because a rote teaching method is used or because of the inherent structure of the knowledge and skill set. Usually language concepts, mathematical operations, and problem-solving strategies each form linear-additive sets. Learning about some member of the set does not teach you how to do the others.

When a class of skills to be tested involves a general-case set, the class can be described by the characteristics of the set. When a linear-additive set is involved, the specific members of the set must be identified.

The steps to follow in constructing progress tests for an instructional program are these: First, identify the main terminal skills. A scope and sequence chart or a teacher's guide is a good place to start. Second, identify the specific directions and response requirements necessary to show mastery of the objectives. Third, find where each skill is taught (if it is taught). This will lead to an analysis of subskills which may be needed and provide a basis for a flowchart showing where each skill is introduced and how long it is taught. Fourth, divide the skills into tracks. The goal is to show what is being taught when, and how tasks or skills build on each other. A track may be defined by a set of skills which are taught in a common format, or as sequence of skills using different formats which build to a terminal objective. Fifth, divide the track into testing units. How many testing units are needed depends on the method of instruction. If instruction is individualized, a test for each two weeks of progress may be needed. If instruction is in large groups and the students stay together, a test every six weeks might be adequate. The sixth step is to decide which skills to test at each testing cycle. Since not everything can be tested, key building blocks and their consolidation into more complex skills are given priority. Testing also focuses on members of sets which are likely to be confused with recently taught members. The seventh and last step involves construction of test items. Five guidelines were suggested:

1 Test what has been taught.
2 Give preference to most recently taught items and to highly similar items taught earlier.
3 Do not test a skill unit until it has been taught for three days.
4 Do not test trivial skills, that is, skills which are never used in the program again.
5 Avoid ambiguous instructions.

When selecting instructional programs, you can apply the same analysis procedures used in building tests for an instructional program.

self-test

If you get nine or ten right, skip the Programed Practice and go on to the next exercise. If you make more than one error, do the Programed Practice, go back to the text to correct mistakes, and then do the next exercise.

1 It makes no sense to try to build an instruction-referenced testing program, if no particular instructional program is _____ .

2 Two kinds of skill sets can be defined, _____-_____ sets and linear-additive sets.

1 followed

2 general-case

3   You have to analyze the _____ sequence to be able to define skill classes that can be tested for a given program of instruction.

4   Language concepts usually form a _____-_____ set. The learning of one concept does not teach you another.

5   Very often the scope and sequence chart in the teacher's manual, or a _____ of terminal skills provided with a program will help to determine the main terminal skills.

6   The vocabulary used in the program should be used for the _____ .

7   Tracks may be defined as a set of skills which are taught with a common _____ , or as a sequence of skills using different formats that build

to a _____ objective.

8   In writing test items, give preference to most _____ taught items and highly _____ items taught earlier.

NUMBER RIGHT _____

exercise 1 programed practice

Cover the answers on the left with your marker. Read each item, and write in your answer. Then check the answer by moving your marker down one step. Accept your answers if the meaning is the same as that given. If you are not sure about the material covered, return to the text.

1   To be most useful criterion-referenced tests should be referenced to an _____ program.

2   Presently, educational materials and tests are not designed in this way, so the teacher needs to know how to _____ and use tests.

3   It makes no sense to try to build an instruction-referenced testing program, if no particular instructional program is _____ .

4   In defining skills for testing, it is most desirable to define a _____ _____ _____ any one of which the student should be able to perform.

5 Two kinds of skill sets can be defined, _____-_____ sets and linear-additive sets.

6 A general case has been taught when, after instruction on some tasks in a particular class, _____ task in that class can be performed correctly.

7 Whether or not an objective forms a general case depends on how it is _____ .

8 One could teach addition as number facts to be learned by _____ , instead of as a set of problem-solving operations to handle any problem of a given type.

9 Thus, you have to analyze the _____ sequence to be able to define skill classes that can be tested for a given program of instruction.

10 For skill classes involving linear-additive sets, each _____ _____ of the class must be taught explicitly.

11 Language concepts usually form a _____-_____ set. The learning of one concept does not teach you another.

12 The first step in constructing an instructional-program-based test is to identify the main _____ skills.

13 Terminal skills should be defined as _____ of tasks, any one of which the student can perform at the end of a program level.

14 Very often the scope and sequence chart in the teacher's manual, or a _____ of terminal skills provided with a program will help to determine the main terminal skills.

15 The next step is to identify the specific _____ and response requirements.

16 The vocabulary used in the program should be used for the _____ .

17 The response requirements taught are the response requirements that should be _____ .

18 Next, locate where instruction occurs on each subskill and terminal skill, and where and how the children make _____ using the skill.

19 Next, divide the skills into tracks. Tracks may be defined as a set of skills which are taught with a common _____ , or as a sequence of skills using different formats that build to a _____ objective.

20 The next step is to decide how many _____ you need.

21 After the testing parts are located, you need to determine the _____ to be tested at each cycle. Key building _____ and their consolidation into complex skills are given priority.

22 Also, when testing related sets of concepts, the testing should emphasize the members which are likely to be _____ with each other.

23 Five rules were suggested for constructing test items:

a. Test what has been _____ . If you are dealing with a _____-_____ set, you can test with examples not used in teaching. If you are dealing with a _____-_____ set, only the set members taught may be used in testing.

b. Give preference to most _____ taught items and highly _____ items taught earlier.

c. Do not test a skill until it has been taught for _____ days.

d. Do not test _____ skills. A trivial skill is one that is taught but _____ again used in the program.

e. Avoid _____ instructions. A test instruction should not be subject to more than one _____ .

24 Some of the analysis procedures used to build a test are also useful in _____ instructional programs.

---

20 tests

21 skills; blocks

22 confused

23a. taught;
   general-case;
   linear-additive

b. recently;
   similar

c. three

d. trivial; never

e. ambiguous;
   interpretation

24 selecting

---

exercise 2   analyzing a program segment and constructing test items

1 Select a segment of any program for elementary school students that could reasonably be covered by the students in 6 to 10 days of daily lessons. It is suggested that you avoid beginning reading programs for this task and that you select a program where tests for the program (beyond workbook exercises) are minimal or absent. If possible, select a segment of a program soon to be actually taught so that you can try out your test before and after the instruction.

2 Analyze the teaching objectives for the program segment selected. List these objectives as statements of sets of tasks the students should be able to perform.

3 Analyze where the objectives are taught in the segment. Note if the students are actually required to perform the tasks assumed by the objectives and if sufficient practice is required. Where sufficient practice is not provided, make suggestions for improving the instruction.

4 Identify any subskills taught in the segment.

5 List special direction words used and response requirements.

6 List the preskills assumed by each objective.

7 Chart the sequence of dependencies among objectives, subskills, and preskills.

8 Build a test for the end of the sequence and build a test of assumed preskills.

Be prepared to present your analysis in class or discussion group and/or to turn in a report if requested by your instructor. Also note that if you can get to try your test out, exercise 2 in unit 4 involves an analysis of the data from the tryout. It is suggested that you read the requirements of exercise 2, unit 4, before proceeding with this exercise.

discussion questions

1 Why is it important for the teacher to know how to build tests?

2 Why is it important that the teacher follow a fairly structured set of procedures in teaching a specified set of skills and information?

3 In defining sets of skills for testing, what is the difference between a general-case set and a linear-additive set?

4 Give examples of general-case sets and linear-additive sets.

5 In analyzing an instructional program, how do you identify the main terminal skills?

6 Why is it important to identify the specific directions and response requirements used in an instructional program?

7 What is the purpose of locating where each skill and subskill is taught in a program?

8 How are skill tracks defined?

9 What determines the number of testing units you will need?

10 How do you define which skills to test at each testing unit or cycle?

11 Give five rules for constructing test items.

12 What exactly does the rule "Test what has been taught" cover?

13 Summarize the main steps to follow in constructing tests for an instructional program.

14 Explain why the procedures used in analyzing a program for test building are also useful in analyzing a program for possible adoption?

15 What additional questions should be asked in evaluating possible programs besides the internal evidence that it can do the job?

unit 4

Evaluating
Instructional-Program-Based Tests

objectives

When you complete this unit you should be able to—

1 Give four criteria for evaluating an instructional-program-based test.
2 Discuss how to decide how many different tests you have.
3 Define test reliability and validity.
4 Show how to compute reliability indexes for a test of a general-case set and a test of a linear-additive set.
5 Specify two criteria for determining the validity of instructional-program-based tests.
6 Define and compute validity indexes that show sensitivity to instruction.

lesson

Building a test is a design problem and like other design problems, solutions are not right or wrong, but better or worse as judged against specific criteria. Usually in judging tests, we are interested in the reliability and validity of the information provided. We should also be interested in the cost of getting the information. Finally, for an instructional-program-based test, we should be interested in the value of the test for evaluating the adequacy of instruction and in pointing to remediation procedures.

How Many Tests Do You Have?

A test usually consists of a group of tasks or items where it is meaningful to add together an individual's performance on the tasks to form a single score. For tests of instruction, it is meaningful to add performances together when they reflect a common teaching outcome. Therefore it is possible to have as many tests as there are different teaching outcomes. The definition of teaching outcomes (and therefore the number of tests needed) depends upon the stage of instruction with respect to an objective and if a general-case objective is dealt with, or one that involves a linear-additive set.

Generally, when an instructional objective defines a general-case set, such as reading regular-sound words, the objective provides the basis for one test, and any members of that set can be sampled in building a test. When an instructional objective defines a linear-additive set, there are conditions when each member of the set should be treated as a separate test. For example, just because a child can say the sound for the letters *sh* says nothing about the child being able to say the sound for *p*. Both might be on a *test of sounds,* but be tests of different teaching outcomes.

The number of tests you have also depends on the stage of instruction. For example, if you are working on the objective for the general case "Addition of numbers with sums up to 20," and have not firmed the more complex skills involved with higher numbers, it may be necessary to break the objective into two tests, the addition of numbers with sums to 10 and the addition of numbers with sums from 11 to 20. Students might pass the first test and fail the second.

Conversely, it may not be necessary to test all members of a linear-additive set if the members have had a relatively equal chance to be learned. A sample could be used as a test of mastery of the whole set. For example, a *test of sounds* with samples from those sounds which have been taught could be treated as one test to evaluate the question "Have all the sounds taught so far been learned?" If some items are failed, the whole set should be tested to find out where more teaching is required.

Reliability

The basic reliability question is "To what degree do different measures of the same thing lead to the same result?" or conversely, "How much error is there in the test?" Errors in a test score can arise from several sources. A person's performance may vary from day to day. Errors can be made in scoring a test. Errors can be made in giving a test. The most critical information about the reliability of a criterion-referenced test can usually be obtained by examining the *consistency* with which a group of items taken from the same test leads to the same result. "Do those who pass one item on the test pass the other items?" Such comparisons reflect errors due to scoring of items, moment to moment individual variations in performance, and variations in item content. First we will examine procedures for determining *response consistency* or reliability for tests of a general-case set.*

---

*Note that in test theory literature, the term reliability is used almost exclusively to refer to the reliability of individual differences within a norm-referenced framework. *Response consistency* is quantified *relative* to the spread of scores on a test. This usage is clarified in unit 12, where the most common measure of reliability, the Pearson correlation coefficient, is discussed. In the present unit, response consistency is quantified as a percentage of the number of items being compared.

Reliability of a General-Case Set

If we have two or more test items which are assumed to be measures of the "same thing," we can determine the degree to which those items produce the same result by seeing if students who pass one item pass other items. For example, suppose we are testing for a solution to regular addition problems of this form $3 + 13 = \boxed{}$ with sums up to 20. These problems form a general-case set, any one of which the student should be able to do if appropriate instruction has been given. Suppose three problems are given to ten students with the following results (+ indicates pass and − indicates fail).

TABLE 4.1 SCORES FOR TEN STUDENTS ON THREE ITEMS

Students	A $3 + 7 = \boxed{}$	B $6 + 3 = \boxed{}$	C $3 + 15 = \boxed{}$
1	+	+	+
2	−	−	−
3	+	+	+
4	+	+	+
5	+	+	+
6	−	−	−
7	+	+	+
8	+	−	+
9	+	+	−
10	+	+	+

A and B: $\dfrac{\text{Agreements}}{\text{Students}} = \dfrac{9}{10} = 90\%$

A and C: $\dfrac{\text{Agreements}}{\text{Students}} = \dfrac{9}{10} = 90\%$

B and C: $\dfrac{\text{Agreements}}{\text{Students}} = \dfrac{8}{10} = 80\%$

Average of A, B, and C: $\dfrac{90 + 90 + 80}{3} = 86.7\% = 87\%$

For items A and B, in every case except one, students who passed A passed B, and those who failed A failed B. A simple reliability index is the percent of agreement between the results for two test items across students. This is determined by taking two items, counting the number of agreements, and dividing by the number of students. For A and B, this index is 90 percent. For A and C, this index is 90 percent and for B and C this index is 80 percent. The average index for A, B, and C is 87 percent.

Let us now look at a more elaborate example. Suppose we give a ten-item test of the same objective to twenty students and obtain the results given in table 4.2. Again +'s indicate an item is passed and −'s indicate an item is failed.

TABLE 4.2 PASS-FAIL SCORES FOR TWENTY STUDENTS ON TEN ITEMS

Student No.	Test Item No.										Sum
	1	2	3	4	5	6	7	8	9	10	
1	+	+	+	+	+	−	+	+	+	−	8
2	+	+	+	+	+	+	+	+	+	−	9
3	+	+	+	+	+	−	+	+	+	+	9
4	−	+	−	+	−	−	−	−	+	+	④
5	+	+	+	+	+	−	+	+	+	−	8
6	+	+	+	+	+	+	+	+	+	−	9
7	−	−	+	−	−	−	−	−	+	+	③
8	+	+	+	+	+	−	+	+	+	−	8
9	+	+	+	+	+	+	+	+	+	−	9
10	−	+	+	+	+	−	+	+	+	−	7
11	+	+	+	+	+	+	+	+	+	−	9
12	+	−	+	−	−	−	+	−	+	−	④
13	+	+	+	+	+	+	+	+	+	+	10
14	+	+	+	+	+	−	+	+	+	−	8
15	−	−	+	−	+	+	−	−	−	−	③
16	+	+	+	+	+	−	+	+	+	+	9
17	+	+	+	+	+	+	+	+	+	−	9
18	+	+	+	+	+	−	+	+	+	+	9
19	+	+	+	+	+	−	+	+	+	−	8
20	+	+	+	+	+	−	+	+	+	−	8
SUM	16	17	19	17	17	⑦	17	16	19	⑥	

+ = Pass
− = Fail

We can calculate a percent agreement index for each item with every other item. We have calculated these indexes for the data in table 4.2 and placed them in table 4.3. Note that the indexes above the diagonal are identical to those below the diagonal. The percent agreement indexes for all items except 6 and 10 are 80 percent or higher. The average reliability index for these 8 items (excluding 6 and 10) is 88.9. The agreement between 6 and 10 and the rest of the items ranges from 25 to 50 percent, therefore items 6 and 10 are obviously measuring something different.

By returning to table 4.2, we can see that the conclusion drawn from examining percent-agreement indexes could also have been reached by examining the sums at the bottom of the table. Item 6 was passed by 7 students and item 10 by 6 students. The rest of the items were passed by 16 to 19 students. In working with criterion-referenced tests where the students have been taught the material being tested, this kind of outcome is expected. Most of the students will pass most of the items. When this does not happen, the items failed should stand out in the pass-fail table. Thus, usually it would not be necessary to compute the percent agreement indexes (as in table 4.3) unless they are needed to summarize a large mass of data.

Note also in table 4.2 that four students consistently did poorly (numbers 4, 7, 12, and 15). This suggests that the reasons most of the items (excluding 6 and 10) are not at 100 percent pass is not the fault of the items,

TABLE 4.3   PERCENT AGREEMENT INDEXES FOR A TEN ITEM TEST

ITEM NUMBER	ITEM NUMBER									
	1	2	3	4	5	6	7	8	9	10
1		85	85	85	85	45	95	90	85	30
2	85		80	100	90	40	90	95	90	35
3	85	80		80	90	40	90	85	90	25
4	85	100	80		90	40	90	95	90	35
5	85	90	90	90		50	90	95	80	25
6	45	40	40	40	50		40	45	30	45
7	95	90	90	90	90	40		95	90	25
8	90	95	85	95	95	45	95		85	30
9	85	90	90	90	80	30	90	85		35
10	30	35	25	35	25	45	25	30	35	
Average	76.1	78.3	73.9	78.3	77.2	41.7	78.3	79.4	75.0	31.7

but rather due to the fact that some students were not taught. They may have been absent a lot; they may have lacked the preskills to profit from the instruction. Whatever the reason, the test shows that those students need special attention.

Further Analysis of Low Agreement Indexes

The analysis of reliability or response consistency begins by determining if the items to be compared for pass-fail patterns are logically measures of the same teaching objectives. Then, empirically, we find out if those items do in fact produce the same results for different students. When the percent-agreement indexes are high, all is well and reliability has been established. When the percent-agreement indexes are low, however, a closer examination of patterns among items is needed. Agreements among some items may possibly be low, but high within *subgroups* of items. Consider the pattern within table 4.4. A and B show 100 percent agreement in pass-fail patterns and so do C and D. However, the agreement between the items in these two subgroups is only 60 percent. Does the fact that C and D produce results that disagree with A and B mean that the items are unreliable? Probably not. It appears that we have two tests rather than one. Some students could not do addition problems with sums over ten, while others could. While all four problems were measures of what we called "adding with sums up to 20," at the stage of learning where these students were working, two separate objectives were being measured. The empirical analysis showed that our assumption was wrong about what items were measures of the same teaching objective. That assumption can be corrected by redefining what constitutes a test.

TABLE 4.4 SCORES FOR TEN STUDENTS ON FOUR ITEMS

Students	A 3 + 7 = □	B 6 + 3 = □	C 3 + 15 = □	D 5 + 14 = □
1	+	+	+	+
2	+	+	−	−
3	+	+	+	+
4	+	+	+	+
5	+	+	−	−
6	+	+	−	−
7	+	+	+	+
8	+	+	+	+
9	+	+	−	−
10	+	+	+	+

Low agreement indexes might also be attributable to items which are subject to more than one interpretation. In that case, rewrite the item to remove the ambiguity and try again.

Reliability of Linear-Additive Sets

Linear-additive sets define groups of essentially different skills. Each member of the set constitutes a different test. If it can be assumed that the students have had an opportunity to learn all members of the set, then a test sampling the separate skills can be treated as a test of mastery of the objective. This procedure is used in much criterion-referenced testing today. However, the procedure gives no basis for evaluating the reliability of individual members of the set, or for knowing precisely what teaching is required if the sample shows students have not mastered the objective. Which members need reteaching can be determined by testing with the whole set in which failures occur. The question of reliability of the set can be answered by including more than one test item for each member of the linear-additive set sampled. Then, the reliability question is focused on the pairs (or larger groups) of *like items.* Scores for different students can be examined for pairs of like items to see if there is pattern agreement (+ + or − −). A percent agreement index can be computed for each pair of like items. These indexes can then be averaged over members of the linear-additive set used as a sample in the test. These computations are illustrated in table 4.5. The table shows the pass-fail results for eight sounds, each tested twice (for example: m_1, m_2) for ten students. The percent agreement indexes for pairs of like items are shown in the right-hand column. The average for the eight pairs of items is given at the bottom. The cost in testing time to achieve this elegance may not be worth it. A good strategy to follow would be to include "double items" in tryout forms of a test. This would be especially necessary if the test format differs in some ways from the teaching-program format. If reliability proves to be high, the extra items can be omitted in later versions of the test. If reliability is low, a re-examination of the test procedures is needed.

TABLE 4.5 RELIABILITY COMPUTATION FOR A LINEAR-ADDITIVE SET (SOUNDS)

| Items | Students | | | | | | | | | | Percent Agreement |
	1	2	3	4	5	6	7	8	9	10	
m_1	+	+	+	+	−	+	+	+	+	+	100
m_2	+	+	+	+	−	+	+	+	+	+	
t_1	−	+	−	+	+	+	+	−	−	+	100
t_2	−	+	−	+	+	+	+	−	−	+	
a_1	−	−	+	−	+	−	+	+	+	+	90
a_2	−	−	+	−	−	−	+	+	+	+	
c_1	+	+	−	−	+	−	−	−	+	+	100
c_2	+	+	−	−	+	−	−	−	+	+	
f_1	+	+	−	+	+	+	+	+	+	+	90
f_2	−	+	−	+	+	+	+	+	+	+	
e_1	+	+	+	−	+	+	−	−	−	−	90
e_2	+	+	+	+	+	+	−	−	−	−	
i_1	+	−	+	−	−	−	−	+	−	−	80
i_2	+	−	+	+	−	−	−	−	−	−	
b_1	−	−	+	+	+	+	−	−	−	−	100
b_2	−	−	+	+	+	+	−	−	−	−	
							Average Percent Agreement				94

Evaluating Validity

The validity question asks, "Does the test measure what it is supposed to measure?" With instruction-based tests this question means, "Does the test measure the objective that was taught, or is it a measure of something else?"

Content Validity

The initial criterion for validity is that items meet the logical requirements of the teaching objective. In the test-construction literature this is known as content validity or logical validity. A teaching objective defines a set of tasks the student should be able to perform. The content validity question asks if each item is a member of the set so defined. Conclusions about the content validity of given items change as the stated objectives change. For "reading comprehension" items, an incredibly large range of items could meet the content-validity requirement. For "reading comprehension for a third-grade reading vocabulary," the range is substantially reduced. If the content-validity requirement is "identification of specific information references for third-grade reading material," the range of items is further limited. The statement of the test objective provides the basis for determining whether or not an item has "content validity." A valid test item must also be content-consistent in terms of the *direction words* and *response requirements* taught in the program.

Sensitivity to Instruction

Beyond the requirement of content validity, the key concept in the analysis of validity of instruction-based tests is *sensitivity to instruction*.[1,2] In the development of norm-referenced tests, an attempt to show sensitivity to instruction is a key concern. A typical procedure has been to show that students in higher grades do better on a given test than students in lower grades. This procedure will show some general changes taking place with age, but cannot demonstrate that the changes are due to instruction. First, actual changes in individual students (pretest to posttest) are not measured. Second, there is no assurance that the presumed instruction actually occurred, and various "good" and "bad" programs are conglomerated in the test results. Third, there is no attempt to control for instruction that might be going on at home, on television, and elsewhere. As we will see later, because of the method of item selection on norm-referenced achievement tests, any kinds of changes occurring with age are likely to be reflected in achievement scores. There is a strong possibility that results on most norm-referenced tests will be highly related to education of parents, since more out-of-school instruction is likely to occur in the homes of better educated parents.[3,4] Instructional-program-based tests offer the possibility (not yet fully documented) of overcoming some of these problems with norm-referenced tests.

To determine whether or not test items are sensitive to instruction, it is necessary to

1 Show that items are logically valid measures of a *specified* instructional program.
2 Show that items are not passed prior to instruction and are passed after the relevant instruction.[5]
3 Show independently that the instructional program can be used to teach the objectives under specified conditions and measure the degree to which these conditions obtain in the setting where the items are evaluated for sensitivity.
4 Show that passage of time, without instruction, does not produce increases in the passing of the items.

We will discuss each of these points in more detail.

1. The procedures to follow in writing content-valid items was described in unit 3 (Constructing Instructional-Program-Based Tests). Those procedures involve defining program objectives and then selecting items that are measures of those objectives, using directions and formats consistent with what is taught.

2. To show sensitivity to instruction it is necessary to follow the pretest-posttest procedure of giving the test items prior to the point where the skills tested are taught in the program, then carry out the instruction, and test again to see what changes occurred. A sensitive item will show a higher per-

centage of students passing after instruction. A useful validity index can be obtained by computing differences between posttest and pretest percentages. The closer the index comes to 100, the more sensitive the item is shown to be to that instructional program. If only 5 percent of the students pass an item before instruction and 95 percent pass after, the validity index would be 90. If 5 percent pass it before instruction and 5 percent pass it after instruction, the validity index would be 0. Similarly, if 95 percent pass the item before instruction and 95 percent pass it after instruction, the index would also be 0.

3. The third point is concerned with the validity of instruction. If students fail test items before and after instruction, it could be that they were not taught the skills. An independent evaluation of the adequacy of the program and use of the program by the teacher is necessary. The validity of the instructional program and the teaching methods are at stake. For example, in developing the Distar programs, initial sequences were tried by skilled teachers with hard-to-teach children. Careful attention was paid to error rates made by students on each step in the program. When error rates were high, the program was modified by inserting additional steps or clarifying the presentation. When error rates were very low, the sequence was accelerated. Before publication, a clear demonstration was provided that the programs were effective when taught in specified ways. The next focus was on specifying the required teaching skills and training procedures. Particularly important were learning key formats, use of signals to get attention and control responses, use of rapid pacing, use of correction procedures, and reinforcing of good responses. Criteria were developed that made it possible to evaluate teacher performance on those variables. Those procedures are discussed in more detail in *Teaching 2*, units 2 and 3. With an independent demonstration that the program can work, what is needed is an evaluation of the degree to which the teaching covered by the testing is adequate. If the children perform well on the test with adequate teaching and perform poorly with less adequate teaching, the test should not be faulted.

4. The final concern in evaluating item validity arises when validity indexes are high. How do we know the information was not learned somewhere else? There is an obvious way to check. A group of children without the relevant skills could be pretested and half of them taken through the instruction. Then, all of the children would be tested again. If outside influences are not important, the children who were taught should show high scores and those who were not should show no improvement. This problem has not been critical for instructional-program-based tests covering short time spans. It is a logical possibility which should be considered in evaluating instruction.

Cost

Testing that takes too much time away from teaching is not desirable. Pencil and paper tests or relatively short tests that can be given by paraprofessionals are preferred. In building the Continuous Progress Tests for the Distar programs, we have attempted to keep testing time under ten minutes per child when given individually and under twenty minutes when given in groups.

Implications for Remedies

A final consideration is the ease with which the test results can be translated into *remediation procedures* when teaching procedures have failed. The following illustration shows how test results lead directly to remediation procedures and is taken from the *Distar Reading 1* Continuous Progress Test. Figure 4.1 shows a filled out record form for testing children who are between Days 21 and 30 in the program.[6]

Test items are arranged in tracks. Items a, b, c, and d are in the SIF (Say It Fast) track. Items e, f, and g are in the SI (Sounds Identification) track. Items slashed are items that were missed by a particular child. Bill R missed five items on the test. Bonnie Z missed one.

Next to each track column is a column headed CRIT, which stands for *failure criterion*. At the top of each of these columns is a number that indicates the failure criterion. For SIF the failure criterion is 2 or more. For SI the failure criterion is 1 or more.*

READING I RECORD FORM
Section I: 21-30

Teacher _____   Site _____
Group _____   Date _____

Name	Track SIF	Crit 2 or more	Track SI	Crit 1 or more	Track SAG	Crit 1 or more	Track COG	Crit 1 or more	Individual Criterion = 3 or more Checks
Bill R.	a b̸ c d̸	✔	e f g̸	✔	h i j k		l̸ m̸	✔	✔
Donna J.	a b c d		e f̸ g̸	✔	h̸ i j k	✔	l m		
Sean M.	a b c d		e f g		h i j k		l m		
Renee P.	a b̸ c d		e f g		h i̸ j̸ k	✔	l m		
Bonnie Z.	a b c d		e f g		h i j̸ k	✔	l m		
Clyde B.	a b c d		e̸ f g̸	✔	h i̸ j̸ k	✔	l m̸	✔	✔
	a b c d		e f g		h i j k		l m		
	a b c d		e f g		h i j k		l m		
	a b c d		e f g		h i j k		l m		
	a b c d		e f g		h i j k		l m		
	a b c d		e f g		h i j k		l m		
Group Totals	SIF = $\frac{1}{6}$		SI = $\frac{3}{6}$		SAG = $\frac{4}{6}$		COG = $\frac{2}{6}$		Group criterion = ⅓ of children or more fail track.

---

*This could also be a passing criterion if one wished. The failure end is counted here because it usually involves less counting.

If a child meets the failure criterion, the tester places a check to the right of the appropriate track. Bill R met the failure criterion for three tracks (SIF, SI, and SAG).

The fractions at the bottom of the tracks give in the numerator the number of children failing the track and in the denominator the number of children in the group. One child met the failure criterion for SIF. Therefore, the fraction at the bottom of the SIF track is $1/6$. Four children failed the SAG track, so the fraction is $4/6$. If more than $1/3$ of the children fail a track, the teacher follows a remedial procedure for the *whole group*. A chart is provided for the teacher which indicates exactly which tasks should be retaught. The record form also leads to prescriptions for individual *remedies*. In the column on the far right is a check mark for Bill R and Clyde B. They failed three or more tracks. Individual remedies are only considered if a problem still remains after group remedies have been completed. An individual remedy might involve moving a child to a lower group. It can also involve tutoring in the skills which were failed. Again, a remedial assignment chart tells exactly which skills should be retaught an individual child.

Detailed specification of remedial procedures is possible when tests are carefully structured to measure important skills and subskills, and when the program of instruction is sufficiently structured so that a remedial key can be constructed to tell what needs to be taught.

Validating a Test for a Bad Program

It is possible to still be in trouble after following all procedures discussed in this unit to establish instruction-based tests which are reliable and valid for a particular program. *A program can be designed to teach misrules or trivia which are then tested.* Good reliability and sensitivity to instruction can be demonstrated for even a bad program. Thus, a prerequisite to the development of tests for a program is a logical analysis of the teaching sequences used in a program with a full knowledge of effective programing procedures as covered in *Teaching 2.*

summary

In evaluating instruction-based tests first decide how many different teaching outcomes you wish to test. This depends on the stage of instruction and whether you are dealing with outcomes involving general-cases or linear-additive sets. Usually, a general-case set provides the basis for one test. Exceptions to this may occur before the set is fully taught. In a linear-additive set, each member should be treated as a separate test unless all members have had a good chance to be taught.

In looking at item reliability we are concerned with the degree to which there is performance consistency on items assumed to measure the same thing. In dealing with a general-case set, a percent-agreement index can be computed for any pair of items by counting the number of students for whom there is an outcome agreement and dividing by the number of students. Then the average agreement for all possible pairs of items on the test can be computed. Usually, inspection of the table of pluses and minuses will reveal the problem items without this computation. Low agreement may occur where items are written ambiguously and need revision. It can also occur between subgroups of items which are consistent within themselves. In this latter case, it is likely that you are testing two different things.

With linear-additive sets, each member constitutes a different teaching objective. An effective measure of reliability would use at least two measures of each member of the set. A percent agreement index can then be computed for each member of the set and averaged over members. It may be economical to use double item testing only in a tryout form of the test. If good reliability is found, then a return to testing with one item for each member of the set is possible. After all members of a linear-additive set have been taught, it is reasonable to consider testing with only a sample of the set. However, where poor performances are found, a full testing of the set should be undertaken to guide remediation.

In looking at test validity we are concerned with whether or not the test is a measure of the specific teaching objective. This can be determined *logically*, by analyzing the content validity of the items, and *empirically* by examining the sensitivity to instruction of the items. Content validity is concerned with if the test item falls in the set of tasks defined by a teaching objective. Sensitivity to instruction is demonstrated by showing that an item is not passed prior to instruction and is passed after instruction. Where items are failed before and after instruction, one has to determine the adequacy of the instruction before a judgment about the test items can be made. Where items are failed before and passed after instruction, it is necessary to evaluate whether the change could have occurred because of instruction taking place elsewhere. A validity index was proposed based on the gain in percentage passing from pretesting to posttesting.

The evaluation of a testing procedure should also consider cost (in terms of money and teaching time) and the usefulness of the test information for determining remedial procedures. A final caution: it is possible to get good reliability and validity data on instruction-based tests even when the underlying program is defective. Many programs teach misrules, trivia, or limited cases where a more general case could be taught. A careful examination of what is being taught should come first.

self-test

1 Generally, when an instructional objective defines a general-case set, such as reading regular-sound words, the objective provides the basis for one test, and any members of that set can be _____ in building a test.

2 When an instructional objective defines a linear-additive set, there are conditions when each member of the set should be treated as a _____ test.

3 The consistency with which groups of items taken from the same test lead to the same result, is used to determine the _____ of a test.

4 Assume that five students receive the following pass (+) and fail (−) scores on two items. What is the percent of agreement for these two items:

Student	Item A	Item B
1	−	−
2	−	+
3	+	+
4	+	+
5	+	+

Write answer here: _____

5 In working with criterion-referenced tests, where the students have been taught the material being tested, it is usually unnecessary to compute _____-_____ indexes. Most of the students will pass most of the items. When this does not happen, the items _____ should stand out in the pass-fail table.

6 With a linear-additive set, if it can be assumed that the students have had an equal opportunity to learn _____ members of the set, then a test sampling the separate skills could be treated as a test of mastery of the objective.

7 The initial criterion for validity is that the items meet the _____ requirements of the teaching objective. In the test-construction literature this is known as _____ validity or logical validity.

8 Beyond the requirement of content validity, the key concept in the analysis of validity of instruction-based tests is _____ to instruction.

NUMBER RIGHT _____

Answers (margin):

1 sampled

2 separate

3 reliability

4 80%

5 percent-agreement; failed

6 all

7 logical; content

8 sensitivity

exercise 1 programed practice

1   A test usually consists of a group of tasks. For tests of instruction, it is meaningful to add performances together when they reflect a common teaching _____ .

2   The definition of teaching outcomes depends upon the _____ of instruction with respect to an objective and if a general-case objective is dealt with or one that involves a _____-_____ set.

3   Generally, when an instructional objective defines a general-case set, such as reading regular-sound words, the objective provides the basis for one test, and any members of that set can be _____ in building a test.

4   When an instructional objective defines a linear-additive set, there are conditions when each member of the set should be treated as a _____ test.

5   It is not necessary to test all members of a linear-additive set if the members have had a relatively _____ chance to be learned.

6   If some items are _____ , it would be necessary to test the whole set to know where more teaching is required.

7   The consistency with which groups of items taken from the same test lead to the same result is used to determine the _____ of a test.

8   The reliability question is "To what degree do the different members of the set produce the _____ results?"

9   If we have two or more test items which are assumed to be measures of the "same thing," we can determine the degree to which they produce the same result by seeing if students who pass one item pass _____ items.

10 A simple reliability index is the percent of _____ between the results for two test items across students. This is determined by taking two items and counting the number of agreements and dividing by the _____ of students.

1 outcome

2 stage; linear-
    additive

3 sampled

4 separate

5 equal

6 failed

7 reliability

8 same

9 other

10 agreement;
    number

11 Assume that five students received the following pass (+) and fail (−) scores on two items. What is the percent of agreement for these two items:

Student	Item A	Item B
1	−	−
2	−	+
3	+	+
4	+	+
5	+	+

Write answer here _____

12 We can calculate a percent-agreement index for each item with _____ _____ item.

13 In working with criterion-referenced tests where the students have been taught the material being tested, it is usually unnecessary to compute _____-_____ indexes. Most of the students will pass most of the items. When this does not happen, the items _____ should stand out in the pass-fail table.

14 The analysis of reliability or response consistency begins by determining whether the items to be compared for pass-fail patterns are _____ measures of the same teaching objectives. Then, empirically, we find out if they do in fact produce the _____ results for different students.

15 When the percent-agreement indexes are high, all is well and _____ has been established.

16 When the percent-agreement indexes are low, however, a closer _____ of patterns among items is needed.

17 The empirical analysis may show that our assumption about what items were measures of the same teaching objective was _____ . This could be corrected by redefining what constituted a _____ .

18 Low agreement indexes might also be attributable to items which are subject to more than _____ interpretation (item ambiguity).

19 Linear-additive sets define groups of essentially different skills. Each member of the set constitutes a _____ test.

---

11 80%

12 every other

13 percent-agreement; failed

14 logically; same

15 reliability

16 examination

17 wrong; test

18 one

19 different

20 The reliability question is focused on _____ of like items. A percent-_____ index can be computed for each pair of like items.

21 If it can be assumed that the students have had an equal opportunity to learn _____ members of the set, then a test sampling the separate skills could be treated as a test of mastery of the objective.

22 The validity question asks, "Does the test measure what it is _____ to measure?" In the case of instruction-based tests this question means, "Does the test measure the _____ that was taught or is it a measure of something else?"

23 The initial criterion for validity is that the items meet the _____ requirements of the teaching objective. In the test-construction literature this is known as _____ validity or logical validity.

24 The definition for a teaching objective defines a _____ of tasks the student should be able to perform. The content validity question asks if each test item is a _____ of the set so defined.

25 Beyond the requirement of content validity, the key concept in the analysis of validity of instruction-based tests is _____ to instruction.

26 To determine whether test items are sensitive to instruction, it is necessary to:

  a. Show that items are logically valid measures of a _____ instructional program.

  b. Show that the items are _____ passed prior to instruction and _____ passed after the relevant instruction.

  c. Show, _____ , that the instructional program can be used to teach the objectives under specified conditions and _____ the degree to which these conditions obtain in the setting where the items are evaluated for sensitivity.

  d. Show that the simple passage of time, without instruction, does not produce _____ in the passing of the items.

27 Another factor to consider in evaluating instructional-program-based tests is _____ .

28 A final consideration is the ease with which the test results can be translated into _____ procedures.

29 Note that it is possible to follow all of the procedures discussed in this unit to establish instructional-based tests which are reliable and valid for a particular program, and still be in trouble. A program can be designed to teach misrules or _____ which are then tested. Good reliability and sensitivity to instruction can be demonstrated for a _____ program.

29 trivia; bad

exercise 2 practice in data interpretation and analysis

1 The result in the table below was obtained from a test on punctuation. The teacher thought she was dealing with one objective.

Students	Items					
	1	2	3	4	5	6
1	+	−	−	+	−	+
2	+	−	−	+	−	+
3	+	+	−	+	+	−
4	−	+	+	+	+	−
5	−	+	+	−	+	−
6	+	−	−	+	−	+
7	−	−	+	−	+	+
8	−	+	+	−	+	−
9	−	+	+	−	+	−
10	−	+	+	−	+	−

First compute the percent-agreement indexes between pairs of items and place them in the table below in the upper diagonal.

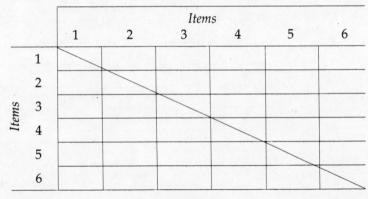

Table A

Next reorganize the percent-agreement indexes in the table with the items in the order indicated below.

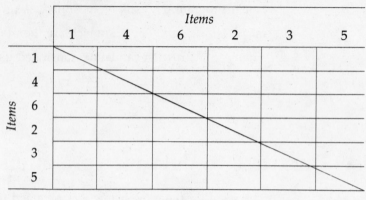

Table B

How would you interpret the results obtained by this teacher? (Write answer here.)

_____

_____

_____

2 Compute the percent agreement indexes for the following data involving five members of a linear-additive set (a, b, c, d, e) on which there were two items for each set member (a_1, a_2). Also compute the overall average agreement.

Items	\multicolumn{10}{c	}{Students}	Percent Agreement
	1	2	3	4	5	6	7	8	9	10	
a_1	+	+	−	+	+	+	−	+	+	+	
a_2	+	+	−	+	+	−	−	+	+	+	
b_1	−	+	−	+	+	−	−	+	+	+	
b_2	−	+	−	+	−	−	−	+	+	+	
c_1	+	+	+	+	+	−	−	+	+	+	
c_2	+	+	+	+	+	−	−	+	+	+	
d_1	+	+	+	−	+	+	−	−	+	+	
d_2	+	+	+	−	+	+	+	−	+	+	
e_1	−	+	+	−	+	−	+	−	+	+	
e_2	−	+	+	+	+	+	+	−	+	+	
								Average Percent Agreement			

3 Given the following pretest and posttest data, compute the validity index for each item, and for the average for the set.

Pretest

Stu-dents	Items					
	1	2	3	4	5	6
1	−	−	−	+	−	−
2	+	−	−	−	−	−
3	−	−	−	+	−	−
4	−	−	−	−	+	−
5	−	+	−	+	−	−
6	−	−	−	+	−	−
7	−	−	−	−	−	−
8	−	−	−	+	−	+
9	−	−	−	+	−	−
10	−	−	−	+	−	−

Posttest

Stu-dents	Items					
	1	2	3	4	5	6
1	+	+	+	+	+	+
2	+	+	+	+	+	−
3	+	+	+	+	+	+
4	+	+	+	+	+	−
5	+	+	+	+	+	+
6	+	+	−	+	+	+
7	+	+	+	+	+	−
8	+	+	+	+	+	+
9	+	−	+	+	+	−
10	+	+	+	+	+	+

Validity index computation:

Item	Percent Pass Posttest	Percent Pass Pretest	Percent Gain
1			
2			
3			
4			
5			
6			

Average Gain _____

What can you say aboout item 4? _____

_____

What can you say about item 6? _____

_____

What can you say about items 1, 2, 3, and 5? _____

_____

Answers for Exercise 2

1

Items	1	2	3	4	5	6
1		20	00	90	00	90
2			80	30	80	10
3				10	100	10
4					10	80
5						10
6						

Table A

Items	1	4	6	2	3	5
1		90	90	20	00	00
4			80	30	10	10
6				10	10	10
2					80	80
3						100
5						

Table B

The results clearly show two clusters of items agreeing highly within clusters, but not between clusters. Thus, the teacher has two reliable tests measuring different things consistently.

2 Percent agreement indexes:

a. 90
b. 90
c. 100
d. 90
e. 80
Average—90

3

Item	Percent Pass Posttest	Percent Pass Pretest	Percent Gain
1	100	10	90
2	90	10	80
3	90	00	90
4	100	70	30
5	100	10	90
6	60	10	50

Average gain 72%

Item 4 was passed by most on pretest. It did not need to be taught to all of the students.

Item 6 was failed by four students on posttest. It apparently was not taught well or there is something wrong with the item.

Items 1, 2, 3, and 5 show excellent validity indexes.

exercise 3 analysis of tests built for unit 3, exercise 2

If it is possible, give the test constructed for exercise 2, unit 3 to a group of students. Give the test of preskills and a test of the objectives *before* the instruction and give the test of objectives *after* the instruction. Where this is not possible, try to give the tests to a group of students who have already been taught the objectives and to a group who have not, and base your computations for part 3 below on the differences in percent passing for these groups.

1 Decide beforehand how many tests you have, both for preskills and objectives.
2 Where you have several items for the same teaching objective (hopefully this is always the case for your tryout test), compute percent-agreement scores. Follow the special procedures for dealing with a linear-additive set, if you have one.
3 Next, examine each test of objectives for sensitivity to instruction by computing the gain in percentage passing the items from pretesting to posttesting.
4 Evaluate your findings in terms of adequacy of your tests and adequacy of the instruction. Suggest where revisions in either might be made.

discussion questions

1 Give four criteria for evaluating an instructional-program-based test.

2 How do you decide how many tests you have?

3 Give examples that show the idea of a single teaching outcome.

4 What is meant by the *reliability* of a test?

5 Describe and illustrate a reliability index that can be used with criterion-referenced tests?

6 What do you do when there are many items on the same test?

7 Why is it usually not necessary to compute all of the agreement indexes to find where there is trouble with a test focused on instruction?

8 Give two reasons why the agreement indexes for some items might be low.

9 How do you determine the reliability of a linear-additive set?

10 What is meant by the *validity* of a test?

11 What criteria are used to determine the validity of instructional-program-based tests?

12 What additional control information is necessary in the evaluation of the validity of instruction-referenced tests?

13 Define and illustrate a validity index for showing sensitivity to instruction?

14 Suggest a procedure for showing that events correlated with time other than the specified instruction are not responsible for the gain in percentage of students passing an item.

15 What are some problems in demonstrating that a program will work under specified conditions and assessing the degree to which these conditions are met?

16 What is required for a test to be useful for remediation?

17 Why is it possible to have a valid test for a bad program?

unit 5

Approaches to Monitoring Student Progress

objectives

When you complete this unit you should be able to—

1 Specify the six general requirements of an effective monitoring system.
2 Give examples of a variety of procedures that can be used to meet each requirement of an effective monitoring system.
3 Describe the monitoring systems used with:
  Learning Activity Packages
  Precision Teaching
  Behavior Analysis Follow Through Model
  Pittsburgh LRDC Follow Through Model
4 State where rate measures of student progress are not likely to be the best procedure.
5 Describe a study by Hofmeister demonstrating the value of a monitoring system.

lesson

In constructing tests for an instructional program, a primary objective is to permit a careful monitoring of student progress so that failure can be eliminated or at least greatly minimized. Through the use of quality control procedures designed to lead to corrective actions within a short period of time, education can come to serve all children. In this unit, we will discuss a variety of procedures which the teacher can consider for use depending on the circumstances. Some of the monitoring systems discussed in this unit do not depend on tests built following the procedures of units 3 and 4. Others do. In the next unit, we will examine a highly detailed system used for monitoring the University of Oregon sponsored Follow Through Programs. This example will illustrate the precision in teacher decision making which can be achieved, given appropriate programs, tests, and record keeping procedures.

General Requirements

The available curriculum materials will determine how much you have to do to complete a monitoring system. If you have the option of selecting your own materials, then look for materials that have clearly stated terminal goals, placement procedures, require frequent student responding in exercises and/or tests, and which provide guides to remedial procedures based on testing outcomes. If your curriculum does not have these features, it is necessary to provide for them. The following procedures need to be considered in developing a monitoring system.

Specify a Placement Procedure

Assuming that some individualization of instruction is going on, a placement procedure is needed to see if students have the assumed preskills or if they should be placed at an advanced point in the program. To assess preskills, take the earliest tasks calling for student responses and analyze them for prerequisite skills. If the student is required to do workbook addition problems with sums up to 20, then he needs to be able to read numbers to 20, count to 20, write numbers to 20, and have a procedure for solving an addition problem. Where the preskills are lacking, they must be taught before placement in the program.

Decisions on advanced placement can be held off for a few days and be based on the early performance of the students in the program. When students are able to complete units rapidly with few errors, allow them to move ahead by doing the key parts of two or three lessons a day until you find the point at which errors increase and mastery is down. Alternatively, a placement test can be made by sampling skills in the program and testing all the children. Be aware, however, that errors in placement are very likely. Students may have the main skills to be taught, but fail the test because the directions are new or the response requirements are new. Placement judgments should always be made tentatively, subject to revisions based on student performance.

Define Progress Units

For beginning levels, a unit may be defined as completion of certain workbook exercises, by a specified number of pages covered in a text, by specified performance on a test of key concepts, or by the amount of work to be covered in a day or a week. At more advanced levels, the unit may be a chapter in a text.

The units provide the teacher with a metric for measuring progress through the curriculum. By charting this progress (as illustrated later), the teacher is able to keep track of progress of individual students and to take steps to improve this progress when necessary.

Specify Checkout Procedures

For each unit, specify checkout procedures and periodic review procedures. The checkout procedures can consist of a written exercise(s) checked by the teacher, an aide, or by the student. Oral reading progress can be checked by reading a passage to the teacher or aide who charts rate and errors. When writing skills are adequate, comprehension and grammar tasks can be checked by the student. A desk can be placed at the back of the room as a checkout station. An answer key can be provided by the teacher so that the students can correct their answers (using a special colored pencil). The answers can then be turned in for spot checking by the teacher. For some activities the checkout can be given by another student who has completed the unit. Checkouts can also consist of unit tests which are corrected by the teacher or students. The point to note is that monitoring procedures can be individualized and need not involve a lot of extra teacher or aide time except at beginning levels where oral responding is very critical to the objectives.

Develop a Guide for Recording Progress Through the Units

The next step is to develop a guide specifying the steps to be followed in working through the units and taking checkouts. The guide should also serve as a record of progress. One teacher we have worked with had a large group (33) of fourth graders with reading skills ranging from beginning second to sixth grade. She devised a system that provided small-group instruction and workbook exercises to the lowest group and a more individualized self-directed approach for the more advanced students. The list of tasks to be completed in reading were placed on dittos in order. The tasks covered the basal series from second grade to sixth grade. Each student was provided with materials appropriate to his or her level, and an appropriate dittoed page was stapled to each student's workbook to provide a checklist to be followed and a record of progress. The following is an example of the kind of instructions provided.

Unit 7	Completion Check	Date
1. Read story on pages 36 to 45 in your reader.		
2. Answer the questions on page 46 in your reader.		
3. Check your answers at checkout station A, and place in box A.		
4. Do workbook exercise 7 on pages 14 and 15.		
5. Check your answers at checkout station B, and place workbook in box B.		
6. Do SRA *Reading Laboratory* level 1b, number 7.		
7. Check your answers at checkout station C, and place in box C.		

A teacher in the University of Kansas Behavioral Analysis Follow Through Model developed a small booklet to provide a guide through a reading curriculum that lacked specific checkpoints.[1] The following is a sample of the guide:

Turn to page 318 in your reading book. There is a word list there of the new words on each page of your reader. Study the words for pages 45, 46, 47, 48, 49, and 50. If you have trouble with some of them, hold up your hand for a teacher to help you. When you can say all of them, pronounce them to a teacher. She must give you an OK and write her initials in the little box here, before you go on to the next part.

Word List, pp. 45-50 .... ☐☐

Now turn to the reading part of your book and study the story from pages 46 to 50. Try to read it to yourself at least three times, so you can read all the words and tell about the people and things that happened in the story. Your teacher will ask you some questions about it and pick out one page for you to read aloud. When you can answer the questions and read well enough to suit her, she will give you an OK and write her initials in this little box.

Questions and Oral Reading .... ☐☐

Now get your workbook and work on page 8, Part 1 of your workbook. Take your time and think, because we want you to get a good grade on this. Then put your name on both sides of the page and hand it in to [the teacher]. She will give you an OK and write her initials in the little box.

Workbook, Part 1, p. 8 .... ☐☐

When you get this paper back with your grade on it, you can fill in the graph at the end of this little book that we will tell you about.

Next turn to Part 2, page 8. Read the questions and answer each one with a complete sentence the way it shows you in Question 1. You will need the words at the top of the page to write your answers. These words have consonant digraphs in them. There are four digraphs:

kn — sounds n.   The k is silent.
wr — sounds r.   The w is silent.
ph — sounds f.
gh — sounds f.

Underline words with these digraphs in them in the sentences you write. Be sure you do all you are supposed to do on this page. Look it over before you hand it in. Write your name on it. Then tear it out and take it to [the teacher] for her OK and initials.

Workbook, Part 2, p. 8 .... ☐☐

When you get it back, you may have to do part of it over before you can fill in the graph for the page. Get an OK from a teacher.

Establish Goals

With a sequenced list of tasks to be followed for each instructional program, an individualized approach must let the students know what is expected of them. Setting weekly goals for progress is a very effective procedure for increasing motivation. Figure 5.6 (p. 92) illustrates a goal chart used within the University of Kansas Follow Through Model.

Establish Remedial Procedures

A monitoring system makes it very evident when students are progressing too slowly through the course or are not learning the material. If the children are progressing too slowly, the solution may involve increasing the amount of instruction provided through the use of an aide or tutor or changing the incentive conditions through any one of a variety of procedures covered in *Teaching 1*. If some children are having trouble with specific skills, special lessons can be provided, the children can be asked to go through some self-instructional materials again, and so forth. The key is to establish a plan for dealing with mistakes that provides new instruction and a *new checkout* on the skills.

Some Illustrative Process Evaluation Systems

Applications of these general procedures in several programmatic approaches will be illustrated. Since our concern is with procedures to guide teacher behavior in setting-up and operating a classroom, we will not cover Computer Assisted Instruction (see *Teaching 2*, unit 1). Obviously, computer systems can be programed to provide highly sophisticated monitoring reports on the progress of many students. Two other important approaches to monitoring not covered here are the use of token reinforcement systems, and point-contract systems. Units 11 and 12 in *Teaching 1* detail procedures for setting up these systems. It would be valuable for the student to review the characteristics of such systems from the current perspective of problems in process evaluation.

Learning Activity Packages

Learning Activity Packages (LAP) provide one approach to individualizing instruction in a more open setting, especially for junior high students for whom exploration of individual interests is often encouraged.[2] The basic idea of the Learning Activity Package is much the same as the *instructional unit* proposed in Keller's system of Personalized Instruction. The idea is also much the same as the Morrison method, introduced by H. C. Morrison around 1930.[3] The instructor following the Morrison method organized his material into units and then would pretest, teach, test, reteach, and retest until mastery was demonstrated. Most systems with good monitoring of progress have similarities to the Morrison method.

The first step in building a Learning Activity Package involves dividing the curriculum objectives into units that take a week to a month to complete. If a large unit is used for cohesiveness, then it may in turn be divided into a number of subunits each focusing on a particular concept or skill.

The next steps involve building the Learning Activity Packages. The procedures are very similar to Popham's outline for a teaching strategy described earlier, except that the instructional materials are specified before hand:

1 Give a rationale which makes the experience to be undertaken personally important. For example, why is it important to know how to use card index files?

2 Specify the goals of the package as a set of behavioral objectives.
3 Devise tests for the objective—pretests, posttests, and where suitable, self-tests. The self-test allows the student to decide when to take a posttest.
4 Select activities which will provide instruction (with teacher assistance as requested). The packages often involve *required* materials and *optional* materials. The use of a variety of media and response requirements are encouraged.

Often each component of a package is color coded, red for tests, green for objectives, and so on. Students learn to use the package in a systematic way. The key to the LAP system lies in organizing the instructional space into learning stations and in teaching the students how to work on their own in using the packages. The instructional space is divided into areas that can be used for listening to various kinds of recordings, a library type area, a science center, work tables, a space for group discussions, individual study areas, and an area for viewing filmed material. An orientation session is used to let the students know how the system operates. Charts are set up so students can sign for various packages, and for use of various spaces at certain times. The teacher functions as a consultant and facilitator when help is needed. At the end of each package, students also sign up for a conference with the teacher. The posttest may be reviewed and possible reworking of some areas suggested. Decisions may be made on which activities to do next. Progress charts kept by students or teachers can be filled in at this point.

Comments. Learning Activity Packages have a lot of potential for individualizing instruction after basics have been mastered. Some can be required of all and some can be elective. Good records of student progress are easy to keep and use to motivate students. Opportunities for student's learning-to-learn on their own should be apparent. A drawback is the effort involved in every teacher "inventing the wheel" again. The amount of time and effort devoted to designing packages for use in only a few classrooms is costly. No doubt more published packages will become available to avoid this problem.

Precision Teaching

Precision teaching is a set of procedures for process evaluation. The approach came out of the teachings of Ogden Lindsley.[4] The heart of the approach is the use of procedures for the daily measurement of improvement on some target behaviors. Most often a rate measures is taken (responses per minute) and the students chart their daily progress on their own graphs. If the behavior requires an oral response, the teacher, aide, or another student will time a 30-second or 1-minute performance each day when the student is ready. If the measure involves a written response, then a group might be tested at the same time. A key to precision teaching is learning to state learning objectives in terms of observable behaviors (pinpointing). Next a way of measuring the rate of pinpointed behavior must be found, and finally, a charting procedure established. Assuming that key teaching goals have been identified by the measurement procedures, teacher and students get daily feedback on their progress. This feedback motivates both students and teachers.

The Regional Resource Center for Handicapped Children at the University of Oregon has developed a set of diagnostic materials in reading and math for use in the elementary grades in implementing a precision teaching approach.[5] Materials involve sequenced sets of tasks on which rate measures can be taken. Tasks are first used as a criterion-referenced diagnostic-placement test, then the tasks are used to guide daily practice and to test progress. Often teaching machines are used to provide daily practice.

The Reading Inventory tests these skills:

1 Sounding consonants
2 Sounding vowels
3 Blending three-letter phonically regular words
4 Blending consonant teams
5 Reading sight words (words which are phonically irregular and cannot be sounded out)
6 Reading four and five letter phonically regular words
7 Orally reading a primer level selection from a phonically regular reader
8 Orally reading a selection from the classroom reader currently used by the student.

Figure 5.1 illustrates inventory pages for vowel sounds. The teacher is free to determine the procedures desired to teach the skills. The following teaching sequence is recommended:

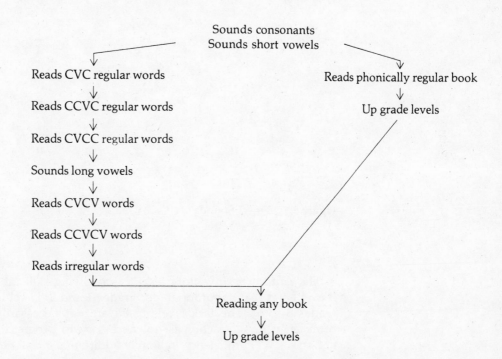

C stands for consonant and V for vowel. Generally, the student should reach proficiency in one skill before going on to the next. Criterion levels of performance are defined on the basis of the performance of average adults or good students. For example, a rate of 60 to 80 sounds per minute is recommended as the criterion level for reading sounds, and 100 to 120 words per minute is recommended as the criterion rate for a classroom reader.

ī   a   ō   i   e   u   ā   ē   o   ū

ē   ū   ā   o   a   ī   e   i   ō   u

e   ī   u   o   i   ā   ū   a   ē   o

ū   o   ē   ā   u   e   i   ō   a   ī

u   ō   i   e   ī   a   o   ā   ū   ē

ō   ē   a   ū   ā   i   o   u   ī   e

ī   a   ō   i   e   u   ā   ē   o   ū

ē   ū   ā   o   a   i   e   ī   ō   u

e   ī   u   o   i   ā   ū   a   ē   ō

Figure 5.1   Vowel Sounds

The Arithmetic Inventory tests the following skills at the levels specified (Level I and II are appropriate for grades 1 and 2, Level III is appropriate for grades 3 to 6). The task levels listed are not necessarily ordered. That is, proficiency in subtraction is not necessary to progress in two-place addition; however, proficiency in simple addition is *necessary*.

Subtest Name	Level
Oral Counting	I and II
Oral Identification of Sets (0-10)	I and II
Reading Numerals (oral)	
0-99	I and II
0-10,000	III
Writing Numerals	I and II, III
Ordering Numerals	
0-99	I and II
0-1,000	III
Basic Addition (single digit + single digit)	I and II, III
Basic Subtraction (single digit − single digit)	I and II, III
Basic Equations (addition)	I and II, III
Basic Equations (subtraction)	I and II, III
Addition Without Carrying (double digit)	I and II, III
Subtraction Without Borrowing (double digit)	I and II, III
Addition With Carrying	III
Subtraction With Borrowing	III
Basic Multiplication	III
Basic Division	III

Figures 5.2 and 5.3 illustrate two test pages from the math inventory.

Addition (with carrying)

$$
\begin{array}{ccccc}
71 & 83 & 35 & 44 & 28 \\
+\ 9 & +\ 8 & +\ 7 & +\ 9 & +\ 6 \\
\end{array}
$$

$$
\begin{array}{ccccc}
57 & 17 & 68 & 13 & 12 \\
+\ 8 & +\ 9 & +\ 9 & +\ 7 & +\ 9 \\
\end{array}
$$

$$
\begin{array}{ccccc}
48 & 29 & 38 & 37 & 42 \\
+12 & +19 & +25 & +37 & +19 \\
\end{array}
$$

$$
\begin{array}{ccccc}
86 & 34 & 46 & 65 & 14 \\
+17 & +66 & +56 & +28 & +49 \\
\end{array}
$$

$$
\begin{array}{ccccc}
73 & 56 & 66 & 37 & 29 \\
+38 & +19 & +16 & +25 & +29 \\
\end{array}
$$

Figure 5.2 Arithmetic Inventory

Equations (Addition)

□ + 5 = 6	1 + □ = 5	□ + 1 = 8	□ + 8 = 10
6 + □ = 7	□ + 9 = 10	3 + □ = 4	2 + □ = 5
□ + 0 = 2	4 + □ = 9	□ + 1 = 9	□ + 0 = 4
2 + □ = 3	2 + □ = 6	6 + □ = 6	□ + 0 = 8
□ + 5 = 10	5 + □ = 8	□ + 4 = 6	7 + □ = 9
□ + 8 = 8	2 + □ = 8	□ + 1 = 6	2 + □ = 4
□ + 4 = 5	□ + 0 = 3	□ + 7 = 10	4 + □ = 8
□ + 3 = 6	4 + □ = 7	□ + 10 = 10	2 + □ = 5
□ + 1 = 10	7 + □ = 8	□ + 5 = 7	6 + □ = 10
1 + □ = 3	□ + 9 = 10	1 + □ = 2	□ + 6 = 9
3 + □ = 8	□ + 5 = 7	□ + 8 = 9	4 + □ = 9

Figure 5.3 Arithmetic Inventory

Comments. The precision teaching approach, particularly as put into operation by the University of Oregon Regional Resource Center, contains all of the essential features of a good monitoring system *except a specified curriculum*. Since the Resource Center objectives focus on skills taught in almost any beginning program, this is not a serious problem. However, the difficulties of defining testing procedures without defining a program of instruction pose potential problems. For example, the testing procedures in math use only *column addition* and *column subtraction* until level III where "equation forms" are introduced. Further, the methods by which the children are taught determine what sequence of testing is appropriate. The authors of the Resource Center program recognize this problem and try to get around it by recommending that teachers adapt the testing procedures to their specific program.

Another potential problem is the heavy reliance on *rate* measures. In reading, for example, a high word-reading rate is not desirable if accompanied by a high error rate. A low error criterion is needed before the focus is placed on rate. Rate-measures are useful in consolidating skills after they have been taught, but an early rate emphasis can hinder some acquisitions. Furthermore, rate measures are inappropriate as a test of concept learning. Whether dealing with language concepts, logical reasoning, or mathematical concepts, testing is primarily concerned with whether the critical discriminations have been learned, not with the rate at which examples can be identified. In identifying sounds, it is initially more important to know which sounds the student can identify correctly and which sounds require more teaching, than to know the rate at which a page of sounds can be read. Thus, there would seem to be a need for a two-stage testing procedure. The first stage tests for the learning of critical concepts. Only after this is passed with 99% accuracy do you move on to the second stage of testing for rate of using the concepts and related operations.

A key procedure in precision teaching, having students chart their daily progress, is a procedure any teacher can profitably use. Most kindergarten and first grade children can be taught to read graphs and to chart their own progress.

Behavior Analysis Follow Through Model

Under the direction of Don Bushell, Jr. and Gene Ramp at the University of Kansas, the Behavior Analysis Follow Through Model has demonstrated the effectiveness of a variety of procedures for building a monitoring system around existing curriculum materials. The program is currently operating in 300 classrooms in 12 communities where there is a high percentage of disadvantaged children. The goal of the program is to substantially improve the children's mastery of basic skills. Most classrooms have a teacher, a Title I (ESEA) supported aide, and two parent aides. Each adult is typically working with six or seven children. The teacher works on reading, the Title I aide on arithmetic, and the parent aides on spelling and handwriting.

Curriculum materials were selected that could be individualized in their use, that required frequent student response, and that contained periodic criterion-referenced tests. The main programs selected for use are *Programed Reading* (McGraw-Hill), *Sets and Numbers* (Singer), and the *Behavior Analysis Handwriting Primer*. *Programed Reading* is augmented by a phonics preprogram using Distar-type small-group instruction, by SRA Reading Laboratories, and by a recommended list of supplementary texts. Praise and tokens are used extensively to motivate the children. Throughout the day, periods of instruction are alternated with periods when tokens can be exchanged for fun activities such as singing, art projects, stories, recess, and even doing extra reading or math.

Like the University of Oregon Follow Through Model described in the next unit, extensive training along with a monitoring process is used to get the program going and to insure quality control. We are most interested in describing here some of the procedures used to monitor child progress.

Both the reading and math programs have frequent in-book tests. *Programed Reading* has a test for each one-fourth book and the end of each book. Seven to eight books constitute a school year program. *Sets and Numbers* has in-book quizzes for each unit. These range in number from 13 in Book 1 to 24 in Book 6. Each curriculum series was broken into progress steps, defined by the number of pages to be completed. The steps were constructed to take about the same amount of time to complete on the average, and, where feasible, break at a testing point. Whenever the student reaches a check point, the test is taken and checked by the teacher or aide. If it is passed at an 80 percent correct rate or higher, the student goes on to the next unit. If the test is failed, an analysis of the problem is made and supplemental materials and tutoring are used to teach the deficient skills. The test is then retaken and if passed, the student progresses to the next unit.

With an individualized program beyond the initial level, and with tests built into the curriculum, it is not difficult to keep track of student progress. Figure 5.4 shows a Class Progress Record for reading.[6] The teacher for this class took the whole class through the first three units and used that as her pretest. By week five she was ready to take twelve of the students back for

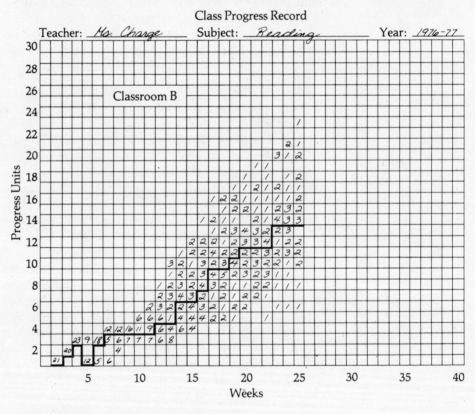

Figure 5.4 Completed Class Progress Record

review of basic sounds. From week 11 on the degree of individualization increased steadily. The dark line on Figure 5.4 shows the progress of the median (middle) child in the class. Progressing at this rate, the median child will complete unit 28 by the end of school. This corresponds to seven books in the *Programed Reading* series and is considered average progress for middle-class children.

Individual progress records are also kept. Figure 5.5 shows an example of a very simple record for six children. The units in arithmetic are listed across the top. A slash is placed in the appropriate box to show each day the unit each student was working on. An *a* indicates an absence. The daily information is readily converted into a weekly or monthly Personal Progress Record as indicated in Figure 5.6.[7]

In the last two years, the University of Kansas Follow Through Model has been using OpScan (Optical Scanning) equipment and telephone lines every Friday to transmit progress data for each child to the University of Kansas Computation Center. Their current placement is evaluated against previous placement and a new individual target for the coming week established and sent back to each school by teletype. It takes about 18 hours to send the data to and receive the feedback from the computer. While this degree of sophistication is useful in keeping track of the progress of 7,000 children, the charts shown earlier can help most teachers to keep track of their progress quite handily.

Comments. The University of Kansas monitoring system contains all of the essential features that we have indicated are required by an adequate monitoring system. There is a specified curriculum, adaptable to individualization, as well as placement procedures, progress measures toward goals, evaluation of student performance and remedial procedures. It should not

Individual Progress Report: Arithmetic												
Teacher: *Mr. Sharp* School: *Rose Garden*												
Grade: *First* Semester: *Fall, 1971*												

Units	1	2	3	4	5	6	7	8	9	10	11	12
ABLE, ALEX	///	///	///	//a/	ЖЖ /	Жa// /	//	//	///	///		
ACCURATE, ALICE	////	///	//	///	ЖЖ	ЖЖ //	//	/	//	///	///	/
BOOMER, Wm.	//	/a/	//	////	ЖЖ //	ЖЖ /	//	//	//a/	////		
CAPABLE, CATHY	///	//	//	///	////	ЖЖ ///	//	/	///	//	////	//
FAST, FRED	//	/	//	/	///	///	/	/	//	//	//	//
FAULTER, FRANK	ЖЖ	///a/	ЖЖ /	////	Жa/ ЖЖ	ЖЖ						

Figure 5.5 Completed Report. Each mark indicates a day spent on that unit. *a* indicates absent.

be too surprising to learn that test data on progress of children in this program are very positive in comparison to control groups.[8] The beauty of the program lies not in the logical niceties of the programing procedures or the completeness of analysis of progress, but in the *simplicity* of the procedures. Any teacher could be expected to do a reasonable job of adapting these procedures for his or her own use, given at least one aide.

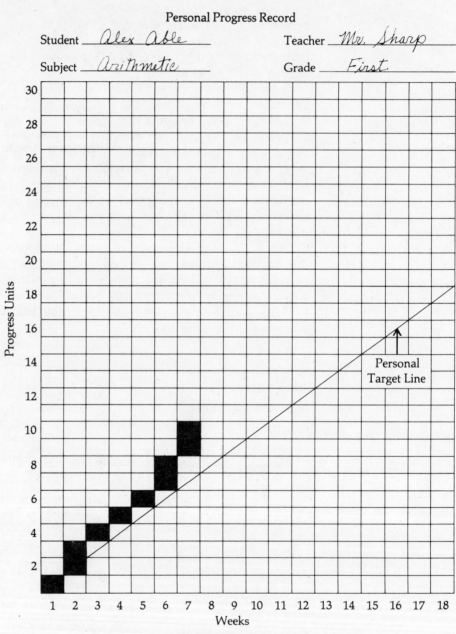

Figure 5.6 Completed Personal Progress Record. This chart is filled in for Alex by seeing how many units are completed at each five-day point for the data in Figure 5.5.

Pittsburgh LRDC Follow Through Model

The Individualized Early Learning Program was developed at the University of Pittsburgh Learning Research and Development Center (LRDC) under the direction of Lauren Resnick. It is a combination of the Primary Education Project and the Individually Prescribed Instruction (IPI) programs. Warren Shepler initially directed the use of these programs as a Follow Through Model. Betty Boston and Tony Eichelberger currently direct the Pittsburgh Follow Through Model. Some of the basic features fo the IPI program were described in unit 1. The use of placement tests, pretests, post-tests, and curriculum embedded tests enables the teacher to monitor student progress through the curriculum sequences. These tests come with the program and do not have to be teacher constructed. There are also carefully established training and monitoring procedures for use by the LRDC field staff to be sure the programs are being used adequately.

Beyond these important feedback systems, there are two additional procedures which add to the current discussion. The first is the Progress Summary Report and the second is the use of individual student assignment folders. Figure 5.7 shows a part of a classroom Progress Summary Report

Progress Summary
Follow Through 1974–75

IPI MATH
(new)
Levels A–D

- Completed last year
X Placement tested out of
M Worked in *and* mastered
P Pre-tested out of
• Currently working

District _Happytown_
Building _Lowel_
Teacher _Brown_
Grade _1_   Room _12_
Date _October 20_

Name	Level A							Level B											Level C												Level D									
	NPI	NPII	ASI	ASII	Fr	Mon	Time	NP	ASI	ASII	Mult	Div	Fr	Mon	Time	SoM	Geom	App	NPI	NPII	ASI	ASII	Mult	Div	Fr	Mon	Time	SoM	Geom	App	NP	AS	Mult	Div	Fr	Mon	Time	SoM	Geom	App
Mark	X	X	X	M	X	M	X	X	M	X	•																													
Julie	X	X	M	X	M	M	•	•																																
Wes	X	X	X	X	X	X	X	X	X	X	X	M	X	X	X	M	M	M	M	•																				
John	X	P	X	P	M	M	X	M	•																															
Angie	X	X	X	M	X	X	M	M	M	M	M	M	•																											
Linda	X	X	X	M	X	M	M	M	X	M	X	M	M	M	M	•																								
Jeff	X	X	X	P	M	M	M	•																																
Ken	X	M	M	M	X	M	•																																	
Jill	M	M	M	M	•																																			

NP	Numeration/Place Value	Mult	Multiplication
AS	Addition/Subtraction	Div	Division
Fr	Fractions	SoM	Systems of Measurement
Mon	Money	Geom	Geometry
Time	Time	App	Applications

Figure 5.7 Completed Progress Summary

which can be brought up to date by an aide on a daily, weekly, or monthly basis depending on the need.[9] The report shows where each student started for the school year and the units mastered to date. An overview of the class is quickly obtained. These forms are used by LRDC to monitor pupil progress quarterly.

The use of individual student folders for keeping track of progress and for making assignments is another key idea in this program which is of general usefulness. Each student folder contains an individual summary of progress and shows the more detailed placement of the student within the units of each skill area. The student folder is also used by teachers to write new assignments (prescriptions). When an assignment involves working with an audio tape or reference book, this is indicated on the assignment sheet. The materials needed to do the assignment can then be placed in the folders. When a test is due, it can also be placed in the folders. The individual progress summary sheet helps student and teacher to see progress through the curriculum sequence. In a very real way, each unit in the LRDC program is like a Learning Activity Package. It has pretests and posttests, multimedia instruction, multiple response requirements, and progress records. In addition, and importantly, the units are sequenced to build on one another.

Comment. The Individualized Early Learning Program contains all of the components of an effective monitoring system. It is a program which is gaining wide acceptance in elementary education today.

A Study of the Effects of Monitoring

Alan Hofmeister studied the effects of the use of a monitoring system on the arithmetic progress of students scoring in the lowest 20 percent on the Wide Range Achievement Test.[10] The students were in first and second grades in two schools in each of two districts in southern Idaho. The experimental group consisted of 32 pupils distributed through five first and five second grades. The control group consisted of 37 pupils distributed through four first and five second grades. In one district, the students were assigned randomly to experimental and control classes. In the other, this was not possible and so a procedure called covariance adjustment (see unit 13) was used to adjust for possible initial differences between experimental and control students. The students were pretested and posttested with the Wide Range (math only) and a criterion-referenced test (of high reliability) based on the math curriculum in use in the two districts.

The experimental program was evaluated over a ten-week period. The teachers in the experimental groups were given:

1 A list of instructional objectives for each pupil
2 A list of references to district texts covering material teaching the objectives
3 Mastery tests for each objective
4 A recording system to monitor progress through the objectives

A one-hour training session was held in the use of the materials and a manual left with the teacher. No further interventions were made. However, an itinerant specialist employed by the district made unobtrusive observations of implementation of the procedures. These observations revealed that most of the first grade teachers in the experimental group did not implement the experimental procedures, while most of the second-grade teachers did.

The results showed a significant difference on the Wide Range and the criterion mastery tests favoring the experimental groups. The difference was attributable to the gains by second graders where the program was clearly implemented. The adjusted posttest mean for second graders was .44 grade levels higher after ten weeks of instruction. On the criterion-referenced tests the control second graders passed 21.4 objectives and the experimentals passed 27.9 (covariance adjusted posttest means).

While Hofmeister was concerned with approaches to mainstreaming special education children and with effective ways for special education resource teachers to use their time, these results also have obvious implications for any teacher concerned with effective educational procedures.

summary

An effective monitoring system first requires a set of procedures for placing students in a program, or at least insuring that they have the preskills assumed by the program. Second, a method for identifying progress steps through a curriculum sequence is needed. Third, a procedure for checking the quality of student work on each progress unit is required. This may consist of formal mastery tests, less formal verbal checkouts, or workbook exercises. The fourth requirement of a monitoring system is a set of procedures for guiding students through an instructional sequence and keeping track of where they are. Fifth, it helps to motivate progress if goals are established for each student or groups of students and a method devised to visually show progress toward the goal. Finally, a set of procedures for correcting errors or recycling the student through objectives not mastered is required.

A variety of examples of monitoring systems were discussed to show the many possible approaches to building a monitoring system. You will have a chance to summarize these points for yourself in exercise 2 which follows.

A study by Alan Hofmeister shows some of the potential benefits for student progress of using an appropriate monitoring system.

self-test

1 To assess preskills, take the _____ tasks calling for student responses and analyze them for prerequisite skills.

2 For beginning levels, a unit may be defined as the point where the student is to do a _____ exercise, or by the number of pages covered in a _____ .

1 earliest

2 workbook; text

3 A plan is needed for dealing with instructional failure that provides new instruction and a new _____ on the skills.

4 The basic idea of the Learning Activity Package is much the same as the _____ _____ proposed in Keller's system.

5 The heart of Precision Teaching is the use of procedures for the _____ measurement of improvement on some target behaviors.

6 The precision teaching approach contains all of the essential features of a good monitoring system except a specified _____ .

7 In the Behavior Analysis Follow Through Model, each curriculum series was broken into progress _____ , defined by the number of _____ to be completed.

8 In a very real way each unit in the LRDC program is like a _____ _____ _____ .

NUMBER RIGHT _____

3 checkout

4 instructional unit

5 daily

6 curriculum

7 steps; units, pages

8 Learning Activity Package

exercise 1   programed practice

1 A primary objective in constructing tests for an instructional program is to permit a careful monitoring of student progress so that _____ can be eliminated or at least greatly minimized.

2 An effective monitoring system first requires a set of procedures for _____ students in a program, or at least insuring that they have the _____ assumed by the program.

3 To assess preskills, take the _____ tasks calling for student responses and analyze them for prerequisite skills.

4 Progress units provide the teacher with a metric for _____ progress through the curriculum.

1 failure

2 placing, preskills

3 earliest

4 measuring

5 For beginning levels, a unit may be defined as the point where the student is to do a _____ exercise or by the number of pages offered in a _____ .

6 For each unit, specify _____ procedures and periodic review procedures.

7 Checkout procedures can be _____ and need not involve a lot of extra teacher or aide time.

8 The next step is to develop a guide specifying the steps to be followed in working through the _____ and taking _____ .

9 The guide should also serve as a _____ of progress.

10 Setting weekly goals for progress is a very effective procedure for increasing _____ .

11 Next a plan is needed for dealing with instructional failure that provides new instruction and a new _____ on the skills.

12 The basic idea of the Learning Activity Package is much the same as the _____ _____ proposed in Keller's system.

13 The instructor organizes the material into units and then _____ , teaches, tests, reteaches, and retests until _____ is demonstrated.

14 In building the Learning Activity Packages, give a rationale which makes the experience to be undertaken _____ important, specify the goals of the package as a set of _____ objectives, devise _____ for the objective, and specify the activities which will provide the _____ .

15 Charts are built so the students can _____ _____ for various packages, and sign up for use of various spaces at certain times.

16 The heart of Precision Teaching is the use of procedures for the _____ measurement of improvement on some target behaviors.

17 Most often a _____ measure is taken (responses per minute) and the students chart their own daily progress.

18 A key to precision teaching is learning to state learning objectives in terms of _____ behaviors (pinpointing).

5 workbook; text

6 checkout

7 individualized

8 units; checkouts

9 record

10 motivation

11 checkout

12 instructional unit

13 pretests; mastery

14 personally; behavioral; tests; instruction

15 sign up

16 daily

17 rate

18 observable

19 The precision teaching approach contains all of the essential features of a good monitoring system except a specified _____ .

20 Another potential problem is the heavy reliance on _____ measures. Rate-measures are useful in _____ skills after they have been taught, but an _____ rate emphasis can hinder some acquisitions.

21 Rate measures are also inappropriate in testing concept learning. Whether dealing with language concepts, logical reasoning, or mathematical concepts, testing is primarily concerned with whether the critical _____ have been learned, not with the rate of which examples can be identified.

22 A key procedure in precision teaching is having students _____ their daily progress.

23 In the Behavior Analysis Follow Through Model, each curriculum series was broken into progress _____ , defined by the number of _____ to be completed. The steps were constructed to take about the same amount of _____ , and, where feasible, break at a testing point.

24 When the student reaches a check point, a _____ is taken and checked by the teacher or aide. If it is passed at an _____ percent correct rate or higher, the student goes on to the next unit. If the test is failed, supplemental materials and _____ are used to teach the deficient skills.

25 Group and individual _____ _____ are used to keep track of the students and to aid in motivation.

26 The beauty of the program lies not in the logical niceties of the programing procedures or the completeness of analysis of progress, but in the _____ of the procedures.

27 In the Individualized Early Learning Program, the use of placement tests, pretests, _____ , and curriculum-embedded tests gives the teacher full control of student _____ through the curriculum sequences.

28 Beyond important feedback systems, there are two additional procedures which add to the current discussion. The first is the Progress Summary Report and the second is the use of individual student assignment _____ .

19 curriculum

20 rate; consolidating; early

21 discriminations

22 chart

23 steps, units; pages; time

24 test; 80; tutoring

25 progress records

26 simplicity

27 posttests; progress

28 folders

29 The Progress Summary Report shows where each student started for the school year and the units _____ to date.

30 Each student folder contains an _____ summary of progress and shows the more detailed _____ of the student within the units of each skill area. The student folder is also used by teachers to write new _____ (prescriptions).

31 In a very real way each unit in the LRDC program is like a _____ _____ _____ . It has pretests and posttests, multimedia instruction, multiple _____ requirements, and _____ records. In addition, and importantly, the units are _____ to build on one another.

29 mastered

30 individual;
   placement;
   assignments

31 Learning
   Activity
   Package;
   response;
   progress;
   sequenced

exercise 2   comparing monitoring systems

For each monitoring system illustrated, identify how that system provides for each of the procedures important to a monitoring system (to the degree covered in the text).

A *Learning Activity Packages*

  1 Placement procedure: _____

  _____

  2 Progress units: _____

  _____

  3 Checkout procedures on objectives: _____

  _____

  4 Student guide and progress record: _____

  _____

  5 Procedure for setting goals: _____

  _____

  6 Correction and remediation procedures: _____

  _____

B *Precision Teaching* (as used by the Oregon Regional Resource Center)

1 Placement procedure: _____

_____

2 Progress units: _____

_____

3 Checkout procedures on objectives: _____

_____

4 Student guide and progress record: _____

_____

5 Procedure for setting goals: _____

_____

6 Correction and remediation procedures: _____

_____

C *Behavioral Analysis Follow Through Model*

1 Placement procedure: _____

_____

2 Progress units: _____

_____

3 Checkout procedures on objectives: _____

_____

4 Student guide and progress record: _____

_____

5 Procedure for setting goals: _____

_____

6 Correction and remediation procedures: _____

_____

D *Pittsburgh LRDC Follow Through Model*

1 Placement procedure: _____

_____

2 Progress units: _____

_____

3 Checkout procedures on objectives: _____

_____

4 Student guide and progress record: _____

_____

5 Procedure for setting goals: _____

_____

6 Correction and remediation procedures: _____

_____

Answers for exercise 2

A *Learning Activity Packages*

1 Placement procedure: Pretests are used to see if students need the package. No test of assumed preskills is usually provided, but it could be.

2 Progress units: Each package is a progress unit.

3 Checkout procedures on objectives: Posttests.

4 Student guide and progress record: Charts for signing up for areas, packages, and teacher conferences. Individual records of progress kept by teacher or students and filled in at teacher conferences.

5 Procedure for setting goals: Not discussed.

6 Correction and remediation procedures: If posttest is failed, the teacher may recommend additional work.

B *Precision Teaching*

1 Placement procedure: The various tasks are used as a pretest to determine placement.

2 Progress units: Provided by the groupings of tasks on the tests.

3 Checkout procedures on objectives: Daily testing of rate.

4 Student guide and progress record: Charting of progress of skill being worked on.

5 Procedure for setting goals: Goals set on charts based on rates by average adults.

6 Correction and remediation procedures: Errors are usually counted when a rate measure is taken, but no systematic procedures for correction, other than more practice, are provided.

C *Behavioral Analysis Follow Through Model*

1 Placement procedure: Not generally described. The one shown for reading, started all the students together and then took some back while the rest moved on at their own rates.

2 Progress units: Defined by number of pages to be completed, designated so that about the same amount of time was required for each unit.

3 Checkout procedures on objectives: In-book tests or teacher-made tests checked by teacher or aide.

4 Student guide and progress record: Teacher-made guides as well as group and individual progress charts.

5 Procedure for setting goals: Goals set on individual progress chart. Also individual targets set by computer on a weekly basis.
6 Correction and remediation procedures: Supplemental materials and tutoring used for deficient skills.

D *Pittsburgh LRDC Follow Through Model*

1 Placement procedure: Placement tests and pretests are used in placement.
2 Progress units: The skills in the learning continuum define progress units.
3 Checkout procedures on objectives: In-program tests and posttests.
4 Student guide and progress record: Student folder contains charts showing progress and assignments.
5 Procedure for setting goals: Not formally considered, but could easily be added to the system.
6 Correction and remediation procedures: When tests are not passed, students may be tutored or recycled through the material as determined by teacher.

exercise 3

Do alternative A or B.

A Develop a small Learning Activity Package. This might be done by taking a chapter (or part of a chapter) in other course texts or in an elementary text and:

1 Identify the objectives.
2 Build a posttest.
3 Specify assumed preskills.
4 Specify a rationale for the student.
5 Specify supplementary activities which can be used to master the goals.

Be prepared to turn in your package and discuss it.

B Give the tests for Consonant Sounds (page 103) and Vowel Sounds (page 104) to two children in beginning reading (first grade). The instructions and forms for giving these tests are provided on the pages which follow. Remove the instructions and score sheets before testing. Use the pages 103 and 104 for the student materials. The time limit for Consonant Sounds Test is 1 minute and for Vowel Sounds is 30 seconds.
     The criteria for proficiency are:
     Consonant Sounds: 60-80 sounds per minute, two or less errors.
     Vowel Sounds: 60-80 sounds per minute, two or less errors.
Make recommendations for where the students should be working with respect to these tasks. Be prepared to turn in a report and discuss it.

Acceptable Consonant and Vowel Sounds

Administrator: The list below provides the key sounds for the first two tests of the *Reading Inventory*. Sounds which are pronounced with an additional sound are not acceptable ("buh" is incorrect for "b").

Consonant Sounds		*Vowel Sounds*
b as in bill	n as in nap	a as in and
c as in cap	p as in pin	e as in egg
d as in did	r as in ran	i as in if
f as in fan	s as in sand	o as in on
g as in gas	t as in tap	u as in up
h as in had	v as in van	ā as in ate
j as in jump	w as in will	ē as in eat
k as in kite	x as in fox	ī as in ice
l as in lap	z as in zoo	ō as in open
m as in mat		ū as in use

Consonant Sounds

m	t	r	d	s	f	v	g	h	z
b	l	c	n	p	k	j	z	k	r
t	v	h	d	f	g	l	c	n	b
m	p	j	s	t	r	d	v	j	f
h	g	z	p	n	c	l	b	m	k
s	j	n	z	t	v	d	r	p	s
l	g	f	h	m	k	r	b	c	s
d	v	t	n	g	l	p	z	j	b
h	m	c	r	k	f	m	t	r	d
s	f	v	g	h	z	b	l	c	n

Vowel Sounds

ī   a   ō   i   e   u   ā   ē   o   ū

ē   ū   ā   o   a   ī   e   i   ō   u

e   ī   u   o   i   ā   ū   a   ē   o

ū   o   ē   ā   u   e   i   ō   a   ī

u   ō   i   e   ī   a   o   ā   ū   ē

ō   ē   a   ū   ā   i   o   u   ī   e

ī   a   ō   i   e   u   ā   ē   o   ū

ē   ū   ā   o   a   i   e   ī   ō   u

e   ī   u   o   i   ā   ū   a   ē   ō

General Instructions to Student

This is a test to see how well you can work with sounds and words. Listen carefully to the directions, they will help you do each test. Do the best you can. Do not expect to finish each test.

Examiner proceeds to "Consonant Sounds."

Consonant Sounds (1 Minute)

Instructions for Administration

Each letter makes a sound. This letter, (show m) makes this sound—mmmmmm. Say the sound that each of these letters makes. (Give student copy.) Go as fast as you can. Point to each letter as you sound it. (Demonstrate pointing left to right on student's copy.) If you do not know a sound, skip it, and go on to the next. Ready . . . . . begin.

At the end of one minute, say *stop.*

Record Sheet

m	t	r	d	s	f	v	g	h	z	(10)
b	l	c	n	p	k	j	z	k	r	(20)
t	v	h	d	f	g	l	c	n	b	(30)
m	p	j	s	t	r	d	v	j	f	(40)
h	g	z	p	n	c	l	b	m	k	(50)
s	j	n	z	t	v	d	r	p	s	(60)
l	g	f	h	m	k	r	b	c	s	(70)
d	v	t	n	g	l	p	z	j	b	(80)
h	m	c	r	k	f	m	t	r	d	(90)
s	f	v	g	h	z	b	l	c	n	(100)

Marking Instructions

1 Slash through each letter sounded incorrectly. Write in above what the student said.
2 Circle each letter that the student skips.
3 Slash *after* the last letter sounded at the end of one minute.

Scoring

Correct _____   Error _____

Vowel Sounds (30 Seconds)

Instructions for Administration

Each letter makes a sound. Some letters make two sounds. When a letter has this mark (point to ā), *it sounds its own name. This sound is—ā. Say the sound that each of these letters makes.* (Give student test copy). *Point to each letter as you sound it.* (Demonstrate pointing left to right on student's copy). *Go as fast as you can. If you do not know a sound, skip it, and go on to the next. Ready . . . . . begin.*

At the end of 30 seconds, say *stop*.

Record Sheet

ī	a	ō	i	e	u	ā	ē	o	ū	(10)
ē	ū	ā	o	a	ī	e	i	ō	u	(20)
e	ī	u	o	i	ā	ū	a	ē	ō	(30)
ū	o	ē	ā	u	e	i	ō	a	ī	(40)
u	ō	i	e	ī	a	o	ā	ū	ē	(50)
ō	ē	a	ū	ā	i	o	u	ī	e	(60)
ī	a	ō	i	e	u	ā	ē	o	ū	(70)
ē	ū	ā	o	a	i	e	ī	ō	u	(80)
e	ī	u	o	i	ā	ū	a	ē	ō	(90)

Marking Instructions

1 Slash through each letter sounded incorrectly. Write in above what the student said.
2 Circle each letter which the student skips.
3 Slash *after* the last letter sounded at the end of 30 seconds.

Scoring

Correct (total) _____   Error (total) _____
Long vowels _____   Long vowels _____
Short vowels _____   Short vowels _____

General Instructions to Student

This is a test to see how well you can work with sounds and words. Listen carefully to the directions, they will help you do each test. Do the best you can. Do not expect to finish each test.

Examiner proceeds to "Consonant Sounds."

Consonant Sounds (1 Minute)

Instructions for Administration

Each letter makes a sound. This letter, (show m) makes this sound—mmmmmm. Say the sound that each of these letters makes. (Give student copy.) Go as fast as you can. Point to each letter as you sound it. (Demonstrate pointing left to right on student's copy.) If you do not know a sound, skip it, and go on to the next. Ready . . . . . begin.

At the end of one minute, say *stop*.

Record Sheet

m	t	r	d	s	f	v	g	h	z	(10)
b	l	c	n	p	k	j	z	k	r	(20)
t	v	h	d	f	g	l	c	n	b	(30)
m	p	j	s	t	r	d	v	j	f	(40)
h	g	z	p	n	c	l	b	m	k	(50)
s	j	n	z	t	v	d	r	p	s	(60)
l	g	f	h	m	k	r	b	c	s	(70)
d	v	t	n	g	l	p	z	j	b	(80)
h	m	c	r	k	f	m	t	r	d	(90)
s	f	v	g	h	z	b	l	c	n	(100)

Marking Instructions

1. Slash through each letter sounded incorrectly. Write in above what the student said.
2. Circle each letter that the student skips.
3. Slash *after* the last letter sounded at the end of one minute.

Scoring

Correct _____   Error _____

Vowel Sounds (30 Seconds)

Instructions for Administration

Each letter makes a sound. Some letters make two sounds. When a letter has this mark (point to ā), it sounds its own name. This sound is—ā. Say the sound that each of these letters makes. (Give student test copy). Point to each letter as you sound it. (Demonstrate pointing left to right on student's copy). Go as fast as you can. If you do not know a sound, skip it, and go on to the next. Ready . . . . . begin.

At the end of 30 seconds, say *Stop*.

Record Sheet

ī a ō i e u ā ē o ū   (10)

ē ū ā o a ī e i ō u   (20)

e ī u o i ā ū a ē ō   (30)

ū o ē ā u e i ō a ī   (40)

u ō i e ī a o ā ū ē   (50)

ō ē a ū ā i o u ī e   (60)

ī a ō i e u ā ē o ū   (70)

ē ū ā o a i e ī ō u   (80)

e ī u o i ā ū a ē ō   (90)

Marking Instructions

1 Slash through each letter sounded incorrectly. Write in above what the student said.
2 Circle each letter which the student skips.
3 Slash *after* the last letter sounded at the end of 30 seconds.

Scoring

Correct (total) _____   Error (total) _____

Long vowels _____   Long vowels _____

Short vowels _____   Short vowels _____

discussion questions

1 Why should teachers be concerned with having testing systems to monitor the process of instruction?

2 What are six general requirements for a monitoring system?

3 Specify an instructional objective and a task which is an example of that objective. Next analyze the task for assumed preskills.

4 What are some placement procedures to use when formal tests are not available?

5 Suggest five ways of defining progress units.

6 Suggest some procedures for checkouts on units that can be individualized and which save teacher time.

7 Describe a procedure that can serve as a guide through a sequence of progress units and related record systems.

8 Why should the teacher help the students to establish individual or group goals?

9 Discuss some possible ways in which corrective action can be taken when failure occurs on a checkout.

10 Describe how Learning Activity Packages provide for the components of an effective monitoring system.

11 Describe how Precision Teaching provides for the components of an effective monitoring system.

12 Describe how the Behavior Analysis Follow Through Model provides for the components of an effective monitoring system.

13 Describe how the Pittsburgh LRDC Follow Through Model provides for the components of an effective monitoring system.

14 What are the potential problems of a high reliance on rate measures in precision teaching?

15 How can the problem with rate measures in precision teaching be overcome?

16 What did Alan Hofmeister do and find in his study of the effects of a monitoring system on student learning?

unit 6

Monitoring System for the University of Oregon Follow Through Model

objectives

When you complete this unit you should be able to—

1 Describe the main features of the Direction-Instruction Follow Through Model.

2 Describe the monitoring system used for this model and explain how the Report of Lessons Taught, the Continuous Progress Test Reports, and supervisors are used to locate and remediate problems.

lesson

The Direct-Instruction Follow Through Model built by Engelmann and Becker is based on the initial assumption that disadvantaged children learn more only if they are taught more.[1] The task therefore was viewed as one of devising a *system* that would get more teaching into classrooms. We began by adding two aides (usually parents of the disadvantaged children) in grades K, 1, and 2, and one aide in grade 3. We then set up plans for the use of the staff throughout the day. Plans vary with local conditions but have common components. The primary teaching mode is small-group instruction, as described in detail in *Teaching 2*. This provides for individual differences in starting points and progress, and emphasizes the importance of verbal communication in teaching beginning skills in reading, arithmetic, and language. The teachers and aides were trained to be specialists in at least one of the three basic programs. The plans for use of space and time were geared to the small-group teaching mode and provided for rotating students through teaching stations. Since three groups are usually taught at the same time, partitions are used to separate the groups and reduce distractions. At the beginning levels, group periods last about 30 minutes for each subject area. At advanced levels, 15 minutes of group instruction is followed by 30 minutes of self-directed practice in workbooks. Structured large-group teaching activities are also included. The goal of the model is to make meximal use of the teaching staff throughout the day and to insure that staff and students know what they should be doing and when.

To implement this model, sequenced daily lessons in reading, arithmetic, and language (now published as *Distar*) were constructed using the principles described in *Teaching 2* aimed at teaching generalized skills. Preservice and inservice training provide teachers and aides with the skills required to teach the programs. Again, these skills were described in some detail in *Teaching 2, Unit 3*. Finally, a monitoring system was established to show if the system was working and to provide a basis for correcting deficiencies before it was too late. It is the monitoring system that is of greatest concern here.

The monitoring system consists essentially of placement procedures, reports of lessons taught in the instructional programs, continuous progress tests (program-based), and supervision of instruction in the classroom. In addition, a project manager from Oregon periodically reviews all monitoring information including supervisor activities.

Placement Tests

Monitoring of progress begins at the start of the year where it is important to determine the skills individual children have relative to the program. At the beginning levels of the Distar programs this is accomplished by tests of preskills, called the *placement tests.*

In Reading 1, the placement test covers some reading preskills such as: (1) listening to a broken-up word (motor . . . cycle) and saying the whole word fast when asked to (motorcycle), (2) repeating actions in sequence, and (3) identifying the sounds *m* and *a.* If no more than one error is made on the pretest the children start the program on day 11. Otherwise they start on day 1. In Arithmetic 1, the children start on day 31 if they can count to ten and can count up to ten objects. Otherwise they start on day 1. In Language 1, the children start on day 16 if the pretest shows they can repeat a whole statement and can identify simple objects. Otherwise they start on day 1. The placement tests can also be used to group the children according to the number of errors made.

At advanced levels, the teacher can use several methods to decide on placement. One approach is to take the records of how far the students advanced in the program the year before and start the children back 10 to 15 lessons, using these lessons as "warm up" and review during the first week of school. From then on, decisions on group assignments are made on the basis of individual performances. Another approach is to use the Continuous Progress Tests to determine placement. This may be especially helpful with new children entering the program. A third approach is to use the review lessons, that precede advance level programs, as a testing device to make placement decisions.

Reports of Lessons Taught

Every two weeks a report is filled out showing which lesson each group is on, the number of lessons gained during that two weeks, and lessons gained from the start of the school year. By taking a school calendar and numbering it consecutively from the first day of school to the last day of school, the *day in the school year* can be determined for any given report date. By comparing day-in-school year with number of lessons taught, important monitoring information is obtained. From this information, a teacher, supervisor, or principal can easily determine the likelihood of any given group completing one of the programs. Table 6.1 gives an example of a Bi-Weekly Report of Lessons Taught. In that report, by December 10, 70 school days had passed. The children in group 1 started on lesson day 10 in reading (as determined by the placement test). They are now at lesson day (LDIP) 90. During the past two weeks they gained 12 lessons. From the start of the school year they have gained 80 lessons or an average of 1.14 lessons a day (80/70). If they continue at this rate they will be on lesson 207 (1.14 × 180) by the end of the year. This means they will be 45 days into the level 2 program. Group 1 is making good progress.

Group 4 started the reading program at the beginning. They are now on lesson day 40. They progressed only 5 lessons in the past two weeks. They are progressing at an average rate of .57 lessons per day (40/70). By the end of the year they will be expected to complete only 103 lessons (.57 × 180). Whether this is an acceptable performance will depend on a more careful analysis of how they are being taught. If analysis shows that the problem is

TABLE 6.1   Bi-Weekly Report of Lessons Taught

Teacher Thomas   Grade   K   School Marshall

Date   Dec. 10   Day in School 70

Group	Reading					Arithmetic					Language				
	L	SDIP	LDIP	2 wk Gain	Year Gain	L	SDIP	LDIP	2 wk Gain	Year Gain	L	SDIP	LDIP	2 wk Gain	Year Gain
1	1	10	90	12	80	1	40	125	13	85	1	60	150	14	90
2	1	0	70	10	70	1	0	65	9	65	1	0	75	11	75
3	1	0	60	9	60	1	0	50	7	50	1	0	65	10	65
4	1	0	40	5	40	1	0	45	4	45	1	0	55	8	55

   L = Program Level
SDIP = Starting Day In Program
LDIP = Lesson Day In Program

one of scheduling teaching time, or if the teacher's skills with low-performing children are weak, then the supervisor would try to adjust the schedule or provide additional training for the teacher. If the group is in fect being taught each day and the teaching method is adequate, this rate of progress would be acceptable. Many groups of children with low skills at entry progress slowly the first year. After mastering skills in the language of instruction, this rate can be expected to improve to .80 or .90 lessons per day.

It is possible to plot the information from the Bi-Weekly Report of Lessons Taught on a graph each two weeks to show more readily the rate of progress toward a goal. Our experience indicates that with proper training and supervision, the top group should progress about 8 lessons every 5 days, the middle group about a lesson a day, and the lowest performing group about 5 lessons every 8 days. Figure 6.1 shows a graph of group progress for group 4. The dark heavy line shows the targeted rate of progress for this group of low-performing children. The lighter line shows the progress each two weeks. Graphs of this sort help to show where things are going well and where additional efforts might be needed.

Reports of Continuous Progress Testing

In the school districts implementing the University of Oregon Follow Through Model, the children are tested every two weeks in one subject area. A testing schedule is set up for testing aides to test reading first, then arithmetic, and then language. The cycle is then repeated during the next six weeks. Five to six cycles occur during the school year. The test results are reported each two weeks in one subject area along with the Bi-Weekly Report of Lessons Taught.

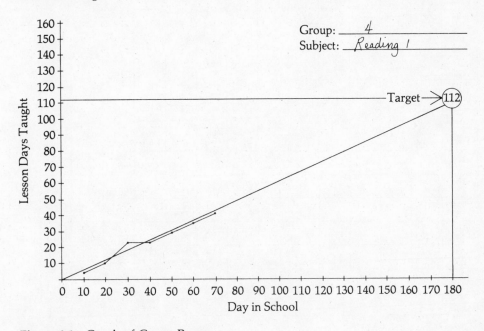

Figure 6.1 Graph of Group Progress

Over the seven years of the program, we have used two kinds of report systems. We have already illustrated one system in our descriptions of the instructional-program-based test for revised *Distar Reading 1* (see units 3 and 4, particularly table 4.4). A test is provided for each 10 days of program, and the Record Form is designed to specify when individual and group remedial procedures are needed. This new system is especially helpful in pinpointing remedial procedures. However, the main system we have been using for several years allows one to follow individual progress more easily. The Arithmetic I Continuous Progress Test will be used to illustrate the monitoring procedure and its uses in decision making.

Like the Reading I test, the arithmetic test is made up of tracks which cover the major skills in the program. Figure 6.2 illustrates an Individual Record Form. The abbreviations across the top stand for the track names such as Object Counting (OC) or Algebra Addition (AA). The testing begins according to the student's current lesson placement in the program. For example, if a student is on Lesson 100, testing would begin with those items

ARITH 1: 1-220

Arithmetic Record Form

Teacher _____

Child _____

Site _____

	Testing	Group	Lesson
1st			
2nd			
3rd			
4th			

Lesson Range	OC	CTN	CET	CFN TN	E	A	AA	FA	POS	SP	CB	AAF	S	SF	AS	C	ASF	Lesson Range
	1	8																
1 / 43	2−, 2+	9−, 9+|	17															
44 / 53	3−, 3+	10−, 10+	18−, 18+															
54 / 63		11−, 11+	19−, 19+															
64 / 73	4−, 4+	12−, 12+	20−, 20+	22														
74 / 83	5−, 5+	13−, 13+	21−, 21+	23−, 23+														
84 / 93	6−, 6+	14−, 14+		24−, 24+|	28	32												
94 / 103	7−, 7+	15−, 15+		25−, 25+	29−, 29+	33−, 33+	46											
104 / 113		16−, 16+		26−, 26+	30−, 30+	34−, 34+	47−, 47+|											
114 / 123				27−, 27+	31−, 31+	35−, 35+	48−, 48+|	56										
124 / 133						36−, 36+	49−, 49+	57−, 57+|	67	77								
134 / 143						37−, 37+	50−, 50+	58−, 58+	68−, 68+	78−, 78+|	87							
144 / 153						38−, 38+	51−, 51+	59−, 59+	69−, 69+	79−, 79+	88−, 88+|	94						
154 / 163						39−, 39+	52−, 52+	60−, 60+	70−, 70+	80−, 80+	89−, 89+	95−, 95+|	99					
164 / 173						40−, 40+	53−, 53+	61−, 61+	71−, 71+	81−, 81+	90−, 90+	96−, 96+	100−, 100+|	106	112			164 / 173
174 / 183						41−, 41+	54−, 54+	62−, 62+	72−, 72+	82−, 82+	91−, 91+	97−, 97+	101−, 101+	107−, 107+	113−, 113+|			174 / 183
184 / 193						42−, 42+	55−, 55+	63−, 63+	73−, 73+	83−, 83+	92−, 92+	98−, 98+	102−, 102+	108−, 108+	114−, 114+|	118		184 / 193
194 / 203						43−, 43+		64−, 64+	74−, 74+	84−, 84+	93−, 93+		103−, 103+	109−, 109+	115−, 115+	119−, 119+|	122	194 / 203
204 / 213						44−, 44+		65−, 65+	75−, 75+	85−, 85+			104−, 104+	110−, 110+	116−, 116+	120−, 120+	123−, 123+|	204 / 223
214 / 220						45−, 45+		66−, 66+	76−, 76+	86−, 86+			105−, 105+	111−, 111+	117−, 117+	121−, 121+	124−, 124+	224 / 243

Figure 6.2 Individual Record Form

in the row identifying the 94-103 lesson range (items 7, 15, 25, 29, 33). The tester goes ahead to the next item in a track if the first is passed, and moves back if it is failed. Since each item (which is actually a set of tasks) is selected to reflect ten days progress in the lessons tested in the track, the scores can be directly interpreted in relation to lesson placement in the program. If a student is two items ahead of where the teacher has him, he is 20 lessons ahead. If a student is two items behind, he is 20 lessons behind. To make the tests useful diagnostically, a key is provided so that for any item missed, the teacher has a direct reference to the tasks which need to be taught. For each new testing cycle, the same form is used, providing a summary of progress over the year.

Data from individual testing are then summarized on a Biweekly Test Report form covering the whole class. (The Biweekly Report of Lessons Taught, illustrated earlier, goes on the bottom of the test report, so that only one form is needed.) Figure 6.3 gives an example of part of a Biweekly Test Report. For each group, numbers in the shaded area give the items the student should pass. For group 1, all students passed item 11 on track 1 as they should have. For tracks 2, 3, 4, and 5, most students were right on target, and only a few were 10 days (one item) ahead or behind. This is acceptable. For group 2, however, there are problems with tracks 2 and 4. Several students in the group are 20 days behind (circled scores). This performance calls for remediation in sounding out words (track 2) and rhyming (track 4).

In group 3 there are problems with tracks 2, 3, and 4. Track 3 involves reading new words using sounds which have been taught. Groups 2 and 3 could be combined for review on tracks 2, 3, and 4.

In group 4, Edward needs special tutoring in tracks 1 and 2 or he won't be able to keep up with the group. He does not know the sounds taught in the past 30 days and cannot sound out words with the sounds he does know. Tam and David need help in track 4.

As noted earlier, from the Report of Lessons Taught, we are able to make projections about where the children will be at the end of the year and to take steps to change those projections if that is needed. However, when we compare the student's *test performance* with *lessons taught*, we are able to get a more complete picture of what is happening. Consider some of the logical possibilities.

Suppose 125 lessons in arithmetic have been taught to the students in the top group and their performance on the addition track indicates that they failed item 29 for lesson days 94-103. The students are performing substantially below (about 25 days) where the teacher has them. This suggests that the teacher may just be taking them through the lessons and not making sure the children have mastered each lesson before going on. It may be necessary to take the students back and reteach some lessons after carefully examining and correcting the teacher's procedures.

Consider a reverse example. The teacher has the students at day 90, but the test shows they can do test items at day 130. The students already have the skills coming up in the program so that it is possible to move them ahead.

Another possibility is that the whole group is behind, but only in one track. In the other tracks, they are at lesson day-in-program on the test. It

SITE: Smithville   SUBJECT: Reading   REPORT NO: 13   DATE: 3-17-75
TEACHER: Selma Salt   GRADE: Kindergarten   SCHOOL DAY AT TEST: 132

	Group No.	Days Absn.	LDIP*	TRACKS 1	2	3	4	5
Level: ① II III			100	11**	23	34	44	53
Shauna	1	0	100	11	23	34	44	53
Susan	1	0	100	11	24	35	45	54
Steven	1	0	100	11	23	35	43	53
Sally	1	1	100	11	24	35	45	54
Laura	1	0	100	11	24	35	45	53
Ken	1	2	100	11	23	35	43	53
Mike	1	0	100	11	23	35	45	53
Level: ① II III			88	10	22	33	43	52
Michelle	2	0	88	10	⑳	33	㊶	52
Shawn	2	0	88	10	⑲	33	㊶	53
Laura	2	1	88	10	⑳	33	43	52
Sandy	2	0	88	10	⑳	33	㊶	52
John	2	½	88	10	22	33	43	52
Level: ① II III			87	10	22	33	43	52
Penny	3	1	87	9	⑲	㉛	㊶	52
David	3	0	87	9	⑳	㉜	42	52
Tony	3	0	87	9	⑲	㉜	㊶	52
Pam	3	2	87	9	㉑	㉛	㊶	52
Brian	3	0	87	9	22	33	43	52
Joe	3	0	87	9	⑲	㉛	㊶	52
Stan	3	1	87	9	⑳	33	㊶	52
Level: ① II III			84	9	21	32	42	
Tam	4	1	84	10	21	33	41	
Jim	4	0	84	10	21	32	43	
Charles	4	3	84	10	21	31	42	
Violet	4	0	84	10	21	33	43	
Edward	4	1	84	⑥	⑱	32	42	
David	4	2	84	10	20	32	41	

*Lesson Day in Program

**Numbers in shaded area indicate expected performance for the given LDIP

Figure 6.3   Sample Biweekly Report

is likely that the teacher may need specific help in teaching the skills in *that track*.

The test results might also show that one or two students in a group are lagging behind the rest. This could happen because the teacher was not teaching every child in the group or because the children are placed in a group too fast for them. The supervisor would give special attention to such a situation and either give the teacher more training or reassign the children to a lower group.

Again, the reverse could be happening. Two students in a group may be far ahead of where the teacher has them. A placement in a higher group would be in order.

The Continuous Progress Test results in combination with the Report of Lesson Taught provide very critical information for monitoring classroom progress and correcting difficulties.

Classroom Supervision

In our Follow Through Model we attempt to have one supervisor for every 200 children (eight classrooms). The supervisor is able to pinpoint possible problems and plan training sessions from the reports discussed above, but final decisions come from a careful examination of the teaching process itself. Supervisors are expected to spend 75 percent of their time in the classroom working with teachers. In working with teachers, the supervisor uses the Teacher Performance Form. The form helps to structure what is to be observed and provides a record of problems and assignments made to correct problems. The Roman numerals refer to the program levels and R, A, and L refer to Reading, Arithmetic, and Language. No more than two "Work on" suggestions are given at any one observation. MANAGEMENT refers to maintaining the students' attention by keeping them close, using praise where appropriate, and following a series of other positive motivational procedures. ORGANIZATION includes having materials ready when needed, moving the groups from place to place, and being prepared for what is coming next. FOLLOWS FORMAT is concerned with being able to present the tasks in the program as they are written. CORRECTIONS is concerned with the way in which corrections are made (which depends on the type of error) and with actually making corrections when they are needed. PACING refers to keeping the teaching moving at a fairly rapid rate in most cases, with pauses at specified points, and also with the way in which phrases are grouped when presenting a format. Different kinds of formats call for different pacing requirements. SIGNALS is concerned with hand signals, inflections, and the like, designed to get the children to respond together. SKIP or MAKE UP is concerned with where the teacher has the group in the program. The tests may show they are performing ahead or behind where the teacher has them. If this is verified by classroom observations, a recommendation to take the group back or move them ahead is made. GROUPING is concerned with whether all members of the group are appropriately placed. By using the Continuous Progress Tests and observations, a recommendation may be made to move a child ahead or back in the program.

	Skills	Good	Work On	Assignment	Follow-Up Date	Good	Work On	Assignment
I	Management							
II	Organization							
III	Follows Format							
R	Corrections							
L	Pacing							
A	Signals							
	Skip or Make Up							
	Grouping							

(Left margin labels: Teacher / Lesson / Date / Title)

Figure 6.4 Teacher Performance Form

When assignments are made that involve a change in teaching technique, our supervisors will very often sit down with the teacher's group and present a model of the skill the teacher needs to learn. It is essential that the supervisor be a skilled teacher or this could not be done.

While the particular program we have been describing is restricted to grades kindergarten through third, the basic ideas of a monitoring system which gives the information needed to do an effective job is adaptable to any *systematic* approach to instruction. As described in *Teaching 2*, unit 12, outcome data using this model has been very positive in teaching disadvantaged children in all sectors of the United States.

summary

We have devoted this unit to a more detailed look at the monitoring system used in the University of Oregon Sponsored Follow Through Projects. The details of the monitoring system show how it is possible to have the information to make *logical decisions* to improve instruction as it is proceeding. With a carefully programed sequence of instruction, it is possible to build a testing, reporting, and supervision system to support that instruction. The important informations in the system are:

1 Placement procedures to get students started in the program where they need to be.
2 A Report of Lessons Taught which can be related to days available for teaching and goals for the year.

3   Continuous Progress Tests which check the *quality* of student progress through the program. When quality of progress is considered along with the rate of progress from 2 above, a strong basis for making instructional decisions is provided.

4   Finally, the teacher supervisor working within this monitoring system is in an excellent position to pinpoint problems in instructional procedures and to aid the teacher in correcting them.

Undoubtedly, to some, a management system such as this must seem confining. However, the majority of teachers working within the system (after the initial shock!) come to consider it the best way, because they know what they are doing and they like the progress the students make.

self-test

1   The Direct-Instruction Follow Through Model built by Engelmann and Becker is based on the initial assumption that disadvantaged children learn more only if they are _____ more.

2   A monitoring system was established to show whether the system was working and to provide a basis for _____ _____ before it was too late.

1 taught

3   The monitoring system consists essentially of placement procedures, _____ of lessons taught in the instructional programs, _____ _____ _____ (program-based), and supervision of instruction in classroom.

2 correcting
   deficiencies

3 reports;
   continuous
   progress tests

4   If a student is on lesson 36 and there have been 48 school days so far, what is his lesson rate per day? _____ .

5   It is possible to plot the information from the Bi-Weekly Report of Lessons Taught on a _____ each two weeks to more readily show rate of progress toward a goal.

4 .75

6   On the Continuous Progress test, if a student is two items ahead of where the teacher has him, he is _____ lessons ahead.

5 graph

7   When we compare a student's test performance with _____ _____ , we are able to get a more complete picture of what is happening.

6 20

7 lessons
   taught

8 If students are performing below where the teacher has them placed, it suggests the teacher is moving ahead without insuring _____ .

9 If students are performing ahead of where the teacher has them placed, it suggests the teacher can _____ some lessons.

8 mastery

9 skip

NUMBER RIGHT _____

exercise 1 programed practice

1 The Direct-Instruction Follow Through Model built by Engelmann and Becker is based on the initial assumption that disadvantaged children learn more only if they are _____ more.

2 Two aides were added to each class (usually _____ of the disadvantaged children) in grades K, 1, and 2, and one aide in grade 3.

3 The primary teaching mode is _____-_____ _____ . This provides for _____ differences in starting points and progress, and emphasizes the importance of _____ communication in teaching beginning skills.

4 Plans for use of space and time were geared to the small-group teaching mode and provided for _____ students through teaching stations.

5 To implement this model, sequenced daily _____ in reading, arithmetic, and language were constructed.

6 Preservice and _____ training provide teachers and aides with the skills required to teach the programs.

7 A monitoring system was established to show whether the system was working and to provide a basis for _____ _____ .

8 The monitoring system consists essentially of placement procedures, _____ of lessons taught in the instructional programs, _____ _____ _____ (program based), and supervision of instruction in the classroom.

1 taught

2 parents

3 small-group
  instruction;
  individual; verbal

4 rotating

5 lessons

6 inservice

7 correcting
  deficiencies

8 reports;
  continuous
  progress tests

9   At beginning levels, placement depends on critical _____ . When the skills are present, the student starts at an _____ point. When the skills are absent, the student starts at the beginning of the program.

9 preskills; advanced

10   At advanced levels, placement is determined by _____ _____ in program achieved the year before or by _____ test results.

10 lesson day; continuous

11   Every two weeks a report is filled out showing which _____ each group was on, the number of lessons _____ during that two weeks, and lessons gained from the _____ of the school year. By comparing day-in-school year with number of _____ _____ , important monitoring information is obtained.

11 lesson; gained; start; lessons taught

12   If a student is on lesson 36 and there have been 48 school days so far, what is his lesson rate per day? _____ . If there are 160 teaching days in the average school year, how far will the student progress by the end of the year? _____ .

12 .75; 120 lessons

13   Whether 120 lessons is acceptable progress will depend on a more careful analysis of how the group is being _____ . If analysis shows that the problem is one of scheduling teaching _____ , or if the teacher's _____ with low-performing children are weak, then the supervisor would try to adjust the schedule or provide additional training for the teacher. If the group is in fact being taught each day and the teaching method is adequate, this rate of progress would be _____ .

13 taught; time; skills; acceptable

14   It is possible to plot the information from the Bi-Weekly Report of Lessons Taught on a _____ each two weeks to more readily show rate of progress toward a goal.

14 graph

15   In the University of Oregon Follow Through Model, children are tested every two weeks in one subject area on the _____ _____ tests.

15 continuous progress

16   Since each item (which is actually a set of tasks) is selected to reflect 10 days of progress in the lessons tested in the track, the scores can be directly interpreted in relation to _____ placement in the program.

16 lesson

17 If a student is two items ahead of where the teacher has him, he is _____ lessons ahead. If a student is two items behind, he is _____ lessons behind.

18 To make the tests useful _____ , a key is provided so that for any item missed, the teacher has a direct reference to the tasks which need to be taught.

19 When we compare the student's test performance with _____ _____ , we are able to get a more complete picture of what is happening.

20 If students are performing below where the teacher has them placed, it suggests the teacher is moving ahead without insuring _____ .

21 If the students are performing ahead of where the teacher has them placed, it suggests the teacher can _____ some lessons.

22 If the group is behind in one track, it implies poor _____ of that track.

23 If some students do poorly in many tracks, it implies a _____ problem in need of diagnosis.

24 The Continuous Progress Test results in combination with the Report of Lesson Taught provide very critical information for _____ classroom progress and _____ difficulties.

25 Teacher supervisors are able to pinpoint possible problems and plan training sessions from the reports discussed above, but final decisions come from a careful examination of the _____ process itself.

17 20; 20

18 diagnostically

19 lessons
taught

20 mastery

21 skip

22 teaching

23 student

24 monitoring;
correcting

25 teaching

discussion questions

1 Describe the main features of the Direct-Instruction Follow Through Model.
2 What placement procedures are used with the program?
3 What is the value of the Report of Lessons Taught?
4 Describe the testing procedure used for the Arithmetic I Continuous Progress Test.
5 How are scores on the Continuous Progress Tests used?
6 How are teacher supervisors used in the program?

unit 7

Outcome Evaluation
with Criterion-Referenced Tests

objectives

When you complete this unit you should be able to—

1 Specify why it is desirable to restrict comparisons of programs to those based on common objectives.
2 Specify the factors to be considered in making between-program comparisons.
3 Specify the problems in evaluating instructional programs which have different objectives and/or formats and, where appropriate, suggest possible solutions.
4 Describe an approach to program comparisons which focuses on minimum common standards.
5 Specify the procedure used in designing the *Survival Skills Reading Test* to make it especially useful in remedial work.
6 Specify two approaches to within-program comparisons which can be used to upgrade instruction.
7 Discuss the potential value of norms for criterion-referenced tests geared to specific instructional programs.

lesson

Ideally, in evaluating instructional outcomes, one of two possible comparisons would be made:

1 Different instructional programs *designed to teach the same objectives* would be compared, or
2 *Different procedures* for teaching the same program would be compared.

123

If comparisons could be restricted in this way, the problems of designing and interpreting outcome studies would be manageable. However, in the live world of educational realities, instructional programs are usually not constructed to teach the same objectives. This situation makes the design of studies to compare different programs difficult. However, today's teacher is likely to be right in the middle of studies of program effectiveness. With an understanding of the minimum requirements for a rational comparison of programs or procedures, the teacher will be in a better position to defend desirable practice against the all-too-common abuses of poor research design. In this unit we will examine some of the requirements for the design of outcome research using criterion-referenced tests. In a later unit, we will return to the issues of design of research and consider the uses of norm-referenced tests in such research.

Comparisons of Different Programs

Testing Common Objectives

Different programs can be readily compared to the degree that it is reasonable to evaluate them on *common objectives*. For example, two English programs are designed to teach punctuation. The objectives of the programs are identified in terms of specific performances such as:

Capitalize the first letter of a sentence.

Use commas to separate items in a series.

Place a question mark at the end of a question.

Use apostrophes to show that one or more letters have been left out.

After the objectives are identified, test items can be written to provide four to six examples of each rule. Test items would look like these:[1]

Directions: Read each sentence carefully and add any punctuation that has been left out. Where a letter should be capitalized, write the capital above the letter.

1 the cat ran in the house

2 Shall i visit you on monday

3 The grocer sells eggs butter bacon and cheese.

In an ideal study, students and teachers would be randomly assigned to each of the programs. Then pretest and posttest data would be gathered on the objectives. Figure 7.1 illustrates a possible outcome.

The data in figure 7.1 show that both programs were effective in producing improvements, but that program B was more effective than program A. The critical question at this point is what else would you want to know to be able to interpret the results? The following questions need to be considered:

1. *Are the students in the two groups equivalent in important characteristics?*
   The similarity of the pretest data suggests that they are.

2. *Were both programs taught in a reasonably adequate way?*

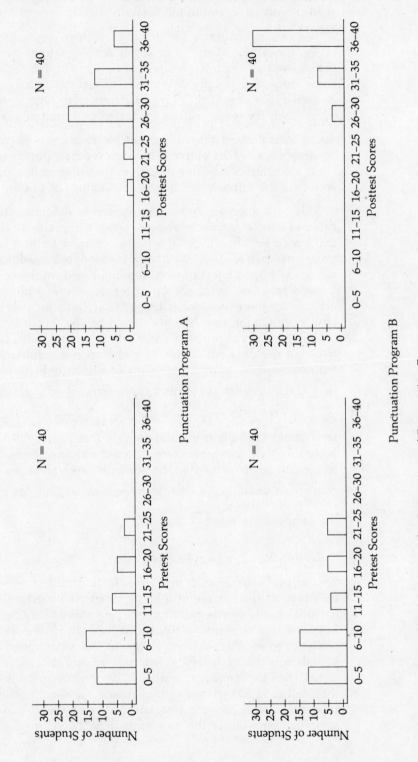

Figure 7.1 Hypothetical Outcome of a Comparison of Punctuation Programs

To insure this requires a specification of teaching procedures before hand, training on the procedures if necessary, and classroom observations to insure that the procedures were followed.

3. *Was the time devoted to teaching both programs comparable?*

Perhaps the students in program A were taught for less time each day. If this were so, the interpretation of the result might be different. In an outcome study, it is usually desirable to record the actual teaching time allotted to each major objective. If large differences in time devoted to an outcome occur, then the results can be evaluated as a ratio of gains to teaching time.

4. *Are there program differences in outcome on the sub-objectives?*

An analysis of the outcome for each separate punctuation objective might show weaknesses for some objectives for program B which the teacher could correct in the future by additions or modifications of the program.

This basic approach to the comparison of program effects is widely applicable as long as common objectives can be specified. The key is to find or make tests which will get at what is common to the program goals. If two programs teach reading by a phonic method, but use different specific words, we can still build a test of word reading based on the common sounds used in each program, but made up of regular-sound words or nonsense words *not used by either program*. If the general skills for decoding regular words have been taught, the students should be able to pass the test.

Another kind of problem arises when two programs have common objectives but use different directions and response requirements. Each program teaches the same information, but uses a restricted task format. One program may teach division problems in this form: $\frac{6}{8} = \square$, another in this form: $6 \div 8 = \square$, and yet another in this form: $8 \overline{\smash{)}6}$. To deal with this problem, tests could be built using the same numerical problems for the different programs, but using program specific response formats. Alternatively, a test might be structured so the students were given an example of how to convert an unfamiliar format into the familiar one, for example, $\frac{6}{8} = \square$ is the same as: $6 \div 8 = \square$.

Testing Not-Common Objectives

Special problems arise in dealing with linear-additive sets, when different members of the set are taught by different programs. A spelling test of irregular-sound words geared to one program will not be suitable to another. The language concepts or vocabulary taught in one program may not be common to another. A comparison in this case might be concerned with *how much* is taught as well as *how well* it is taught.

Let's say the language vocabulary for one program is 1,000 concepts and for another is 500. A test is built based on the concepts common to each program (say, a 20-word test sampled from the 200 common words) and samples from each of the not-common sets (say, a 40-word test out of the

800 remaining in one program, and a 40-word test out of the 300 remaining in the other). The test of common concepts gives one comparison of the programs. This can be augmented by an estimate of the size of the not-common vocabulary actually taught. For example, if for the first program the average was 80 percent correct, this would lead to an estimate of 640 words (80 percent of 800) learned. Similarly, an 80 percent performance on the second program test would lead to an estimate of only 240 (80 percent of 300) words learned. One could also see how well the students in one program do on a test of the other program, but the outcome would be difficult to interpret and would violate the rule, *Test what was taught*.

Interpreting the results on not-common objectives requires a careful judgment concerning the value of the objectives, as well as an appraisal of the comparability of the students, the adequacy of the teaching, and the time devoted to producing the outcome. This problem has been a major one in the national evaluation of programs instituted by different Follow Through sponsors. Programs designed by different sponsors had different goals. Some focused on work with parents, some community action, some affective goals for students, and others cognitive goals for students. The initial attempts to produce an evaluation design gave a lot of attention to not-common objectives. This approach led to a morass of possible measures, none of which was useful in *comparing* programs. Eventually, by focusing on a minimum set of *common objectives*, an approach to comparative evaluations was possible. It is much easier to tell whether one orange is better than another, than to tell if an orange is better than a banana. Test comparisons are helpful in the first case, but in the second case it might be better if people could take their choice. The problems of choice or alternatives in educational goals is a most important one. It enters into the task of evaluating any programs and *it won't go away*. At present it can only be dealt with through some kind of consensus among educators and community. Needless to say, that is the subject of a book in itself and goes beyond the goals of this text.

Testing Minimal Standards of Competency

There is another approach to the comparison of programs which is designed around the criterion-referenced test. School systems and states are beginning to specify minimal standards of competency in language, reading, writing, math, American government, personal finance, and the like, which all students must meet in order to earn a high school diploma. Once these minimal goals are specified, any programs designed to meet such goals can be compared with criterion-referenced tests of the *minimum common standards*. At various points in making progress toward such goals, the question can be asked: "What percentage of students are below minimum criterion?" This information can be used to compare different programs. Furthermore, if the tests are properly designed, they can also be used to pinpoint the remedial efforts that should be undertaken; and the remediation prescription can be evaluated by its successfulness. Alan Hofmeister has called this latter concern the "treatment validity" of a test.[2] An example of this approach is provided by the *Survival Skills Reading Test* developed by Engelmann and

Hanner.[3] We will describe this test in some detail because the logic used in its development may provide an important model for the future development of one variety of criterion-referenced tests.

The *Survival Skills Reading Test* was designed and tested for use in comparing different programs to determine the degree to which basic skills in language and reading have been taught and to provide for remediation where they have not. The test focuses on those basic reading and language skills that any program would say it is trying to teach. It is not tied to a specific instructional program. Rather, it is tied to the basic survival skills a school system would like to teach to every child. This testing model could easily be extended to other basic skills areas. The testing system has these components:

Level A. This provides an individually administered test of preskills to be used in kindergarten and first grades. Its aim is to identify children in need of special instruction before they can enter into a typical first grade basal series. The test covers oral blending, rhyming, sound identification, sequencing, inferences, statement repetition, and simple writing and copying skills.

Levels B, C, and D. Test batteries for levels B, C, and D are each divided into three parts. Level B is designed for use in grades 2 to 4, Level C in grades 5 to 7, and Level D in grades 8 to 12. Batteries B, C, and D contain: (1) a Screening Test, (2) a Diagnostic Test for those who fail the Screening Test, and (3) an Elaborated Test for those who *pass* the Screening Test. The Screening and Diagnostic Tests are given individually and take five and twenty minutes to give, respectively. The Elaborated Test is a group-administered paper-and-pencil test which requires about thirty minutes to complete.

The Level B Screening Test tests *decoding* of words and sentences and *following instructions.* The words used in the Decoding Test are those research has shown are often missed by the poor reader, such as *the, then, where, left, felt.* The sentences used on the Decoding Test are the same ones used for the Following Instructions Test, for example, "Cross out the ball," "Fill in the circle under something you find in the kitchen." If the student can decode, but cannot follow instructions, a different remedy is called for. But exactly what is needed cannot be determined without the Diagnostic Test. The Diagnostic Test examines decoding skills in sufficient detail to provide teaching prescriptions for students who fail the test. The Diagnostic Test also tests sentence repetition, comprehension, and sequencing skills, each of which is essential to being able to follow instructions. Sequencing is also an important skill in decoding.

The Level B Elaborated Test focuses on advanced comprehension skills such as reading for information, deductions, inductions, sequencing of ideas, and following instructions.

Table 7.1 summarizes the skills tested at each level with each type of test.

One key to Engelmann's approach is the focus on *common objectives;* the other key is the *item cluster.* Items are designed and grouped so that deficient component skills are isolated. A student could fail to follow written instructions because he could not decode the words, he could not remember what he had decoded (statement repetition), he did not understand the words, he lost the sequence of ideas, and so forth. By designing clusters of test items to assure that a component skill is tested in isolation before it is required

TABLE 7.1 SUMMARY OF SURVIVAL SKILLS READING TEST

Test	Skills
A	Sequencing, Blending, Rhyming, Letter Identification, Following Instructions, Writing/Copying, Statement Repetition, Inferences
B-1 Screening	Decoding, Following Instructions
B-2 Diagnostic	Decoding, Statement Repetition, Comprehension, Sequencing
B-3 Elaborated	Sequencing, Informational Reading, Deductions, Inductions, Following Instructions
C-1 Screening	Reading Rate, Accuracy, Comprehension
C-2 Diagnostic	Decoding, Statement Repetition, Comprehension, Sequencing
C-3 Elaborated	Sequential and Informational Reading, Inferential Reading, Deductions, Inductions, Library Skills
D-1 Screening	Reading Rate, Accuracy, Comprehension
D-2 Diagnostic	Decoding, Statement Repetition
D-3 Elaborated	Deductions and Inferential Reading, Informational Reading, Library Skills, Following Instructions (complete Job Application Form)

for use in a more complex task involving an additional skill, it is possible to pinpoint deficiencies and prescribe remedial procedures.

Engelmann and Hanner recommend precise procedures for teaching skills found to be deficient. For the most part these recommendations follow instructional procedures already demonstrated to work in various parts of the Distar system. In some cases, teachers will actually want to use Distar sequences or the *Corrective Reading Program*.[4] Engelmann is also working on extensions of *Corrective Reading* which cover advanced comprehension, spelling, and other aspects of a basic language competency. It is too early to say how much this approach can help school districts having trouble teaching basic skills to some children. It can do a good job in locating students needing help and in providing comparative information on programs. At this time, tests of the "treatment validity" of the remedial recommendations that go with the testing program are needed.

Within-Program Comparisons

So far, we have primarily looked at the use of criterion-referenced tests for comparing outcomes with common objectives for different programs. Outcome evaluations can also be used to upgrade the quality of ongoing programs by *experimentally studying variations in procedures,* or by *identifying the natural variations* that occur between teachers, and capitalizing on them. This latter procedure we will call the *bootstrap* approach.

The Vermont Title I Evaluation 1973-74[5]

The Title I programs of the Elementary and Secondary Education Act provide supplementary educational funds for children from low income families. For the 1973-74 school year, the Vermont State Department of Education helped organize a Title I program based on criterion-referenced tests and prescriptions based on those tests. The area of focus was reading.

Thirty-five of fifty-five school districts in the state participated in the program. A test of reading objectives for grades 2 through 8 (the Prescriptive Reading Inventory)[6] was administered to all Title I students in October. A different test was used for first graders and will not be considered here. The Prescriptive Reading Inventory (PRI) tests 90 different objectives on four levels. There are 34 to 42 objectives tested at a level with many objectives occurring at several levels. Each objective is measured with three or four items. Figure 7.2 shows some objectives in the area of interpretive comprehension. Figure 7.3 shows some test questions for level D, which are answered after the student reads the story *The Emperor's New Clothes.*[7]

At each grade level, the objectives were rated according to whether the instructional emphasis for that objective was heavy, moderate, or light. Those with light emphasis were omitted from the data summaries.

OBJECTIVE	LEVEL			
	Red A	Green B	Blue C	Orange D
65. The student will identify the clues in reading material that lead to a conclusion. (Conclusions: Factor Identification)				X
66. The student will draw inferences in anticipating or predicting future action or events based upon the content of reading material. (Predicting Future Actions)		X	X	X
67. The student will demonstrate recognition of the main idea of a passage or story by selecting the most appropriate title; by choosing the word, phrase, or sentence that tells the main idea; or by identifying the theme, moral (lesson), or best summary statement for a given selection. (Main Idea: Summary, Title, or Theme)	X	X	X	X
68. The student will employ character analysis in identifying or describing the feelings of a character at a particular time or throughout a story. (Character Analysis: Feelings)	X	X		
69. The student will employ character analysis in indicating or describing the reason for, or justification of, a story character's action. (Character Analysis: Motive or Cause)	X	X		

Figure 7.2 Some PRI Objectives for Interpretive Comprehension

DIRECTIONS: Now do Items 64–81. There is only one answer to each item. Look at the story again if you want to.

64. When did the emperor order the weavers to make the clothes?

F after the looms were set up

G during a parade through the town

H before the weavers had come to the court

J after he heard that the cloth was magic

K after he realized that he could not see the cloth

65. Which of these is the best word to describe the emperor?

A wise

B foolish

C blind

D beautiful

E splendid

66. The author makes us believe early in the story that the emperor won't really get a beautiful suit, He does this by saying that

F the emperor spent a lot of money on clothes

G the emperor was fond of new clothes

H the weavers came to the emperor's court

J the emperor lived many years ago

K the weavers were really clever robbers

67. How does the story treat the emperor and his people?

A It shows us they were clever.

B It makes us feel sorry for them.

C It makes fun of them.

D It shows how they were happy.

E It shows how they were sad.

Figure 7.3 Some PRI Test Questions

The tests were scored by machine, and individual reports and classroom summaries were provided, along with prescriptions tying objectives to local textbooks. Workshops were conducted in November on the use of the results. The aim was to individualize instruction using the prescriptions. Except for a project attitude questionnaire given in January, the teachers were on their own the rest of the year. The students were posttested in May.

Because the Title I students were below average in grade-level performance, the test levels were assigned as follows:

Level	Suggested Grade	Actual Grades Tested
A	1.5-2.5	2,3
B	2.0-3.5	4
C	3.0-4.5	5
D	4.0-6.5	6,7,8

Over 1800 students were tested in grades 2 to 8. Table 7.2 gives the results for four of the grade levels.

TABLE 7.2   NUMBER OF MODERATELY OR HEAVILY EMPHASIZED OBJECTIVES MASTERED ON THE PRETEST AND ON THE POSTTEST AND GAIN

	Skills Area	Number of Objectives	Average Objectives Mastered on Pretest	Average Objectives Mastered on Posttest	Gain	Percentage Gain in Mastery
Grade 2	Vocabulary	5	2.5	4.1	1.6	64%
	Comprehension	12	4.7	8.8	4.1	56
	Work attack skills	6	3.0	5.0	2.0	67
	Language skills	10	4.9	8.3	3.4	67
	Total	33	15.1	26.2	11.1	62
Grade 3	Vocabulary	5	3.6	4.5	.9	64%
	Comprehension	12	7.7	10.1	2.4	56
	Work attack skills	6	4.2	5.4	1.2	67
	Language skills	11	7.8	9.9	2.1	66
	Total	34	23.3	29.9	6.6	62
Grade 4	Vocabulary	6	3.5	4.7	1.2	48%
	Comprehension	15	5.3	9.1	3.8	39
	Work attack skills	11	5.3	7.7	2.4	42
	Language skills	8	4.0	5.7	1.7	43
	Total	40	18.1	27.2	9.1	42
Grade 6	Vocabulary	7	2.3	3.6	1.3	28%
	Comprehension	20	1.9	3.4	1.5	8
	Work attack skills	4	1.9	2.5	.6	29
	Language skills	3	.6	1.1	.5	21
	Total	34	6.7	10.6	3.9	14

The Percentage Gain in Mastery Score is based on the objectives not mastered on pretest which were mastered on posttest. Gain can only occur on items failed on pretest. To compute this percentage, the *actual gain* is divided by *possible gain* for each student.

The interpretation of these results poses some problems because there is nothing to make a *comparison* with. There is no basis for making a between-programs comparison, or a within-program comparison. Furthermore, there is no basis for knowing to what degree "the program" was implemented, nor, in fact, the precise nature of the instruction given. What is known is the number of objectives mastered by the students. For example, an average of 11.1 objectives was mastered at the second grade level, 6.6 at the third grade level, 9.1 at the fourth grade level, and 3.9 at the sixth grade level. We also know the Percentage Gain in Mastery was 62, 62, 42, and 14, respectively. Is this good or bad? Did some grades do more poorly than others? We cannot tell. There is no basis for a valid comparison.

An additional problem is that the assignment of test levels according to grade levels was a mistake. The level A test seems to be "too easy" for the third graders, and the level D test "too hard" for the sixth graders. This essentially means the students could not show much progress on the tests because they did not cover what they were taught. The "easy test" covers what already has been taught, and the "hard test" covers something to be taught later after other skills have been mastered. This problem arises because the test ranges on the PRI are too narrow to cover the range of skills found in a typical grade level.

The publisher of PRI suggests that this problem be handled in the future by mixing the levels of tests used at a given grade level. Such mixing would require some kind of screening test (not available) to decide which level to give which student. A better solution was proposed by Glaser in building the IPI continuum of objectives. Skills were ordered within tracks covering nine typical grade levels. A placement test was used as a screening test to roughly locate the student level. Then, pretests were used to give a more detailed fix on what the student could and could not do. With this approach, evaluation of gains focuses on the number of units on the continuum of objectives each student gained. Restrictions arising from the tests being "too easy" or "too hard" are avoided except at the ends of the continuum.

The Bootstrap Approach

This Title I evaluation could have been more meaningful if comparisons to other programs had been made, or if measures had been taken of the ways in which the program was implemented by different teachers. It is this latter possibility that we would like to consider in more detail.

Suppose supervisors observed some of the teachers at each grade level during the first two weeks and began to formulate a checklist of performance differences that might affect student outcomes. For example:

1 Devotes X time to planning for group and individual instruction.
2 Sequences instructional activities effectively.
3 Develops a high rate of student participation.
4 Has procedures for checking and correcting student responses.
5 Uses good reinforcement procedures.
6 Uses instructional time fully. Does not waste time.
7 Keeps good progress records.

The checklist would depend on what supervisors and teachers see as important. Overall judgments of good and poor implementation strategies and ratings on specific variables could be compared with high and low student outcome. If teachers using certain procedures have better outcomes, a basis is provided for helping other teachers through inservice training.

A simple extension of this idea would be to develop *norms on criterion-referenced tests* based on applications of the *same program* around the country. For example, in monitoring test results on our Continuous Progress Tests in Follow Through, we have developed norms for teachers based on within-grade-level comparisons of the performance of the students. The basic measure on the student is rate of gain of the Continuous Progress Tests. If the student has been in school 30 days and gains 45 lesson days on the test, his rate is 1.5 lessons per day. For each subject area and each grade level, we can determine standard scores for a teacher based on the average rate of gain of the students. If the students are gaining more than the average gain made by other teachers at that grade level, the standard score is positive. If the gain is less than average the standard score is negative. The size of the standard score, of course, tells you where the teacher's performance stands in the distribution of teachers. A study of high and low performing teachers would be helpful in isolating important skills to work on in inservice training.

Interpreting the standard scores as *reflections of teacher behaviors* can only be considered if the students being taught are roughly comparable. Because we find large differences between school districts in pupil characteristics, we have restricted our comparisons to those which can be made within districts in identifying teachers needing help. Between-district comparisons can be made, however, if appropriate information on student comparability is provided.

Experimental Studies of Effective Procedures

Within-program comparisons can also be used to experimentally evaluate new procedures for using a current program. Suppose you wished to know whether it was worthwhile to provide inservice training on a regular basis to facilitate implementation of a program. Special training could be provided to a group of five to ten teachers, while a second group was not provided training. Criterion-referenced tests of the program objectives would be given as pretests and posttests. With random assignment of students to teachers or a check of the pretests to be sure students are comparable, it becomes possible to draw conclusions about the contribution of the inservice training program to the outcome. If it looks like training makes a difference, the procedures could be extended to others in the district who are using the same program.

The range of teaching behaviors that can be studied using experimental comparisons is unlimited. It is a good way of finding out whether some new procedures really work in your setting.

summary

Criterion-referenced tests are particularly useful in outcome evaluations where different instructional programs can be compared on the same objectives, or where different procedures for teaching the same programs can be compared. In order to interpret the findings from the comparison of programs, we must (1) demonstrate that the students in the programs are equivalent on important characteristics, (2) insure that the programs were appropriately implemented, (3) evaluate the time devoted to the teaching of the programs, and (4) consider differential outcomes for sub-objectives. When programs have common objectives, but use different directions and response requirements, this difference needs to be considered in constructing tests.

When the objectives of two programs are different, interpretation of any comparisons of the different objectives is most difficult. Attempts can be made to show if one program teaches more than another, but we are likely to end up with value judgments that are hard to defend except where a group consensus can be found.

Criterion-referenced tests are ideally suited for comparing programs on their ability to produce standards of competency. The *Survival Skills Reading Test* was described to illustrate how such tests can be constructed to be maximally useful in diagnosis and remediation of deficiencies, as well as in comparing programs.

We suggested that within-program comparisons could be used to experimentally study procedures and to capitalize on natural variations in teacher performance. The Vermont Title I Evaluation was used to illustrate some potential problems in making within-program evaluations with a criterion-referenced test. The outcome of the study was difficult to interpret because there was no basis for making valid comparisons. It was suggested that if measures had been taken concerning program implementation by different teachers, the measures could have been related to different student outcomes and provided a basis for program improvement. An extension of this idea is the possibility of developing norms on criterion-referenced tests based on the same instructional program as implemented in different settings. These norms would, for any given application of a program, allow teachers to make judgments about whether they were doing a good job or not (relative to the norm), especially where the norms were based on comparable students.

self-test

1a. objectives

b. program

2a. equivalent

1   Ideally, in evaluating instructional outcomes, one of two possible comparisons would be made:

(a) Different instructional programs designed to teach the same _____ would be compared, or

(b) Different procedures for teaching the same _____ would be compared.

2   In comparing programs on common objectives, it is important to consider the following questions:

(a) Are the students in the two groups _____ in important characteristics?

(b) Were both programs _____ in a reasonably adequate way?,

(c) Was the _____ devoted to teaching both programs comparable?, and

(d) Are there program differences in outcome on the _____-_____ ?

3 Another approach to the comparison of programs focuses on tests of the minimum _____ standards. Program can be compared by asking "what _____ of the students meet the standards"?

4 Outcome evaluations can also be used to upgrade the quality of ongoing programs by _____ studying variations in procedures, or by identifying the _____ variations that occur between teachers, and capitalizing on them.

NUMBER RIGHT _____

b. taught

c. time

d. sub-objectives

3 common;
   percentage

4 experimentally;
   natural

exercise 1 programed practice

1 Ideally, in evaluating instructional outcomes, one of two possible comparisons would be made:

(a) Different instructional programs designed to teach the same _____ would be compared, or

(b) Different procedures for teaching the same _____ would be compared.

2 In the live world of educational realities, instructional programs are usually not constructed to teach the same _____ . This situation makes the design of studies to compare different _____ difficult.

3 In comparing programs on common objectives, it is important to consider the following questions:

(a) Are the students in the two groups _____ in important characteristics?

1a. objectives

b. program

2 objectives;
   programs

3a. equivalent

(b) Were both programs _____ in a reasonably adequate way?

(c) Was the _____ devoted to teaching both programs comparable?

(d) Are there program differences in outcome on the _____-_____ ?

4   If two programs have common objectives but use different directions and have different response requirements, tests could be built with program-specific _____ but using common problems.

5   Special problems arise in dealing with _____-_____ sets, when different members of the set are taught by different programs. Comparisons in this case might be concerned with _____ _____ is taught as well as how well it is taught.

6   Interpreting results on not-common objectives requires a careful judgment concerning the _____ of the objectives, as well as an appraisal of the comparability of the students, the adequacy of the _____ , and the _____ devoted to producing the outcome.

7   Another approach to the comparison of programs focuses on tests of the minimum _____ standards. Programs can be compared by asking, "What _____ of the students meet the standards"?

8   Furthermore, if the tests are properly designed, they can also be used to pinpoint the _____ efforts that should be undertaken.

9   One key idea in the *Survival Skills Reading Test* is the focus on _____ objectives, the other key is the item _____ . Items are designed and grouped so that deficient component skills are _____ .

10   By designing clusters of test items to assure that a _____ skill is tested in isolation before it is required for use in a more complex task involving an additional skill, it is possible to pinpoint deficiencies and prescribe _____ procedures.

11   Outcome evaluations can also be used to upgrade the quality of ongoing programs by _____ studying variations in procedures, or by identifying the _____ variations that occur between teachers, and capitalizing on them.

12 The Vermont Title I evaluation program was used to illustrate a criterion-referenced test, and the problems which arise in interpretation of outcomes when appropriate _____ are lacking.

13 The study also showed that the assignment of test levels according to _____ levels was a mistake. The level A test was "too easy" for the third graders, and the level D test was "too hard" for the sixth graders.

14 The "easy test" covers what _____ has been taught, and the "hard test" covers something _____ _____ _____ later, after other skills have been mastered.

15 This Title I evaluation could have been made more meaningful if comparisons to _____ _____ had been made, or if measures had been taken of the ways in which the program was _____ by different teachers.

16 Suppose supervisors observed some of the teachers at each sixth grade level during the first two weeks and began to formulate a checklist of performance differences that might affect _____ _____ .

17 If teachers using certain procedures have better outcomes, a basis is provided for helping _____ _____ through inservice training to produce better outcomes. This was called the _____ approach.

18 A simple extension of this idea would be to develop norms on criterion-referenced tests based on applications of the _____ _____ around the country.

19 These norms would make it possible for any given application of a program to make judgments about whether they were doing a good job or not (relative to the norm), especially where the norms were based on _____ students.

---

12 comparisons

13 grade

14 already;
   to be taught

15 other
   programs;
   implemented

16 student
   outcomes

17 other teachers;
   bootstrap

18 same program

19 comparable

discussion questions

1 Why is it desirable to restrict the comparisons of instructional programs to those based on common objectives?

2 In evaluating the results of program comparisons, what factors have to be considered in addition to the actual outcomes on the tested objectives?

3 What can you do when two programs have the common objectives but use different words and have different response requirements?

4 What can you do when in comparing objectives involving linear-additive sets where the members taught are not all common?

5 Describe an approach to program comparisons based on testing minimum common standards.

6 Why is the *Survival Skills Reading Test* especially useful in targeting remedial efforts?

7 What are two approaches to making within-program comparisons which may help upgrade instruction?

8 What were the deficiencies in the use of criterion-referenced tests in the Vermont Title I evaluation of 1973-74?

9 What does it mean to say that a criterion-referenced test is "too easy" or "too hard"?

10 What is the Bootstrap approach to program evaluation?

11 What are some measures of teacher behavior which might be gathered to relate to student outcomes?

12 Why might it be valuable to have norms on criterion-referenced tests geared to specific instructional programs?

unit 8

Review 1

objectives

This review unit is designed to remind you of some of the material covered earlier in the course. This unit is *not* designed to teach you new material. If any terms or concepts are mentioned that you do not understand, you should go back to the original material and study it carefully. In addition, you should go back through the exercises you did for each unit and make sure that you know the correct answer for each item.

review

Unit 1. Kinds of Tests: Norm Referenced and Criterion-Referenced Tests

Tests are systematic procedures for assessing behavior under specified stimulus conditions. Norm-referenced tests compare people to each other. Criterion-referenced tests compare a person's performance to some standard. Norm-referenced tests are especially useful in selecting relatively high and low members of a group. Criterion-referenced tests are useful in specifying those who meet or fail to meet a standard of performance. A good item on a norm-referenced test is one that some pass and some fail. An item that everybody (or most) passed would be eliminated from a norm-referenced test. On the other hand, on a criterion-referenced test being used to evaluate instruction, such an item might be very valuable.

One of the main uses of criterion-referenced tests in education is to evaluate the process of instruction to show where it has occurred and where it has not. There are two approaches to developing criterion-referenced tests. One bases the tests on a set of instructional objectives, the other ties the tests to a specified instructional program. Objectives-based tests have had considerable popularity in the past 10 years. They required the teacher to

INFORMATIONAL USES OF THE VARIOUS KINDS OF TESTS

Information Provided	Norm Referenced Tests	Criterion Referenced Tests	
		Objectives-Based	Instructional-Program-Based
1. Pre-program to post-program gains	Depends on the fit of the specific test and program	Yes, on the objectives tested	Yes, on program skills
2. Process evaluation	No	Depends on fit of test and the specific instruction used.	Yes
3. Comparison of programs	Yes. To the extent the tests are acceptable as criteria	Depends on fit of test with the programs to be compared.	No
4. Identifying weaknesses for specific children and teachers	No. Most errors can occur for many reasons	Unlikely. No basis for telling why items were failed	Yes, for program skills
5. Implying specific remedies for weaknesses	No	No	Yes, earlier tasks in the program
6. Showing continuity in skill development from grade to grade	Only in the sense of grade-norm progress. The skills tested change from grade to grade and fail to show sequenced mastery	No	Yes, if same program (or program series) is used
7. Identification of extremely high or low performances	Yes. Especially useful here	Possibly useful as a screening device, but not especially sensitive to extreme performances	Possibly useful as a screening device, but not especially sensitive to extreme performances

specify what he is trying to teach, to pretest the students, and to get feedback after instruction through posttesting. Such procedures can assist in improving programs.

The difficulties with objectives-based tests are:

1 It is a lot of work to write objectives and build tests. If every teacher had to do it, the waste of effort would be considerable.

2 It is difficult to evaluate good and bad test items without an instructional program. The test might be failed because of poor teaching, use of different directions and response requirements from those taught the students, use of examples beyond the range of those taught, and so forth.

3 It is not possible to specify how specific or how general an objective should be in the absence of an instructional program.

As Baker noted, to be maximally useful tests must be specifically referenced to defined instructional materials. When this is done, it is possible to monitor the process of instruction throughout the program and provide for corrective action when it is needed. Precise diagnosis of problems and their remediation is possible with such tests. Also, when working with a program that has been previously demonstrated to work, it is possible to analyze the test results to determine if failures are due to poor teaching (most students fail items which have been "taught"), or to student difficulties (one or more students fail many tasks on the test which are not failed by most students).

Unit 2. Understanding Test Scores

Tests are used to measure behavior. Measurement is a comparison procedure. In norm-reference testing, comparisons are made to the performance of other people. In criterion-referenced testing, comparisons are made with some standard of performance. Five statistical concepts were introduced to permit examination in more detail of the nature of norm-referenced and criterion-referenced scores.

A *frequency distribution* graphically depicts how many people received what scores on a test. The vertical axis on the graph shows the "how many" people, the horizontal axis shows the "what scores." Two important statistics for describing the set of scores that make up a frequency distribution are the mean and the standard deviation. The *mean* (M) is an average. All of the scores (Xs) are summed and then divided by the number of scores (N). This tells us where the "middle" of the frequency distribution is.

$$M = \frac{\text{Sum Xs}}{N}$$

The *standard deviation* (SD) is a measure of the degree to which scores in a distribution deviate from the mean. It can be thought of as the average of the deviations from the mean, except that the deviations are squared and then the average is later "unsquared" by taking the square root. The standard deviation tells us how far the scores in a distribution spread out from the mean on the average.

$$SD = \sqrt{\frac{\text{Sum}(X-M)^2}{N}} \quad \begin{matrix} \leftarrow \text{unsquaring} \\ \leftarrow \text{squared deviations from mean} \\ \leftarrow \text{taking the average} \end{matrix}$$

The mean and the standard deviation of a distribution can be used to convert each score in the distribution to *standard scores* (SS). The raw scores are expressed as a deviation from the mean, and then they are divided by the standard deviation.

$$SS = \frac{X - M}{SD}$$

The sign of a standard score tells you immediately whether the score is above or below the mean. Most raw scores will fall between +3 and −3 on a standard score scale. Standard scores provide one kind of "standard frame of reference" for comparing scores of individuals within a distribution, and between distributions involving different measurements.

The most common approach to comparing scores in criterion-referenced testing is to compute the percent right. These scores tell how close one comes to meeting the objective the test was designed to measure.

An example involving spelling and arithmetic was presented to show how widely different conclusions could be drawn from the test scores using standard scores rather than percent right scores. "How much is much?" depends on the comparison standard. Standard scores discard the absolute level of performance in looking at score distributions. Percent right scores retain this information and are generally more informative when one is concerned with teaching mastery or competency.

This unit is only the first step in understanding test scores. In future units, we will be examining both criterion-referenced and norm-referenced scores in more detail with respect to the questions:

> How much is much?
> How reliable are the scores?
> How valid are the scores?

Norm Referenced	*Criterion Referenced*
Given a set of scores, a *mean and standard deviation* can be computed to describe the *frequency distribution* for those scores. The mean and standard deviation can then be used to express raw scores in *standard score* form. Standard scores readily tell where a score falls in a frequency distribution relative to other scores.	Given a set of scores, we can compute a mean and standard deviation, but it is unlikely that the latter would be used if computed. A frequency distribution can be plotted if desired. Standard scores would not be used. Instead, *percent right scores* would be computed to see how many students met a criterion of say 85 or 90 percent right.

Unit 3. Constructing Instructional-Program-Based Tests

It makes no sense to try to build a test based on an instructional-program if in fact no consistent program is followed. So be sure first that the program can be used with consistency before spending time building tests to use with it.

It is also important in building tests to be able to tell the difference between sets of skills that define a general case and those that do not. A general case has been taught when after teaching some members of a defined set, all members can be performed correctly. Examples or applications of concepts, operations, or problem-solving rules form general-case sets. Linear-additive sets involve skill sets where each new member has to be taught. This can occur because a rote teaching method is used or because of the inherent structure of the knowledge and skill set. Usually language concepts, mathematical operations, and problem-solving strategies each form linear-additive sets. Learning about some member of the set does not teach how to do the others.

When a class of skills to be tested involves a general-case set, the class can be described by the characteristics of the set. When a linear-additive set is involved, the specific members of the set must be identified.

The steps to follow in constructing progress tests for an instructional program are these: First, identify the main terminal skills. A scope and sequence chart or a teacher's guide is a good place to start. Second, identify the specific directions and response requirements necessary to show mastery of the objectives. Third, find where each skill is taught (if it is taught). This will lead to an analysis of subskills which may be needed and provide a bases for a flowchart showing where each skill is introduced and how long it is taught. Fourth, divide the skills into tracks. The goal is to show what is being taught when, and how tasks or skills build on each other. A track may be defined by a set of skills which are taught in a common format, or as sequence of skills using different formats which build to a terminal objective. Fifth, divide the track into testing units. How many testing units are needed depends on the method of instruction. If instruction is individualized, a test for each two weeks of progress may be needed. If instruction is in large groups and the students stay together, a test every six weeks might be adequate. The sixth step is to decide which skills to test at each testing cycle. Since not everything can be tested, key building blocks and their consolidation into more complex skills are given priority. Testing also focuses on members of sets which are likely to be confused with recently taught members. The seventh and last step involves construction of test items. Five guidelines were suggested:

1 Test what has been taught.
2 Give preference to most recently taught items and to highly similar items taught earlier.
3 Do not test a skill unit until it has been taught for three days.
4 Do not test trivial skills, that is, skills which are never used in the program again.
5 Avoid ambiguous instructions.

When selecting instructional programs, you can apply the same analysis procedures used in building tests for an instructional program.

Unit 4. Evaluating Instructional-Program-Based Tests

In evaluating instruction-based tests it is first necessary to decide how many different teaching outcomes you wish to test. This depends on the stage of instruction and whether you are dealing with outcomes involving general-cases or linear-additive sets. Usually, a general-case set provides the basis for one test. Exceptions to this may occur before the set is fully taught. In a linear-additive set, each member should be treated as a separate test unless all members have had a good chance to be taught.

In looking at item reliability we are concerned with the degree to which there is performance consistency on items assumed to measure the same thing. In dealing with a general-case set, a percent-agreement index can be computed for any pair of items by counting the number of students for whom there is an outcome agreement and dividing by the number of students. Then the average agreement for all possible pairs of items on the test can be computed. Usually, inspection of the table of plusses and minuses will reveal the problem items without this computation. Low agreement may occur where items are written ambiguously and need revision. It can also occur between subgroups of items which are consistent within themselves. In this latter case, it is likely that you are testing two different things.

With linear-additive sets, each member constitutes a different teaching objective. An effective measure of reliability would use at least two measures of each member of the set. A percent agreement index can then be computed for each member of the set and averaged over members. It may be economical to use double item testing only in a tryout form of the test. If good reliability is found, then a return to testing with one item for each member of the set is possible. After all members of a linear-additive set have been taught, it is reasonable to consider testing with only a sample of the set. However, where poor performances are found, a full testing of the set should be undertaken to guide remediation.

In looking at test validity we are concerned with whether the test is a measure of the specific teaching objective. This can be determined *logically*, by analyzing the content validity of the items, and *empirically* by examining the sensitivity to instruction of the items. Content validity is concerned with if the test item falls in the set of tasks defined by a teaching objective. Sensitivity to instruction is demonstrated by showing that an item is not passed prior to instruction and is passed after instruction. Where items are failed before and after instruction, one has to determine the adequacy of the instruction before a judgment about the test items can be made. Where items are failed before and passed after instruction, it is necessary to evaluate whether the change could have occurred because of instruction taking place elsewhere. A validity index was proposed based on the gain in percentage passing from pretesting to posttesting.

The evaluation of a testing procedure should also consider cost (in terms of money and teaching time) and the usefulness of the test information for determining remedial procedures. A final caution: it is possible to get good reliability and validity data on instruction-based tests even when the underlying program is defective. Many programs teach misrules, trivia, or limited cases where a more general case could be taught. A careful examination of what is being taught should come first.

Unit 5. Approaches to Monitoring Student Progress

An effective monitoring system first requires a set of procedures for placing students in a program, or at least insuring that they have the preskills assumed by the program. Second, a method for identifying progress steps through a curriculum sequence is needed. Third, a procedure for checking the quality of student work on each progress unit is required. This may consist of formal mastery tests, less formal verbal checkouts, or workbook exercises. The fourth requirement of a monitoring system is a set of procedures for guiding students through an instructional sequence and keeping track of where they are. Fifth, it helps to motivate progress if goals are established for each student or groups of students and a method devised to visually show progress toward the goal. Finally, a set of procedures for correcting errors or recycling the student through objectives not mastered is required.

A variety of examples of monitoring systems were discussed to show the many possible approaches to building a monitoring system. You will have a chance to summarize these points for yourself in exercise 2 which follows.

A study by Alan Hofmeister shows some of the potential benefits for student progress of using an appropriate monitoring system.

Unit 6. The Oregon Follow Through Monitoring System

We have devoted this unit to a more detailed look at the monitoring system used in the University of Oregon Sponsored Follow Through Projects. The details of the monitoring system show how it is possible to have the information to make *logical decisions* to improve instruction as it is proceeding. With a carefully programed sequence of instruction, it is possible to build a testing, reporting, and supervision system to support that instruction. The important informations in the system are:

1 Placement procedures to get the students started in the program where they need to be.
2 A Report of Lessons Taught which can be related to days available for teaching and goals for the year.
3 Continuous Progress Tests which check the *quality* of student progress through the program. When quality of progress is considered along with the rate of progress from 2 above a strong basis for making instructional decisions is provided.
4 Finally, the teacher supervisor working within this monitoring system is in an excellent position to pinpoint problems in instructional procedures and to aid the teacher in correcting them.

Undoubtedly, to some, a management system such as this must seem to be confining. However, the majority of teachers working within the system (after the initial shock!) come to consider it the only way to go, because they know what they are doing and they like the progress with the students.

Unit 7. Outcome Evaluation with Criterion-Referenced Tests

Criterion-referenced tests are particularly useful in outcome evaluations where different instructional programs can be compared on the same objectives, or where different procedures for teaching the same programs can be compared. In order to interpret the findings from the comparison of programs it is important to: (1) demonstrate that the students in the programs are equivalent on important characteristics, (2) insure that the programs were appropriately implemented, (3) evaluate the time devoted to the teaching of the programs, and (4) consider differential outcomes for sub-objectives. When programs have common objectives, but use different directions and response requirements, this difference needs to be considered in constructing tests.

When the objectives of two programs are different, interpretation of any comparisons of the different objectives is most difficult. Attempts can be made to show if one program teaches more than another, but you are likely to end up with value judgments that are hard to defend except where a group consensus can be found.

Criterion-referenced tests are ideally suited for comparing programs on their ability to produce standards of competency. The Survival Skills Reading Test was described to illustrate how such tests can be constructed to be maximally useful in diagnosis and remediation of deficiencies, as well as, in comparing programs.

It was suggested that within program comparisons could be used to experimentally study possibly important procedures and to capitalize on natural variations in teacher performance. The Vermont Title I Evaluation was used to illustrate some potential problems in making within program evaluations with a criterion-referenced test. The outcome of the study was difficult to interpret because there was no basis for making valid comparisons. It was suggested that if measures had been taken concerning program implementation by different teachers, the measures could have been related to different student outcomes and provided a basis for program improvement. An extension of this idea is the possibility of developing norms on criterion-referenced tests based on the same instructional program as implemented in different settings. These norms would make it possible for any given application of a program to make judgments about whether they were doing a good job or not (relative to the norm), especially where the norms were based on comparable students.

review exercises

Unit 1

1 What is a test?
2 How do the comparison standards differ for criterion-referenced and norm-referenced tests?
3 Give examples of criterion-referenced and norm-referenced tests.
4 Describe two approaches to developing criterion-referenced tests to evaluate instruction.
5 What are the four steps for teachers to follow in planning for instruction as recommended by Popham?
6 Why is Popham's strategy of potential valuable to the teacher?
7 Give three common problems with objectives-based test approach.

8 What are some possible solutions to these problems?

9 What advantages do instructional-program-based tests have over objectives-based tests?

10 What are the essential features of IPI?

11 What are the essential features of Distar?

12 Explain how the results of testing a group in a Distar program can be used to identify teacher problems and student problems.

13 When are norm-referenced tests especially useful?

14 When are objectives-based tests especially useful?

15 When are instructional-program-based tests especially useful?

Unit 2

1 What does it mean *to measure* something?

2 How are the mean and standard deviation related to a frequency distribution of test scores?

3 How many standard deviations would include most scores in most frequency distributions?

4 Give the formula for computing a mean of a set of scores.

5 Give the formula for the standard deviation of a set of scores.

6 Explain the five steps you would follow to compute a standard deviation from the formula in 5 above.

7 Draw a smoothed frequency distribution. Then draw on the same scale a distribution with a standard deviation that is half as large.

8 Give the formula for computing a standard score.

9 Suppose you have a raw score frequency distribution and you wish to rescale the distribution to show where the various standard scores fall. You know the mean and standard deviation. What would you do?

10 What does it tell you to know that a person's standard score is +3, 0, or −2?

11 How are standard scores useful?

12 Why are percent-right scores often preferred in evaluating instruction?

13 What determines the answer to a "How much?" question?

Unit 3

1 Why is it important for the teacher to know how to build tests?

2 Why is it important that the teacher follow a fairly structured set of procedures in teaching a specified set of skills and information?

3 In defining sets of skills for testing, what is the difference between a general-case set and a linear-additive set?

4 Give examples of general-case and linear-additive sets.

5 In analyzing an instructional program, how do you identify the main terminal skills?

6   Why is it important to identify the specific directions and response requirements used in an instructional program?

7   What is the purpose of locating where each skill and subskill is taught in a program?

8   How are skill tracks defined?

9   What determines the number of testing units you will need?

10   How do you define which skills to test at each testing unit or cycle?

11   Give five rules for constructing test items.

12   What exactly does the rule "Test what has been taught" cover?

13   Summarize the main steps to follow in constructing tests for an instructional program.

14   Explain why the procedures used in analyzing a program for test building are also useful in analyzing a program for possible adoption?

15   What additional questions should be asked in evaluating possible programs besides the internal evidence that it can do the job?

Unit 4

1   Give four criteria for evaluating an instructional-program-based test.

2   How do you decide how many tests you have?

3   Give examples that show the idea of a single teaching outcome.

4   What is meant by the *reliability* of a test?

5   Describe and illustrate a reliability index that can be used with criterion-referenced tests?

6   What do you do when there are many items on the same test?

7   Why is it usually not necessary to compute all of the agreement indexes to find where there is trouble with a test focused on instruction?

8   Give two reasons why the agreement indexes for some items might be low.

9   How do you determine the reliability of a linear-additive set?

10   What is meant by the *validity* of a test?

11   What criteria are used to determine the validity of instructional-program-based tests?

12   What additional control information is necessary in the evaluation of the validity of instruction-referenced tests?

13   Define and illustrate a validity index for showing sensitivity to instruction.

14   Suggest a procedure for showing that events correlated with time other than the specified instruction are not responsible for the gain in percentage of students passing an item.

15   What are some problems in demonstrating that a program will work under specified conditions and assessing the degree to which these conditions are met?

16   What is required for a test to be useful for remediation?

17   Why is it possible to have a valid test for a bad program?

Unit 5

1. Why should teachers be concerned with having testing systems to monitor the process of instruction?
2. What are six general requirements for a monitoring system?
3. Specify an instructional objective and a task which is an example of that objective. Next analyze the task for assumed preskills.
4. What are some placement procedures to use when formal tests are not available?
5. Suggest five ways of defining progress units.
6. Suggest some procedures for checkouts on units that can be individualized and which save teacher time.
7. Describe a procedure that can serve as a guide through a sequence of progress units and related record systems.
8. Why should the teacher help the students to establish individual or group goals?
9. Discuss some possible ways in which corrective action can be taken when failure occurs on a checkout.
10. Describe how Learning Activity Packages provide for the components of an effective monitoring system.
11. Describe how Precision Teaching provides for the components of an effective monitoring system.
12. Describe how the Behavior Analysis Follow Through Model provides for the components of an effective monitoring system.
13. Describe how the Pittsburgh LRDC Follow Through Model (IPI) provides for the components of an effective monitoring system.
14. What are the potential problems of a high reliance on rate measures in precision teaching?
15. How can the problem with rate measures in precision teaching be overcome?
16. What did Alan Hofmeister do and find in his study of the effects of a monitoring system on student learning?

Unit 6

1. Describe the main features of the Direct-Instruction Follow Through Model.
2. What placement procedures are used with the program?
3. What is the value of the Report of Lessons Taught?
4. Describe the testing procedure used for the Arithmetic I Continuous Progress Test.
5. How are scores on the Continuous Progress Tests used?
6. How are teacher supervisors used in the program?

Unit 7

1 Why is it desirable to restrict the comparisons of instructional programs to comparisons based on common objectives?

2 In evaluating the results of program comparisons, what factors have to be considered in addition to the actual outcomes on the tested objectives?

3 What can you do when two programs have the common objectives but use different words and have different response requirements?

4 What can you do when in comparing objectives involving linear-additive sets where the members taught are not all common?

5 Describe an approach to program comparisons based on testing minimum common standards.

6 Why is the Survival Skills Reading Test especially useful in targeting remedial efforts?

7 What are two approaches to making within-program comparisons which may help upgrade instruction?

8 What were the deficiencies in the use of criterion-referenced tests in the Vermont Title I evaluation of 1973-74?

9 What does it mean to say that a criterion-referenced test is "too easy" or "too hard"?

10 What is the Bootstrap Approach to program evaluation?

11 What are some measures of teacher behavior which might be gathered to relate to student outcomes?

12 Why might it be valuable to have norms on criterion-referenced tests geared to specific instructional programs?

unit 9

Norm-Referenced Achievement Tests

objectives

When you complete this unit you should be able to—

1 Describe how norm-referenced tests are built.
2 Specify the similarities and differences in the construction of norm-referenced and criterion-referenced tests.
3 Describe three types of achievement tests.
4 In general terms, state what is measured by achievement test batteries and give examples of the kinds of test items used to measure different skill areas.
5 Describe some uses for the *Mental Measurement Yearbook*.
6 Evaluate the pros and cons for the use of norm-referenced tests in diagnostic-remedial work, in placement, in process evaluation, in a "norm-referenced evaluation" of program outcomes, in program comparisons, in teacher evaluation, in selection, and in guidance.
7 Discuss the value issues involved in using tests for selection of high and low students.

lesson

Hundreds of millions of standardized achievement tests are sold each year for use in the evaluation of student learning and educational programs. Much of this evaluation is done in an attempt to satisfy requirements for the evaluation of federally financed programs. Much of it is carried out to satisfy local concerns about student progress. In this unit we examine some of the procedures used to build such tests, the tests themselves, and their uses.

152

Constructing Norm-Referenced Achievement Tests

Steps followed in building a norm-referenced achievement test are in some ways quite similar to those followed in developing a criterion-referenced test. First there is a concern with the instructional objectives in a particular curriculum area. The test publishers usually convene a group of curriculum specialists in a particular subject matter and use their skills to analyze textbooks and programs most commonly used throughout the country. A list of instructional objectives is developed. Objectives provide the skeleton framework for the development of test items. Classroom teachers and curriculum specialists then write items to flesh out the framework provided by the statement of objectives. Those items are reviewed and edited for logical consistency, difficulty level, and ambiguity. Next, instructions are prepared and the items are given a tryout on an appropriate group. The data are then subjected to an item analysis (discussed further in unit 12) to weed out poor items and to provide a basis for further editing. Finally, the test is given to a representative sample of students (called a norm population) to provide a basis for constructing test norms.

The key differences in procedures used to construct norm-referenced achievement tests and criterion-referenced tests are these:

1 Objectives for norm-referenced tests *cover more material* which is usually taught over longer time units. Objectives for criterion-referenced tests are usually geared to the goals of shorter units of instruction.
2 Objectives for norm-referenced tests attempt to reflect what is *common to most instructional programs* in a content area. Objectives for criterion-referenced tests are either the basis of an instructional program in themselves (as in Popham's use), or directly derived from an instructional program (as in Distar).
3 Methods of item analysis differ greatly. For example, in selecting items for norm-referenced tests, items are eliminated that most students pass or fail. In selecting items for criterion-referenced tests, one would seek items that are failed by many prior to instruction, but passed by many after instruction. The effects of methods of item analysis on test structure and norms are discussed further in unit 12.
4 Scores for norm-referenced achievement tests are interpreted in relation to the frequency distribution of scores obtained by the norm group. Scores for a criterion-referenced test are usually interpreted directly in terms of the degree (percentage) of mastery of an objective.

Types of Norm-Referenced Achievement Tests

There are basically three types of norm-referenced achievement tests: diagnostic tests, which attempt to isolate particular weaknesses, single-subject tests, and achievement batteries.

Diagnostic Tests

Diagnostic tests using norm-referenced test construction procedures can be found mainly in the areas of reading and arithmetic. In the area of reading, diagnostic tests are presumed to be useful in analyzing the types of errors students make (omission, reversals, etc.) and providing a basis for remedial programs. Three of the more popular tests are the Gray Oral Reading Test (1963), the Durrell Listening-Reading Series (1969-70), and the Gilmore Oral Reading Test (1968). The Gilmore will be used to illustrate a test format.

The Gilmore Oral Reading Test consists of ten paragraphs carefully graded for increasing difficulty and length. Each paragraph is appropriate for a grade level. The student is usually started two years below grade level. If more than two errors are made, easier paragraphs are read until a "basal level" is found. Then, reading of more difficult paragraphs progresses until ten errors are made. Three scores are provided. An Accuracy score is based on the number of errors made in each paragraph. A Comprehension score is based on answers to five factual questions asked after reading each paragraph. A Rate score is based on time to read each paragraph. The Accuracy score is the most reliable and probably the most valuable. A basis for analyzing types of errors is provided, but is of dubious value.

Following two examples are from form A.[1]

The girl is in the yard.
The girl has a big ball.
The boy is back of the girl.
He is playing with his dog.
The cat looks at the girl.
He wants to play ball, too.
The girl does not see the cat.
She is looking at the ball.

TIME ———— Seconds

——— 1. Where is the girl?
——— 2. What does the girl have?
——— 3. What is the boy doing?
——— 4. What does the cat want?
——— 5. What is the girl looking at?

NUMBER RIGHT ————

ERROR RECORD	Number
Substitutions	
Mispronunciations	
Words pronounced by examiner	
Disregard of punctuation	
Insertions	
Hesitations	
Repetitions	
Omissions	
Total Errors	

Nearly every family living in the city suburbs takes a vacation sometime during the summer. When the weather becomes warm, usually during July, Bob and Jane accompany their parents to the seaside. In order to reach their destination on the shore, they are obliged to travel over a mountain range. If they begin their journey before sunrise the first day, they can see many impressive scenes in the mountains. The exciting but lengthy trip requires two full days. While at the beach Bob and Jane spend many blissful hours bathing in the surf and relaxing on the sunny sand. Summer vacations help Bob and Jane keep healthy.

TIME _____ Seconds

____ 1. What does almost every city family do in summer?
____ 2. What month do Bob and Jane usually go to the seashore with their parents?
____ 3. What must they do to reach the shore?
____ 4. How long is their trip?
____ 5. How do summer vacations help Bob and Jane?

NUMBER RIGHT _____

ERROR RECORD	Number
Substitutions	
Mispronunciations	
Words pronounced by examiner	
Disregard of punctuation	
Insertions	
Hesitations	
Repetitions	
Omissions	
Total Errors	

A measure of oral reading rate and accuracy can be a useful addition to a battery of tests designed to evaluate a beginning reading program or a corrective reading program.

Diagnostic arithmetic tests can be especially effective in locating deficiencies because one is dealing with a finite set of basic facts, logical operations, and symbols. A good example is the Diagnostic Tests and Self-Helps in Arithmetic (California Test Bureau, 1955). This test system provides four screening tests which help to pinpoint problem areas. Then, diagnostic tests can be selected from a group of 23 to detail deficient skills. Remedial exercises are provided in the form of Self-Helps. By current standards, the better older diagnostic arithmetic tests are actually criterion-referenced tests. Many of them do not even pretend to provide norms. The newer diagnostic-prescriptive tests in arithmetic are usually clearly identified as criterion-referenced tests (for example, the *Diagnostic Mathematics Inventory*[2]). What is still needed in the evaluation of these diagnostic tests is evidence on the validity of the diagnoses and prescriptions in terms of improvement in student skills.

Single-Subject Tests

Single-subject tests can be found for all levels of curriculum. Such tests are particularly common for elective areas of study in high school and college in sciences and foreign languages. At the beginning elementary level, reading readiness tests have been popular for use in placing young children. The *Seventh Mental Measurement Yearbook*[3] by Oscar Buros provides a detailed listing and also critical reviews on most single-subject tests.

Achievement Batteries

The four most commonly used achievement batteries each have three letter abbreviations: the SAT, MAT, CAT, and SRA. The Stanford Achievement Test (SAT) is the granddaddy of them all. The first edition came in 1923. The Metropolitan Achievement Test (MAT) first appeared in 1931. The California Achievement Test (CAT) followed closely in 1934, and the Science Research Associates (SRA) Achievement Series is a latecomer, first published in 1954. Each of these tests was revised and renormed between 1968 and 1971.

Table 9.1 gives the titles of the major tests and subtests. In most cases, subtests under Reading, Mathematics, and Language are also combined into total scores for those areas. In some cases, Spelling is kept separate when Language tests are added together. Science and Social Studies are kept as separate tests. A total score based on all subtests is also obtained from each test.

TABLE 9.1 Structure of Four Common Achievement Batteries

Test: Stanford Achievement Test (SAT)

Test Levels	Grades Covered	Major Tests and Subtests			
		Reading	Mathematics	Language	Other
Primary 1	1.5– 2.4	Word Reading, Paragraph Meaning, Vocabulary, Word Study Skills	Arithmetic	Spelling	
Primary 2	2.5– 3.9	Word Meaning, Paragraph Meaning, Word Study Skills	Computation, Concepts	Spelling, Language	Science and Social Studies
Intermediate 1	4.0– 5.4	Word Meaning, Paragraph Meaning, Word Study Skills	Computation, Concepts, Applications	Spelling, Language	Social Studies, Science
Intermediate 2	5.5– 6.9	Word Meaning, Paragraph Meaning	Computation, Concepts, Applications	Spelling, Language	Social Studies, Science
Advanced	7.0– 9.9	Paragraph Meaning	Computation, Concepts, Applications	Spelling, Language	Social Studies, Science
High School Basic Battery	9.0–12.0	Reading	Numerical Competence, Mathematics	English, Spelling	Social Studies, Science

Test: Metropolitan Achievement Test (MAT)

Test Levels	Grades Covered	Major Tests and Subtests			
		Reading	Mathematics	Language	Other
Primer	K– 1.4	Listening for Sounds, Reading	Numbers		
Primary 1	1.5– 2.4	Word Knowledge, Reading (comprehension), Word Analysis	Mathematics		
Primary 2	2.5– 3.4	Word Knowledge, Reading, Word Analysis	Computation, Concepts, Problem Solving	Spelling	
Elementary	3.5– 4.9	Word Knowledge, Reading	Computation, Concepts, Problem Solving	Spelling, Language	
Intermediate	5.0– 6.9	Word Knowledge, Reading	Computation, Concepts, Problem Solving	Language, Spelling	Science, Social Studies
Advanced	7.0– 9.5	Word Knowledge, Reading	Computation, Concepts, Problem Solving	Language, Spelling	Science, Social Studies
High School	9.0–13.0	*Language Arts:* Reading, Spelling, Language, Study Skills	*Mathematics:* Computation and Concepts Analysis and Problem Solving	*Social Studies:* Study Skills, Vocabulary, Information	*Science:* Concepts and Understanding Information

Test: California Achievement Test (CAT)

Test Levels	Grades Covered	Major Tests and Subtests			
		Reading	Mathematics	Language	Other
1	1.5– 2.0	Vocabulary Comprehension	Computation, Concepts and Problems	Auding, Mechanics, Usage and Structure, Spelling	
2	2.0– 4.0	Vocabulary Comprehension	Computation, Concepts and Problems	Mechanics, Usage and Structure, Spelling	
3	4.0– 6.0	Vocabulary Comprehension	Computation, Concepts and Problems	Mechanics, Usage and Structure, Spelling	

CAT continued

		Vocabulary	Computation,	Mechanics,
4	6.0– 9.0	Vocabulary Comprehension	Computation, Concepts and Problems	Mechanics, Usage and Structure, Spelling
5	9.0–12.0	Vocabulary Comprehension	Computation, Concepts and Problems	Mechanics, Usage and Structure Spelling

Test: Science Research Associates (SRA) Achievement Series

Test Levels	Grades Covered	Major Tests and Subtests			
		Reading	Mathematics	Language	Other
1	1.0–2.0	Verbal Pictorial Associations, Language Percep- tion, Comprehension, Vocabulary	Concepts, Reasoning, Computation		
2	2.0–3.0*	Comprehension, Vocabulary	Concepts, Reasoning, Computation	Capitalization and Punctuation, Grammatical Usage, Spelling	
3	3.0–4.0*	Comprehension, Vocabulary	Concepts, Reasoning, Computation	Capitalization and Punctuation, Grammatical Usage, Spelling	
4	4.0–9.0	Comprehension, Vocabulary	Concepts, Reasoning, Computation	Capitalization and Punctuation, Grammatical Usage, Spelling	Social Studies, Science

*Levels 2 and 3 come as one test in the hand-scored edition.

Following are sample items from these four tests. The CAT[4] was used to give examples for the end of grade 1, the MAT[5] for grade 2, the SAT[6] for grade 5 and the SRA[7] for grades 7 and 8. These examples illustrate the test formats and some of the content coverage of the tests. Note in particular the complexity of some directions and response requirements.

For first to third grades, the content of these four tests is quite similar, although formats and specific vocabulary requirements differ. After fourth grade, there is more variability in the topics tested and their time emphasis. Some tests cover science and social studies, others do not. Some spend up to 30% of test time on comprehension, others only 15%. The tests differ very little in technical qualities such as reliability and adequacy of the norm group used to standardize the tests.

CAT—Level 1, Grades 1.5-2.0 (Form A)

Reading   *Vocabulary*

Page 1, item 4. Teacher says: "The chicken ate the corn." The student is to fill in the space by the picture that shows something the sentence is about.

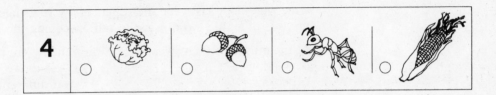

Page 5, item 6. Fill in the space under the word that tells what the picture is.

6		gate	goat	got	great
		○	○	○	○

Mathematics   *Concepts*

Page 3, item 17. Teacher reads item as the student reads it and answers.
c. Which of these boys is sixth in line?

Computation

Page 5, item 16. Fill in the space next to the answer you choose.

9	0 ○	2 ○
−8	1 ○	3 ○

Page 6, item 4.

7 − 3 = ☐	4 ○	6 ○
	5 ○	9 ○

Reading Stories   Page 8, story 1. Teacher says (after a demonstration): "Fill in the space in front of the correct answers to the questions that go with each story."

1

Tom's class visited the art museum. They saw many beautiful paintings. Some were done last year and others many years ago. Tom's favorite picture was of a little girl dressed in red, sweeping the floor.

14 At the museum, there were—
   o paintings
   o books
   o dogs

15 Tom went to the museum with—
   o his father
   o his class
   o his aunt

16 When were the paintings done?
   o yesterday
   o at different times
   o after school

17 Tom's favorite painting might be called—
   o Wild Horses
   o Girl with a Broom
   o Blue Boy

Mathematics   *Computation*
Page 12. Teacher says (after a demonstration): "Do all the examples on this page and the next."

Item 11.	
55	o 27
−32	o 23
	o 87
	o NG (not given)
	o DK (don't know)
Item 18.	
40 − ___ = 37	o 76
	o 3
	o 13
	o NG
	o DK

Concepts   Page 14, item 3. Teacher says: "Now look at the pen. Fill in the space beside the sentence that best describes the length of this pen."

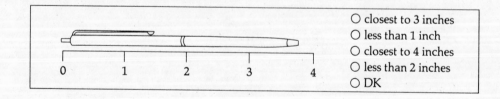

   O closest to 3 inches
   O less than 1 inch
   O closest to 4 inches
   O less than 2 inches
   O DK

Reading *Paragraph Meaning*

Directions: page 5, items 29 to 33. Read each paragraph below. Decide which of the numbered words or phrases below the paragraph is best for each blank. Look at the answer spaces at the right. Fill in the space which has the same number as the word(s) you have chosen.

Belgium is a small European country between France and the Netherlands. Although the country is small in size, a great many people live in Belgium. They grow grain and vegetables, raise farm animals, and manufacture many products. The most famous of the latter are glass and lace.

Belgium is a 29 country.

29	1 middle-sized	3 large		1 2 3 4
	2 little	4 very large	29	o o o o

The word "latter" in the last sentence refers to 30.

30 5 vegetables
    6 grain
    7 farm animals   5 6 7 8
    8 manufactured products   30 o o o o

This passage is most probably from a book on 31.

31 1 geography
    2 agriculture
    3 languages   1 2 3 4
    4 America   31 o o o o

Arithmetic *Concepts*

Page 19, item 2. What does XXIX mean?

			e f g h
e. 31	g. 24		
f. 29	h. 39	2.	o o o o

Page 19, item 7. What is one fourth of 12?

			a b c d
a. 3	c. 8		
b. 4	d. 16	7.	o o o o

Applications

Page 21, item 6. How many boys came out for practice on the second day? Thirteen came out the first day and twice as many came out the second day.

f. 26   g. 15   h. 25   i. 13   j. NG   f g h i j
                                                  6. o o o o o

Page 21, item 11. Diane bought 3 pounds of fruit for $1.20. What was the cost per pound?

                                                  a b c d e
a. 40¢   b. $1.20   c. $2.40   d. $4.80   e. NG   11. o o o o o

This is a multilevel test. The Blue battery is used for grades 4.5 to 6.4, the Green battery is used for grades 6.5 to 8.4, and the Red battery is used with grades 8.5 through grade 9. Our examples are drawn from the Green and Red levels. The student must mark a separate IBM answer sheet.

Language   *Grammatical Usage*

A Family Vacation in Mexico

All the members of the Miller family had been planning a trip for some time. Eva and Charles, the twins, were even more impatient than their parents to be on $\begin{smallmatrix}A.\ there\\B.\ their\end{smallmatrix}$ way to Mexico. Charles, the $\begin{smallmatrix}A.\ taller\\B.\ tallest\end{smallmatrix}$ twin, didn't

$\quad\quad\quad\quad\quad\quad$ 48 $\quad\quad\quad\quad\quad\quad\quad\quad\quad$ 49

want to pack his bags hastily, so he came home from camp a week early.

He knew that his prompt arrival would cause $\begin{smallmatrix}A.\ less\\B.\ fewer\end{smallmatrix}$ worries for his parents.

$\quad\quad\quad\quad\quad\quad\quad\quad\quad\quad\quad\quad\quad\quad\quad\quad\quad\quad\quad$ 50

When he walked into the house, Eva was packing clothes into a suitcase that was $\begin{smallmatrix}A.\ lying\\B.\ laying\end{smallmatrix}$ on her bed.

$\quad\quad\quad$ 51

The Millers had agreed $\begin{smallmatrix}A.\ between\\B.\ among\end{smallmatrix}$ themselves that they would fly to Mexico City by jet. Travel in a jet plane would be the quickest way to go. Since

$\quad\quad\quad\quad\quad\quad\quad\quad\quad$ 52

the twins had never $\begin{smallmatrix}A.\ flew\\B.\ flown\end{smallmatrix}$ in a jet before, they could scarcely wait to

$\quad\quad\quad\quad\quad\quad\quad\quad\quad$ 53

get started.

Social Studies

Page 92, Item 51   The reason Columbus called the natives he saw in America "Indians" was that
A. he thought he had sailed to the shores of India
B. he realized he was in the West Indies and not in North America
C. this was the name the natives gave to themselves when he talked to them
D. the natives were fierce and warlike as many Indians were

Page 92, Item 53   Which of the following does NOT extend from the United States into Canada?
A. Rocky Mountains
B. Great Plains
C. Great Basin
D. St. Lawrence River Valley

Science

Page 83, Item 46   The volume of the sun is about
A. the same as that of the earth
B. ten times that of the earth
C. a thousand times that of the earth
D. a million times that of the earth

Page 83, Item 48   Most limestone is made of
A. the ashes from volcanoes of earlier times
B. the shells of dead sea animals
C. rocks that have been heated deep in the earth
D. decayed plants covered by layers of earth

Page 85, Item 81   The electrical circuit below, composed of a battery and two light bulbs is called a

Circuit

A. phase circuit
B. parallel circuit
C. series circuit
D. short circuit

Page 86, Item 85   If a man wearing a space suit should step out of the door of a space platform in true orbit round the earth, he is most likely to
A. fall rapidly toward the earth as soon as he steps out of the door
B. fly off into space very quickly
C. continue moving slowly away from the platform in the direction he steps
D. quickly fall behind the speeding platform

Other Normative Tests

The *Seventh Mental Measurement Yearbook*[8] by Oscar Buros provides detailed reviews of most tests which teachers might be interested in. This reference book may be found in most college libraries and should be consulted when you need more information on some test.

In considering general achievement batteries, besides the four tests already described, consideration should be given to the following:

Cooperative Primary Tests (1965) (grades 1 to 3).[9]
Comprehensive Tests of Basic Skills (1968) (grades 2 to 12).[10]
Iowa Test of Basic Skills (1971) (grades 1 to 8).[11]
Wide Range Achievement Test (1965) (ages 5 to 11, and 12 and over).[12]

In considering single-subject reading tests, the Gates-MacGinitie Reading Tests (1965, 1969) (grades 1 to 12) should be given consideration.[13]

The Wide Range Achievement Test (WRAT) is unique in its range of coverage. It provides scores in oral word reading, arithmetic, and spelling, and is suitable for use from preschool levels through high school. The test is built in two levels, but comes in only one, four-page form. We have found the reading test especially valuable for evaluation of progress of disadvantaged children over long periods of time. The fact that oral testing is required makes it possible to test the children at the beginning kindergarten level and follow them for many years. While the test is criticized because it does not measure reading comprehension, does not have an alternate form, and was normed on a narrow sample, we have found the reading test to have good reliability and to show systematic relations to reading instruction. The test is also useful as a screening test for educational placement of children on whom there is no other information.

Uses of Norm-Referenced Achievement Tests

In the first unit of this text, we suggested that norm-referenced achievement tests were most likely to be useful in showing pre-post gains, in comparing different programs, in showing continuity of progress against a grade or age norm, and in the selection of extremely high or low performers. Because of our increased knowledge of these tests, the question of uses can be re-examined.

Diagnosis of Weaknesses

In table 1.2 we suggested that norm-referenced tests were of little value in pinpointing specific weaknesses and suggesting remedial procedures. In the case of the achievement batteries, this conclusion still holds. The general batteries would be useful only as a screening device to find the kids who are in trouble. Other procedures would have to be used to pinpoint the weaknesses.

In the case of the reading diagnostic tests, our earlier conclusion still holds. The diagnostic use of reading tests is very questionable. Most poor readers will not even make the same errors the second time they read the *same passage* (see *Teaching 2*, pages 234-35 for a discussion of the problems in designing corrective reading programs). In our judgment, the primary value that can be served by these tests is to provide measures of *oral reading accuracy and rate* which can be converted to approximate grade-norms. Decoding words is a most important component of reading behavior, yet the major achievement batteries makes no provision for testing oral responding. Many of the diagnostic reading tests can be used to fill this gap.

In the case of the arithmetic diagnostic tests, several of them are basically adequate criterion-referenced tests which will pinpoint weaknesses. The problem remaining is to be sure the test selected for diagnostic use provides a basis for relating deficiencies to teaching strategies. Many older tests now in print do provide such information, and they are likely to be sold today as criterion-referenced tests.

Placement

Norm-referenced achievement tests can be useful in the crude assignment of students to curriculum levels. In fact, the Wide Range Achievement Test is often used as a starting point when nothing else is known about a student. However, placement assignments through norm-referenced tests can be off by two years or more. More precise testing of the skills taught in particular instructional programs is needed, along with actual tryout within a program. Hofmeister[14] illustrates this point with an analysis of 24 pupils referred for special education services as spelling failures. The students were given a norm-referenced spelling test which expressed their score as a grade equivalent, and a criterion-referenced test specified placement in a specific curriculum in terms of grade level. The results showed that the mean grade level on the two tests differed by only .14 grade levels. However, the norm-referenced test systematically underestimated the placement of the younger children (third graders) and overestimated the placement of the older children (sixth graders). The actual discrepancies in placement ranged from .1 to 1.2 grade levels, and the mean *difference* in placement by the two methods was .42 grade levels or nearly half of a year.

Because norm-referenced achievement tests are designed in an attempt to satisfy the goals of many programs, they are likely only to be a crude placement device for any particular program. Hofmeister's study gives some notion of the magnitude of error involved.

It was noted earlier that there are a large number of reading readiness tests on the market for use in deciding when to start children in reading programs. Readiness is defined by a variety of auditory and visual discrimination skills, writing skills, and language competencies assumed by most basal reading programs. As such the tests are misnamed and should be called tests of preskills for basal reading programs. As our experience has shown in teaching reading to some 15,000 disadvantaged five-year olds using Distar, when the reading program starts where the students are and teaches the needed skills, nearly all children are ready to learn to read long before the first grade. The readiness tests have helped to create a fiction that allows the first grade teacher not to teach reading to those children for whom the *program* is inappropriate. It would be better to use tests to specify the skills that should be taught to such children and then use methods that will accomplish the teaching.

Process Evaluation

Just as norm-referenced tests are not program-specific enough to be useful in placement, so too they are inappropriate for evaluating the process of instruction. In the attempt to satisfy the goals of many instructional programs, there is a good likelihood that the goals and subgoals of particular programs are not measured. Also, it is unlikely that the format and timing requirements of particular programs are satisfied.

Pre-Post Outcomes

It is possible to assess the effects of a given instructional program using norm-referenced tests. The basic idea is to see if the program being tested shows an improvement in standard score norms in going from pretest to posttest. This is called a "norm-referenced evaluation." The first requirement is that the test used reflects appropriately the objectives of the instructional program. The second requirement is that the testing dates relative to the school year correspond as closely as possible to those used in norming the test. These procedures are discussed in more detail in unit 14.

Comparisons of Programs

Norm-referenced achievement tests may also be useful in comparing different instructional programs. In this case it is necessary to examine the match between test objectives and program objectives for each program. *This requirement poses a major problem.* While test developers often provide content lists, these are usually too general to be useful. If the student will return to Table 10.2 and start reading items carefully, noting the preskills assumed, the range of vocabulary concepts implied, and the response requirements, it should be readily seen that making judgments about the fit of a test with an instructional program is a most difficult task, requiring a complete program analysis and test analysis. Then it is necessary to match the two. Until a better recognition of this problem is given in the specification of tests and instructional programs, the comparison of instructional programs remains a risky task.

Evaluation of Teachers

Norm-referenced tests are inappropriate instruments for the evaluation of teachers. Differences in student outcomes can be produced for many other reasons than teaching skills. In unit 12, we suggest that differences in home backgrounds will be reflected on such tests and therefore favor the teacher of children with better educated parents. Also, teachers may be saddled with inadequate instructional materials. At this point, monitoring of classroom processes and relating teacher behaviors to student outcomes (as discussed in unit 7) provides a more realistic basis for evaluating teachers and improving their effectiveness.

Selection

Various kinds of norm-referenced tests are currently used to select students for special programs. For example, IQ tests are used to determine eligibility for special education. More often than not, tests are used to place the economically disadvantaged in special classes that do little. Why should the educationally disadvantaged continue to be placed in disadvantaged educational settings? Decisions made with such tests need to be made with a fuller understanding of needs of children and *what can* be done for children. Currently achievement tests are used to determine Title I eligibility. This leads to a situation where, although there may be an effective program for disadvantaged children, they might be declared ineligible for the program long before it can have its long-term impact.

Other issues can arise when norm-referenced tests are used to select more capable students for special programs. Is this use of tests discriminatory? In the land of freedom of opportunity, there are some tough issues facing educators in the use of tests for selection. Broader social justifications for their uses need to be established. The fact that the tests are really effective in selecting high and low performers is not enough.

Guidance

Although not a consideration in the goals of this text, in closing this unit we should mention that quite an important use of achievement tests is to assist students in making wise decisions about curriculum options and longer term educational and occupational goals. Special strengths can be capitalized on in making decisions which are likely to be more rewarding.

summary

Norm-referenced achievement tests attempt to test the "common core" of what is happening in elementary and secondary education today. The most popular tests have been revised in the past five to eight years. Most of the achievement tests are constructed by starting with a group of general objectives defined by a group of curriculum experts on the basis of texts and programs in use in the schools. Test items are then written, tried out, and edited for ambiguities, logical consistency, difficulty level, and item information relating to reliability and validity. Finally, a representative sample of students is tested to provide a basis for constructing test norms. In contrast to criterion-referenced tests, the objectives of norm-referenced tests are usually broader and not specific to particular instructional programs. Items are preferred which discriminate among persons taking the test, and scores are interpreted according to placement in the distribution of scores obtained by the norm group.

Three types of tests were discussed. *Diagnostic tests* in reading and arithmetic have been used in planning remedial programs. We have suggested that the reading tests be used primarily to obtain norm-referenced measures (although crude) of oral reading rate and accuracy. The diagnostic arithmetic tests, which are essentially criterion-referenced tests, are also useful in remedial work when tied to appropriate corrective procedures. *Single-subject tests* can be found for almost any subject area. The most common tests used in elementary schools are measures of reading readiness. In discussing their use we have suggested that such tests might best be thought of as tests of preskills assumed by basal reading programs. Keep in mind that with proper analysis and procedures, these preskills can be taught.

Four of the most commonly used *achievement batteries* were illustrated and discussed in more detail. Each of the tests is technically quite sophisticated. They enjoy a widespread use in the evaluation of educational programs today. Such tests are sometimes useful in making gross decisions about student placement, but are not designed for use in making precise placements in a particular curriculum. Similarly, they are not sensitive enough nor program-specific enough for use in evaluating the process of instruction. These tests may be useful in the "norm-referenced evaluation" of a single program or in the experimental comparison of two or more programs. The major problem in such use is one of forming a careful judgment of the degree to which the tests measure program objectives. Test builders could do much to aid this judgment by giving more precise specifications of the objectives being measured by the tests. Norm-referenced tests are not useful in teacher evaluation, but may have many uses in student selection for special programs and in guidance. Some tough ethical issues must be considered when tests are proposed for use in the selection of students for special programs.

self-test

1 Objectives for norm-referenced tests attempt to reflect what is _____ to most instructional programs in a content area.

2 Diagnostic tests using norm-referenced test construction procedures can be found mainly in the areas of _____ and arithmetic.

3 By current standards, the better older diagnostic arithmetic tests are actually _____-_____ tests.

4 Major test batteries differ very little in technical qualities such as _____ and adequacy of the _____ group used to standardize the tests.

5 In a study by Hofmeister, the average placement in spelling using a norm-referenced test was off by _____ grade levels on the average.

6 The authors believe that reading readiness tests have helped to build a _____ that some first graders are not ready to learn to read, when the problem lies with inappropriate _____ .

1 common

2 reading

3 criterion-referenced

4 reliability; norm

5 .4 to .5

6 fiction; programs

7 Just as norm-referenced tests are not program-specific enough to be useful in placement, so too are they inappropriate for evaluating the _____ of instruction.

8 Norm-referenced achievement tests may be useful in comparing different in-structional programs when common _____ are covered by the test.

NUMBER RIGHT _____

exercise 1 programed practice

1 Steps followed in building a norm-referenced achievement test are in some ways quite similar to those followed in developing a _____- _____ test.

2 Key differences in procedures used are:

    a. Objectives for norm-referenced tests cover _____ material which is usually taught over _____ time units.

    b. Objectives for norm-referenced tests attempt to reflect what is _____ to most instructional programs in a content area.

    c. Methods of item analysis differ. For example, in selecting items for norm-referenced tests, items are eliminated that _____ students pass or fail. In selecting items for criterion-referenced tests, one would seek items that are _____ by many prior to instruction, but _____ by many after instruction.

    d. Scores for norm-referenced achievement tests are interpreted in relation to the frequency _____ of scores obtained by the norm group. Scores for a criterion-referenced test are usually interpreted directly in terms of the _____ of mastery of an objective.

3 There are basically three types of norm-referenced achievement tests: diag-nostic tests, single-subject tests, and achievement _____ .

4 Diagnostic tests using norm-referenced test construction procedures can be found mainly in the areas of _____ and arithmetic.

5 In reading, diagnostic tests are presumed to be useful in analyzing the types of _____ students make and providing a basis for _____ programs.

6 As measures of _____ reading rate and accuracy some diagnostic tests can be a useful addition to a battery of tests designed to evaluate a beginning reading program.

7 Diagnostic arithmetic tests can be especially effective in locating _____ because one is dealing with a finite set of basic facts, logical operations, and symbols.

8 By current standards, the better older diagnostic arithmetic tests are actually _____-_____ tests.

9 Single-subject tests are common for _____ areas of study in high school and college.

10 At the beginning elementary level, reading _____ tests have been very popular for use in placing young children.

11 Four most commonly used achievement batteries are the SAT, MAT, _____ , and SRA.

12 For first to third grades, the content of these four tests is quite _____ , although formats and specific _____ requirements differ. After fourth grade, there is more _____ in the topics tested and their time emphasis.

13 The tests differ very little in technical qualities such as _____ and adequacy of the _____ group used to standardize the test.

14 Norm-referenced tests are of little value in pinpointing specific _____ and suggesting remedial procedures.

15 Diagnostic _____ tests also have a questionable usefulness in planning for remedial work.

16 Norm-referenced achievement tests can be useful in the crude _____ of students to curriculum levels. In fact, the _____ _____ Achievement Test is often used as a starting point when little is known about a student's abilities.

---

5 errors; remedial

6 oral

7 deficiencies

8 criterion-
  referenced

9 elective

10 readiness

11 CAT

12 similar;
   vocabulary;
   variability

13 reliability;
   norm

14 weaknesses

15 reading

16 assignment;
   Wide Range

17 two years

18 .4 to .5

19 fiction;
programs

20 process

21 standard

22 objectives;
dates

23 objectives

24 inappropriate

25 select; little

26 values

27 goals

---

17 However, placement assignments through norm-referenced tests can be off by _____ _____ or more.

18 In a study of Hofmeister, the average placement in spelling using a norm-referenced test was off by _____ grade levels on the average.

19 The authors believe that reading readiness tests have helped to build a _____ that some first graders are not ready to learn to read, when the problem lies with inappropriate _____ .

20 Just as norm-referenced tests are not program-specific enough to be useful in placement, so too they are inappropriate for evaluating the _____ of instruction.

21 It is possible to assess the effects of a given instructional program using norm-referenced tests. The basic idea is to see if the program being tested shows an improvement in _____ score norms in going from pretest to posttest.

22 The first requirement is that the test used reflect appropriately the _____ of the instructional program. The second requirement is that the testing _____ relative to the school year correspond as closely as possible to those used in norming the test.

23 Norm-referenced achievement tests may also be useful in comparing different instructional programs when common _____ are covered by the test.

24 Norm-referenced tests are _____ instruments for the evaluation of teachers.

25 Various kinds of norm-referenced tests are currently used to _____ students for special programs. This use is often rightly questioned by minorities who find too many of the economically disadvantaged placed in special classes that do too _____ .

26 The fact that the tests are really effective in selecting high and low performers is not enough. It is also important to justify the social _____ implicit in such selection.

27 An important use of achievement tests is to assist students in making wise decisions about curriculum options and longer term educational and occupational _____ .

exercise 2   test review

Choose a test of oral reading and write a two-page (double spaced) review of the test for turn-in next week. Your review should start with the test manual. These are usually kept in a special place for tests in the Education part of the library. Then, go to Buros' *Seventh Mental Measurement Yearbook* for additional specifications and reviews. If there are no reviews current, go back to the *Sixth Mental Measurement Yearbook* to find reviews.

Your review should:

1 Identify the test and who it is for.
2 Specify the scores the test gives.
3 For each score indicate what it measures and give its reliability or reliabilities.
4 Present and evaluate any evidence for the test's validity, including content validity.
5 Specify how norms were determined and discuss their adequacy.
6 Draw your conclusions as to circumstances where you would recommend using or not using the test.

discussion questions

1 What are the key steps in building a norm-referenced test?
2 What are four ways in which the construction of norm-referenced and criterion-referenced tests differ?
3 Name and give examples of three kinds of achievement tests.
4 Describe three kinds of response conventions used in the MAT, CAT, SAT, and SRA.
5 What is the Mental Measurement Yearbook series?
6 Discuss the uses of norm-referenced achievement tests in diagnostic-remedial work.
7 Discuss the use of norm-referenced tests in student placement.
8 What is a "norm-referenced evaluation"?
9 What two requirements must be met in making a "norm-referenced evaluation"?
10 What is the major problem in using norm-referenced tests to compare the effects of different programs?
11 Should norm-referenced test data be used in teacher evaluation? Why?
12 What value issues arise in the use of tests in selection of students?
13 How might norm-referenced tests be used in guidance?

unit 10

Interpreting Norm-Referenced Test Scores

objectives

When you complete this unit you should be able to—

1   Describe the normal distribution and explain how it can be useful in interpreting norm-referenced test scores.

2   Define the following terms:

z-score   percentile ranks
transformed standard score   age-equivalent scores
expanded standard score   grade-equivalent scores
ranks   norm population

3   Convert any z-score value to a statement of percent of cases falling above or below that value, assuming a normal distribution.

4   Find the percent of cases falling between any two z-score values, assuming a normal distribution.

5   Transform a set of z-scores into standard scores with any specified mean and standard deviation.

6   Convert any transformed standard scores back to z-scores.

7   Assign ranks to a set of scores.

8   Assign percentile ranks to a set of scores.

9   Explain how grade-equivalent scores are determined.

10   Intelligently interpret grade-equivalent scores.

11   Explain how norm-groups are selected in norming the major achievement test batteries.

12   Describe the Anchor Test Study and its value.

13   Use norm tables to convert raw test scores to various normed scores.

lesson

No matter where you are in education, you are likely to encounter people making statements about test scores such as percentile ranks, grade-equivalency scores, IQ's, and standard scores. It is important to understand what these scores mean, so that you can critically evaluate statements made with reference to such scores. We begin the development of this understanding by examining the normal curve or normal distribution. This distribution provides a practical basis for interpreting standard scores in terms of the percentage of persons likely to have higher or lower scores.

The Normal Distribution

In norm-referenced testing, scores are usually expressed in relation to the distribution of scores obtained by some reference group. As noted in unit 2, standard scores (SS) can be computed to express any given score (X) in relation to the mean (M) and standard deviation (SD) of a reference group's scores.

$$SS = \frac{X - M}{SD}$$

For most tests, the distribution of standard scores tends to be bell-shaped. An idealized form of the bell-shaped distribution known as the *normal curve* is useful in interpreting test scores stated in standard score form. The normal distribution can be thought of as a smoothed frequency distribution generated by making the score intervals very, very small. Figure 10.1 shows two frequency distributions and a normal distribution. Distribution A has 9 fairly large intervals. Distribution B has 19 smaller intervals. The normal curve in C can be imagined to have an infinite number of very small intervals. The effect of having more intervals that are small is to convert a jagged frequency distribution into a smooth curve. The area under the normal curve can be divided into portions which sum to one. The proportion of area between any two points on the curve gives the *relative frequency* of persons falling between those two points. Thus, if we know that a given distribution of scores is approximately normal, we can immediately find out the proportion of students which fall above or below a given standard score. Multiplying by 100, these proportions become percentages. For example, figure 10.1C shows that 2.28 percent of the cases (2.15 plus .13) score higher than +2 standard deviations. Conversely, 97.72 percent score below that point.

Note that 99.74 percent of the cases fall between plus or minus 3 standard deviations and only .26 percent fall beyond this point. Because of these relations, a convenient approximation for remembering the percent of cases covered by standard deviation units is this:

Mean to 1 SD = 34%
1 SD to 2 SD = 14%
2 SD to 3 SD = 2%
Mean to 2 SD = 48%
Mean to 3 SD = 50%

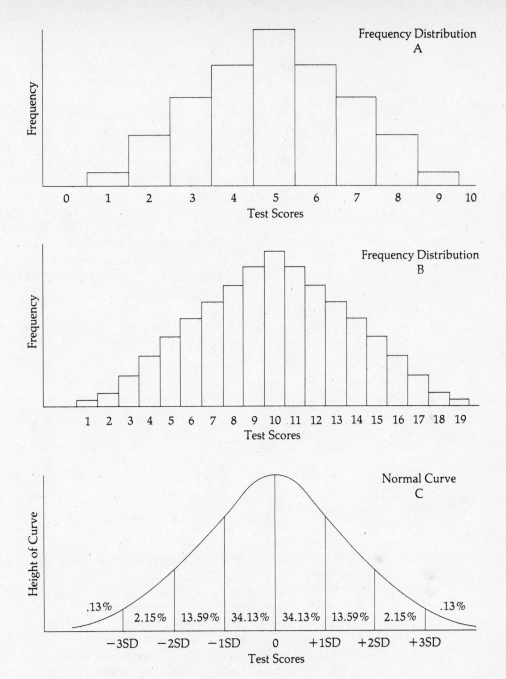

Figure 10.1 From Frequency Distribution to Normal Curve

This approximation can be used, of course, with SD units above or below the mean.

Appendix B gives the percentage of cases falling above or below any given standard deviation unit, assuming a normal distribution. Since many different standard scores can be made through transformations, the standard score defined by $\frac{X-M}{SD}$ has been given the special symbol z. It is also known as a z-score.

$$z = \frac{X-M}{SD}$$

To use appendix B, simply express a given score in z-score form. Then find that z in the table (closest approximation) and read the percentage of cases falling above or below that z. For example, for a z of 2.50, .62 percent of the cases fall above and 99.38 percent fall below. Thus, a z-score of 2.50 occurs in less than one percent of the cases. This is an extremely high score. A z-score of zero, of course, would be right at the mean. Since the normal curve is symmetrical, it is also at the median, with 50 percent falling above and 50 percent falling below that point. Find the percent of cases falling above and below the following z-scores:

z-Score	Percent Above	Percent Below
0	_____	_____
+1.00	_____	_____
+2.00	_____	_____
+3.00	_____	_____
−1.00	_____	_____
−2.00	_____	_____
−3.00	_____	_____
−1.20	_____	_____
−2.60	_____	_____
+1.25	_____	_____
+ .75	_____	_____

(Check answers on page 193.)

Appendix B can also be used to find the percentage of cases falling in between any two z-scores. Find the *percent below* in appendix B for the lower z-score and subtract it from the *percent below* for the higher z-score. The difference is the percent of cases falling in the interval defined by the two z-scores. For a z-score of 0 and a z-score of 1, the percent below values are 50.0 percent and 84.1 percent. The difference is 34.1 percent. This means that 34.1 percent of the cases fall between a z-score of 0 and 1. Find the percent of cases that fall between the following z-scores:

z-Scores	Percent of Cases Between
−1.0 to +1.0	_____
−2.0 to +2.0	_____
−3.0 to +3.0	_____

(Check your answers on page 194.)

Transformed Standard Scores

When standard scores are reported for various educational tests, they are usually in a form other than z-scores. Explaining a zero standard score to a parent might be difficult. Also, the negative numbers and decimal points can be a nuisance. Standard scores can be transformed in a variety of ways to make them more convenient. This is done by changing the mean (M) and standard deviation (SD) of the z-score distribution. The general transformation is:

$$\text{Transformed standard score} = z \cdot SD + M$$

where SD is the standard deviation of the transformed distribution and M is the mean of the transformed distribution. To produce transformed standard scores, the z-scores are multiplied by the desired standard deviation of the new distribution and the mean desired for the new distribution is added to each score.

Some common transformed standard scores are given in table 10.1. IQ's are transformed standard scores with a mean of 100 and a standard deviation usually of 15 (16 for the Stanford-Binet). The subscales on the Wechsler Intelligence Tests are transformed standard scores with a mean of 10 and a standard deviation of 3. Many achievement tests use transformed standard scores with means of 50 and standard deviations of 10. These are called T-scores. The College Board Examination and the Graduate Record Examination use transformed standard scores with a mean of 500 and a standard deviation of 100. The final entry in the table 10.1 is stanines. Stanines are *standard nines*; they are transformed standard scores with a mean of 5 and a standard deviation of 2. All of the other scores illustrated in table 10.1 can take

TABLE 10.1   SOME COMMON STANDARD SCORES

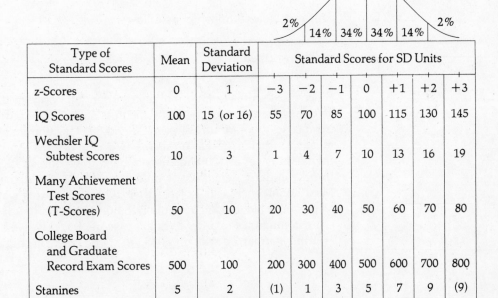

Type of Standard Scores	Mean	Standard Deviation	Standard Scores for SD Units						
			−3	−2	−1	0	+1	+2	+3
z-Scores	0	1	−3	−2	−1	0	+1	+2	+3
IQ Scores	100	15 (or 16)	55	70	85	100	115	130	145
Wechsler IQ Subtest Scores	10	3	1	4	7	10	13	16	19
Many Achievement Test Scores (T-Scores)	50	10	20	30	40	50	60	70	80
College Board and Graduate Record Exam Scores	500	100	200	300	400	500	600	700	800
Stanines	5	2	(1)	1	3	5	7	9	(9)

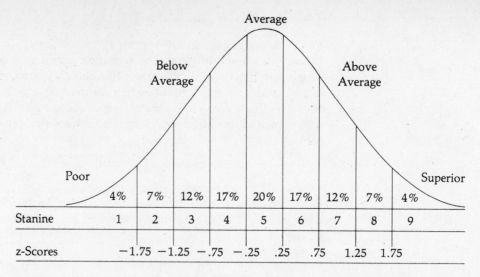

Figure 10.2 Relations of Stanines to the Percentage of Area Under the Normal Curve and to z-scores

on any precise three or four digit value. Stanines are restricted to one digit values from 1 to 9. Figure 10.2 illustrates how the normal curve is divided into stanines. Each stanine covers about one-half of a standard deviation or one-half of a z-score unit. Stanines are relatively easy to explain to parents. Five is average, one is low, and nine is outstanding.

Suppose we wish to convert the following z-scores to standard scores in a distribution with a mean of 50 and a standard deviation of 10:

$$z_1 = -1.5$$
$$z_2 = 0$$
$$z_3 = +2.1$$

This can be accomplished as follows:

Transformed $z_1 = -1.5 \cdot 10 + 50 = 50 - 15 = 35$
Transformed $z_2 = 0 \cdot 10 + 50 = 50$
Transformed $z_3 = 2.1 \cdot 10 + 50 = 21 + 50 = 71$

Since most scores in a normal distribution fall between plus and minus three standard deviation units, if the mean is 50 and the standard deviation is 10, most scores would fall between 20 and 80. This eliminates the negatives and gives a sufficient range of scores (without decimals) for most purposes. If the mean is set at 100 and the standard deviation at 15, then plus or minus three standard deviations would place most scores between 55 and 145. Most intelligence tests express their IQ scores in this way.

It is possible to use appendix B to help interpret any transformed standard score if you first convert it back to a z-score. Suppose we know the mean is 100 and the standard deviation is 15, an IQ of 125 would give a z-score of:

$$z = \frac{X - M}{SD} \quad \text{or}$$

$$z = \frac{125-100}{15} = \frac{25}{15} = 1.67$$

From table B we can determine that approximately 95 percent of the population would get a z-score lower than 1.67 and 5 percent would get one higher. Knowing this is of considerable help in interpreting the IQ of 125. We know it falls in the top 5 percent. See if you can find out what percentage of students would have IQ's higher or lower than 80, assuming the mean is 100 and the standard deviation is 15.

IQ of 80 = z-score   _____

Percent below z   _____

Percent above z   _____

(Check your answers on page 194.)

Expanded Standard Scores

The most commonly used achievement test batteries provide another kind of standard score which allows the standard scores to increase over grades covered by the tests. For example, on the Metropolitan Achievement Test, the various levels of the test are interrelated through the use of expanded standard scores. At a given grade level, the standard deviation for reading or math is approximately 10, but the mean grows from grade to grade. Table 10.2 shows the relationship between mean expanded standard scores and grade level for the Metropolitan Achievement Test (MAT). Table 10.2 shows that when reading and mathematics are expressed in standard score units the amount of gain in those two subjects decreases in successive years. The spread of scores on these tests decreases as basic skills are mastered by more children. Table 10.2 also illustrates the fact that expanded standard scores in reading are not comparable to those in math. Only the scores from different forms of the same subject area test can be compared legitimately.

Rank-Order Scores

Rank-order scores offer a simple method for comparing the members of a group. Johnny was first, Sally was second, Melissa was third, and so forth. Let us rank-order these scores:

Person	Score	Rank
Jim	21	7
Julie	16	9
Jack	42	1
Joan	21	7
Jane	35	2.5
Joe	35	2.5
Jason	21	7
Jeb	28	5
Jennifer	32	4

TABLE 10.2 RELATION BETWEEN GRADE LEVELS AND MEAN STANDARD SCORES ON THE METROPOLITAN ACHIEVEMENT TEST

Grade Level	Total Reading Mean Standard Score	Total Math Mean Standard Score
2.0	43	46
	(13)*	(14)*
3.0	56	60
	(10)	(13)
4.0	66	73
	(8)	(10)
5.0	74	83
	(7)	(7)
6.0	81	90
	(6)	(7)
7.0	87	97
	(5)	(5)
8.0	92	102
	(4)	(6)
9.0	96	108

*The figures in parentheses show the gain in mean expanded standard score units for each grade level increase.

Jack has the highest score and is given the rank of 1. Jane and Joe are tied for the next highest score, so ranks 2 and 3 are averaged (2.5) and given to each of them. Jennifer then is given rank 4 and Jeb rank 5. Jim, Joan, and Jason each have 21, so the next three ranks are averaged ($\frac{6+7+8}{3} = 7$) and each is given rank 7. Finally, Julie is given the last rank of 9. Assign ranks to the following scores:

Score	Rank
4	_____
7	_____
9	_____
6	_____
7	_____
4	_____
10	_____
3	_____
7	_____
5	_____

(Check your answers on page 194.)

Percentile Ranks

Percentile ranks (also called percentiles or centiles) are often used to interpret test scores to parents and others, because they are a little easier to interpret directly than are standard scores. The most common procedure for interpreting standard scores is to state how many students in the norm population achieve a higher or lower score. With percentile ranks, it is unnecessary to convert standard scores to a percentage statement. A percentile rank specifies the percentage of scores which are *lower* than a given score. For example, if a person ranks 25 in a group of 500, 475 people have lower scores. The percentile rank would be $\frac{475}{500} \cdot 100 = .95 \times 100 = 95$th percentile.

Saying that a person ranks at the 95th percentile is a little easier to interpret than saying he ranks 25 out of 500, or that he has a z-score of +1.65. A person ranking at the 95th percentile is in the top 5 percent of the group. Lower scores are obtained by 95 percent of the group. If a person ranks 90 in a group of 100, his percentile rank is 10. This indicates that only 10 percent of the group had a lower score ($\frac{10}{100} \cdot 100 = 10$).

A percentile *scale* is distinctly different from a standard score scale. This difference can be illustrated placing percentiles on a z-score scale and a percentile scale. Assuming that standard score units best express differences among people on some test (and this is a reasonable assumption most of the time), then it can be seen from figure 10.3 that percentiles exaggerate differences in the middle of a distribution and minimize differences at the extremes of a distribution. A percentile change from 50 to 60 is a z-score change of only .25. A percentile change from 90 to 100 is a z-score change of more than 1.7. The latter change is over *seven times larger* in standard score units. Problems in interpretation arise mainly when looking at *differences* between students or at gains by students. When expressed in percentiles, a gain or difference of 10 points in the middle of the distribution is much less significant than a gain or difference of 10 points at the extremes of the distribution.

Practice Problems

1 Find the percentiles for rank 12 and rank 37 in a distribution of 200 persons. (Round to the nearest whole number.)

Rank	Percentile
12	_____
37	_____

2 Use appendix B to find the percentile rank (rounded) for the following z-scores:

z-Score	Percentile
+1.30	_____
+ .30	_____

Find the gain in percentile units for the 1 unit gain in z-score units above:

Gain in percentiles = _____

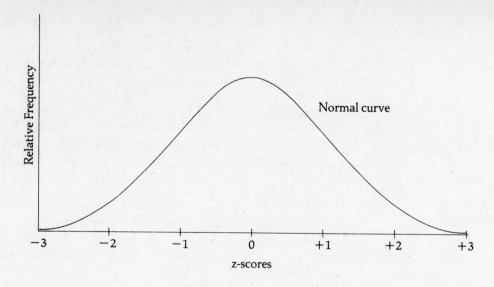

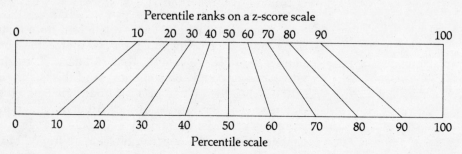

Figure 10.3 A Comparison of Frequency Distributions For z-scores and Percentile Scores

3 Use appendix B to find the percentile ranks (rounded) for the following z-scores:

z-Score	Percentile
+1	_____
+2	_____
+3	_____

(Check your answers on page 194.)

Age- and Grade-Equivalent Scores

Standard scores and ranks allow one to locate a person's position within some reference group. "He is in the top 10 percent of 10 year olds." "She is right in the middle of the group of second graders." Age-equivalent scores and grade equivalent scores assign scale scores on the basis of the average raw score earned by a group of a given age or grade. A student with a grade equivalent of 2.0 has a score obtained by the *average* beginning second grader.

Suppose we design a concept mastery test (vocabulary) to cover ages six to 18 or grades 1 to 12. The test is built so that concepts are ordered from easy to difficult and it contains 100 items. Now, suppose Jimmy, a third grader who is nine years old, gets 25 words right. Is that good or bad? We need some basis for comparison. We could find out how Jimmy stands in his class by comparing his score to the rest of the class. This could lead to a conversion of his score to a z-score or a rank. An alternative comparison procedure is to test a group of children at a number of ages, or a number of grades and plot the mean score obtained by each age or grade group. Some hypothetical data for such an analysis is presented in figure 10.4. Age- or grade-equivalent scores are determined by "smoothing out" the plotted mean data (with the best fit line or curve), and then finding a possible age or grade equivalent for each possible raw score. For example, a raw score of 47 has an age-equivalent score of 11 and a grade-equivalent score of 5.0. These scores can then be placed in a table for easy use.

In constructing an achievement test battery, one test cannot be given to all students, so overlapping testing is used to permit a tying together of different levels of a test battery. If one test is appropriate for third graders and another for second graders, some second and third graders would take both tests to permit a linking of the tests.

Age- and grade-equivalent scores, while seemingly easy to interpret, have a number of problems connected with them. The scores usually increase in a linear way, with time, but learning does not. Reading skills may increase rapidly in the early grades and then level off, so that the raw score of the average sixth grader is not much different from that of the average 12th grader. A "ceiling" effect is encountered with basic competencies. What seems like "twice as much" (eighth grade versus fourth grade reading level) may represent only a small change. The standard score changes on the MAT presented in table 10.2 illustrate this kind of effect. Conversely, some skills such as knowledge of social studies may accelerate rapidly during grades 6 to 12 and represent a great deal of learning. A change from grades 6 to 12 may represent four times as much learning as took place from grades 1 to 6. Unless one can somehow weigh test items in terms of critical criteria such as time-to-teach, scales which are a function of time can be quite deceptive. Using grade- or age-equivalents to study gains must be done very cautiously, if at all. These issues are discussed further in unit 14.

Another problem lies in the concept of *grade equivalence*. It is usually assumed that the second grader who receives a 6.5 grade-equivalent score can do sixth grade work. Except for a few cases, such as the Wide Range Achievement Test or the Gilmore Oral, *where the same test is given to all students,* the second grader with a 6.5 grade equivalent score does not even take the sixth grade test. What the 6.5 grade equivalent score means is that the second-grade student can do second-grade work as well as the average sixth grader is *estimated* to be able to do second-grade work.

Norm Populations

Norm-referenced test scores, whether they be standard scores, percentile scores, or grade-equivalent scores, are determined by giving a test to a sample drawn from a reference population or norm group. The performance of this

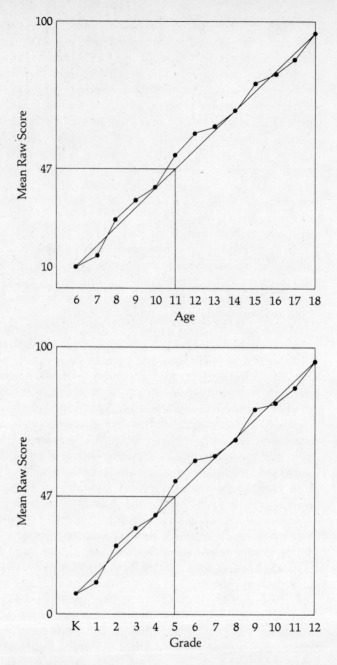

Figure 10.4 Mean Concept Mastery Score by Age and by Grade

group is used to determine how the raw scores are to be converted to norm-referenced scores. The norm population is used as the standard of comparison in interpreting test scores. It provides the test user with a frame of reference for score interpretation. "A score this high is obtained by only 10 percent of *second graders in the United States*." "This score is two standard deviations above the mean of scores obtained by *high school seniors in California.*" It is possible for teachers to build their own norms for teacher-made tests by comparing scores obtained to the distribution for the class. If the same test is used for several years, the comparison group can be enlarged.

The key step in building norms for a test is the selection of the norm group. The major achievement batteries provide norms based on a representative national sample of students. Schools are selected in a sample of geographic regions and on an urbal-rural basis. An attempt is made to construct a sample that will match census figures for the United States in terms of its representation. Representativeness is also sought on student IQ and social class. Samples for norms for major test batteries range as high as 50,000 to 100,000 students across all grade levels.

Because different tests are based on different samples as well as different items, they are likely not to produce the same result. One check of comparability was made in the Anchor Test Study.[1] The study was designed to permit a comparison of reading test scores from different tests at grades 4, 5, and 6. The Metropolitan Achievement Test was given to a sample of students along with one other test. The MAT served as the anchor test. The "other test" was varied so that eight commonly used tests were represented. The study was designed so that raw scores from the different tests could be converted to a common norm through the comparison with the anchor test. When the norm values obtained by the Anchor Test Study for various tests were compared with the published norms for those tests, they were found to be surprisingly close, especially for scores near the mean.

For some purposes it would be desirable to have norms based on a population just like yours. If you are teaching in a southern rural school, national norms will likely show you are behind no matter how effective your teaching. Similarly, if you teach in a New England suburb, national norms will likely show your students to be above the national average even if you have done ineffective teaching. If norms are to be used to compare teachers or schools, they should be based on comparable student groups, similar curricula and organizational structures. Even the policy on promotion of students is important. For example, if 90 percent of Spanish speaking children are retained each year in first grade, the levels of performance at each *grade level* would possibly be quite different than if most of them were promoted each year. Students with two years of first grade are likely to perform better than those with only one.

Keep in mind that grade norms are based on the average performance of a group of students at a given grade level. That means if your class average is at grade level, 50 percent of the children will be below this grade level and 50 percent will be above.

Using Norm Tables

A number of norm-referenced scores are provided for each of the major tests. We will use the CAT and the MAT to provide examples and to get practice in obtaining and interpreting norm-referenced scores. Most achievement batteries provide for conversion of raw scores to stanines, percentiles, grade equivalents, and expanded standard scores that place different test forms and different test levels on a common scale.

Raw Scores to Grade Equivalents

Table 10.3 is used to convert raw scores to grade equivalents for the CAT Level 1, Form A.[2] Suppose Jimmy Blake scores 77 in Vocabulary and 10 in Comprehension. This gives him a Reading Total Score of 87 (77 + 10). By going down the Reading-VOCAB column until we find 77, and then looking left on the same row, we find his grade equivalent score to be 2.3. For COMPR it is 2.2, and for TOTAL it is 2.3. Find the grade equivalent scores for the following:

	Raw Score	Grade Equivalent
Mathematics—Computation	39	_____
Mathematics—Concepts & Problems	31	_____
Mathematics—Total Score	70	_____
Language—Mechanics	9	_____
Language—Spelling	14	_____

(Check your answers on page 194.)

Note that grade equivalents are constructed so that each tenth is equal to a month of school. The school year is divided into nine months and one month is counted for the summer. Thus a grade equivalent score of 4.2 would be the average score expected from a fourth grader in November. The following table shows the relationship of months to grade placement in tenths:

Date of Testing	Sept.	Oct.	Nov.	Dec.	Jan.	Feb.	March	April	May	June
Grade Placement	.0	.1	.2	.3	.4	.5	.6	.7	.8	.9

Raw Scores to Percentiles and Stanines

Table 10.4 is used to convert raw scores to percentile ranks and stanines for the CAT Level 1, Form A, *if the student is tested during December, January, or February.*[3] Similar tables are available covering September, October, November and March, April, May, and June. Note first that the raw scores on this table go in the opposite direction from the previous table. For a given test raw score we find the raw score in the table and look for the percentile or stanine score on the same row. For example, for Reading VOCAB a raw score of 77 gives a percentile of 86 or a stanine of 7. A raw score of 34 gives a percentile of 8 and a stanine of 2.

TABLE 10.3 RAW SCORE TO GRADE EQUIVALENT

Grade Equiv-alent	Reading			Mathematics			Language					Total Battery	Grade Equiv-alent
	Vocab	Compr	Total	Compu	Concpt & Prob	Total	Audg	Mech	Usg & St	Total	Spell		
0.6	0-51	0-4	0-58	0-10	0-19	0-31	0-7	0-6	0-6	0-21	0-3	0-119	0.6
0.7	52-53		59	11		32-33			7	22		120-123	0.7
0.8	54		60-61	12	20	34		7		23		124-128	0.8
0.9	55-56	5	62	13-14	21	35-36			8	24		129-132	0.9
1.0	57		63	15	22	37-38	8	8		25	4	133-137	1.0
1.1	58		64-65	16	23	39-40			9	26		138-143	1.1
1.2	59-60		66-67	17	24	41-43		9		27		144-147	1.2
1.3	61	6	68	18-19	25	44-45		10	10	28		148-152	1.3
1.4	62		69	20	26	46				29-30	5	153-156	1.4
1.5	63-64		70	21	27	47-48		11	11	31		157-161	1.5
1.6	65		71-72	22-23	28	49-51		12		32-33		162-167	1.6
1.7	66-67	7	73-74	24-25	29	52-54	9	13		34	6	168-174	1.7
1.8	68-69	8	75-77	26	30	55-56		14	12	35-36		175-181	1.8
1.9	70		78-79	27-28	31	57-59		15-16		37-38	7	182-188	1.9
2.0	71-72	9	80-81	29-30	32	60-62		17		39-40	8	189-195	2.0
2.1	73-74		82-83	31-32	33	63-64		18	13	41		196-201	2.1
2.2	75-76	10	84-85	33	34	65-67		19-20		42-43	9	202-208	2.2
2.3	77	11	86-88	34	35	68-69	10	21		44-45	10	209-215	2.3
2.4	78-79	12	89-90	35	36	70-71		22	14	46		216-221	2.4
2.5	80-81	13	91-94	36	37	72-73		23		47-48	11	222-228	2.5
2.6	82	14	95-96		38	74-75		24		49	12	229-234	2.6
2.7	83	15	97-100	37	39	76		25		50-51		235-241	2.7
2.8	84	16	101-102	38	40	77-78		26	15	52	13	242-247	2.8
2.9	85	17	103			79	11	27		53		248-252	2.9
3.0		18	104-105		41	80		28		54	14	253-257	3.0
3.1	86		106	39		81		29		55	15	258-261	3.1
3.2	87	19	107		42	82				56		262-265	3.2
3.3		20	108			83		30	16	57	16	266-268	3.3
3.4	88		109	40	43	84	12	31		58		269-270	3.4
3.5						84				59	17	271-273	3.5
3.6	89	21	110		44	85		32				274-275	3.6
3.7										60		276	3.7
3.8			111								18	277	3.8
3.9						86		33		61		278-279	3.9
4.0	90								17			280	4.0
4.1		22	112		45	87		34		62		281	4.1
4.2											19	282	4.2
4.3										63		283	4.3
4.4	91							35				284	4.4
4.5			113				13			64		285	4.5
4.6												286	4.6
4.7					46					65		287	4.7

TABLE 10.4   RAW SCORE TO PERCENTILE RANK AND STANINE MIDDLE OF GRADE 1:1.3 TO 1.5 (DEC, JAN, FEB)

CAT Level 1   CAT Form A

Sta	Nat. %ile Rank	Reading			Mathematics			Language					Total Battery	Nat. %ile Rank	Sta
		Vocab	Compr	Total	Compu	Concpt & Prob	Total	Audg	Mech	Usg & St	Total	Spell			
	99	88-92	20-24	107-116	39-40	44-47	80-87	14-15	32-38	19-20	59-73	15-20	249-296	99	
	98	87	18-19	104-106			79		30-31	18	57-58	14	242-248	98	
9	97	86	16-17	101-103	38	42	78		29		56	13	235-241	97	9
	96	85	15	98-100		41	77		28		55	12	230-234	96	
	95	84	14	96-97	37		76	13	27	17	54		226-229	95	
	94	83	13	94-95		40	75		26		53	11	222-225	94	
8	93	82		92-93			74		25		52		218-221	93	8
	92	81	12	91	36	39	73		24		51		216-217	92	
	91	80		90			72				50	10	213-215	91	
	90			88-89		38	71		23	16	49		210-212	90	
	89	79	11	87	35		70						209	89	
	88	78				37	69		22		48		206-208	88	
	87			86	34			12			47		204-205	87	
	86	77	10	85		36	68		21			9	202-203	86	
	85			84			67				46		201	85	
	84	76			33	35	66		20	15	45		198-200	84	
	83	75		83			65						197	83	
7	82				32				19		44		196	82	7
	81	74		82			64					8	193-195	81	
	80		9		31	34	63				43		192	80	
	79			81			62		18		42		190-191	79	
	78	73		80	30			11					189	78	
	77	72				33	61				41		187-188	77	
	76				29		60		17	14			186	76	
	75			79							40		185	75	
	74	71		78		32	59					7	183-184	74	
	73				28				16		39		182	73	
	72	70	8		27		58						181	72	
	71			77		31	57				38		179-180	71	
	70						56		15				178	70	
6	69	69		76	26						37		176-177	69	6
	68						55			13			175	68	
	67					30					36		174	67	
	66	68		75	25		54	10	14				172-173	66	
	65												171	65	
	64	67		74			53				35	6		64	
	63		7		24	29	52		13				169-170	63	
	62			73							34		168	62	
	61	66			23					12			166-167	61	
	60						51				33		165	60	
	59	65		72		28	50						163-164	59	
	58				22				12					58	
	57						49				32		162	57	
	56	64		71									160-161	56	
	55					27		9					159	55	
	54	63		70	21		48		11	11	31		157-158	54	
	53				20		47						156	53	
	52						46							52	
	51			69		26					30	5	154-155	51	
5	50	62	6										153	50	5

Sta	Nat. %ile Rank	Reading Vocab	Reading Compr	Reading Total	Math Compu	Math Concpt & Prob	Math Total	Lang Audg	Lang Mech	Lang Usg & St	Lang Total	Spell	Total Battery	Nat. %ile Rank	Sta
	49			68	19		45				29		151-152	49	
	48	61							10				150	48	
	47					25	44							47	
	46			67	18					10	28		148-149	46	
	45	60											147	45	
	44			66			43						145-146	44	
	43	59				24	42	8	9		27		144	43	
	42			65	17		41						142-143	42	
	41				16									41	
	40	58		64						9	26		141	40	
	39					23	40						139-140	39	
	38	57		63									138	38	
	37				15		39		8		25	4	136-137	37	
	36	56	5	62									135	36	
	35					22	38						133-134	35	
	34	55			14					8	24			34	
	33			61			37						132	33	
	32	54					36						130-131	32	
4	31			60	13	21		7			23		129	31	4
	30	53							7				127-128	30	
	29			59			35						126	29	
	28	52		58	12	20	34		7				124-125	28	
	27			57							22		123	27	
	26	51					33						121-122	26	
	25	50		56	11		32				21		120	25	
	24					19			6			3	118-119	24	
	23	49	4	55									117	23	
	22			54			31	6		6	20		116	22	
	21	48			10	18	30						114-115	21	
	20	47		53									111-113	20	
	19			52	9		29				19		110	19	
	18	45-46		51									109	18	
	17			50		17	28		5	5	18		107-108	17	
3	16	44		49			27						105-106	16	3
	15	42-43			8	16	26						104	15	
	14			47-48				5			17		102-103	14	
	13	41	3	46			25			4		2	100-101	13	
	12	39-40		45	7	15	24		4		16		97-99	12	
	11	38		44			23						96	11	
	10	36-37		43	6	14	22				15		94-95	10	
	9	35		42									91-93	9	
	8	34		40-41		13	21	4		3	14		89-90	8	
2	7	32-33	2	38-39	5		20		3		13		85-88	7	2
	6	30-31		37		12	18-19					1	83-84	6	
	5	28-29		35-36	4	11	17	3		2	12		79-82	5	
	4	25-27	1	32-34		10	16		2		11		75-78	4	
	3	22-24		29-31	3	9	14-15				10		70-74	3	
1	2	17-21	0	25-28	2	8	12-13	2	1	1	8-9	0	63-69	2	1
	1	0-16		0-24	0-1	0-7	0-11	0-1	0	0	0-7		0-62	1	

Find the percentiles and stanines for each of the following:

	Raw Score	Percentile	Stanine
Reading Total	70	_____	_____
Mathematics—Computation	13	_____	_____
Language—Usage and Structure	11	_____	_____
Total Battery	211	_____	_____
Total Battery	135	_____	_____

(Check your answers on page 194.)

Table 10.5 is from the MAT Primary II.[4] It provides for the conversion of raw scores to expanded standard scores. The use of this table is the opposite from the last two. The raw score is found on the outside column and then you move right on the row until you find the standard score for the right subtest and form (F, G, or H). A raw score of 35 in Word Knowledge would have a standard score of 61 on form F. As noted earlier, expanded standard scores have a standard deviation of approximately ten for a given grade level, and the increase progressively from grade to grade.

Find the standard scores for the following raw scores.

	Raw Score	Standard Score
Form F, Word Knowledge	20	_____
Form G, Spelling	15	_____
Form H, Total Mathematics	35	_____

(Check your answers on page 195.)

TABLE 10.5 RAW SCORE TO STANDARD SCORE CONVERSION TABLE
Standard Scores (Expanded)

Raw Score	Word Knowledge F G H	Word Analysis F G H	Reading F G H	Total Reading F G H	Spelling F G H	Math Computation F G H	Math Concepts F G H	Math Prob. Solving F G H	Total Mathematics F G H	Raw Score
55				52 53 51					53 53 53	55
54				51 53 51					53 53 53	54
53				51 52 51					52 52 52	53
52				51 52 50					52 52 52	52
51				51 52 50					52 52 52	51
50				50 51 50					51 51 51	50
49				50 51 50					51 51 51	49
48				50 51 49					51 51 51	48
47				50 50 49					50 50 50	47
46				49 50 49					50 50 50	46
45				49 50 49					49 49 49	45
44			86 86 86	49 49 48					49 49 49	44
43			77 77 77	49 49 48					48 48 48	43
42			70 70 70	48 49 48					47 47 47	42
41			65 66 65	48 48 47					46 46 46	41
40	87 87 87		62 63 62	48 48 47			97		45 45 45	40
39	74 77 74		60 62 62	48 48 47			91		44 44 44	39
38	67 70 67		59 61 61	47 47 46			86		43 43 43	38
37	64 67 64		57 60 60	47 47 46			81		41 41 41	37
36	62 65 62		56 59 59	47 47 46			76		40 40 40	36
35	61 64 61	72	55 58 58	46 46 45			73	94 94 94	39 39 39	35
34	59 62 59	67	55 57 57	46 46 45			71	87 87 87	38 38 38	34
33	58 61 58	63	54 56 56	45 45 44		89 89 89	69	82 82 82	37 37 37	33
32	57 60 57	61	54 56 56	45 45 43		82 82 82	67	78 78 78	36 36 36	32
31	56 59 56	59	53 55 55	44 44 42		77 77 77	65	74 74 74	36 36 36	31
30	55 58 55	58	53 54 54	43 43 42	76 76 76	73 73 73	63	71 71 71	35 35 35	30
29	55 57 54	56	52 54 54	42 42 41	69 69 69	69 69 69	61	68 68 68	34 34 34	29
28	54 56 53	55	52 53 53	41 41 40	64 65 64	67 67 67	59	66 66 66	33 33 33	28
27	54 55 52	54	52 53 53	40 40 39	62 62 62	65 65 65	58	65 65 65	33 33 33	27
26	53 54 52	53	51 52 52	39 39 38	60 61 60	62 63 63	56	64 64 64	32 32 32	26
25	53 53 51	52	51 52 52	38 38 37	59 60 59	60 61 61	54	62 62 63	31 31 31	25
24	52 53 51	51	50 51 51	37 37 37	58 59 58	58 60 60	53	61 61 62	30 30 30	24
23	52 52 50	50	50 50 50	36 36 36	57 58 57	57 59 59	52	60 60 61	30 30 30	23
22	51 52 50	49	49 50 50	35 35 35	56 57 56	56 57 57	51	58 58 59	29 29 29	22
21	51 51 49	47	49 49 49	34 34 34	56 56 56	55 56 56	50	57 57 58	28 28 28	21
20	50 50 49	46	48 48 48	32 32 32	55 56 55	54 54 54	49	55 55 56	27 27 27	20
19	50 50 48	45	47 47 47	31 31 31	54 55 54	53 53 53	48	54 54 55	26 26 26	19
18	49 49 48	44	46 46 46	29 29 29	53 54 53	52 52 52	46	52 52 53	25 25 25	18
17	48 48 47	43	44 44 44	28 28 28	52 53 52	51 51 51	44	51 51 52	24 24 24	17
16	47 47 46	42	42 42 42	27 27 27	51 52 51	50 50 50	42	50 50 51	23 23 23	16
15	46 46 44	41	40 40 40	25 25 25	50 51 50	49 49 49	40	49 49 50	22 22 22	15
14	44 44 43	40	38 38 38	23 23 23	49 50 49	48 48 48	38	47 47 48	21 21 21	14
13	43 43 42	38	36 36 36	21 21 21	49 49 49	46 46 46	36	45 45 47	20 20 20	13
12	42 42 41	37	34 34 34	19 19 19	48 49 48	45 45 45	34	43 43 45	20 20 20	12
11	41 41 39	35	32 32 32	17 17 17	47 48 47	43 43 43	32	41 41 43	19 19 19	11
10	39 39 37	33	30 30 30	16 16 16	46 47 46	40 40 40	31	38 38 39	18 18 18	10
9	37 37 35	31	28 28 28	14 14 14	45 46 45	37 37 37	29	35 35 36	17 17 17	9
8	35 35 33	29	26 26 26	13 13 13	44 45 44	35 35 35	28	33 33 33	15 15 15	8
7	33 33 31	26	24 24 24	11 11 11	43 44 43	33 33 33	27	30 30 30	14 14 14	7
6	31 31 30	24	22 22 22	9 9 9	41 43 41	32 32 32	26	28 28 28	13 13 13	6
5	29 29 28	21	20 20 20	8 8 8	40 41 40	30 30 30	25	26 26 26	11 11 11	5
4	26 26 26	19	18 18 18	6 6 6	39 40 39	28 28 28	24	25 25 25	10 10 10	4
3	24 24 24	17	15 15 15	5 5 5	38 39 38	27 27 27	24	23 23 23	9 9 9	3
2	20 20 20	15	13 13 13	4 4 4	36 37 36	26 26 26	23	22 22 22	7 7 7	2
1	14 14 14	12	9 9 9	2 2 2	35 35 35	25 25 25	23	21 21 21	6 6 6	1

summary

The normal curve or normal distribution is useful in interpreting norm-referenced test scores because it provides a practical basis for converting standard scores to statements about the percentage of persons likely to have scores higher or lower than a given score. The area under the curve can be divided into portions which sum to one. The proportion of area between any two points gives the relative frequency of persons likely to fall between those two points. By multiplying the proportion by 100, the percentage of persons falling under a section of the curve can be obtained. A table based on the normal distribution (appendix B) can be used to convert any standard score (in z-score form) to a statement of the percentage of persons having higher or lower scores. It can also be used to find the percentage of persons likely to fall between any two z-scores. The following are important examples:

Normal Curve Section	Percent of Cases Included	Bases
Mean to 1 SD	34%	
1 SD to 2 SDs	14%	
2 SDs to 3SDs	2%	
Mean to 2 SDs	48%	(34% + 14%)
Mean to 3 SDs	50%	(34% + 14% + 2%)
−1 SD to +1 SD	68%	(34% + 34%)
−2 SDs to +2 SDs	96%	(48% + 48%)
−3 SDs to +3 SDs	100%	(50% + 50%)

Transformed standard scores are desirable because they eliminate negative scores and decimal parts. To transform a set of z-scores, multiply the z-scores by the desired standard deviation for the transformed distribution and then add the desired mean for the transformed distributions. T-scores are transformed standard scores with a mean of 50 and a standard deviation of 10. IQ scores are transformed standard scores with a mean of 100 and a standard deviation of 15 (or 16). Graduate Record Examination scores are transformed standard scores with a mean of 500 and a standard deviation of 100. Stanines are transformed standard scores with a mean of 5 and a standard deviation of 2 which can only take on the whole numbers 1 to 9.

Appendix B can also be used to help interpret any transformed standard score. Simply convert it back to a z-score using the following:

$$z = \frac{X - M}{SD}$$

where X is the transformed standard score, M is the mean of the transformed distribution and SD is the standard deviation of the transformed distribution.

Most popular achievement test batteries use an *expanded standard score* to interrelate different levels of tests. The standard deviation is kept at approximately 10 for any given level, and the means are allowed to progress from level to level.

Ranks assign 1 to the best score, 2 to the next best, and so on. A percentile rank specifies the percentage of scores which are lower than a given score. Percentiles allow for a direct statement of the percent of persons in the norm group who score lower than a given score. This feature makes percentiles useful in presenting test data to parents. However, percentiles can be misinterpreted when used to evaluate gains or compare different students. Percentiles tend to exaggerate differences near the mean and undervalue differences near the ends of a distribution.

Grade-equivalent scores assign scale scores on the basis of the average raw score earned by a group at a given grade. A similar procedure is followed to develop age-equivalent scores. Interpreting *changes* in grade-equivalent scores can be deceptive. Some skills may develop rapidly in the early grades and then level off, so that a change in grade-norm from fourth to eighth grade might represent very little learning. Knowledge of the relation of grade-equivalents and expanded standard scores can alert one to the problem areas. There is also a problem in the meaning of grade-equivalence. A second grader with a grade-equivalent score of 6.5 cannot necessarily do sixth-grade work. He doesn't even take the sixth-grade test. He can do second-grade work as well as the average sixth grader is estimated to do second-grade work.

Norm-referenced scores are based on the performance of some norm population on the test. The norm population provides a frame of reference for score interpretation. An obtained score is high or low *in relation to* a specified norm group, such as, all *second graders in the United States*. The major achievement batteries provide norms based on a representative national sample. Tests using norms from different samples are not likely to produce the same result because of norm sample differences and test differences. However, the Anchor Test Study suggests that for reading at grades 4, 5, and 6, these differences are not very great. The study also provides a basis for comparing groups tested with different achievement tests.

Local norms and norms based on students "like yours" are desirable when using norm-referenced tests to evaluate program effectiveness.

In the last section of this unit, practice was provided in using norm tables to convert raw scores to norm-referenced scores.

Answers to in-lesson exercises

Page 176

z-Score	Percent Above	Percent Below
0	50.00	50.00
+1.00	15.87	84.13
+2.00	2.28	97.72
+3.00	.13	99.87
−1.00	84.13	15.87
−2.00	97.72	2.28
−3.00	99.87	.13
−1.20	88.50	11.50
−2.60	99.50	.50
+1.25	10.60	89.40
+ .75	22.70	77.30

Page 176

z-Scores	Percent of Cases Between
−1.0 to +1.0	68.26
−2.0 to +2.0	95.44
−3.0 to +3.0	99.74

Page 179

IQ of 80 + z-score	− 1.33
Percent below z	9.18
Percent above z	90.82

Page 180

Score	Rank	Score	Rank
4	8.5	4	8.5
7	4	10	1
9	2	3	10
6	6	7	4
7	4	5	7

Page 181–182 *Practice Problems*

1

Rank	Percentile
12	94
37	82 (or 81)

2

z-Score	Percentile
+1.30	90
+ .30	62

Gain in percentiles = *28*

3

z-Score	Percentile
+1	84
+2	98
+3	100

Page 186

	Raw Score	Grade Equivalent
Math—Computation	39	3.1
Math—Concepts and Problems	31	1.9
Math—Total Score	70	2.4
Language—Mechanics	9	1.2
Language—Spelling	14	3.0

Page 190

	Raw Score	Percentile	Stanine
Reading Total	70	54	5
Math—Computation	13	31	4

	Raw Score	Expanded Score	
Language—Usage and Structure	11	54	5
Total Battery	211	90	8
Total Battery	135	36	4

Page 190

	Raw Score	Expanded Score
Form F, Word Knowledge	20	50
Form G, Spelling	15	51
Form H, Total Mathematics	35	39

self-test

1 percentage

2 34%

3 multiplied; added

4 100

5 20; 80

6 z-score

7 lower

8 average

1 The normal distribution provides a practical basis for interpreting standard scores in terms of the _____ of persons likely to have higher or lower scores.

2 The percent of cases falling between the mean and one standard deviation is _____ .

3 To produce transformed standard scores, z-scores are _____ by the desired standard deviation of the new distribution, and the mean desired for the new distribution is _____ to each score.

4 IQ's are transformed standard scores with a mean of _____ and a standard deviation usually of 15.

5 Since most scores in a normal distribution fall between plus and minus three standard deviation units, if the mean of a transformed distribution is 50 and the standard deviation is 10, most scores would fall between _____ and _____ .

6 It is possible to use appendix B to help interpret any transformed standard score if you first convert it back to a _____ .

7 A percentile rank specifies the percentage of scores which are _____ than a given score.

8 Grade-equivalent scores assign scale scores on the basis of the _____ raw score earned by a group of a given grade.

NUMBER RIGHT _____

exercise 1 programed practice

1   The normal distribution provides a practical basis for interpreting standard scores in terms of the _____ of persons likely to have higher or lower scores.

2   The normal distribution can be thought of as a smoothed frequency distribution generated by making the score intervals very, very _____ .

3   The area under the normal curve can be divided into _____ which sum to one.

4   The proportion of area between any two points on the curve gives the _____ _____ of persons falling between those two points.

5   Multiplying by 100, these proportions become _____ .

6   A convenient approximation for remembering the percent of cases covered by standard deviation units is this:

Mean to 1 SD = _____

1 SD to 2 SDs = _____

2 SDs to 3 SDs = _____

Mean to 2 SDs = _____

Mean to 3 SDs = _____

7   Appendix B gives the percentage of cases falling above or below any given _____ deviation unit, assuming a normal distribution.

8   To use appendix table B, simply express a given score in _____ form.

9   Appendix B can also be used to find the percentage of cases falling in _____ any two z-scores.

10   Transformed standard scores are desirable because they eliminate _____ scores and decimal parts.

11   To produce transformed standard scores, the z-scores are _____ by the desired standard deviation of the new distribution and the mean desired for the new distribution is _____ to each score.

12   IQ's are _____ standard scores with a mean of 100 and a standard deviation usually of 15.

---

1 percentage

2 small

3 portions

4 relative frequency

5 percentages

6 34%; 14%; 2%; 48%; 50%

7 standard

8 z-score

9 between

10 negative

11 multiplied; added

12 transformed

13 500; 100

14 5; 2

15 20; 80

16 z-score

17 expanded;
   progress

18 parents

19 percentage

20 lower

21 compare;
   exaggerate;
   undervalue

22 average

23 over-lapping

13 The College Board Examination and the Graduate Record Examination use transformed standard scores with a mean of _____ and a standard deviation of _____ .

14 Stanines are standard nines; they are transformed standard scores with a mean of _____ and a standard deviation of _____ .

15 Since most scores in a normal distribution fall between plus and minus three standard deviation units, if the mean of a transformed distribution is 50 and the standard deviation is 10, most scores would fall between _____ and _____ .

16 It is possible to use appendix B to help interpret any transformed standard score if you first convert it back to a _____ .

17 Most popular achievement test batteries use _____ standard scores to interrelate different levels of tests. The standard deviation is kept at approximately 10 for any given level, and the means are allowed to _____ from level to level.

18 Percentile ranks are often used to interpret test scores to _____ and others, because they are a little easier to interpret directly than are standard scores.

19 With percentile ranks, it is unnecessary to convert standard scores to a _____ statement.

20 A percentile rank specifies the percentage of scores which are _____ than a given score.

21 Percentiles can be misinterpreted when used to evaluate gains or _____ different students. Percentiles tend to _____ differences near the mean and _____ differences near the ends of a distribution.

22 Grade-equivalent scores assign scale scores on the basis of the _____ raw score earned by a group of a given grade.

23 In constructing an achievement test battery, one test cannot be given to all students, so _____ testing is used to permit a tying together of different levels of a test battery.

24 Interpreting _____ in grade-equivalent scores can be deceptive. Some skills may develop rapidly in the early grades and then level off, so that a change in grade-norm from 4.0 to 8.0 might represent very _____ learning.

25 When a second grader gets a grade-equivalent score of 6.0, this means that the second-grade student can do second-grade work as well as the average sixth grader is estimated to be able to do _____ grade work.

26 A norm population provides the test user with a frame of _____ for score interpretation.

27 The major achievement batteries provide norms based on a _____ national sample of students. An attempt is made to construct a sample that will match _____ figures for the United States in terms of its representation.

28 Tests using norms from different samples are not likely to produce the same result because of norm sample _____ and test differences. However, the _____ Test Study suggests that for reading at grades 4, 5, and 6, these differences are not very great.

29 Keep in mind that grade norms are based on the average performance of a group of students at a given grade level. That means if your class average is at grade level, 50 percent of the children will be _____ this grade level and 50 percent will be _____ .

30 The way grade equivalents are constructed, each _____ is equal to a month in school. The school year is divided into nine months and one month is counted for the _____ .

24 changes; little

25 second

26 reference

27 representative; census

28 differences; Anchor

29 below; above

30 tenth; summer

exercise 2 transformations

1 A student has an IQ of 130 on a test where the mean is 100 and the SD is 15. What percentage of students might be expected to get higher scores? _____ . What is this student's percentile rank? _____ .

2 You obtain a score of 650 on the quantitative part of the Graduate Record exam. What percent of students are likely to receive scores lower than you? _____ .

3 A student receives a T-score of 42 on an achievement test. What is his percentile rank? _____ .

4 What percent of a set of normally distributed scores would you expect to receive a stanine of 5? _____ .

5 If a student showed a percentile gain from 25 to 50, pretest to posttest, what would be the gain in z-score units? _____ .

6 If a student showed a percentile gain from 5 to 25, what would be the gain in z-score units? _____ .

7 If IQ's were truly normally distributed, what percent of population would you expect to have IQ's below 25? (severely retarded) Assume the mean is 100 and the SD is 15 for the IQ scores. _____ .

8 Transform the following z-scores to a distribution where the mean is 50 and the SD is 10: −1.35, .75, 2.10. _____ _____ _____ .

9 Transform the same z-scores (in 8 above) to a distribution where the mean is 100 and the SD is 15. _____ _____ _____ .

10 Convert these IQ's (M = 100, SD = 15) to T-scores: 100, 115, 70, 145.

_____ _____ _____ .

Answers for Exercise 2

1 IQ is 130. This is equivalent to a z of $\frac{130\text{-}100}{15}$ = 2.00. A z higher than 2.00 is found 2.28% of the cases. The percentile rank is *98*.

2 GRE is 650. This is equivalent to a z of $\frac{650\text{-}500}{100}$ = 1.50. A z lower than 1.50 is found in 93.32% of the cases.

3 T-score is 42. This is equivalent to a z of $\frac{42\text{-}50}{10}$ = −.8. A z-score lower than this is found in 21.19% of the cases. The percentile rank is *21*.

4 *20%* (figure 10.2) or compute percent between ± .25% z-scores.

5 The 25th percentile corresponds to a z-score of −.67. (Use appendix B and start with percent lower column.) The 50th percentile corresponds to a z-score of 0. Thus, the gain is *.67* z-score units.

6 The 25th percentile corresponds to a z-score of −.67. The fifth percentile corresponds to a z-score of −1.65. The gain is *.98* z-score units.

7 $\dfrac{25-100}{15} = \dfrac{-75}{15} = -5.0$ z-score units. A z-score of -5.0 is extremely improbable in a normal distribution. Actually the IQ distribution shows a small hump at the lower end which appears to be due to genetic, traumatic, and infectious accidents.

8   36.50   57.5   71.0

9   79.75   111.25   131.50

10   Convert first to z-scores than back to T-scores.
      50   60   30   80

discussion questions

1 Why is the normal distribution useful in interpreting norm-referenced test scores?

2 What percentage of the cases (approximately) falls between the following standard score units on the normal curve? 0 to 1 SD, 1 SD to 2 SDs, 2 SDs to 3 SDs, 0 to 2 SDs, 0 to 3 SDs.

3 What are z-scores?

4 What is a transformed standard score and how is the transformation accomplished?

5 Give three examples of transformed standard scores.

6 How wide is the band covered by a stanine unit in z-score units?

7 How is appendix B used to interpret transformed standard scores?

8 What is an expanded standard score?

9 How can one interpret the fact that on the Metropolitan, for reading and math, the mean expanded standard score progresses less and less each year (table 10.2)?

10 How do you rank order a set of scores?

11 What are percentile ranks (percentile, centiles)?

12 Why are percentiles useful?

13 What problems arise in interpreting gain scores, or difference scores when expressed as percentiles? Give an example.

14 How are age- and grade-equivalent scores determined?

15 Suppose a fifth grader obtains a grade-equivalent score of 9.3 grades. What does this mean?

16 On the MAT, would a grade-equivalent gain in reading going from 2.0 to 4.0 be as much of a gain as going from 6.0 to 8.0? Explain your answer.

17 What is a norm population?

18 How are norm groups determined in standardizing the major achievement test batteries?

19 What was found in the Anchor Test Study?

20 How do you interpret a grade-equivalent score of 5.6?

unit 11

Interpreting Correlations

objectives

When you complete this unit you should be able to—

1 State what a joint-frequency distribution (or scatter diagram) is and display data in that form.

2 Relate a scatter diagram to a four-fold table.

3 Draw scatter plots and four-fold tables to illustrate positive, negative, and zero correlations.

4 Explain how correlations are useful in prediction.

5 Judge the size of a correlation (relatively) from its scatter plot.

6 Define the Pearson correlation coefficient in z-score terms.

7 Compute the Pearson correlation coefficient from z-scores or from raw scores, given the formula.

8 Explain why r takes on positive or negative values in terms of the positive and negative products being summed.

9 Relate the slope of a best-fit prediction line to r.

10 State what the biserial correlation and four-fold point correlations might be used for in test construction.

lesson

The concept of correlation provides the key to understanding how normative tests are built. The concept of correlation underlies the procedures for selecting items in constructing a test and for evaluating tests for their reliability and validity.

The term correlation is made up of the terms *co* and *relation*. A correlation is an index of the degree of relationship between two variables. A correlation is a co-relationship. Let us first look at correlations as expressed in fourfold tables.

Correlations in Four-Fold Tables

Suppose we give a spelling test to a class. The test contains two words, *during* and *caution*. The results are as follows:

Student	during	caution
1	+	+
2	−	−
3	−	+
4	+	+
5	−	−
6	+	−
7	−	−
8	+	+
9	−	−
10	+	+
11	+	+
12	−	−

One question that might interest the teacher is, "How does the performance on *during* relate to the performance on *caution*?" Do students who do well on the first word do well on the second? Actually, this turns out to be the same kind of question we asked in unit 4, in trying to determine if different criterion-referenced test items were measuring the same thing. In unit 4, we suggested that a *percent agreement* index could be used to answer the question. The agreements in outcome (+ + and − − patterns) were divided by the number of students (N) to get a percent agreement index. For the performances on the two spelling words *caution* and *during*, the index shows 83 percent agreement. Another way of looking at the spelling data in a four-fold table is this:

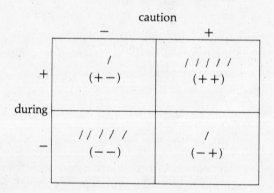

Student 1 passed both words, so a mark is placed in the top right quadrant; student 2 failed both, so a mark for him is placed in the lower left quadrant; student 3 failed *during* and passed *caution* so a mark is placed in the lower right quadrant, and so on. When most of the cases fall in the + + and − − quadrants, as in this example, it implies a high *positive* correlation.

Now consider the following two possible outcomes:

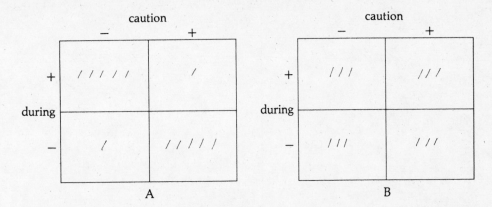

In example A, most of the students fall in the + − and − + quadrants. This is an example of a high *negative* relation. In example A, if students passed *during*, they tended to fail *caution*, and if they failed *during*, they tended to pass *caution*. When there is a positive correlation between two measures, a high score on one measure goes with a high score on the other. When there is a negative correlation, a high score on one measure goes with a low score on the other.

Example B shows no correlation between the outcomes for *during* and *caution*. Half the students who pass *during* pass *caution*, and half fail *caution*. Half the students who fail *during* pass *caution* and half fail. It is possible for two measures to be correlated positively, negatively, or to have no correlation. Positive and negative correlations can vary in degree.

The Joint Frequency Distribution

Now, let us consider the case where the scores on two measures are not simply pass-fail, but can vary over a range of possibilities. Suppose the two measures are IQ and grade-point average (GPA).

Student	IQ	GPA
One	125	3.8
Two	100	2.5
Three	88	2.0
Four	115	3.0
Five	95	2.3
Six	120	3.5
Seven	90	2.3
Eight	130	4.0
Nine	110	2.8
Ten	105	2.6

We can plot these scores on a joint-frequency distribution (or scatter diagram) as shown in figure 11.1.

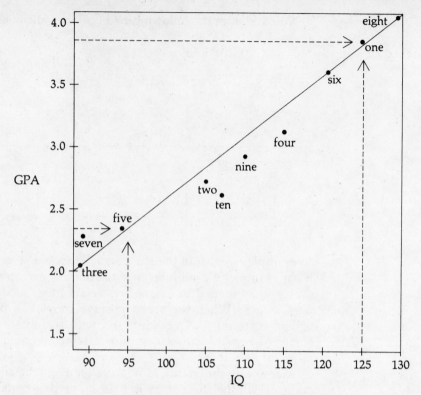

Figure 11.1 A Joint Frequency Distribution (The numbers written out on the graph above are student identification numbers)

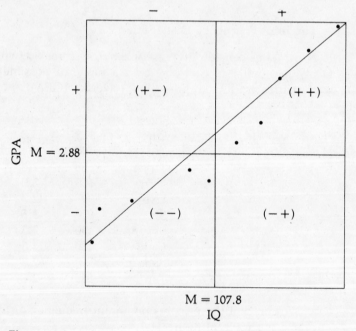

Figure 11.2 A Joint Frequency Distribution Divided Into Quadrants

Student One scored 125 on the IQ test and had a 3.8 grade-point average. A dot is made to represent him where 125 and 3.8 intersect on the graph. Similarly, Student Five had an IQ of 95 and a GPA of 2.3. A dot to represent him is made at the intersection of 95 and 2.3. Usually, in making a joint frequency distribution we do not include student numbers as was done in figure 11.1. We did it to show explicitly how each dot got where it is. Drawing a line through the dots helps to show the relationship. These data show that the higher the IQ, the higher the GPA, and vice versa. They show a high positive correlation.

Now, consider figure 11.2. This figure is the same as 11.1 except that we have eliminated the student numbers and drawn in a line at the mean for each measure. We will call scores above the mean +'s, and those below the mean −'s. Suppose we count how many students fall into each of the four quadrants produced by the lines through the means. The results would look as follows:

IQ

		−	+
+		0	5
GPA			
−		5	0

Thus, the four-fold tables we first used to illustrate positive, negative, and zero relations can be seen to be special cases of joint frequency distributions where the scores were forced into only two categories.

Consider each of the following scatter diagrams. Decide whether each one represents a high positive correlation, a medium positive correlation, a zero correlation, a medium negative correlation, or a high negative correlation. Record your answers and check them on page 214.

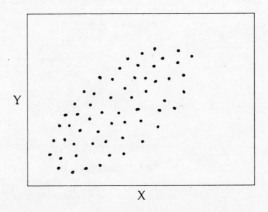

Y

X

1 This represents: (check)

If a or b was checked, check one of the following:

a. _____ positive correlation

b. _____ negative correlation

c. _____ zero correlation

d. _____ it is a high correlation

e. _____ it is a medium correlation

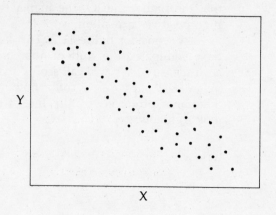

2 This represents: (check)

If a or b was checked, check one of the following:

a. _____ positive correlation

b. _____ negative correlation

c. _____ zero correlation

d. _____ it is a high correlation

e. _____ it is a medium correlation

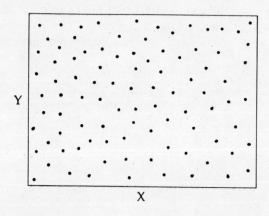

3 This represents: (check)

If a or b was checked, check one of the following:

a. _____ positive correlation

b. _____ negative correlation

c. _____ zero correlation

d. _____ it is a high correlation

e. _____ it is a medium correlation

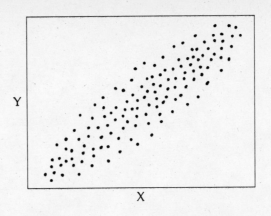

4 This represents: (check)

a. _____ positive correlation
b. _____ negative correlation
c. _____ zero correlation

If a or b was checked, check one of the following:

d. _____ it is a high correlation
e. _____ it is a medium correlation

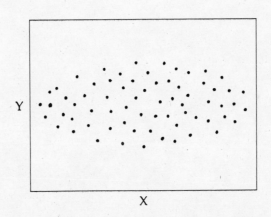

5 This represents: (check)

a. _____ positive correlation
b. _____ negative correlation
c. _____ zero correlation

If a or b was checked, check one of the following:

d. _____ it is a high correlation
e. _____ it is a medium correlation

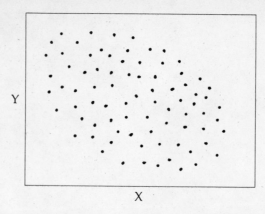

6 This represents: (check)

a. _____ positive correlation

b. _____ negative correlation

c. _____ zero correlation

If a or b was checked, check one of the following:

d. _____ it is a high correlation

e. _____ it is a medium correlation

Predictability

Another way of thinking about a correlation is in terms of the degree to which you can predict one variable from another. Suppose the relationship between IQ and GPA for a given school is as follows:

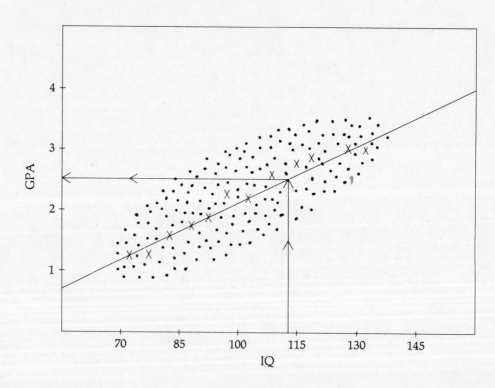

The X's represent the mean GPA for each grouping of 5 IQ points. For example, the first X on the left is the average GPA for all students with IQ's from 70 to 74. It is the mean of the scores in that vertical column. The sloping line which runs approximately through the X's is a best-fit line to the averages represented by the X's. If we know a person's IQ to be 114, we can predict his GPA by proceeding vertically from 114 to the sloping line and from there going horizontally to 2.50. This gives the predicted GPA for an IQ of 114. An important point to note is that the higher the correlation, the better the prediction. The more the data scatter away from the best-fit prediction line, the more error is likely in the prediction. In looking at a scatter plot, it is useful to think of the length of the scatter along the best-fit prediction line in relation to the average scatter from this line. High correlations have small scatter relative to the length of the best-fit prediction line when both measures are expressed in standard deviation units. For low correlations, the length of the average scatter approximates the length of the best-fit prediction line. For example:

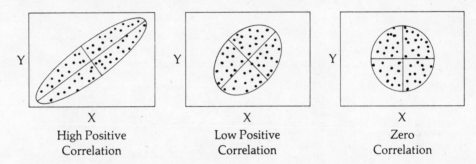

| High Positive Correlation | Low Positive Correlation | Zero Correlation |

The size of a correlation is also directly related to the slope of the prediction line when both variables are expressed in standard deviation units (z-scores). As the slope approaches 45 degrees, the correlation increases to its maximum value of 1. As the slope approaches zero, the correlation approaches zero. Correlations are often used in predicting future performances based on current performances. In the example given, IQ was used to predict GPA. A battery of tests is used by the Air Force to predict success in flight training. Predictive validity is an important property of tests which the correlation coefficient helps us to summarize. This topic is discussed further in the next unit.

The Pearson Correlation Coefficient

So far we have talked about correlations in terms of four-fold tables and the shape of joint-frequency distributions or scatter plots. Most of the basic understandings required for interpreting correlations can be derived from such analysis. However, a more technical understanding of measures of correlation is useful in understanding the basic tenets of normative test theory.

The most frequently used index of the degree of relation between two variables is the Pearson correlation coefficient which has been given the symbol r. Karl Pearson, an English statistician, invented r. The Pearson r is defined as:

$$r = \frac{\text{Sum } z_X \cdot z_Y}{N}$$

This formula can be interpreted as follows: Given a set of scores on two variables (X and Y) for N persons, r is obtained by multiplying each z_X times its pairmate z_Y, summing these products, and then averaging them by dividing by the number of cases (N). Thus, r is the mean of the z-score products. The Pearson r can take on values from +1 to −1. A +1 correlation is a perfect positive correlation. A −1 correlation is a perfect negative correlation. A zero correlation indicates no relationship.

Computing r from z-Scores

Table 11.1 shows the computation of r using z-scores. X and Y stand for raw scores on two variables.

TABLE 11.1   COMPUTATION OF r USING z-SCORES

X	Y	z_X	z_Y	$z_X z_Y$
30	15	1.65	1.70	2.8050
27	13	1.23	1.21	1.4883
24	12	.82	.97	.7954
21	8	.41	.00	.0000
20	9	.27	.24	.0648
16	7	− .27	− .24	.0648
14	6	− .55	− .49	.2695
12	5	− .82	− .73	.5986
9	4	−1.23	− .97	1.1931
7	1	−1.51	−1.70	2.5670

$M_X = 18$ $M_Y = 8$ Sum $z_X \cdot z_Y = 9.8465$

$SD_X = 7.29$ $SD_Y = 4.12$

$$r = \frac{\text{Sum } z_X z_Y}{N} = \frac{9.8465}{10} = .98$$

The mean and the standard deviation of X and Y are computed first so that z-scores can be computed. Then r is computed as the mean of the products of z_x and z_y. The r for the variables in table 11.1 is .98. This is a very high positive correlation. Figures 11.3 and 11.4 show scatter diagrams for the data in table 11.1. Figure 11.3 plots the raw scores and figure 11.4 plots the z-scores. The raw score scatter plot confirms that the relationship is very high and positive. The z-score scatter plot shows that all of the scores fall in the + + and − − quadrants. This is often the case for a high positive correlation. Two positives multiplied together make a positive, and two negatives multiplied together make a positive. So, when most scores fall in the + + and − − quadrant, a positive sum is produced. When most scores fall

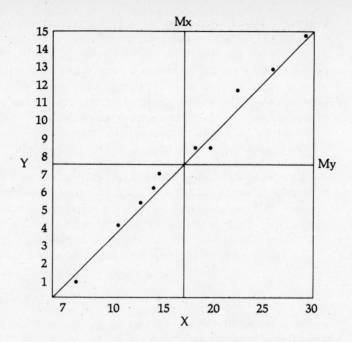

Figure 11.3 Raw Score Scatter Plot of Data From Table 11.1

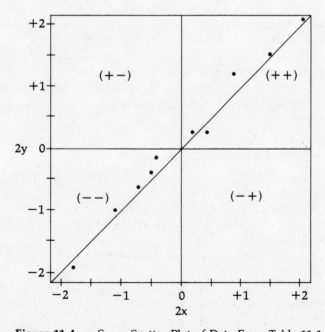

Figure 11.4 z-Score Scatter Plot of Data From Table 11.1

in the + − and − + quadrants, negative products are produced leading to a negative correlation. Finally, if some of the scores fall in quadrants that produce positive products and some in the quadrants that produce negative products, they would cancel each other out and produce a low or zero correlation. This analysis should provide an understanding of how the correlation coefficient, in ranging from +1 to −1, can provide a summary statement of a relationship shown by a scatter diagram.

Computing r from Raw Scores

We first presented the calculation of r from z-scores to show clearly that *r is an average*. Using z-scores also made it easier to show the quadrants which produce positive products (+ +, − −) and those which produce negative products (+ −, − +) to clarify how correlations take on positive and negative values. Using z-scores, however, is not the easiest way to compute r.

The Pearson r is usually best computed directly from raw scores as follows:

$$r = \frac{N\Sigma XY - (\Sigma X) \cdot (\Sigma Y)}{\sqrt{N\Sigma X^2 - (\Sigma X)^2} \ \sqrt{N\Sigma Y^2 - (\Sigma Y)^2}}$$

In this formula, the symbol Σ stands for *sum* of the cases. To compute r we need the following terms:

(1) ΣX
(2) ΣX^2
(3) ΣY
(4) ΣY^2
(5) ΣXY

With many mechanical calculators, it is possible to put an X score in on one side of the keyboard, a Y score on the other, push a squaring operator, and obtain all five sums at the same time. Sum X and Y come out in the upper dial, Sum X^2 and Y^2 come out in the lower dial, and *two* times Sum XY comes out in the middle of the lower dial.

Compute the correlation for the data in table 11.2 by hand using the raw score formula above and appendix A to find squares and square roots. Check your answer on page 214.

TABLE 11.2 COMPUTATION OF r

Student	X	Y
One	1	9
Two	2	7
Three	4	6
Four	6	4
Five	7	2
Six	7	3
Seven	5	4
Eight	3	9
Nine	1	7
Ten	5	5

(1) ΣX = _____
(2) ΣX^2 = _____
(3) ΣY = _____
(4) ΣX^2 = _____
(5) ΣXY = _____

N = <u>10</u>

r = _____

Other Kinds of Correlation Coefficients

Two other kinds of correlation coefficients are of interest in test development. The *biserial correlation* provides a procedure for computing a correlation between a pass-fail item and some continuous variable such as the total score on a test. The *four-fold point correlation* gives a useful measure of association when correlating two pass-fail items with each other (as in our earlier example on *during* and *caution*). The classroom teacher need not be concerned with how these correlations are computed. However, it is important to realize that measures of association can be computed for dichotomous (pass-fail) variables. These measures are often used in item analysis.

summary

The concept of correlation is important for understanding how norm-referenced tests are constructed and evaluated. In a four-fold table, a high positive correlation exists when most of the cases fall in the $++$ and $--$ quadrants. A high negative correlation exists when most of the cases fall in the $-+$ and $+-$ quadrants. No correlation exists when the cases are equally distributed throughout the four quadrants.

When there is a range of scores for two different measures we can plot these scores on a joint-frequency distribution or scatter diagram. It is possible to judge the nature of the correlation from the shape of the scatter diagram. In a high correlation, the data points tend to fall along a line. If the correlation is positive, this line slopes from the bottom left to the top right quadrant. If the correlation is negative, this line slopes from the bottom right to the top left quadrant. Low or zero correlations have scatter plots where the data points spread all over.

The most important index of the degree of relation between two variables is the Pearson correlation coefficient or r. Starting with z-scores, the Pearson r is obtained by multiplying each z_X by its pairmate z_Y, summing these products, and taking the average by dividing by N.

$$r = \frac{\text{Sum } z_X \cdot z_Y}{N}$$

When computing r from raw scores the formula is:

$$r = \frac{N\Sigma XY - (\Sigma X) \cdot (\Sigma Y)}{\sqrt{N\Sigma X^2 - (\Sigma X)^2} \ \sqrt{N\Sigma Y^2 - (\Sigma Y)^2}}$$

The symbol Σ in this formula stands for *sum* of the cases.

When the properties of r are examined in z-score form, it is easier to see what it means when r takes on positive and negative values. The Pearson r is positive when more cases fall in the quadrants which produce positive products ($++$ and $--$), and r is negative when more of the cases fall in the quadrants which produce negative products ($-+$ and $+-$). The Pearson r can take on values from +1 to −1. A correlation of +1 is a perfect positive correlation. A correlation of −1 is a perfect negative correlation. A zero correlation indicates that two measures are unrelated.

Measures of association can also be computed with dichotomous variables, although the details of how it is done are not important here.

Answers to In-Lesson Exercises

Pages 205–208
1. a, e
2. b, d
3. c
4. a, d
5. c
6. b, e

Correlation Computation Problem on page 212.

X	Y	X²	Y²	XY
1	9	1	81	9
2	7	4	49	14
4	6	16	36	24
6	4	36	16	24
7	2	49	4	14
7	3	49	9	21
5	4	25	16	20
3	9	9	81	27
1	7	1	49	7
5	5	25	25	25
$\Sigma X = 41$	$\Sigma Y = 56$	$\Sigma X^2 = 215$	$\Sigma Y^2 = 366$	$\Sigma XY = 185$ N = 10

$$r = \frac{10 \cdot 185 - (41) \cdot (56)}{\sqrt{10 \cdot 215 - (41)^2} \ \sqrt{10 \cdot 366 - (56)^2}} = \frac{-446}{\sqrt{469} \ \sqrt{524}}$$

$$r = \frac{-446}{21.66 \cdot 22.89} = -\frac{446}{496} = -.899 \text{ or } -.90$$

self-test

1 A correlation is an index of the degree of _____ between two variables.

2 The scores on two tests or measures can be plotted on a joint-frequency distribution (or _____ diagram).

3 In a four-fold table, a positive correlation is indicated by more cases in the lower-left and _____-_____ quadrants.

4 In a scatter-diagram, a _____ correlation is indicated by a spread of data points equally throughout the four quadrants.

5 Another way of thinking about a correlation is in terms of the degree to which you can _____ one variable from another.

6 The size of a correlation is also directly related to the _____ of the prediction line when both variables are expressed in standard deviation units (z-scores). As the slope approaches 45 degrees, the correlation increases to its maximum value of _____ . As the slope approaches zero, the correlation approaches _____ .

7 The Pearson r is the mean of the _____ score products.

8 In the formula for computing r, the symbol Σ stands for _____ of the cases.

NUMBER RIGHT _____

1 relationship

2 scatter

3 upper-right

4 zero

5 predict

6 slope; 1; zero

7 z-

8 sum

exercise 1 programed practice

1 A correlation is an index of the degree of _____ between two variables.

2 It is possible for two measures to be correlated positively, _____ , or to have no correlation. Positive and negative correlations can vary in _____ .

3 The scores on two tests or measures can be plotted on a joint-frequency distribution (or _____ diagram).

4 Four-fold tables are special cases of _____ frequency distributions where the scores are forced into only two categories.

1 relationship

2 negatively; degree

3 scatter

4 joint

5 In a four-fold table, a positive correlation is indicated by more cases in the lower left and _____-_____ quadrants.

6 In a scatter diagram, a positive correlation is indicated by a trend for the data points to fall along a _____ going from the lower-left corner to the upper-right corner.

5 upper-right

7 The higher the correlation, the more the data points tend to form a _____ _____ .

6 line

8 In a scatter-diagram, a _____ correlation is indicated by a spread of data points equally throughout the four quadrants.

7 straight line

9 Another way of thinking about a correlation is in terms of the degree to which you can _____ one variable from another.

8 zero

10 The higher the correlation, the _____ the prediction. The more the data scatter away from the "best fit" prediction line, the more _____ is likely in the prediction.

9 predict

11 The size of a correlation is also directly related to the _____ of the prediction line when both variables are expressed in standard deviation units (z-scores). As the slope approaches 45 degrees, the correlation increases to its maximum value of _____ . As the slope approaches zero, the correlation approaches _____ .

10 better; error

12 The most frequently used index of the degree of relation between two variables is the _____ coefficient which has been given the symbol _____ .

11 slope; 1; zero

12 Pearson; r

13 The Pearson r is the mean of the _____ score products.

14 When most scores fall in the + + and − − quadrant, a _____ sum is produced. When most scores fall in the + − and − + quadrants, _____ products are produced leading to a negative correlation.

13 z-

15 If some of the scores fall in quadrants that produce positive products and some in the quadrants that produce negative products, they would _____ each other out and produce a _____ correlation.

14 positive; negative

16 In the formula for computing r, the symbol Σ stands for _____ of the cases.

15 cancel; low, zero

17 Measures of association can also be computed for dichotomous (_____-_____) variables.

16 sum

17 pass-fail

exercise 2   computational practice

1   Plot the data from table 11.2 on the graph below.

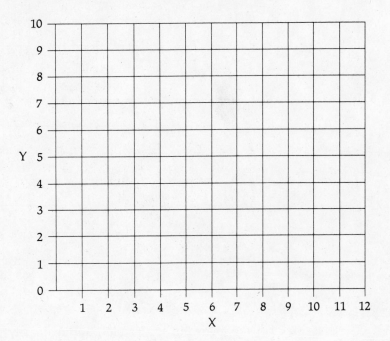

2   Compute r for the following data from raw scores using appendix A for squares and square roots.

Students	X	Y
One	5	5
Two	1	10
Three	9	3
Four	4	6
Five	7	2
Six	6	4
Seven	9	9
Eight	1	6
Nine	7	7
Ten	4	9

(1) ΣX = _____

(2) ΣX^2 = _____

(3) ΣY = _____

(4) ΣY^2 = _____

(5) ΣXY = _____

N = __10__

r = _____

3 Plot the data from problem 2 on the graph below.

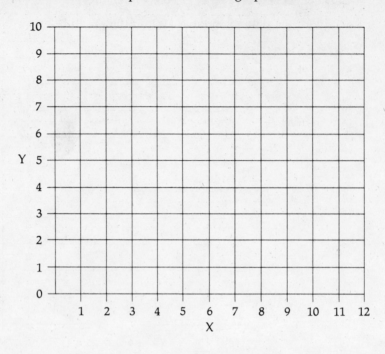

4 For the following scatter plot, approximately what Y value would you predict for a person whose X value is 25?

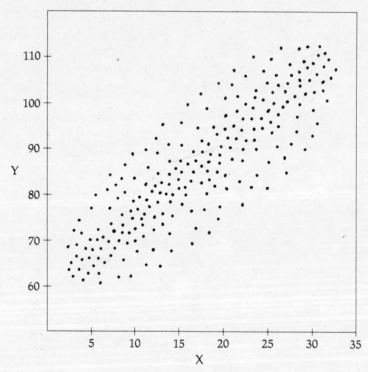

Answers for Exercise 2

1

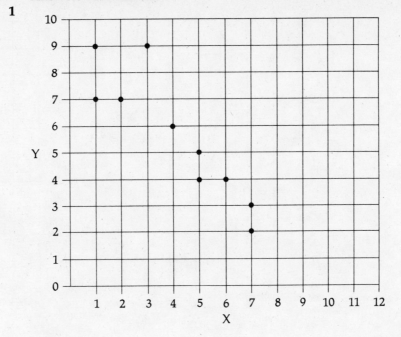

2

Students	X	Y
One	5	5
Two	1	10
Three	9	3
Four	4	6
Five	7	2
Six	6	4
Seven	9	9
Eight	1	6
Nine	7	7
Ten	4	9

(1) $\Sigma X = 53$
(2) $\Sigma X^2 = 355$
(3) $\Sigma Y = 61$
(4) $\Sigma Y^2 = 437$
(5) $\Sigma XY = 296$
        $N = 10$

$$r = \frac{10 \times 296 - 53 \times 61}{\sqrt{10 \times 355 - 53^2} \ \sqrt{10 \times 437 - 61^2}}$$

$$r = \frac{-273}{\sqrt{741} \ \sqrt{649}} = \frac{-273}{693.6} = -.39$$

3

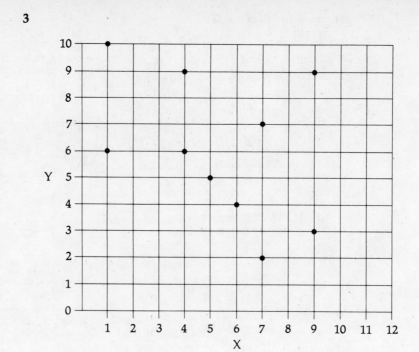

4

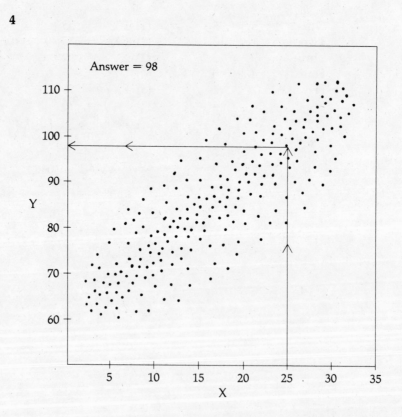

discussion questions

1   Be prepared to fill in the headings and entries on three four-fold tables to show a positive correlation, a negative correlation, and a zero correlation. Label each quadrant as $++$, $--$, $-+$, $+-$.

2   What is a joint-frequency distribution?

3   What is another name for a joint-frequency distribution?

4   How can a scatter plot be related to a four-fold table?

5   Draw scatter plots to illustrate each of the following:
     a. a high positive correlation.
     b. a high negative correlation.
     c. a medium positive correlation.
     d. a medium negative correlation.
     e. a zero correlation.

6   What do correlations have to do with predictability?

7   In looking at a scatter plot, how does the length of the best-fit prediction line, relative to the scatter from this line, relate to the size of a correlation?

8   When both variables are in z-score units, how does the slope of the best-fit prediction line relate to the size of the correlation?

9   State exactly what kind of an average a Pearson r is.

10   What values can r take on?

11   Explain why r must be positive if most of the data points fall in the lower-left and upper-right quadrants of a scatter plot.

12   In analyzing items for test construction, we often are dealing with a dichotomous (pass-fail) score rather than a continuous variable as is necessary to compute r. How is this problem handled?

unit 12

Test Theory as It Applies to Achievement Tests

objectives

When you complete this unit you should be able to —

1 State the basic procedure for determining the reliability of a test and describe three kinds of reliability coefficients.

2 Define three kinds of validity a test might have.

3 Define these terms: variance, standard error of measurement, and confidence interval.

4 Explain reliability in terms of error variance, true-score variance, and obtained-score variance.

5 Provide a guide for interpreting the size of a reliability coefficient and interpreting the size of a criterion-oriented validity coefficient.

6 Explain why norm-referenced achievement tests cannot be universally valid.

7 State in general terms the relation between test length and reliability.

8 Compute the confidence interval for a test score.

9 Explain how reliability affects validity.

10 State three principles central to item analysis in achievement test construction.

11 Explain why the procedures used to determine sensitivity to instruction in constructing achievement tests may be inadequate.

12 Explain how the criterion of item discriminability may bias what a test is measuring toward a measure of intelligence and language competence.

13 Suggest two ways in which the validity of norm-referenced achievement tests, as measures of the effects of school instruction, might be improved.

lesson

Test theory is concerned with principles for maximizing the reliability and validity of norm-referenced tests. Through an understanding of a few principles underlying the construction of norm-referenced achievement tests, wiser decisions can be made in evaluating and using such tests.

Test theory begins with any test score, X, and partitions this score into two parts, $T + E$.[1] T represents that part of X attributable to the *true score* on the test, and E represents that part of X attributable to *error*. To make a test reliable, the test constructor tries to reduce the contribution of E to the total score X. To make a test valid, the test constructor tries to show that the reliable part of the test (T) is measuring what it is suppose to measure. This is done through logical analysis of test items and through correlating test scores (or items) with various criteria of validity.

One further concept is needed before we can proceed. This is the concept of *variance*. The variance of a set of test scores is simply the square of the standard deviation of those scores. Variance is a measure of the spread of scores from the mean of a distribution. If the standard deviation is 6, the variance is 36. If the standard deviation is 3, the variance is 9. Much of statistical theory and test theory deals with variances, since *variances can be added* when dealing with uncorrelated variables. Hypothetical (T) true scores and error scores (E) on a test are uncorrelated, so their variances can be added to obtain a total score (X). This relationship provides the basis for some interesting derivations in test theory. We will use the symbol SD^2 (standard deviation squared) to refer to a variance. The Greek symbol sigma (σ) when squared (σ^2) is usually used to refer to a variance in books on statistics and test theory.

Test Reliability

The error in a measurement can be estimated by making a number of independent measurements of the same thing. These measurements (X) can be thought of as consisting of a measure of the true score (T) plus the measurement error (E). Two measures of the same thing will correlate +1.0 with each other if there is no error. To the degree that error in measurement exists (random error), the correlation between two measures of the same thing will be reduced. Let the symbol r_{XX} stand for a reliability coefficient, that is, the correlation of one measure of X with another measure of X. The reliability coefficient can be expressed in terms of X, T, and E as follows.

$$(1) \qquad r_{XX} = 1 - \frac{SD_E^2}{SD_X^2}$$

$$\text{or} \qquad (2) \qquad r_{XX} = \frac{SD_T^2}{SD_X^2}$$

The first expression states that the reliability coefficient is equal to 1 minus the error variance (SD_E^2) over the total variance of X. This means that as error goes up *relative to* test variance, reliability goes down. The second expression states that the reliability coefficient is equal to the variance of true scores (SD_T^2) divided by the variance of obtained scores (SD_X^2). This means the higher the reliability, the closer an obtained score approximates theoretical true score. This second expression also means that a reliability coefficient can be directly interpreted as the *proportion of variance in a test attributable to true-score variance*. Thus, a reliability coefficient of .80 indicates that 80 percent of the variance in whatever is being measured can be attributed to true scores and 20 percent to errors in measurement. Reliability is a necessary, but not sufficient, condition for test validity. The more error in a measure, the less it can measure what it is supposed to measure.

Reliability Coefficients

In evaluating the reliability of achievement tests we are primarily concerned with the internal consistency of the test items, that is, the degree to which items which are summed to a total score measure the same thing. One way to evaluate this is to use the same rules to build two forms of the same test. The correlation between the *parallel forms* will give an estimate of how well the items in each test measure the same thing. Another approach is to treat a single test as if it were two tests, by determining a score for the odd items and the even items. The correlation between the halves can be used to compute a *split-half* reliability coefficient (r_{XX}) using the Spearman-Brown formula:

$$r_{XX} = \frac{2 r \text{ (between halves)}}{1 + r \text{ (between halves)}}$$

The most general approach to a measure of internal consistency of test items is to compute an *alpha coefficient*[2] using a procedure called analysis of variance. The alpha coefficient is the reliability coefficient one would obtain if all possible split-half estimates of reliability were made and averaged. Test manuals and test reviews also refer to alpha as K-R 20 (Kuder-Richardson formula 20), or as one type of internal consistency reliability.

Another type of reliability coefficient that could be encountered is one based on giving the same test at different times (test-retest coefficient). With achievement tests, if the time interval between testings is short, this procedure could show the degree to which short-term variations in the students and in testing conditions affect scores.

Standard Error of Measurement

When the reliability of a test is known, the standard error of measurement can be computed and used to determine a confidence interval for a given score. The standard error of measurement (SD_E) is defined as follows:

$$SD_E = SD_X \sqrt{1 - r_{XX}}$$

This is the standard deviation of a person's scores that would be expected if he were tested a large number of times on parallel forms of the same test. The mean of this distribution would be the person's true score. Suppose the internal consistency reliability (r_{XX}) for a MAT Reading test is .90, and the standard deviation (SD_X) is 10 using expanded standard scores. The standard error of measurement (SD_E) would be:

$$SD_E = 10 \sqrt{1 - .90} = 10 \sqrt{.10} = 10 \times (.316) = 3.16$$

If a student obtains a standard score of 35, assuming a normal distribution, we would expect that his true score would be within ±2 standard errors of this score, 95 percent of the time.* Knowing the reliability of a test score permits us to determine a score interval in which a student's true score would fall with a certain level of confidence. Now, keeping with this same example, let us see how the SD_E and the 95 percent confidence interval change for different reliability coefficients. Table 12.1 shows how the standard error of measurement increases as reliability coefficient decreases.

TABLE 12.1   CHANGE IN THE STANDARD ERRORS MEASUREMENT AS A FUNCTION OF RELIABILITY OF A TEST WITH STANDARD DEVIATION OF 10

Reliability Coefficient	SD_E	95% Confidence Interval ($\pm 2\ SD_E$)
1.00	0	0
.98	1.41	± 2.8
.95	2.24	± 4.5
.90	3.16	± 6.3
.85	3.88	± 7.8
.80	4.47	± 8.9
.70	5.48	±11.0
.60	6.32	±12.6
.50	7.07	±14.1
.25	8.66	±17.3
.00	10.00	±20.0

Table 12.2 gives an actual reliability table with standard errors of measurement from the MAT Primary II Teacher's Handbook.[4] The first reliability given (r_{ke}) is an alpha coefficient. The second reliability (r_{tt}) is a split-half based coefficient. The alphas, which tend to run a little lower, appear to have been used in the calculation of the standard errors. The importance of reliability to score interpretation can be better appreciated by looking at the confidence intervals in grade-level terms. In most cases, the confidence interval produced by multiplying the standard error by 2 is on the order of ±.6 grade levels. Basically, when test scores are used to make decisions about individual students, reliabilities below .90 are not very tolerable. Test handbooks and the reviews in Buros's *Mental Measurement Yearbook* should be used to assure tests have adequate reliability for your purposes.

---

*The standard error of measurement specifies the probable spread of test scores about a person's true score. In stating a confidence interval we reverse this logic and say the true score must be within ±2 standard errors of measurement from the obtained test score. Cronbach[3] cautions that this logic is not likely to hold for persons with extreme observed scores.

TABLE 12.2 RELIABILITY COEFFICIENTS AND STANDARD ERRORS OF MEASUREMENT FOR PRIMARY II SUBTESTS (MAT)

Test	r_{ke}	r_{tt}	Std. Error of Meas.		
			RS	SS	GE
Word Knowledge	.93	.95	2.0	2.5	.3
Word Analysis	.90	.93	2.0	2.8	.3
Reading	.93	.95	2.3	2.7	.3
Total Reading	.96	.97	3.1	1.9	.2
Spelling	.94	.96	1.7	2.2	.2
Math. Computation	.86	.91	1.8	3.0	.2
Math. Concepts	.85	.89	2.2	3.9	.4
Math. Problem Solving	.88	.92	1.9	3.5	.3
Total Mathematics	.95	.96	3.5	2.1	.2

Test Length and Reliability

The reliability of a test can be increased by increasing the length of the test. The reliability of a test K times as long as test X is:

$$r_{K \cdot XX} = \frac{K\, r_{XX}}{1 + (K-1)\, r_{XX}}$$

Figure 12.1 shows how the reliability can be increased as K goes from 1 to 10 for different beginning reliabilities.[5] The figure also shows how the reliability would be decreased if the initial test were shortened (K goes from one to zero). Thus, one possible way of improving the reliability of a test is to lengthen the test.

Test Validity

Tests can have different validities for different uses. When norm-referenced achievement tests are used in outcome evaluations, the question of validity rests largely on the appropriateness of the test *content* and secondarily on the *sensitivity* of the test items *to instruction*. The following quote is from the MAT Teacher's Handbook:

> The validity of an achievement test is defined primarily in terms of *content validity*. A test has content validity if the test items adequately cover the curricular areas that the test is suppose to evaluate. Since each school has its own curriculum, the content validity of *Metropolitan Achievement Tests* must be evaluated by each school. It cannot be claimed that the tests are universally valid.[6]

Cronbach[7] considers three types of validity: content-oriented validity, criterion-oriented validity, and construct-oriented validity. As noted above, for most of their uses, the validity of normative achievement tests rests on the appropriateness of the content. However, the *criterion* of sensitivity to instruction is also considered in examining the validity of specific items

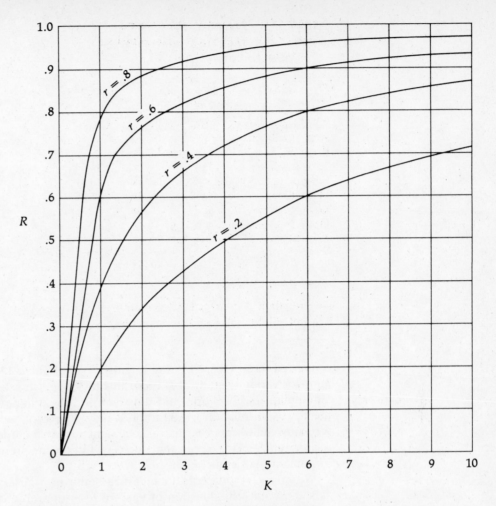

Figure 12.1 Effect of Length on Reliability (General Case)

during test construction. Items that are passed by more students in higher grades than lower grades are considered more valid. This criterion will be examined more closely later in this unit.

Other criteria that enter into the question of validity of achievement tests vary with their use. If achievement tests are used to select students for college, then their validity might depend on the correlation of the test scores with grade-point average in college. GPA becomes a criterion for a validity statement. If an achievement test is being used to diagnose and prescribe remediation, some measure of the remedial successes and failures could provide a criterion for the validity of this use.

When validity is expressed as a correlation between a test score and some *criterion,* it is helpful to know how to interpret the size of a correlation. The basic rule is to *square the validity coefficient* to find the proportion of variance in the criterion that is predictable from the test. (Of course, a proportion is

TABLE 12.3 Interpreting r as
the Percentage of Variance
Accounted For

Given this r	$r^2 \cdot 100$ gives the percentage of variance in Y predictable from X
.00	0%
.10	1%
.20	4%
.30	9%
.40	16%
.50	25%
.60	36%
.70	49%
.80	64%
.90	81%
.95	90%
.98	96%
.99	98%
1.00	100%

converted to a percent by multiplying by 100.) Table 12.3 shows what happens for various values of r. From this table we can see that a correlation of .50 implies that only 25% of the variance in the criterion is predictable from the test; a correlation of .20 implies only 4 percent predictable variance. If we know that scores on an achievement test and grade-point average correlate .70, then we know that there is 49 percent predictable variance and 51 percent that is not predictable.

When a test purports to measure some non-observable *construct* such as self-esteem, the question of validity rests upon the degree to which correct predictions can be made within some theory, involving that construct. For example, a theory might predict that students with higher self-esteem will achieve better. A correlation between the score on a test of self-esteem and achievement could be interpreted as evidence for the construct validity of the test.

It was noted earlier that reliability is a necessary condition for validity. Any unreliability will reduce the correlation between any variables. Given a test X and a criterion Y, the relation of reliability to validity is as follows:

$$r_{XY} = r_{TT} \sqrt{r_{XX}} \ \sqrt{r_{YY}}$$

An obtained correlation (r_{XY}) will be reduced from the true correlation between X and Y (r_{TT}) by the product of the square roots of the reliabilities for X (r_{XX}) and Y (r_{YY}). If a test is perfectly valid ($r_{TT} = 1$), but the test reliability is .80 and the criterion reliability is .80, the obtained validity index (r_{XY}) would be .80 ($1 \cdot \sqrt{.80} \sqrt{.80}$). Squaring this, we see that only 64 percent of the variance in Y is predictable from X because of the unreliability of both X and Y. The implication of this relation for test theory is that one possible way to improve the validity of a test is to improve its reliability.

Test Theory Applied to Item Analysis

The goal in test construction is to build a reliable and valid test. As noted previously, the task begins with a logical analysis of what is to be measured. This analysis permits a definition of a pool of test items from which a test can be built. After trial items have been written and edited, they are given to a tryout group. Principles of item analysis derived from test theory are then used to guide the selection of the final test items to be used in the standardization of the test. Three principles are central: (1) items are preferred if they have larger standard deviations,* (2) if they correlate highly with total test score (a reliability index), and (3) if they correlate highly with an index of validity.

Maximizing The Test Standard Deviation

A desirable test characteristic is to produce a broad spread of scores among the persons taking the test (a large standard deviation relative to measurement error). It is therefore important that all of the items be neither "too easy" nor "too hard." If they are too easy, everyone will get them right and there will be no way to spread people out. The test standard deviation would be zero. If they are too hard, everyone will get them wrong, and again, there will be no way to spread people out. Items of middle difficulty tend to produce larger test standard deviations. Two steps are usually followed in selecting achievement test items so that they will spread people out. The first step is to determine the "middle difficulty level." This is defined as the mid-point between a chance level of performance and a perfect performance. If there are four response options, the chance level is 25 percent right (one out of four). The middle difficulty level would be half way between 25 percent and 100 percent, or 62.5 percent. For a true-false test, chance level would be 50 percent (one out of two) and the middle difficulty level would be 75 percent.

Once the middle difficulty level is determined, it is common to select sets of items covering a range of difficulty on either side of the middle level. For example, a test might be built of six items with difficulty levels from each of the ranges as follows:

Ranges Where Middle Difficulty Level Is 62.5 Percent	Ranges Where Middle Difficulty Level Is 75 Percent
32-40	58-64
41-49	65-71
50-58	(72-78)
(59-67)	79-85
68-76	86-92
77-85	
86-93	

---

*The standard deviation of a pass-fail item is $\sqrt{p \cdot q}$, where p is the proportion who pass the item and q is the proportion who fail the item or $1 - p$.

There are some situations in building normative tests where one might restrict item selection only to those in the middle range. However, this is not the common procedure for achievement tests where a given test has to cover several grade levels of skills.

Item Reliability

To build a reliable test, an index of item reliability (or discriminability) is used. Items are preferred if they correlate higher with what the rest of the test is measuring, that is, they correlate higher with the total score. A biserial correlation coefficient is used with pass-fail items to obtain the correlation of each item with the total score. If an item pool is designed to measure Reading Vocabulary, then different vocabulary items should correlate with the total score. Another way of looking at it is this: The goal is to select the items that best *discriminate* those who score high on the test from those who score low. For example consider items A and B below:

		Item A					Item B		
		Percent Fail	Percent Pass				Percent Fail	Percent Pass	
TEST SCORE	Highest 25%	10	90	100		Highest 25%	50	50	100
	Lowest 25%	90	10	100		Lowest 25%	50	50	100
		100	100				100	100	

For item A, 90 percent of those in the highest 25 percent on total test score pass the item. The item is failed by 90 percent of those in the lowest 25 percent on total test score. The item discriminates well between those who score high and low on the total test. The item measures what the average of the rest of the test is measuring, so it is considered to be reliable. On the other hand, item B is not answered differently by high and low scorers. Item B does not measure what the rest of the test is measuring and is considered unreliable.

Item Validity

While some reliability is always important for test items, validity considerations are more important. Item validity is usually based on two kinds of considerations. First, there is the validity of the content. If the objective being tested involves different kinds of performances, as might occur in a test of reading comprehension (e.g., inductive reasoning, deductive reasoning, summarizing, identifying the theme), then, it would be important to include items covering the different kinds of performances in the final test, even if they did not discriminate best between high and low scorers. A *structured sampling* of different kinds of content is an important consideration in maintaining content validity.

The second validity consideration is whether or not the items meet the criterion of being sensitive to instruction. Usually, this criterion is examined to see if students in higher grades pass an item more than do students in lower grades. Consider items A and B below:

| | Item A Grade Level | | | Item B Grade Level | |
	3	4		3	4
Percent Pass	50	50	Percent Pass	25	75
Percent Fail	50	50	Percent Fail	75	25

Item A shows no improvement in the percent of students passing in going from third to fourth grade. Item B goes from 25 percent pass (chance level for a four-choice item) to 75 percent pass. Item B shows better validity than item A. With data over several grade levels, one can plot the percent passing at each grade level to help identify valid items. For example, determine whether item C or D is more valid:

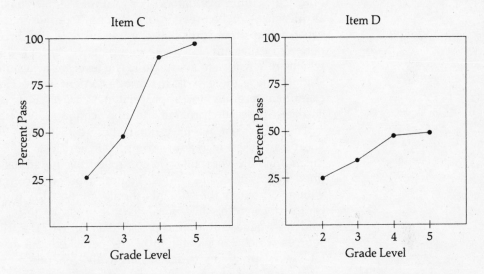

If you selected item C, you are right. Item C shows a better discrimination of students in grades 2, 3 and 4. If *items* are selected to correlate with a criterion such as grade level, the *total score* made up of such items will correlate with the criterion.

Some Potential Problems and Implications

The criterion of sensitivity to instruction. The most common procedure for standardizing achievement tests is to test groups at various grade levels with a sample of items that cover several grade levels. Items are preferred that show a higher increase in percent passing with increasing grade level. Whether or not this increase in percent passing is actually a function of classroom instruction is not examined. As we noted in unit 4, the improvement in performance with grade level can be due to other changes that occur with age, such as general mental ability or instruction occurring at home and elsewhere. The basic flaw in this test construction procedure is not the use of a criterion to select items, *but in the criterion chosen.* Unless there is pretesting and posttesting on the *same students* under conditions where *instruction is monitored* to show that it has occurred, the evidence of item validity is at best presumptive and the likely biasing of the test content to reflect non-school learning is strong.

The criterion of discriminability. Items are selected for inclusion on the tests because they discriminate those who score high on the test from those who score low. If general intellectual skills brought to the teaching situation help determine good and poor test performance, then this criterion will also likely *move* what is being measured *toward* a measure of *general intelligence.* If language development at home or home-directed instruction contributes to test performance, then the test is likely to reflect social class variables. This reliability criterion can bias item selection toward any non-instructional factors that contribute to pupil achievement.

The possibility that these criteria will produce achievement tests that do not accurately reflect the effects of school instruction has been noted by other curriculum evaluators. For example, Stake[8] has described these tests as measures of "correlates of learning," rather than learning itself. Test construction procedures bias the measures in the direction of general competence, especially language competence, rather than toward measures which are sensitive to instruction. The tests are well suited for showing which students have more skills in various content areas. However, they must be examined carefully for appropriateness *when used to evaluate instructional programs,* especially programs for the economically disadvantaged.

The area where we have noted the greatest difficulty is in the admissible vocabulary used in reading comprehension tests. Up through third grade, this admissible vocabulary is controlled by the admissible vocabularies defined by basal reading series. Logical aspects of comprehension are tested with a vocabulary the students should know. After third grade, there is little control over admissible vocabulary in texts or tests. On the average, the evidence suggests that much vocabulary growth is attributable to non-school sources which favor children of the better educated.[9,10] It is very possible for special programs to teach effectively general-case comprehension skills which will not show on a norm-referenced reading test because the presumed vocabulary skills (largely a linear-additive set) are missing.

Possible solutions to these problems are: (1) use of a more effective criterion of sensitivity to instruction in building achievement tests, (2) better recognition of the fact that vocabulary growth is a continuous process through high school at least,[11] and therefore, that language growth contributes to the development of standards for vocabulary control in texts and tests through ninth grade at least.

This analysis also provides another basis for questioning the use of some norm-referenced tests at some levels in teacher accountability evaluations. The teacher of more advantaged children is going to look better on the average, even if the instruction is not exceptional.[12]

summary

Reliability of a test is concerned with the contribution of errors of measurement to test scores. If there is no error, reliability is 1. As the proportion of error variance to total variance increases, reliability decreases. The contribution of error to test scores is determined by correlating two measures (or the average of all possible measures) of the same thing. This can be done with parallel form measures, dividing a test into odd-item and even-item halves, or by computing an alpha coefficient, which gives the average of all possible split halves. A reliability coefficient, when multiplied by 100, gives the percent of the variance in a test score that can be attributed to true scores.

The standard error of measurement is found by taking the square root of 1 minus the reliability coefficient and multiplying this by the standard deviation of a test. In evaluating an individual test score, plus or minus 2 times the standard error of measurement will give the interval within which the true mean should fall with a 95 percent confidence. With standardized achievement tests, 2 times the standard error of measurement is most typically about six-tenths of a grade level. Reliabilities under .90 are not very tolerable when the test scores are used for decisions about individuals. One way to improve the reliability of a test is to make it longer.

A test can have different validities for different uses. With norm-referenced achievement tests, the question of validity for program evaluation rests largely on the appropriateness of the test content and a criterion of sensitivity of the test to instruction. The criterion for sensitivity to instruction used for most achievement tests is that more students in higher grades pass the item than do students in lower grades. Predictive validity of a test depends on its correlation with some future performance, such as success in college. When validity is expressed as a correlation between a test and some criterion, the correlation is best interpreted by squaring the validity coefficient. This gives the proportion of variance (or *percent*, if multiplied by 100) in the criterion that is predictable from the test. Unreliability in tests or criteria will reduce validity coefficients in a predictable way.

Item analysis of the tryout form of a test is used to build a final test form with maximum reliability and validity. This is accomplished by eliminating items that most persons pass and fail, by keeping items that best discriminate between high and low scorers on the test (item reliability index), and by keeping items that students in higher grades pass but in lower grades fail (validity index). While use of these procedures will generally lead to good measures of individual differences, they have potential problems when used to build measures to evaluate effects of *school instruction*. Use of the criterion of higher percent passing with increasing grade level biases item selection away from measures sensitive to school instruction and toward other characteristics that change with age such as mental age and/or non-school instruction. Selecting items that discriminate high and low test scorers can serve to accentuate this bias away from measures of the effects of school instruction. If language development at home or home-directed instruction contributes to test performance, and such instruction is associated with parental education, then the achievement test measures will reflect social class-related variables.

In our judgment the test area most biased by these factors is that of *reading comprehension*. This bias may occur because of a failure to control the choice of vocabulary words used in tests after third grade. Logical aspects of comprehension should be tested mainly with words whose meaning all students have been taught. Vocabulary can be tested separately. These problems could be overcome by using a more direct measure of sensitivity to instruction (pretest, instruction, posttest), and by the control of permissible vocabulary used so that it is appropriate to vocabulary actually taught in school.

self-test

1 standard
  deviation

2 measurements

3 proportion; 80

4 two

5 content;
  sensitivity

6 64

7 higher; lower

1 The variance of a set of test scores is simply the square of the _____ _____ of those scores.

2 The error in a measurement can be estimated by making a number of independent _____ of the same thing.

3 A reliability coefficient can be directly interpreted as the _____ of variance in a test attributable to true-score variance. Thus, a reliability coefficient of .80 indicates that _____ percent of the variance in whatever is being measured can be attributed to true scores and 20 percent to errors in measurement.

4 An interval within which one would expect a true score to fall 95 percent of the time (the 95 percent confidence interval) is the interval defined by going plus and minus _____ standard errors from the obtained score.

5 When norm-referenced achievement tests are used in outcome evaluations, the question of validity rests largely on the appropriateness of the test _____ and secondarily on the _____ of the test items to instruction.

6 If a test and a criterion correlate .80, _____ percent of the variance in the criterion is predictable from the test.

7 In item analysis the usual validity index employed is that students in _____ grades pass an item more often than students in _____ grades.

NUMBER RIGHT _____

exercise 1 programed practice

1   Test theory begins with any test score, X, and partitions this score into two parts, T + _____ . T represents that part of X attributable to the _____ _____ on the test, and E represents that part of X attributable to _____ .

1 E; true score; error

2   Variance of a set of test scores is simply the square of the _____ _____ of those scores.

2 standard deviation

3   Reliability of a test is concerned with the contribution of _____ of measurement to test scores.

3 errors

4   Error in a measurement can be estimated by making a number of independent _____ of the same thing.

4 measurements

5   Two measures of the same thing will correlate _____ with each other if there is no error.

5 +1.0

6   Let the symbol r_{xx} stand for a reliability coefficient, that is, the correlation of one measure of _____ with another measure of _____ .

6 X; X

7   As error goes up relative to test variance, _____ goes down.

7 reliability

8   The reliability coefficient is equal to the variance of true scores (SD_T^2) divided by the variance of obtained scores (_____).

9   A reliability coefficient can be directly interpreted as the _____ of variance in a test attributable to true-score variance. Thus, a reliability coefficient of .80 indicates that _____ percent of the variance in whatever is being measured can be attributed to true scores and 20 percent to errors in measurement.

8 SD_X^2

10 Reliability is a necessary, but not sufficient, condition for test _____ . The more _____ in a measure, the less it can measure what it is suppose to measure.

9 proportion; 80

10 validity; error

11 One way to evaluate reliability is to use the same rules to build two _____ forms of the same test.

11 parallel

12 odd; even;
   split-half

13 alpha; all
   possible

14 confidence; r_{xx}

15 two

16 3; 24-36

17 .6

18 .90

19 length

20 content;
   sensitivity

21 content;
   criterion

12 Another approach to reliability is to treat a single test as if it were two tests, by determining a score for the _____ items and the _____ items. The correlation between the halves can be used to compute a _____-_____ reliability coefficient.

13 The most general approach to a measure of internal consistency of test times is to compute an _____ coefficient. The alpha coefficient is the reliability coefficient one would obtain if _____ _____ split-half estimates of reliability were made and averaged.

14 The standard error of measurement can be computed and used to determine a _____ interval for a given score. The standard error of measurement (SD_E) is defined as follows: $SD_E = SD_X \sqrt{1 - \underline{\hspace{1.5cm}}}$

15 An interval within which one would expect a true score to fall 95 percent of the time (the 95 percent confidence interval) is the interval defined by going plus and minus _____ standard errors from the obtained score.

16 If the obtained score is 30, the reliability is .91 and the test standard deviation is 10, what is the 95 percent confidence interval?
    Step 1. Compute $SD_E = SD_X \sqrt{1 - r_{XX}} = $ _____
    Step 2. Determine $\pm 2SD_E$: _____

17 In grade-equivalent scores, the confidence interval produced by multiplying the standard error by 2 is on the order of $\pm$ _____ grade levels.

18 Basically, when test scores are used to make decisions about individual students, reliabilities below _____ are not very tolerable.

19 The reliability of a test can be increased by increasing the _____ of the test.

20 When norm-referenced achievement tests are used in outcome evaluations, the question of validity rests largely on the appropriateness of the test _____ and secondarily on the _____ of the test items to instruction.

21 Cronbach considers three types of validity: _____-oriented validity, _____-oriented validity, and construct-oriented validity.

22 If achievement tests are used to select students for college, then their validity might depend on the correlation of the test scores with grade-point average (GPA) in college. GPA becomes a _____ for a validity statement.

23 To interpret the size of a validity coefficient, the basic rule is to _____ the validity coefficient to find the _____ of variance in the criterion that is predictable from the test.

24 If a test and a criterion correlate .80, _____ percent of the variance in the criterion is predictable from the test.

25 Any unreliability will reduce the correlation between any variables. An obtained correlation will be reduced from the true correlation between X and Y by the product of the _____ _____ of the reliabilities for X and Y.

26 The implication of the above relation for test theory is that one possible way to improve the validity of a test is to improve its _____ .

27 Three principles are central in item analysis. Items are preferred (1) if they have _____ standard deviations, (2) if they correlate more highly with _____ _____ score (a reliability index), and (3) if they correlate more highly with an index of _____ .

28 The usual validity index used is that students in _____ grades pass an item more often than students in _____ grades.

29 Whether or not this increase in percent passing is actually a function of _____ _____ is not examined. Improvement in performance with grade level can be due to other changes that occur with age, such as general _____ ability or instruction occuring at _____ and elsewhere.

30 The usual evidence of item validity is at best presumptive and the likely biasing of the test content to reflect non-school _____ is strong.

31 Items are also selected for inclusion on the tests because they _____ those who score high on the test from those who score low. If general intellectual skills brought to the teaching situation help determine good and poor test performance, then this criterion will also likely move what is being measured toward a measure of _____ _____ . If language development at home or home-directed instruction contributes to test performance, then the test is likely to reflect _____ _____ variables.

32 While the tests are well suited for showing which students have _____ skills in various content areas, they must be examined carefully for appropriateness when used to evaluate _____ _____ , especially programs for the economically _____ .

33 The area where we have noted the greatest difficulty is in the admissible vocabulary used in reading _____ tests. Up through third grade, this admissible vocabulary is _____ by the vocabularies defined by basal reading series. After third grade, there is _____ control over admissible vocabulary in texts or tests.

34 Possible solutions to these problems are: (1) the use of a more effective criterion of _____ to instruction in building achievement tests, (2) a better recognition that vocabulary growth is a _____ process through high school at least, and, therefore, the development of standards for _____ control in texts and tests through ninth grade at least.

exercise 2   computational practice

1 SD_X is 15. r_{XX} is .75. Find the 95 percent confidence interval for a score of 110. _____ .

2 What is the percentage of error variance if the reliability coefficient is .83? _____ .

3 What is the percentage of reliable variance if the reliability coefficient is .62? _____ .

4 If the standard deviation of X is 5, what is the variance of X? _____ .

5 If the total variance (X) is 100, and the variance attributable to error (E) is 36, what is the variance attributable to true scores? _____ .

6 For the data in (5), what is the reliability of (X)? _____ .

7 If the correlation between the split halves of a test is .70, what is the test reliability? _____ .

8 If the correlation between the split-halves of a test is .82, what is the test reliability? _____ .

9 What is the standard error of measurement, if SD_X is 10 and reliability is .50? _____ .

10 If the correlation between a test and a criterion is .90, what is the percentage of variance in the criterion predictable from the test? _____ .

11 If a test has a reliability of .40, what would be the reliability of a test five times longer? _____ .

12 If a test has a reliability of .60, what would be the reliability of a test 3 times longer? _____ .

13 If the obtained correlation between a test (X) and a criterion (Y) is .60, and the reliability of X is .90 and the reliability of Y is .70, what is the true correlation between X and Y (r_{TT}). (hint: solve the equation—

$$r_{XY} = r_{TT} \sqrt{r_{XX}} \ \sqrt{r_{YY}} \text{ for } r_{TT}.)$$

Answers to exercise 2

1 $SD_E = 15 \cdot \sqrt{1 - .75} = 15 \cdot \sqrt{.25} = 15 \cdot (.5) = 7.5$
$2SD_E = 15$
95 percent confidence interval = 95 − 125.

2 $100 - 83 = 17\%$

3 62%

4 $5^2 = 25$

5 $100 - 36 = 64$

6 $\dfrac{64}{100} = .64$

7 $r_{XX} = \dfrac{2\,(.70)}{1 + .70} = \dfrac{1.40}{1.70} = .82$

8 $r_{XX} = \dfrac{2\,(.82)}{1 + .82} = \dfrac{1.64}{1.82} = .90$

9 $SD_X = 10 \sqrt{1 - .50} = 10 \sqrt{.50} = 10\,(.71) = 7.1$

10 $.90^2 \times 100 = 81\%$

11 $r_{KK} = \dfrac{5\,(.40)}{1 + (5-1)\,(.40)} = \dfrac{2.0}{1 + 1.6} = \dfrac{2.0}{2.6} = .77$

12 $r_{KK} = \dfrac{3\,(.60)}{1 + (3-1)\,(.60)} = \dfrac{1.8}{1 + 1.20} = \dfrac{1.8}{2.2} = .82$

13 $r_{TT} = \dfrac{r_{XY}}{\sqrt{r_{XX}}\ \sqrt{r_{YY}}} = \dfrac{.60}{\sqrt{.90}\ \sqrt{.70}} = \dfrac{.60}{(.95)\,(.84)} = \dfrac{.60}{.798} = .75$

discussion questions

1 Explain the equation $X = T + E$.
2 Relate reliability and validity to the equation in 1.
3 What is a variance?
4 Why does test theory (and much of statistical theory) deal with variances rather than standard deviations?
5 What is the basic procedure for determining the reliability of a measure?
6 What are some implications of the fact that a reliability coefficient can be expressed as the ratio of true-score variance to total variance, or as 1 minus the ratio of error variance to total variance?
7 What is parallel-form reliability?
8 What is a split-half reliability?
9 What is an alpha coefficient?
10 Define the standard error of measurement and explain how it can be used to determine the confidence interval for a test score.
11 How would you determine the range for a 99 percent confidence interval?
12 Use table 12.2 and determine the 95% confidence interval for a reading grade-equivalent score of 2.5.
13 If a unit length test has a reliability of .20, what would be the reliability of a test four times as long? (use figure 12.1).
14 What are the two main criteria for evaluating the validity of a norm-referenced achievement test?
15 How is sensitivity to instruction usually examined in item analysis for achievement test?
16 Name and define three types of validity.
17 Why is it that achievement tests cannot be claimed to be universally valid?
18 How does one judge the size of a criterion-oriented validity coefficient?
19 What is the explicit relation of reliability to the validity of a test?
20 What are three principles central to item analysis in constructing a test?
21 What is the trouble with the usual criterion of sensitivity to instruction?
22 What potential biases are introduced by the criterion of discriminability?

23 Why would Stake refer to norm-referenced achievement tests as measures of "correlates of learning"?

24 What can norm-referenced tests do well?

25 Why do authors suspect these tests would be biased in the norm-referenced evaluation of instructional programs for the disadvantaged, especially in the art of reading comprehension?

26 What are the possible solutions to the potential biases in norm-referenced tests?

unit 13

Research Design and Evaluation

objectives

When you complete this unit, you should be able to—

1 Distinguish between descriptive, correlational, and experimental research.
2 Describe two major kinds of experimental research designs.
3 Explain the logic of good research design in terms of what is being controlled and how.
4 Give examples of various kinds of group and individual-subject designs.
5 Discuss how alternative explanations for research outcomes can be ruled out.
6 Define these concepts:
     statistical regression
     statistical significance
     standard error of the difference
     norm-referenced comparison
     reversal design
     multiple-baseline design
     critical ratio
7 Provide an outline of procedures to follow (rules) in drawing conclusions from a research study.
8 Use the concepts and procedures given in this unit to evaluate published research.

lesson

In this unit, we turn from our study of norm-referenced tests to an examination of the design and evaluation of research studies. When we complete this unit, we will be ready to look at the rather complex problem of outcome evaluations that may involve norm-referenced tests.

Most persons in our society have been taught that "research is good." We tend to be accepting of statements that begin with "Research has shown. . . ." The problem, however, is that there is good research and bad research. You need to know how to tell the difference. The analyses and exercises in this unit are aimed at assisting the teacher in: (1) more critically evaluating the claims made about instructional programs, (2) more critically evaluating the implications of research for training practices, and (3) more expertly defending or criticizing possible research studies involving his or her classroom.

Research may be classified as descriptive, correlational, or experimental. Descriptive research simply takes measures in a group and summarizes them to describe the group. For example, we might show that 29 percent of fourth graders in June of the year have reading grade-equivalent scoresibelow 3.0. Descriptive research is often helpful in finding problems to work on. The solving of the problems, however, usually requires correlational or experimental research.

Experimental Versus Correlational Research[1]

Much research begins with "why." "Why are children aggressive?" "Why are there so many reading failures?" "Why do kids drop out of school?" It is usually necessary to rephrase a "why" question into a "what" question to study possible answers. "What are the conditions under which children are more or less aggressive in the classroom?" "What teaching methods lead children to succeed or fail in reading?" "What home, community, or school conditions increase or decrease the dropout rate?"

One approach to assessing the conditions under which children show more aggression in the classroom would be to identify a group of classes in which the level of aggressive interactions is high and a group in which it is low. We would then see if these two groups of classes differed in how the teachers handle the classes, in characteristics of students' home lives or their neighborhoods. The data would then be analyzed to find factors which *correlate* with high and low aggressive behavior. This approach is not experimental, but rather correlational. Relations between variables are studied in terms of things that already exist but no variable is manipulated. In an experimental approach, possible important conditions are identified and the experimenter manipulates these conditions to see if aggression increases or decreases. Usually, an experimental approach is required to validly answer a "what" question.

The difficulties with the correlational approach are easily illustrated. Suppose that in using a correlational approach we found that children who show more aggressive behavior in the classroom have teachers who criticize them more. What would we conclude? Does the criticism make the children more aggressive? Are more aggressive children criticized more? *Or*, is some other factor (like defective air ventilation in some classes) causing both increased criticism by the teacher and increased aggressive behavior by children. There is no way to know from correlational research if it is dealing with cause and effect or not. What is required to show cause and effect is the experimental manipulation of possible causes to show what controls an effect. For example, we might have the teacher increase his or her level of criticism and find that aggressive behavior increases. When level of criticism is decreased, aggressive behavior decreases. Under these conditions, the direction of causality would be clear.

> *Evaluation Rule 1. In evaluating a research study or claim, first determine if the method used was correlational or experimental.* If the method was not experimental, withhold judgments about cause and effect. Your basic response should be, "That might be a cause, but it is only a maybe."

Designs for Experimental Research

Experimental research requires at a minimum: (a) the changing of one or more variables (independent variables), (b) the making of at least two measurements on some dependent variable, and (c) the comparison of two (or more) measurements to provide the basis for a conclusion. How the two (or more) measurements are made provides the basis for two types of research designs. In *group designs*, measurements are taken on two (or more) groups which are treated differently. In *individual-subject designs*, the measurements are taken from different treatment conditions on the same subjects.

Experimental designs are concerned with *when* measurements are taken on what persons. The object of a design is to permit a clear-cut conclusion to be drawn from the study. To permit unambiguous interpretations of a study, good design must provide for control of variables that might lead to alternative interpretations of findings. Inability to achieve such control in practical situations has made much research in education inconclusive.

Alternative Explanations of Results

Since research on learning-teaching processes takes time, other events which change with time can offer possible alternative explanations.[2] The main classes of competing effects in educational research are:

1 *Other experiences.* Experiences occurring at the same time as a special program (parental teaching, television, etc.) can be said to account for a change.
2 *Maturation.* Biological and psychological maturation might be said to account for change.
3 *Test practice.* Taking a pretest can raise scores on a posttest.
4 *Changes in group membership.* Early drops or late adds to a classroom may differentially affect treatment and comparison groups.
5 *Changes in tests.* Scores may change simply because different tests (or levels of tests) are used for pretest and posttest.
6 *Unreliability.* Scores may change from one testing to the next because of errors of measurement. The concern here is if an obtained difference is greater than one would expect given the size of the measurement error.
7 *Extreme-group-selection-effects.* This effect is called *statistical regression.* It means that if a group is selected for extreme scores on a given test such

as an IQ test, their average scores on retest will be closer to the mean. Thus, a group selected with IQ's below 80 might have a mean IQ of 71, and, with no other changes occurring, they would score higher on retest (say mean 75). This "regression toward the mean" occurs because of errors of measurement in the test (unreliability). By selecting only students falling below 80, the sample *includes* those with true scores above 80 whose obtained scores were below 80 by chance, but *excludes* those with true scores below 80 whose obtained scores were above 80 by chance. On retest, the mean of the selected group with IQ's below 80 will approximate their true mean, that is, be higher.

In group designs, control of these potential influences is accomplished by the use of a *control* (or comparison) *group*. Hopefully, the seven kinds of effects listed above would have an equal impact on the control group and the treatment group, leaving the treatment effect to account for any difference in outcome. However, use of a control group raises a new problem: *persons in the control group might not be comparable to persons in the treatment group in terms of important background characteristics, (such as learning history)*. To overcome this problem, group designs try to use random assignment of persons to treatment and control groups. The object is to allow the treatment and control groups to differ (on the average) *only* with respect to the experimental treatment.* Where random assignment is not possible, greater care must be exercised in ruling out alternative interpretations.

In individual-subject designs, each person serves as his or her own control over possible important background variables. Effects of prior learning, and so on, will be reflected in the baseline measurement. A significant treatment effect has to produce a change that is operating on top of the baseline effect on the dependent variable. To rule out alternative interpretations of possible effects associated with time, individual-subject designs use reversals of effects, multiple baselines, and replications. Most of the studies reported in *Teaching 1* in the section on *Broadening Your Perspective* used individual-subject designs. Some of the more important designs are summarized next.

Group Designs

Random assignment—pretest and posttest. In this design, subjects are randomly assigned to groups and then pretested. Next, one group is given the special treatment, and *everything* else is kept the same. Finally, both groups are posttested. This is a strong design, but one that is often difficult to put into effect in field settings such as public schools. When coupled with tests for statistical significance of a difference (discussed later) it serves to control each of the seven possible threats to a valid interpretation listed above.

Example: All 150 second-grade students in Carver elementary are assigned randomly to one of six teachers. Teachers are randomly assigned to treatment and control groups with the restriction that three teachers be assigned to each

---

*Another approach to controlling possible group differences is to make matched pairs of subjects (matched on critical background variables such as age, IQ, and preskills for the subject to be evaluated), and then randomly assign pair members to control and treatment groups. This approach is often difficult to carry out. In the designs which follow, the random assignment designs could be modified to cover random assignment of matched pairs.

condition. Students are pretested on all multiplication facts with one-digit numbers. Math instruction in both groups is kept to the same time, materials, and procedures, except that in the special treatment group the students chart their daily progress on a graph attached to their workbook. At the end of eight weeks, all students are retested on multiplication facts. On pretest the treatment group had 12 percent right and the control group 15 percent. On posttest the treatment group was at 82 percent and the control group was at 57 percent. The difference at posttest was statistically significant and represented an important gain in skill. The special graphing procedure was judged to be valuable.

Random assignment—posttest only. In this design, subjects are randomly assigned to groups as discussed in the example above. The treatment procedure is given to one group. Then both groups are tested. If truly random assignment can be obtained, the pretest may be unnecessary. However, in the study of an instructional program, the pretest-posttest comparison can often add weight to the judgment that a special program is having *educationally significant effects.* Both of these designs can be complicated by adding additional treatment groups to permit comparisons of different treatments.

No random assignment—pretest and posttest. If it is not possible to use random assignment, one can seek a comparison group that is like the treatment group in important characteristics. If at pretest these characteristics show minimal differences, the possible effects on the outcome of other experiences, maturation, test practice, changes in group membership, and changes in tests, are *minimized.* As the groups differ increasingly, possibilities of misleading results from statistical regression and changes in tests increase.

Example: Students coming to the learning center for remedial reading in two high schools are provided with different programs. To be included in the comparison groups, students must make between 14 and 35 errors on a placement test. Twelve students in school A and fifteen in school B met the criterion. The students in group A were placed in a corrective reading program which gave systematic practice in advanced decoding. The students were taught in two groups. The students in school B were given individual assignment which the teacher designed daily on the basis of her judgment of individual student needs. All students were pretested in early October on Gilmore Oral Reading Test to measure rate and accuracy, and the Wide Range for accuracy in word decoding, and on the MAT Intermediate Reading Test to measure comprehension. At the end of the school year, the students were retested on the same tests. The pretest data showed only minor differences between the two groups. The posttest data showed the procedures used in school A to be more effective on all measures but the MAT Reading Test (comprehension), where there was no difference. It was concluded that the corrective reading program significantly improved decoding skills. The average gain on the Gilmore and Wide Range was more than 2.5 grade levels in group A and 1.2 in group B.

Simple replication. One way to increase confidence in the outcome of a treatment where no control group is possible, is simply to repeat the treatment on a new group. This is called replication. If the same effect is found on different groups at different points in time, one can begin to rule out other interpretations associated with time.

Norm-referenced comparisons. Probably the most common design used in project evaluation in education where there is no control group, is to compare the project performance against the norm group used to standardize a test. Students are pretested, given a special program, and posttested. Without the special program, the expectation is that students will hold their same position relative to the norm group on which the test was standardized. With the special program, the expectation is that they will improve in standing on the norms.

Example: A group of disadvantaged second graders are tested fall and spring on the Metropolitan Achievement Test Primary I Battery. At the beginning of second grade, they score at the 10th percentile in Total Reading and at the 16th percentile in Total Math. After an intensive special program, testing in the spring on the same test shows they now average at the 48th percentile in Total Reading and the 44th percentile in Total Math. The gain in reading is about 2.5 standard score units and the gain in math is about 2 standard score units. Usually, gains of one-fourth to one-half a standard score unit are considered to be educationally significant. The program was judged to be more effective than the average program in the United States.

Norm-referenced design is very convenient and certainly better than making comparisons with a control group which is not truly comparable with the treatment group. One weakness in the design is that the normative tests may be insensitive to the program effects (lack content validity) and lead to a false conclusion of no program effect. Another is the assumption that the achievement status of the group under study would remain the same relative to the norm group over time. Evidence for this assumption is lacking, although the assumption is reasonable in most cases.

In using this design, it is important that pretesting and posttesting occur at the dates used for testing the norm group (see table 14.1). It is also important not to *select* the treatment group on the basis of low or high scores on the pretest. This would produce a statistical regression effect as discussed earlier.

A final caution in using a norm-referenced design is to be sure the same test (or a parallel form of the same test) is used at pretest and posttest. This is important to insure that the comparisons are made on the *same norm group*. When expanded standard scores are available to interrelate several levels of a test battery, it is not critical that the same level of the test be given at pretesting and posttesting, but it is still desirable.

Individual-Subject Designs

The goal of an individual-subject design[3] is to use the individual as his or her own control for differences in personal history. This is accomplished by comparing a treatment effect with baseline measurements. By taking several measurements during a baseline period, it is possible to demonstrate that systematic changes are not occurring over time before the experimental treatment starts. Individual-subject designs are most useful in the fine-grain analysis of the teaching process to show explicitly what specific teacher behaviors produce what specific effects on the students. They are less useful in the more global evaluation of a total program. Three procedures are commonly used to demonstrate that an experimental treatment is producing an effect and to rule out competing explanations. One is the reversal procedure, the second is the multiple-baseline procedure, and the third is simple replication.

Reversal design.   In a reversal design, a baseline condition (A), is followed by an experimental condition (B). Then, the experimental treatment is withdrawn and the baseline condition is reinstated. Given the definitions of A and B above, these designs can take many forms such as the following: ABA, BAB, ABAB. If a second experimental treatment (C) is studied, the design can take the form ABACA, or variations on this.

Example of an ABA design: With a Distar I Reading group, measures are taken on the dependent variable "percent correct responding." In the baseline condition (A), the teacher follows her normal pacing in presenting tasks for ten days. Her pacing is quite rapid with less than 1.5 seconds pause between the end of one task and the start of the next. In the experimental conditions (B), a pause of two seconds is introduced after each task. Correct responding goes down from 95 percent to 81 percent over a 15-day period. The more rapid pacing is again introduced (return to A condition) and "percent correct responding" increases to 93 percent during the following week.

Multiple-baseline design.   Where it is not feasible to withdraw or reverse a treatment effect (like unteaching a child to count to ten), a multiple-baseline design can be used to guard against alternative interpretations associated with time. In this design, the treatment effects are introduced at different times for: (a) different dependent behaviors of the same subject, or (b) for the same behaviors for different subjects.

Example: After taking baseline measurements on hand-raising and time-on-task, praise might be used with Johnny to increase hand-raising this week, and to increase working-on-task next week. The fact that each behavior changed only when the treatment variable (praise) was introduced increases confidence that praise produced the change. The other kind of multiple-baseline design would change Johnny's behavior one week and Mary's the next.

Designs Combining Group and Individual-Subject Procedures

It is possible to use individual-subject designs on a group of subjects, and at the same time to use a control group where only a continuing baseline measure is taken. The control group adds assurance that there is no systematic change occurring with time or allows one to control for systematic changes that might be going on. The use of groups also permits more refined statistical inferences to be drawn and increases confidence in the generality of a finding across persons.

Example: There are 24 students in a third grade basal reading program. The program lasts one hour each day and involves group reading with the teacher, silent reading, and workbook activities. Three times a week, the students take a checkout on a 200-word passage taken from a story just ahead of where their group is reading. Reading rate and errors are charted. Data are taken in this way for five weeks. Now, half the students (Group 1) randomly picked from each reading group are assigned to a special program carried out in the learning center for one hour a day. Group 2 continues in the basal program. All students continue to be tested three times a week on a 200-word passage. For group 1 the passages are selected from stories as if they were progressing at the same rate as before. Hypothetical results are illustrated in figure 13.1. Two types of comparisons are now possible with this design for both the rate measure and the error measure. The first comparison is *between* the two groups. They were comparable on rate and errors during the base condition, but group 1 performed better in the special program. This is a between-group comparison. Also the students in group 1 are doing better in the special program than they did during their own baseline. Rate is increasing and errors are decreasing. *This provides a within-group comparison.*

Use of Multiple Control Groups

It is sometimes necessary to add additional control groups to a study to eliminate alternative interpretations for an outcome. For example, a special program for teaching the disadvantaged may have: (a) a lower teacher-student ratio, as well as (b) an innovative instructional approach. Is the difference in performance over a traditional classroom due: (a) to the change in the teacher-pupil ratio, or (b) to the special program? To answer this question, two control groups might be used: (a) using traditional classrooms, and (b) using traditional classrooms where the teacher-pupil ratio was the same as in the innovative program. A thoughtful choice of control conditions is important in setting up a study and should be carefully considered in evaluating research claims.

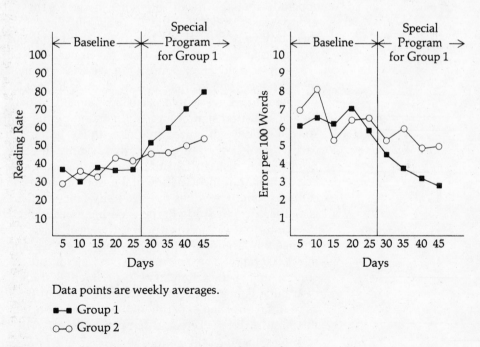

Data points are weekly averages.

■–■ Group 1
○–○ Group 2

Figure 13.1 Hypothetical Data From a Reading Study

Monitoring of Conditions

Another problem that can arise is unplanned happenings that effect one group or condition but not others. The control group may be placed in a special program by an administrator not in on the study. There may be snowstorm or perhaps a strike closing school for one group and not the other. Some teachers might not follow the experimental conditions. A careful monitoring of the actual conditions of an experiment is needed to assure such events are not ignored in evaluating the research.

Drawing Conclusions from Research

Given this background on experimental designs and alternative interpretations of findings, we are ready to consider three questions to be answered in drawing conclusions from research:

1 Is there a difference?
2 If there is a difference, to what can it be attributed?
3 How general is this finding?

Question 1. Is there a difference?

Group designs. In most group designs, the question of whether or not a difference exists is often answered by an appeal to the concept of *statistical significance*. Statistical significance statements give the probability of finding a given difference between two groups if the experiment were to be repeated many times and there was no real difference. For example, a study might conclude that the mean difference between the experimental and control groups was significant at the .05 probability level ($p < .05$). This means that if the study were carried out 100 times, a difference as large as the one found would occur by chance less than five times. The groups selected for study are samples from larger populations we wish to generalize to. Sampling errors may produce group differences by chance. If the p level is .01, it indicates the obtained difference would occur by chance less than one time in a 100. The idea of statistical significance is illustrated by the distributions in figure 13.2. Assume that we did three studies with 50 students in each experimental and each control group. In each study, assume the SDs are the same (1.5). In Study A, the distributions of scores for the two groups did not even overlap. *Every* student in the experimental group did better than every student in the control group. One does not need any fancy statistics to conclude that there is a difference. In Study B, the experimental mean is three points higher than the control mean. Is this a real difference? The probability of finding a difference this large *by chance* (when there is no real difference) is less than one in a 1,000 times. The difference is very significant even though some control students did better than some experimental students. In Study C, the two distributions nearly overlap. The probability of finding a difference as large as .4 in favor of the experimental group is about ten times out of 100. Since this large a difference could happen quite often by chance, it would not be considered statistically significant.

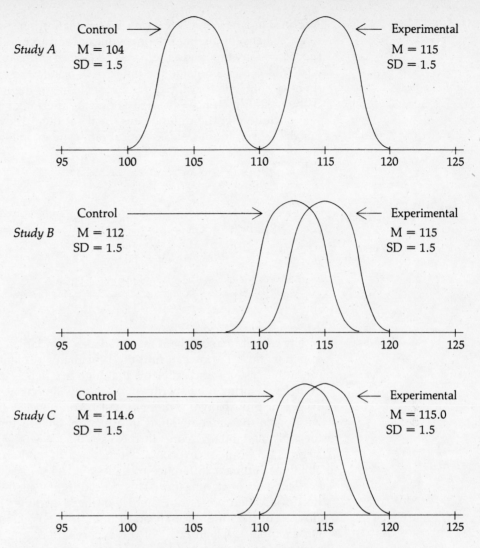

Figure 13.2   A Comparison of Score Distributions for Different Experimental and Control Groups

When an experiment involves only two groups, statistical significance can be determined by computing what is called a *critical ratio*. This is the ratio of the difference between two means to the *standard error of the difference* between the means. The standard error of the difference between the means is the denominator in the following expression and is a function of the standard deviations of the two distributions and the size of the groups (N).

$$\text{Critical Ratio} = \frac{M_e - M_c}{\sqrt{\dfrac{SD_e^2}{N_e} + \dfrac{SD_c^2}{N_c}}}$$

The standard error is the standard deviation (in z-score units) of the differences between the means one would expect to find if the experiment were repeated many times and there was *actually no difference*. If the obtained difference ($M_e - M_c$) is outside the range of two standard errors of the difference, then we conclude that the difference is "real" at the .05 level of significance. If the mean difference obtained is outside the range of 2.6 standard errors, we conclude that the difference is "real" at the .01 level of significance.*
For data given in figure 13.3 critical ratios are as follows:

$$\text{Study A} \quad CR = \frac{115 - 104}{\sqrt{\dfrac{1.5^2}{50} + \dfrac{1.5^2}{50}}} = \frac{11}{.3} = 36.7 \quad p < .001$$

$$\text{Study B} \quad CR = \frac{115 - 112}{\sqrt{\dfrac{1.5^2}{50} + \dfrac{1.5^2}{50}}} = \frac{3}{.3} = 10.0 \quad p < .001$$

$$\text{Study C} \quad CR = \frac{115.0 - 114.6}{\sqrt{\dfrac{1.5^2}{50} + \dfrac{1.5^2}{50}}} = \frac{.4}{.3} = 1.3 \quad p > .05$$

The critical ratio can be interpreted as a standard score (z-score). By using appendix table B, one can find the probability of obtaining a standard score (or in this case a standard error) that high by chance. A standard score of 1.3 or *higher* favoring the experimental group will occur 9.68 percent of the time. To get the probability of a difference of 1.3 or higher in *either direction* (+ or −), we double the percent found in appendix table B under "Percent Higher" for a given standard score. In this case $9.68 + 9.68 = 19.36$. Thus, a CR as large as 1.3 would be expected 19 times in a 100. When we consider the probability of getting a difference of a given size in *either* direction, it is called a *two-tailed test* of significance. This procedure is usually used when the direction of a difference is not predicted ahead of time. If we hypothesize the *direction* of the difference ahead of time, it is possible to use a *one-tailed test*. For example, a CR in favor of the experimental group of at least 1.3 would occur about ten in a hundred ($p = .10$).

When more than two means are involved, significance testing uses a procedure called analysis of variance rather than the critical ratio. However, the basic idea is the same.

It is not our objective to teach the fine nuances of using statistics to make probability inferences. Our concern is in understanding concepts important to deciding if a difference is real. We have found one answer. A difference is real if it is statistically significant. However, this answer contains a problem. From the formula for the critical ratio, it can be seen that the standard error of the difference between the means gets smaller as the number of cases (N) gets larger. This means that a small difference would be judged to be statis-

---

*When N is small, it is common to use a t-test rather than a CR. The logic of the tests are identical. The only difference is that in computing the standard error of the difference, N-1 is used rather than N in the denominator.

tically significant if the N were large enough. Or, a large difference might be judged to be insignificant if the N were small. For example, for Study C (figure 13.2), if the N were increased from 50 to 200 in each group, the difference of .4 would be highly significant. Thus, in evaluating the question, "Is there a difference?" using group designs, it is necessary to first find out if the results are statistically significant, and second, to find out if the size of the difference is *educationally significant.* A gain of one-fourth to one-half of a standard deviation on most achievement measures is likely to be educationally important, but there is no pat answer to the question. It remains a question to be answered by careful judgment.

> *Evaluation Rule 2. In evaluating a difference based on a group design, note the size of the sample (N), the size of the difference in standard deviation units, and the probability of finding a difference that large. If the difference does not show statistical significance, do not consider it further. If it does show statistical significance, evaluate the size of the difference for educational significance (especially when N is large).*

Individual-subject designs. The idea behind using a test for statistical significance is to rule out chance differences. Another way of increasing the confidence in a difference is to repeat the finding. In an individual-subjects design, this can be done by using an ABAB design and showing replication with the same subjects. It also can be accomplished by replicating a finding for different subjects or different behaviors.

> *Evaluation Rule 3. In evaluating a difference based on an individual-subject design, if the difference appears to be educationally significant, determine whether or not the difference was replicated.* Treat with caution those differences presented without replication. The more replications demonstrated, the more confidence you can place in a difference.

Question 2. To What Can The Difference Be Attributed?

When a substantial difference is found, it is necessary to evaluate the possible alternative interpretations for the difference. First, consider whether the study used an individual-subject design or a group design. If it is group design, determine the nature of the control group. Did the selection of the control group permit control for interpretations based on other changes that can take place with time? If not, there is a problem in drawing any clear conclusion. Also consider whether or not the groups were equal at the start as shown by pretest data. Be cautious when the groups were not equivalent at pretest. Next, consider if there is monitoring evidence to show that the effects were actually produced by the experimental treatment. Finally, consider any other possible interpretations for the finding.

If an individual-subject design was used, note whether procedures were used to demonstrate that other factors associated with time could not account for the result. Usually a reversal procedure or some form of multiple-baseline procedure is required to accomplish this. Also, look carefully at the changes made as the experimental treatment. Was the change called the experimental treatment the *only* change made? If not, alternative interpretations are possible.

Evaluation Rule 4. In evaluating a research study or claim, determine if the nature of the design and the experimental procedures adequately control for alternative interpretations of the findings.

Question 3. How General Is This Finding?

Generality depends on what is sampled. If a spelling test is built by *drawing randomly* from the 10,000 most common words in print, then we can generalize a given test performance to this list. If a study of classroom management samples first- and second-grade teachers in a given city, then we can generalize to the first- and second-grade teachers in that city. If we have reason to believe that other teachers do not differ in relevant ways from those in the sample, we might expect the finding to hold for these others too. If we evaluate an instructional program for the disadvantaged by sampling Title I eligible schools in urban and rural areas, and including all ethnic backgrounds, then the finding can be generalized to other Title I eligible schools.

If a study is done on a single subject, we cannot generalize to other subjects until the results are repeated on a variety of subjects. If a study is done with a single teacher, we cannot generalize to other teachers until similar studies prove effective with other teachers.

Evaluation Rule 5. To evaluate the generality of a finding from a given study, find out what was sampled (or covered completely). Replication across a sample of similar things provides the basis for a generalization. Sampling (and thus a generalization) may involve:

1 Student or teacher behaviors measured as dependent variables
2 Student or teacher behaviors measured as independent variables
3 Students selected
4 Teachers selected
5 Schools selected
6 Places in which the dependent behavior occurs
7 Durability of an effect over time

---

summary

There are two kinds of research concerned with relating causes and effects—correlational research and experimental research. In correlational research, relations between variables as they now exist are studied. The difficulty with correlational research is that knowledge of a relation is not sufficient evidence to make an inference about a cause. The relations *might* be pointing to a cause, but we don't know if that is really so. In general, we should be very skeptical about drawing causal conclusions from correlational studies.

Experimental research requires the changing of an independent variable, making at least two measurements on some dependent variable, and comparing the measures to draw a conclusion. In group design, the measurements are taken on two (or more) groups which are treated differently. In individual subject designs, the measurements are taken from different treatment conditions on the same subjects.

To permit unambiguous interpretations of an experimental study, use a design that will control for alternative interpretations of the results. In research or teaching, this usually involves other events which change with time which might account for an outcome, such as:

1 *Other experiences* that involve learning
2 *Maturation*
3 *Test practice*
4 *Changes in group membership*
5 *Changes in tests*
6 *Score changes due to unreliability of tests*
7 *Extreme-group selection effects* (statistical regression)

In group designs, control of these potential influences is best achieved by the use of a control group. However, the use of a control group raises a question of comparability of control group and treatment group in terms of important background characteristics. Random assignment of persons to treatment and control groups is the most effective means of coping with this problem. Where random assignment is not possible, caution must be exercised in interpreting results.

In individual-subject designs, control is achieved over differences in personal history by using the same persons under baseline and various treatment conditions. A significant treatment effect has to produce an effect on the dependent variable that is in addition to that shown during baseline measurements. To rule out other interpretations of effects associated with time, reversal designs, multiple-baseline designs, and simple replications are used.

Some of the more important group designs are:

1 Random assignment to groups, pretest and posttest.
2 Random assignment to groups, posttest only.
3 No random assignment (intact groups), pretest and posttest. Check for initial differences on critical variables. Adjust outcomes for pretest differences.

4 Simple replication.

5 Norm-referenced comparison. Use the norm group of a standardized test as the comparison group. The goal is to show a significant improvement in standings on the norms (pretest to posttest) for the experimental group.

The two main individual-subject designs are:

1 Reversal designs, where baseline and experimental conditions are alternated.

2 Multiple-baseline designs, where for the same subject, different behaviors are changed at different times; or where the same behavior is changed at different times for different subjects.

Group and individual designs can be combined to make both within-group and between group comparisons. When a baseline shows systematic changes over time this may be especially helpful. Multiple control groups are sometimes useful in isolating different possible interpretations of an outcome. Monitoring of experimental and control conditions is necessary to insure that unplanned happenings do not influence outcomes.

Three questions need to be answered in drawing conclusions. First, is there a difference? Second, if there is, to what can it be attributed? Third, how general is the finding?

In answering the first question for group designs, the answer focuses on the question of statistical significance. Is the difference obtained large enough, relative to the standard error of the difference, to justify a conclusion of statistical significance? The critical ratio provides one basis for making this decision when two means are involved. When more than two means are being compared, analysis of variance can be used. If a difference is statistically significant, it is still necessary to decide if the difference is educationally significant. With a large enough N, almost any difference can be found to be statistically significant. A difference of one-fourth to one-half standard deviation on most achievement tests is likely to have educational significance. In answering the question, "Is there a difference?" for individual-subject designs, the basic procedure for building confidence that an effect is real is to use *replication* within the same study or in the new study.

In answering the second question, "To what is the difference attributable?" it is necessary to determine the degree to which the design controls for alternative interpretations. Is a control group used which is *comparable* to the treatment group? Is there monitoring evidence to show that the difference was actually produced by the experimental treatment? In individual subject designs, are procedures used to rule out other things that change with time? Was the change called the experimental treatment the only change made?

In answering the third question, "How general are the findings?" it is necessary to find out what was sampled in building the experimental procedures or groups. When replication of an effect is shown across a sample of similar things, a basis for a generalization is provided.

self-test

1 One approach to answering a "what" question studies the correlation between existing conditions and outcomes, but does not _____ any condition.

2 Experimental research requires at a minimum: (a) the _____ of one or more variables (independent variables), (b) the making of at least _____ measurements on some dependent variables, and (c) the _____ of two (or more) measurements to provide the basis for a conclusion.

3 To permit unambiguous interpretations of a study, good design must provide for control of variables that might lead to _____ interpretations of findings.

4 To rule out alternative interpretations of possible effects associated with time, individual-subject designs use _____ of effects, _____ baselines, and replications.

5 The strongest group designs involve _____ assignment of persons to conditions.

6 In using a norm-referenced design, it is important that pretesting and post-testing occur at the _____ used for testing the norm group.

7 The standard error is the standard deviation (in z-score units) of the differences between the means one would expect to find if the experiment were repeated many times and there was actually _____ difference.

1 manipulate

2 changing; two; comparison

3 alternative

4 reversals; multiple

5 random

6 dates

7 no

NUMBER RIGHT _____

exercise 1 programed practice

1 Much research begins with a "why" question. However, it is usually necessary to rephrase a "why" question into a "_____" question to study possible answers.

2 A "what" question seeks to determine the _____ which produce a given outcome.

1 what

2 conditions

3 One approach to answering a "what" question studies the correlation between existing conditions and outcomes, but does not _____ any condition.

4 A more powerful approach for demonstrating a causal influence is to experimentally _____ a condition to see how it effects an outcome of interest.

5 Experimental research requires at a minimum: (a) the _____ of one or more variables (independent variables), (b) the making of at least _____ measurements on some dependent variable, and (c) the _____ of two (or more) measurements to provide the basis for a conclusion.

6 In group designs, the measurements are taken on two (or more) groups which are treated _____.

7 In individual-subject designs, the measurements are taken from different treatment conditions on the _____ subjects.

8 To permit unambiguous interpretations of a study, good design must provide for control of variables that might lead to _____ interpretations of findings.

9 Since research on learning-teaching processes takes _____, other events which change with _____ can offer possible alternative explanations.

10 In group designs to rule out the effects of the many factors which can effect changes over time, a _____ or comparison group is used.

11 To be sure that control and experimental groups are equivalent or important variables, it is best to assign persons _____ to groups. An alternative procedure is to _____ the groups on some critical variables.

12 In individual-subject designs, the individual's unique history will be reflected in the _____ measures. A significant _____ effect must operate on top of this.

---

3 manipulate

4 change, manipulate

5 changing; two; comparison

6 differently

7 same

8 alternative

9 time; time

10 control

11 randomly; match

12 baseline; treatment

13   To rule out alternative interpretations of possible effects associated with time, individual-subject designs use _____ of effects, _____ base-lines, and replications.

14   The strongest group designs involve _____ assignment of persons to conditions.

15   When random assignment is not possible, it is necessary to demonstrate group _____ on important variables or to statistically adjust for differences.

16   In a norm-referenced comparison, one attempts to show that a special treatment group shows a significant _____ on the test norms in going from pretest to posttest.

17   In using a norm-referenced design, it is important that pretesting and post-testing occur at the _____ used for testing the norm group. It is also important not to select the treatment group on the basis of low or high scores on the pretest. This would produce a statistical _____ effect.

18   Individual-subject designs are most useful in the fine-grain analysis of the _____ process to show explicitly what specific teacher behaviors produce what specific effects on the students. They are less useful in the more global evaluation of a _____ _____.

19   In a reversal design, a baseline condition (A) is followed by an experimental condition (B). Then, the experimental treatment is _____ and the baseline condition is _____.

20   In a multiple-baseline design, the treatment effects are introduced at different times for: (a) different dependent _____ of the same subject, or (b) for the same behaviors for _____ subjects.

21   In group designs the found differences may be evaluated for statistical significance. A statement of statistical significance is a statement of the probability of finding a difference of *that size* by _____ if no real difference existed. The differences which may occur by chance are attributed to _____ errors in selecting groups.

---

13 reversals; multiple

14 random

15 comparability, equivalence, similarly

16 increase

17 dates; regression

18 teaching; total program

19. withdrawn; reinstated

20 behaviors; different

21 chance; sampling

22 When an experiment involves only two groups, statistical significance can be determined by computing what is called a _____ ratio. This is the ratio of the difference between two means to the standard _____ of the difference between the means.

23 The standard error is the standard deviation (in z-score units) of the differences between the means one would expect to find if the experiment were repeated many times and there was actually _____ difference.

24 The standard error of the difference between the means gets smaller as the _____ of cases (N) gets larger. This means that a small difference would be judged to be statistically significant if the _____ were large enough.

25 In evaluating the question, "Is there a difference?" using group designs, it is necessary to first find out if the results are statistically significant, and second, to find out if the size of the difference is _____ significant. A gain of one-fourth to _____-_____ of a standard deviation on most achievement measures is likely to be educationally important.

26 The idea behind using a test for statistical significance is to rule out _____ differences. Another way of increasing the confidence in a difference is to _____ the finding.

27 To evaluate the generality of a finding from a given study, find out what was _____ (or covered completely). Replication across a sample of _____ things provides the basis for a generalization.

22 critical;
   error

23 no

24 number; N,
   number of
   cases

25 educationally;
   one-half

26 chance;
   repeat

27 sampled;
   similar

exercise 2   practice in classifying of research

1   *Read the following:*

In the teaching of sound-symbol relations for beginning reading, a *corrections* condition was compared with a *no-corrections* condition. Five four-year-old children were taught individually throughout the study. A 20-minute lesson was planned for each day. New symbols were introduced only at the beginning of a new lesson. Every five days the conditions were changed from no-corrections to corrections to no-corrections to corrections. The experiment lasted 20 days. Rates of right and wrong responses were compared under each condition, and the percent of sound-symbols mastered was tested at the beginning of the study and at the end of each condition.

Answer the following:

a. Is this study: correlational _____   (check one)
   experimental _____

b. Is the design: group _____   (check one)
   individual-subject _____
   mixed _____

c. What subtype of design is it? _____

_____

d. What kinds of replications of conditions occur? _____

_____

e. What kinds of generalizations could be made about the findings? _____

_____

_____

_____

_____

2   *Read the following:*

The Illinois Test of Psycholinguistic Abilities (ITPA) and other tests were given to 21 children, ages seven to nine, who had normal IQ's but were behind in reading. It was found that the poor readers could understand what they saw (Visual Decoding) better than the norm population, but were below norms on memory for visual sequences, finding objects hidden in pictures, sound blending, mazes, memory for designs, and a measure of perceptual speed. It was suggested that these deficiencies be considered in planning remediation.[4] Bateman has interpreted the findings as suggesting deficient decoding skills rather than comprehension skills.[5]

Answer the following:

a. Is this study: correlational _____   (Check one)
   experimental _____

b. It cannot be experimental because there is no experimental treatment. The comparisons made are of this sort:

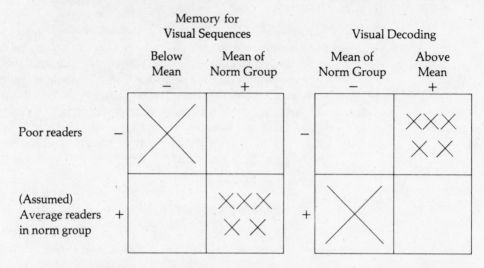

The comparisons are basically correlations based on the assumption that the norm group for the tests given would be average readers. Thus, poor reading is correlated with several low scores and one high score (visual decoding) for the tests given. How would you treat the suggestion that these findings be used in planning remediation? _____

_____

_____

3 *Read the following:*

The study examined the test data and history data available on 360 adolescents who were admitted to a state hospital because of emotional problems.[6] Thirty-one percent of the adolescents were classified as disabled readers (reading below the fourth grade level). The disabled-reader group was compared with the remaining adolescents for whom there were records. The results showed the disabled readers had full scale IQ's on the Wechsler-Bellevue Scale that were nearly identical to the non-disabled readers. However, the disabled readers were higher on the Performance Scale of the Wechsler-Bellevue and lower on the Verbal Scale. There was no evidence to separate the groups because of factors such as brain damage, mixed dominance, physical handicaps, or emotional problems. Boys were more likely to be poor readers than girls. It was concluded that the results support the position that verbal ability is needed to learn to read and that girls are higher in this skill and thus have fewer reading difficulties than boys. Beyond this finding, the results fail to support other assumed causes of poor reading. The author suggests the answer to the problem may lie in better teaching methods.

Answer the following:

a. Is this study: correlational _____ (check one)
           experimental _____

b. How would you interpret the negative evidence about causes? _____

_____

_____

c. How would you interpret the conclusion concerning the positive findings?

_____

_____

_____

_____

4 *Read the following:*

Bishop[7] compared the amount of transfer obtained when reading was taught by sounds versus the sight-word method. The letters were 12 Arabic characters, eight consonants and four vowels. They were combined to form two sets of eight words (see below). The 12 letters appeared at least once in both sets of words. A native speaker of Arabic recorded the sounds and the words on tape. The forms of the letters and words were printed on cards. College sophomores were used as subjects and randomly assigned to three groups of 20 each.

Training words	Phonetic symbols	Transfer words	Phonetic symbols
و ر ا ف	fa:ru:	ى ر ى م	mi:ri:
ى د ا ف	fa:di:	و ت و م	mu:tu:
ا ف ى ت	ti:fa:	ا ش و ك	ko:sa:
ى ن و ت	tu:ni:	ى ف ا ك	ka:fi:
ا ش ى ش	si:sa:	ا ف ى ن	ni:fa:
ش ى م ى ش	si:mi:	ى د ا ن	na:di:
ى ف ا د	da:fi:	ا ش ى ر	ri:sa:
و ك و د	do:ko:	ى ف ى ر	ri:fi:

Stage 1. All subjects *listened* to the eight words in the transfer set and learned to pronounce them. They did not see the words.

Stage 2. The three groups were treated differently:

    Group L This letter-sound group listened and repeated the 12 sounds and then learned to associate them with their graphic shapes.

    Group W This whole-word group listened and repeated eight words and then learned to associate them with their graphic form.

    Group C This control group spent the same time as the others but on an unrelated task.

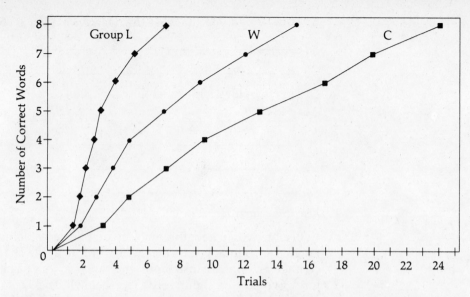

Figure 13.3 Learning curves on transfer task for group trained originally with whole words (W), group trained with single letters (L), and control group (C)

Stage 3. All subjects learned to read the words that they had heard and pronounced in stage 1. This was the transfer test. Figure 13.3 shows the results.[8] The group taught the letter-sound relations was superior on transfer to new words.

Answer the following:

a. Is this study: correlational _____ (check one)
    experimental _____

b. What kind of design was used? Describe its exact type. _____

_____

_____

c. What kinds of replications of conditions occur? _____

_____

d. What kinds of generalizations could be made about the results? _____

_____

_____

_____

5 *Read the following:*

Most educators accept the idea that instruction should be geared to the student's individual *learning style.* In this study, Bateman[9] tests this idea for beginning reading. Some have suggested that one should teach to the weakness, others that one should teach to the strength. Bateman also explores this issue.

Auditory and visual learners were defined by the difference in scores on the Illinois Test of Psycholinguistic Abilities (ITPA) subtests for Auditory Sequential Memory and Visual Sequential Memory. These subtests basically measure the length of an orally presented sequence of random digits one can remember and state, and the length of a sequence of nonsense figures one can remember and reproduce. As a group, in terms of age norms, the children scored nine months higher on the auditory task than the visual task. Thus, to be called an auditory learner, a student had to do nine months better on the auditory task than the visual task.

Using the test results, 87 students were assigned to four classes. Two classes were for auditory learners and two were for visual learners. Two teaching methods were defined. The *auditory method* class utilized the Lippincott beginning reading program where sound-symbol relations are emphasized before being *synthesized* into words. The *visual method* class used the Scott-Foresman beginning reading program which starts with sight words and then goes through *analysis* to sounds. Teachers did not know what type of learner they had. Inservice training was held to keep teachers effective with the method in use.

The children were tested at the end of first grade with the Gates Primary Word Recognition and Paragraph Reading tests. A spelling test of 12 words and six nonsense words was constructed by the author and given to all.

The results show (see table 13.1) that the auditory method was superior to the visual method and that the auditory subjects were superior to the visual subjects on both reading and spelling. On the reading test, method effects accounted for 14 percent of the variance, while subject effects accounted for seven percent of the variance. Of the 16 good readers, 14 had received the auditory method, two the visual. Of the 18 poor readers, 16 were visual subjects and 12 of these had the visual method.

TABLE 13.1   REReading Grade-Equivalent Scores, Spelling Scores, and IQ's for the Four Groups

| Class | N | Subjects | Method | IQ | Average Reading Grade | | Spelling |
					Mean	SD	Mean No. Right
1.	24	Aud	Aud	126.0	3.63	.37	11.29
2.	24	Vis	Aud	124.7	3.43	.38	7.92
3.	20	Aud	Vis	124.8	3.34	.59	7.85
4.	19	Vis	Vis	126.2	2.90	.51	1.79

The effects of the two teaching methods were also examined in four additional classes where the students were not assigned by learner-type, but in terms of the usual district policy (heterogeneous grouping). The "auditory method" was found to be superior in terms of both reading and spelling performance.

Bateman concludes: "The data from this study suggests the answer would then be to teach to his strengths if he is an auditory learner or to his weaknesses if he is a visual learner. However, a much simpler way of stating all this is to say that the auditory method is superior, regardless of the child's own pattern of learning."

Answer the following:

a. What kind of experimental study is this? (Note: consider only the four classes assigned by learner type.) _____

_____

_____

b. In what way is this also a correlational study? _____

_____

_____

c. What kinds of generalizations could be made about the results? _____

_____

_____

_____

d. What restrictions should be placed on conclusions? _____

_____

_____

Answers to Exercise 2

1 a. Experimental.
   b. Individual-subject. (It is not a mixed design because there is no separate control group, or a group treated differently.)
   c. Subtype: reversal design ABAB.
   d. Each experimental condition is replicated once. The basic experiment is replicated for five different individuals.
   e. The findings could be generalized to other four-year olds if consistent effects for different children were found. The findings could be generalized to the teaching of other sound-symbol relations not included in the study if consistent effects for symbols were found.

2 a. Correlational. A study can be correlational without computing correlation coefficients.
   b. I would probably ignore them and directly test reading skills. I would also examine the procedures being used to teach decoding skills.

3 a. Correlational. Again, a four-fold table can help. The relations reported are of this sort:

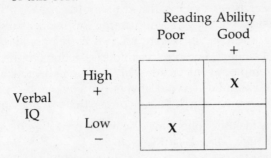

Reading Ability

	Poor −	Good +
High +		X
Low −	X	

Verbal IQ

    b. The reliability and validity of the measures of possible causes must be examined first. If they are high, then the evidence is strong against those possible causes. If the measures are low in reliability and/or validity, the study has no bearing on the importance of those causes.

    c. As a tenable hypothesis.

4 a. Experimental.

    b. Group design involving random assignment and posttesting. It also involved pre-teaching of the pronunciation of the transfer words.

    c. None. We cannot treat the findings for each subject as replications of conditions because there is no basis for a within-subject comparison that could be examined for each subject. In a group design, the randomly formed groups must be treated as a unit for analysis.

    d. Can be generalized to other Arabic sounds and words, maybe to English. Can be generalized to learning by other college students, maybe to younger and older persons.

5 a. This is a group design, with posttesting and with *matching* for selection on learner type. The matching on subject characteristics has not been considered in detail in this unit, but is another way of insuring comparability of experimental and control groups.

    b. When we separate the students into two learner types we can correlate learner type with outcomes for each type of treatment. Do auditory types do better with auditory or visual instruction?

    c. (1) The "auditory" method (teaching sounds and blending) is superior to the whole word method regardless of learner-type. (2) "Auditory-learners" do better than "visual learners" in beginning reading.

    d. (1) The conclusions are restricted to the Lippincott and Scott-Foresman instructional systems, and are not generalizable to phonic and whole-word systems. (However, research by Bliesmer and Yarborough[10] supports a more general interpretation.)

    (2) The conclusions are restricted to brighter children (average IQ was about 125). (Again, the Bliesmer and Yarborough results suggest they are more general.)

    (3) The conclusions are restricted by the definition of auditory learner and visual learner in terms of memory span. Also, there was not a good separation of "types." There was an average superiority on the auditory test for these bright students. This could favor the "auditory method."

exercise 3 evaluating research reports

This exercise can be expanded or contracted according to the wishes of your instructor. We suggest you use the Research Evaluation Report Form. Summarize one descriptive study, two correlational studies, and three experimental studies. Try to restrict your selections to the less complicated designs. For example, avoid factor analytic studies in looking for descriptive or correlational studies. Avoid analysis of covariance studies in looking at group experimental designs. Select studies that are relevant to your area of interest.

a. Consider the following research journals as resources:

American Educational Research Journal

American Journal of Mental Deficiency

Child Development

Elementary School Journal

Exceptional Children

International Reading Association Journal

Journal of Applied Behavior Analysis

Journal of Educational Psychology

Journal of Educational Research

Journal of Experimental Child Psychology

Journal of Learning Disabilities

Journal of School Psychology

Journal of Special Education

Journal of Teacher Education

Journal of Verbal Learning and Verbal Behavior

Psychology in the Schools

Teachers' College Record

The Reading Teacher

b. These reviews may help you target studies in an area of interest:
Review of Educational Research
The School Review
Encyclopedia of Educational Research, 4th edition (ed.) Robert L. Ebel
Yearbook of the National Society for the Study of Education

c. These collections of research studies may contain what you need:
R. C. Anderson et al. (eds.), *Current Research on Instruction* (Englewood Cliffs, N. J.: Prentice-Hall, 1969).
B. D. Bateman, *Reading Performance and How to Achieve It* (Seattle: Bernie Straub Publishing Company and Special Child Publications, 1973).
W. C. Becker, *An Empirical Basis for Change in Education* (Palo Alto, Calif.: Science Research Associates, 1971).
K. D. O'Leary, and S. G. O'Leary, *Classroom Management—The Successful Use of Behavior Modification* (New York: Pergamon Press, 1972).
R. Ulrich, T. Stachnik, and J. Mabry, *Control of Human Behavior*, vol. 3 (Glenview, Ill.: Scott, Foresman, 1974).
R. K. Parker, *Reading in Educational Psychology* (Boston: Allyn and Bacon, 1968).

d. Now you should have the skills to read this classic . . . a must for the teacher of reading.
J. Chall, *Learning to Read—The Great Debate* (New York: McGraw-Hill, 1967). This could be a source of studies of historical and contemporary interest in reading research.

An alternative assignment: A term paper which is a research review of a topical area of interest to you or as suggested by your instructor.

Research Evaluation Report Form

1 *Title of Study* _____

2 *Author*(s) _____

3 *Reference* _____

4 *Type of Study:* Experimental _____ Correlational _____ Descriptive _____
If descriptive: describe subjects, measures, and conclusions (items 6, 7, and 14).
If correlational: describe subjects, measures, relations found, alternative explanations, and conclusions (use items 6, 7, 10a, 12 and 14).

5 *Design of experimental studies* (fill out a, b, or c):

a. Group _____

		Not	Norm	
Random	Random	Random	Referenced	Simple
pre-post ___	post only ___	pre-post ___	Comparison ___	Replication ___

b. Individual-subject _____

| | Multiple | Simple | No |
| Reversal _____ | Baseline _____ | Replication _____ | Replication _____ |

c. Mixed or other (specify below) _____

_____

_____

6 *Subjects* (Describe characteristics, give *N*) _____

_____

_____

7 *Dependent Measures* (Describe and give evidence for reliability and validity).

_____

_____

_____

8 *Independent Variables* (Treatments) _____

_____

_____

9 *Were conditions monitored?* Yes _____ No _____. If yes, specify evidence that experimental and control conditions were or were not satisfactory. _____

_____

_____

(Note: For mixed designs, fill out 10 for between-group effects and 11 for within-group effects.)

10 *For Group Designs:*

a. What outcomes showed statistically significant effects? _____

_____

_____

_____

b. Which in 10a are educationally significant effects? Give basis for answer.

_____

_____

_____

11 *For Individual-Subject Designs:*

a. What outcomes showed replicated effects? _____

_____

b. Which in 11a are educationally significant effects? Give basis. _____

_____

_____

12 Does the design provide adequate control of alternative explanations? Where not controlled, specify alternative explanations. _____

_____

_____

13 In what ways can the results be generalized? Where can the results not be generalized? _____

_____

_____

14 What firm conclusion can you draw from this study? _____

_____

_____

_____

_____

_____

_____

discussion questions

1 Give an example of descriptive research.
2 Describe the essential differences between correlational and experimental research.
3 Give an example of a correlational study.
4 Why should we be concerned with experimental designs?
5 What are some of the common alternative explanations for outcomes in educational research which are related to changes with time?
6 Explain the concept of statistical regression.
7 How do group designs control for individual differences in subject history and for other variables that can change with time?
8 How do individual-subject designs control for individual differences in subject history and for other variables that can produce changes with time?
9 Describe how a norm-referenced comparison is made and the cautions to be exercised.
10 Give an example of a reversal design.
11 What are some advantages of combining group and individual-subject designs?
12 Give some examples to show why it is important to monitor the experimental conditions to see what actually is happening.
13 What are three important questions to ask in drawing a conclusion from a research study?
14 In group designs, how would you answer the question, "Is there a difference?"
15 What is meant by the concept statistical significance?
16 What is a standard error of a difference?
17 What is a critical ratio?
18 Explain why a critical ratio can be interpreted as a standard score (z-score).
19 What questions should you ask in deciding to what to attribute a difference *for a group design? for an individual-subject design?*
20 How do you decide on what generalizations can be made from a study?
21 Give an example describing sampling in a study which would permit generalization across a class of dependent behaviors, a class of people, and a class of independent stimulus events.

unit 14

Outcome Evaluation Revisited

objectives

When you complete this unit you should be able to—

1 Describe the general steps to follow in planning an outcome evaluation study.
2 Explain the principles to be considered in selecting an experimental design.
3 Explain the problems which might be encountered with some designs.
4 Describe the kinds of premeasures that are necessary or desirable for different kinds of designs.
5 State some possible approaches to evaluating programs with different objectives.
6 Describe the outcome measures that might be considered for a study.
7 Describe two kinds of process measures that are important in evaluating an outcome study.
8 Summarize the key steps in data analysis.
9 Summarize the key elements of a report on an outcome study.

lesson

An increasingly important fact of educational life today is that practices must be defended with data and that data must be provided to facilitate the improvement of practices. This is particularly the case when new programs are brought into a system. Outcome evaluations can serve a *political function* within a system by providing a rational basis for accepting something new; they can also serve an *educational function* by providing a basis for program selection and improvement. In unit 7 we considered some of the ways in which criterion-referenced tests could be used to compare program outcomes and to provide a basis for program improvement. In this unit, we return to the question of outcome evaluation within a framework which now includes norm-referenced tests and considerations of research design. Systematic planning of an outcome study should answer the following six questions:

272

1 *Design*. Who will be tested when?
2 *Premeasures*. What initial assessments will be made?
3 *Outcome measures*. What final assessments will be made?
4 *Process measures*. What measures will be taken to show continuous student progress and/or the effectiveness of program implementation?
5 *Analysis*. How are the data to be summarized?
6 *Reporting*. How are the findings to be communicated to others?

Selection of a Design

Control-Group Designs

Usually, a group design will be needed for an outcome study. Individual-subject designs are more likely to be helpful in studying the effects of possible variations in procedures. In choosing a design, select the strongest design possible under the local circumstances. This means that you should first strive for random assignment of students (or the random assignment of members of matched pairs). Where possible, teachers should also be randomly assigned to the treatments to be compared, given the condition that they volunteer for such assignment. The key design consideration is that the groups differ only in their programs of instruction. Random assignment helps to insure this. Where random assignment of teachers is not possible, then strive to select teachers who are especially competent in the programs to be compared and obtain some measures of the teaching process to support this. Where random assignment of students is not possible and intact groups are used, try to select groups that are comparable and obtain premeasures to support their comparability as discussed in the section on premeasures.

Norm-Referenced Comparisons

When a control group is not available, consider a norm-referenced comparison. The key here is to find tests which will fairly measure the objectives of the programs to be compared. As suggested in the last unit, this design assumes that without the special program the students would maintain the same position on pretest and posttest, relative to the norm group. The demonstration of an improvement on the norm from pretest to posttest, which is greater than the change shown by the norm group for the same time period, is taken as evidence in favor of the program being evaluated. Standard scores should be used for computing all summary statistics, rather than grade equivalents or percentiles. However, a conversion to percentiles expressed on a standard-score scale is useful in making an interpretation. For example, suppose the Total Reading expanded standard score on the Metropolitan Achievement Test, Primary II (Form F), shows a mean of 39 at pretest and 53 at posttest. To interpret this gain, we look in the table which converts standard scores to percentiles for beginning second graders and ending second graders. A standard score of 39 is at the 26th percentile for beginning second graders. A standard score of 53 is at the 52nd percentile for ending second-grade students. This represents a gain of 27 percentile points over the average gain of the norm group. Now if we plot these percentiles on a special graph paper (which anyone can make by noting the way the vertical axis is labeled), significance of effects in quarter-standard deviation units is directly shown, percentiles are shown, and relations to the national average (50th percentile) are shown. Figure 14.1 illustrates the MAT Reading data just discussed. The gain of three-fourths of a standard deviation is directly read off the graph by noting the length of the arrow. The graph also shows the pretest and posttest percentiles and the relation of the outcome to the norm group average. It is quite clear that the effect is important and that the experimental group has caught up with the norm group.

A potential problem for norm-referenced comparisons arises because the

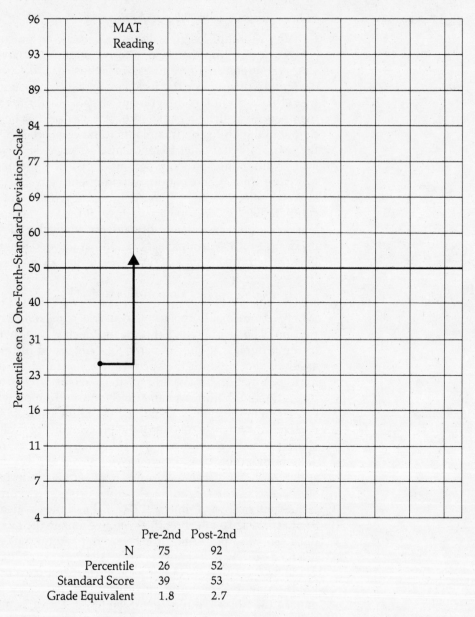

	Pre-2nd	Post-2nd
N	75	92
Percentile	26	52
Standard Score	39	53
Grade Equivalent	1.8	2.7

Figure 14.1 An Easily Interpreted Graph Form

norms are often based on data obtained at only one or two times during the year. The monthly norms are interpolations based on drawing a best-fit line through the data for several years. It is unlikely that gains in learning follow this smooth-line function. A norm-referenced comparison can be greatly distorted because of this. The problem can be avoided by designing the study to test students at the same times that the norm group was tested. Table 14.1 shows the dates when norms were determined for commonly used achievement tests. The table also shows where the Anchor Test Study can be used to provide missing fall or spring norm data.

TABLE 14.1 DATES WHEN NORM DATA WERE OBTAINED FOR FREQUENTLY USED ACHIEVEMENT TESTS[1]

Test	Norm Dates	Comments
California Achievement Test (1971)	February-March	Norms for beginning and end of year are interpolations and should not be used in norm-referenced evaluations.
CAT Anchor Test norms for grades 4, 5, 6—reading	Mid-October Mid-April	Pretest mid-April or mid-October and posttest mid-April using Anchor Test study tables.
Metropolitan Achievement Test (1970)	Mid-October Mid-April	Anchor Test norms for the same testing times are available for reading grades 4, 5 and 6 (using Form F).
SRA Achievement Series (1971)	Mid-April	Beginning- and middle-of-year norms and interpolations and should not be used in norm-referenced evaluations.
SRA Anchor Test norms for grades 4, 5, 6—reading (Form E)	Mid-October Mid-April	Pretest mid-April or mid-October and posttest mid-April using Anchor Test study tables.
Stanford Achievement Test (1973)	October, February, and May	Some of the February norms are interpolations. Check Horst et al. page 107 if information is needed.
SAT (1964) Anchor Test norms for grades 4, 5, 6—reading	Mid-October Mid-April	Can be used with the earlier SAT, but the 1973 SAT has many advantages.
Cooperative Primary Tests (1965)	Late October-early November Late April-early May	Not in Anchor Test Study because no tests for grades 4, 5, and 6.
Comprehensive Test of Basic Skills (1968)	Last week of February and first week of March	Beginning- and end-of-year norms are interpolations and should not be used in norm-referenced evaluations.

TABLE 14.1 (*continued*)

Test	Norm Dates	Comments
CTBS Anchor Test norms for reading at grades 4, 5, 6	Mid-October Mid-April	Pretest mid-April or mid-October and posttest mid-April using Anchor Test Study tables.
Gates-MacGinitie Reading Test (1964)	October and April (except for first grade)	The May norm is probably usable, but not the February norm. Pre-test mid-October and posttest mid-May. First grade tested in January only.
Gates Anchor Test norms for Survey D Form iM Reading	Mid-October Mid-April	Pretest mid-April or mid-October and posttest mid-April using Anchor Test Study tables.
Iowa Test of Basic Skills (1971)	Last half of October and first half of November	Mid-year and spring norms are interpolations and should not be used for norm-referenced evaluations.
Iowa Anchor Tests for reading in grades 4, 5, 6	Mid-October Mid-April	Pretest mid-April or mid-October and posttest mid-April using Anchor Test Study tables.
Sequential Test of Educational Progress II (1969)	Last week of April and first three weeks of May	Fall norms are identical to those for preceding spring and should not be used in norm-referenced evaluation.
STEP Anchor Test norms for Level 4 Form A reading	Mid-October Mid-April	Pretest mid-April or mid-October and posttest mid-April using Anchor Test Study tables.

Individual-Subject Designs

A final alternative is to consider an individual-subject design where repeated measures are taken on a number of students. In certain areas of basic skill competencies, it might be possible to take baseline measures on rate and errors and then to continue these measures as a special program is introduced to first some students and then others (multiple baseline design). An example illustrating such a design is provided later in discussing process measures.

Selection of Premeasures

The premeasures selected depend on the design. With a random assignment of students to conditions, it is possible to use post measures only, although it is desirable to know levels of student performance in making judgments about outcome performances. When intact groups are used, premeasures should include an assessment of social-class-related variables, such as child IQ, parent education and income, and perhaps race or language spoken in the home when these might be relevant in making judgments about the initial equivalence of groups. This information can be used to say the groups are equal on some probably important background variables, or to permit a statistical adjustment of outcomes when differences are found. (See Horst, et al.,[2] for details on the use of a covariance adjustment evaluation design.) With intact groups, pre-assessment on each outcome measure should also be made. When using a norm-group referenced design, pre-assessment on outcome measures is necessary, and a measure of IQ is useful in describing the group on whom a given outcome is obtained. With an individual-subject design, a series of baseline measurements are made on the chosen dependent variables before instituting a new procedure or program.

Selecting Outcome Measures

Norm-Referenced Tests

In previous units we have indicated that the validity of a norm-referenced test has to be judged separately for each instructional program being evaluated. This problem is particularly serious for new programs of instruction that are really different. To the degree that a program deviates from traditional approaches on which the tests were based, norm-referenced achievement tests lose their validity for that program. For example, in evaluating the first edition of Distar Arithmetic II, we found our students showed only four months gain on the Wide Range Achievement Test for a year's work. The new Distar program taught addition and subtraction by focusing on row operations because they are important in teaching algebra. The test focused on column operations, which our students did not get until later. Furthermore, we could find no test which assessed knowledge of negative numbers and fractions at grade levels 1 and 2, although these were taught in the Distar program.

Another illustration from our experiences in evaluating Distar programs, as used in Follow Through, is instructive. The *format* of the in-book tests used in basal reading series is very much like that of the MAT, CAT, SAT, and SRA tests. The students in a basal series get lots of practice in the test formats commonly in use. They learn to read a passage, read four alternative answers, and circle the correct one. They also learn how to do all the items on a page. The first grader who is primarily taught through oral instruction, and tested orally, does not get practice in these test-taking skills. If tests like the MAT are used for such children, practice should be given in the test formats (but not the specific test content). This problem has been reduced for the revised Distar programs, by providing more workbook exercises with formats similar to those in common achievement tests.

It is important to analyze the content and format fit between test and program before deciding to use a given test. Even beyond this, it would be most desirable to know that a given test has already demonstrated *sensitivity to instruction* for the instructional sequence you are using. That is, you would like to know that when the program is taught well, students clearly improve their scores on the test. One can usually learn from the publishers of new materials about evaluations that others have made with those materials. Examination of those evaluations can be helpful in deciding which tests might be most useful in your case.

In unit seven we pointed out that programs can be readily compared when they can be evaluated on *common objectives*. In selecting tests to compare two or more programs, very likely some tests will favor one approach and some another. For example, a test of contemporary mathematics would favor students taught with the new math curriculum, while a test of fundamental operations would seem to favor more traditional programs. The new math and "old math" have different objectives and normative tests are available now slanted toward each. How then does one compare such programs? One can begin by identifying the common objectives as far as *the school system* is concerned and focusing on the initial evaluation questions on them. If schools using the new math still expect their students to have competence in basic operations, then a comparison on these skills is appropriate. A comparison might be made on attitude toward mathematics, since a common goal is to foster a desire to pursue advanced learning in this area. One can then ask questions about the unique contributions of each kind of program—the not-common objectives. To do this requires tests which cover the not-common goals of each program. In making interpretations it would be valuable to know how much time was devoted to the teaching of various outcomes. It may also be useful to do item analyses to demonstrate more clearly the basis for the difference in norm test scores.

The problem of common and not-common objectives can also arise in comparing two reading programs. Some programs argue that a focus on comprehension is more important from the beginning. Others believe that decoding is primary for without it there can be no comprehension. Normative reading tests vary greatly in the kinds of measures they produce. Some measure only word decoding (Wide Range), others measure paragraph decoding for rate and accuracy (Gilmore Oral, Gray Oral), and others measure a variety of language comprehension skills (as illustrated in table 9.1 for the MAT, SAT, CAT, and SRA). A school district which believes that both decoding and comprehension skills should be taught could ask for comparisons of both kinds of measures in deciding which approach would be best for them. Keep in mind the difficulty in assessing comprehension skills (especially between third and fourth grade) using a full adult vocabulary. The disadvantaged are likely to be said to have poor reading comprehension, when in fact the limitation may be more narrow than that. They may well be able to comprehend what they read, if the basic vocabulary used has been taught.

Be careful in selecting test levels. If tests are assigned by grade level, some students may get nearly all items right and some may miss nearly all items. A "ceiling" effect occurs in the first case and a "floor" effect in the second. If the test is too easy (ceiling effect), the student's score will be underestimated. If the test is too hard (floor effect), the student's score will be overestimated. A way around this problem is to select test levels on the basis of student achievement, not on the basis of grade level. If this is done, then it is important to keep the proportion of tests from different levels the same for both treatment and control groups. It would also be important to use a test battery when different levels of the test can be interrelated through the use of expanded standard scores. Because some test contents change with test levels, the above solution may add more complexity to an evaluation than is reasonable. An alternative is to choose the most reasonable test level for a group, rather than for the individual, and adjust the interpretation of the results for possible ceiling and floor effects.

Criterion-Referenced Tests

The addition of criterion-referenced tests to a test battery can aid in the evaluation of programs by showing how well various common objectives are mastered and by giving a more program-specific basis for comparing not-common objectives. Since this topic has already been covered in detail in unit 7, it will not be repeated here. The key point is that an outcome evaluation does not have to use norm-referenced or criterion-referenced tests exclusively. There can be great advantages to using a mixture when it comes to making final decisions about instructional programs.

Attitude Measures

An assessment of attitudes toward instructional procedures by students, teachers, and parents can be very helpful. Short questionnaires can be devised for these different groups to get personal views of different aspects of the programs. For students questions might be of this sort:

I am interested in your opinion about the reading program we used this year. Please answer the following by placing an x on the line to express your opinion:

Did the program improve your skills as you see them?

very little	some	very much

Did you enjoy working with the teacher on the reading lessons?

very little	in between	very much

Do you think we should use this program next year?

no	no opinion	yes

Did you enjoy reading lessons this year more than last year?

much less	same	much better

If the children cannot read the questions and have trouble making ratings, read the questions for them and put a smiling face on one end of the scale and a frowning face on the other to cue positive and negative attitudes.

The positive acceptance of a program by students or parents, does not mean it is doing anything for the students. The students may just like the teacher a lot. But, positive attitudes by parents, teachers, and students, *when coupled with positive outcome data,* can add to the case for a new program.

Cost

An attempt should also be made to assess the relative costs of the programs being compared. This requires an assessment of teacher (and aide) time devoted to the program and cost of materials (spread over their useful life). Express all costs on a per-pupil basis.

Selecting Process Measures

There are two kinds of process measures which are of central importance. The first assesses *teacher behavior* and is aimed at showing the degree to which an instructional program is implemented. The second assesses *student behavior* and is aimed at demonstrating the effect of instruction on the student. The student measure can also provide additional evidence for the adequacy of instruction in the form of quality of student performance.

Cronbach[3] and others have noted that, in evaluating an instructional program, finding out what was actually delivered is as important as assessing outcome. Without such information when a program fails, there is no way of knowing if the program is inadequate or if the problem lies with its implementation. If special training is required, teacher performance can be assessed before and after the training. An on-going monitoring of teacher performance provides an evaluation of the degree to which program procedures are followed and a guide for corrective action. In unit 6, we describe an approach to monitoring teacher behavior used in the schools implementing the University of Oregon Follow Through Model. The supervisor checks various aspects of teacher performance such as signals, pacing, and use of reinforcers. Where there are problems, an assignment is given to be practiced and checked again later. With an observation of each teacher several times a week, the supervisor is in a position to rate the adequacy of program implementation in terms of teacher performance. Two other key measures are the number of lessons taught each week to each group by each teacher and the time devoted to a given subject matter. Instead of lessons taught, an alternative would be to record the number of pages covered in a textbook or workbook.

Continuous measures of student progress are important in spotting when the teacher needs help and in showing a cumulative effect of instruction. Instruction-referenced tests such as those discussed in units 3 and 5 are helpful as process measures. When coupled with a measure of lessons taught, one has a measure of lessons *taught effectively*. As illustrated in unit 6, these can be useful measures for judging how well a program has been implemented.

Another kind of student monitoring measure involves samples of generalizable student behavior that can be tested on a regular basis to show the development of skills which extend beyond the examples used in instruction. For example, Horton[4] assessed the effects of a corrective reading program by demonstrating a decreasing error rate on stories within the program and a decreasing error rate on stories in the basal series back in the classroom. A 100-word sample in the basal reader was taken for ten days prior to the start of the corrective reading program. Then for each week that the corrective reading program was in effect, the measure was continued progressing to new stories in the basal series. The measure provided a convincing demonstration of improved reading behavior. The students could read new materials with fewer errors or no errors. A similar approach is possible with many generalizable basic skills.

Analysis

The goal of a data analysis is to summarize the information in a way that facilitates interpretation. The design selected will dictate the required analysis. If markedly different kinds of students or different grade levels are present in experimental and comparison groups, analyze the data separately and draw separate conclusions.

Horst[5] recommends the following steps be followed for a preliminary analysis.

A. For students with both pre- and posttest scores:
   (1) Plot the distribution of the pretest raw scores and compute the mean and standard deviation.
   (2) Plot the distribution of the posttest raw scores and compute the mean and standard deviation.
   (3) Plot the joint pretest-posttest distribution and compute the . . . correlation. [Pearson r]

B. For students with pretest scores only:
   Plot the distribution of the pretest raw scores and compute the mean and standard deviation.

C. For students with posttest scores only:
   These scores are usually not interpretable by themselves, but may be saved for student files or used as baseline data for following-year evaluations.

In general, the size of any achievement gains will be apparent from the above analyses. The differences in mean scores which are tested statistically . . . can be inspected graphically by comparing the appropriate distributions. However, an equally important use of the plotted distributions is to permit inspection of the data for irregularities which may influence the interpretation of results. It is not possible to list *all* the kinds of irregularities that might be encountered, but the following occur frequently and are important.

Floor or ceiling effects: Pretest and posttest distributions should be inspected to see whether they are bunched near the top or the bottom of the score range. The top of the score range is simply the highest possible raw score. The bottom may be zero, but for multiple choice tests it is usually taken to be the score that could be expected if students were simply guessing. For example, in a typical four-choice test students could be expected to get about one fourth of the items correct by guessing. . . .

Large changes in standard deviations from pretest to posttest: A large increase in standard deviation may simply indicate that there were problems with post-testing but it may also indicate that the project is spreading the students out by helping the initially better students relatively more than the others. A decrease may indicate that initially low scoring students are helped relatively more. Either effect would be an important finding and should be described in any evaluation report on the project.

Differences between pretested students who took the posttest and those who didn't: If students who have only pretest scores appear to be much different on the pretest from those who took both pre- and posttests, some investigation is required. There are many possible explanations. The better students may graduate, or poorer students may drop out, or both. Such findings are themselves important, and may also be relevant to the interpretation of posttest distributions.

Usually, the results will be clear from the distribution of the raw score data. Computation of the means and standard deviations helps in summarizing the distribution. Beyond this, tests of statistical significance can be made appropriate to the design. Such tests should be made with *standard scores* as the basic data, *not grade-equivalent scores*. Horst provides an excellent summary of the procedures which can be used with various designs.[6] As noted earlier, considerations of models for testing statistical significance goes beyond the objectives of this text. The teacher facing a problem in selecting a design or method of analysis should consult Horst and a local research specialist.

Cautions in Measuring Pre-Post Gains

Two common mistakes in project analysis involve the use of gain scores and the inclusion of students on whom there is partial information. A gain score involves taking the difference between the posttest and pretest scores for the experimental group and comparing it with a similar difference for the comparison group. This procedure is usually inappropriate. If there is no difference between groups on pretest, then all that is needed is a simple comparison of groups at posttest. If the groups do differ at pretest, then the gain score method will exaggerate the effect for the group that was initially lower. A procedure called *covariance analysis* can be used to correct this problem. The method basically adjusts posttest scores for treatment and comparison groups on the basis of the initial difference *and* the size of the correlation between pretest and posttest.

Another common problem in analysis of a project's effects is using means based on all available data to determine the gain. Because of student absences at testing times, late additions to the class, and early drops, the pretest and posttest measures will not be truly comparable, since they are not based on the same students. This problem can be overcome by basing the comparisons on only those students for whom there are *both* pretest and posttest scores. Such analysis will more truly show the effects of the special program.

As noted in unit 13, how big a difference needs to be for educational importance is a judgmental issue. In part, the judgment must depend upon the cost of obtaining a given difference. However, a difference of at least one-fourth to one-half of a standard deviation should be given careful consideration.

Reporting

The final stage in an evaluation study is the reporting of the outcome to others. In general, the nature of the report should be adapted to the technical sophistication of the audience. The technical consultant will usually be responsible for preparation of reports. We will mention here a few suggestions for reporting to nontechnical audiences, a task which may be assigned to the teachers involved.

Keep the report under three pages. Begin by stating the purpose of the study. Describe the students and the teachers in the study and the special program. Give an overall evaluation of the outcome. Then back this up with a statement of the nature of the differences on key measures. State that differences are significant without going into detail as to how this was determined unless that is asked for. Then, describe the nature of the differences in percentages for criterion-referenced scores, and use percentiles or grade norms for norm-referenced scores. (Note that while statistics are computed using standard scores, grade-equivalent scores or percentiles are best for communication purposes.) Grade-norms should be reported only where there is little danger of misinterpretation. For example, with basic skills, grade norms give a fair picture of what is happening during the first four or five grades. In reporting *percentiles*, be sure they are not confused with the percentage of items right and that care is taken in not overinterpreting percentile differences in the middle range. Remember that percentile changes at the extremes have greater significance than those in the middle range. A graphic representation of the results on key measures is often helpful. For example:

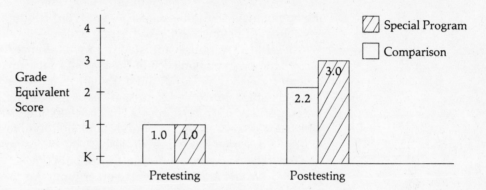

Be sure to include in the report informal impressions of student reactions if formal measures were not taken. End the report with a recommendation appropriate to the findings.

Two Illustrative Studies

A Comparison of Ten Reading Programs

A study by Bliesmer and Yarborough compared ten different beginning reading programs as used in first grade.[7]

Design. Two boroughs in suburban Virginia were selected for the study. One borough was largely middle class, the other was more lower class. There were two schools in each borough. Two classrooms were selected for each of ten reading programs. For nine of the ten programs, one room was in a middle-class school and the other in the lower-class school. For the tenth program, both classes were in the lower-class school. Within schools, kids were assigned randomly to classes. There were 484 kids in the study. Nineteen of the twenty teachers had been rated at least average by their supervisors. The one new teacher received good ratings during the program year. Thus, this is a group design with an attempt to match groups on social class, to select teachers for a minimum standard of quality, and to randomly assign students within schools. This is not a true random design, so care must be taken to check for group equivalences on pretest.

Premeasures. The Metropolitan Reading Readiness Test Form S was given in September. The Short Form of the California Mental Maturity Test (Primary) was given in October. The latter is an IQ test. Analysis of the premeasures showed significant group difference on age, language IQ, and the readiness test. For this reason it was necessary to use a covariance adjustment of the criterion posttest scores in evaluating the outcome.

Process Measures. Formal process measures were not reported. The authors state that each publisher was asked to provide consultant services during the year for their classrooms. Inservice training was provided two to three times for each teacher. In the classes where a teacher-designed individualized approach was used, an appropriate supervisor was provided. (Note: In our judgment, a closer monitoring procedure would have been desirable for this study.)

Outcome Measures. The Stanford Achievement Test (SAT) was given at the end of May. The subtests used were Word Reading, Paragraph Meaning, Vocabulary, Spelling, and Word Study Skills.

Analysis. Covariance adjusted mean differences were tested between each of the programs on each of the five SAT measures.[8] Out of 225 possible differences, 115 were significant at the .01 level. When the reading programs were classified into two groups, a more interesting result emerged. Five programs used a *synthetic* approach. These are linguistically based programs which focus very early on sounds and building sound components into words. The programs were published by Houghton Mifflin, Lippincott, McGraw-Hill *(Programmed Reading)*, Economy *(Phonetic Keys to Reading)*, and Singer *(Structural Reading)*. The five other programs used an analytic method, which is taken to mean an approach that begins with a sight-word vocabulary, focuses on meaning, and only later deals with some phonics. The programs were by American Book, Ginn, Scott-Foresman, an individualized approach supplemented with *SRA Reading Laboratory 1 (Word Games)*, and a completely individualized approach using diverse books but no specific sets of commercial materials. When the five synthetic programs were tested against the five analytic programs (the upper right block in table 14.2), 92 out of the 125 differences were significant in favor of the synthetic group at the .01 level. Only 3 differences favored the analytic group and these did not reach the .01 level of significance. The data clearly imply that during the first grade greater reading progress is made on a variety of measures using an approach that focuses on sounds which can be hooked together to form words. Codes for Table 14.2 are as follows:

HO: Houghton Mifflin
LI: Lippincott
SI: Singer
EC: Economy
MC: McGraw-Hill
IN: Individualized Completely
IS: Individualized Supplemented
GI: Ginn
AM: American
SC: Scott, Foresman

WR: Word Reading
PM: Paragraph Meaning
VO: Vocabulary
SP: Spelling
WS: Word Study Skills

TABLE 14.2 ADJUSTED MEAN CRITERION SCORES, AND DIFFERENCES AMONG MEANS, OF VARIOUS TREATMENT GROUPS

Program Groups		Adjusted Mean Scores**	Differences Among Program Group Means								
			LI	SI	EC	MC	IN	IS	GI	AM	SC
(HO)	WR	1.89	−0.21	−0.07	0.19	0.06	0.22*	0.27*	0.43*	0.33*	0.44*
	PM	1.81	−0.17	−0.12	−0.11	−0.06	−0.03	0.21	0.19	0.39*	0.28*
	VO	2.47	0.30	0.54*	−0.10	0.54*	0.58*	0.67*	0.51*	0.72*	0.67*
	SP	2.48	0.17	0.23	0.35*	0.64*	0.74*	0.82*	1.10*	1.01*	0.87*
	WS	2.58	−0.06	−0.09	0.43	0.56*	0.72*	0.71*	0.95*	0.83*	1.11*
(LI)	WR	2.10		0.14	0.40*	0.29*	0.43*	0.43*	0.64*	0.54*	0.65*
	PM	1.98		0.05	0.06	0.11	0.31*	0.38*	0.36*	0.56*	0.45*
	VO	2.17		0.24	−0.40*	0.24	0.28	0.37*	0.21	0.42*	0.37*
	SP	2.31		0.06	0.18	0.47*	0.57*	0.65*	0.93*	0.84*	0.70*
	WS	2.64		−0.03	0.49*	0.62*	0.78*	0.77*	1.01*	0.89*	1.17*
(SI)	WR	1.96			0.26*	0.15	0.29*	0.34*	0.50*	0.40*	0.51*
	PM	1.93			0.01	0.06	0.26*	0.33*	0.31*	0.51*	0.40*
	VO	1.93			−0.64*	0.00	0.04	0.13	−0.03	0.18	0.13
	SP	2.25			0.12	0.41*	0.51*	0.59*	0.87*	0.78*	0.64*
	WS	2.67			0.52*	0.65*	0.81*	0.80*	1.04*	0.92*	1.20*
(EC)	WR	1.70				0.11	0.03	0.08	0.24*	0.14	0.25*
	PM	1.92				0.05	0.08	0.32*	0.30*	0.50*	0.39*
	VO	2.57				0.64*	0.68*	0.77*	0.61*	0.82*	0.77*
	SP	2.13				0.29	0.39*	0.47*	0.75*	0.66*	0.52*
	WS	2.15				0.13	0.29	0.28	0.52*	0.40	0.68*
(MC)	WR	1.81					0.14	0.19	0.35*	0.25*	0.36*
	PM	1.87					0.20	0.27*	0.25*	0.45*	0.34*
	VO	1.93					0.04	0.13	−0.03	0.18	0.13
	SP	1.84					0.10	0.18	0.46*	0.37*	0.23
	WS	2.02					0.16	0.15	0.39	0.27	0.55*
(IN)	WR	1.67						0.05	0.21	0.11	0.22*
	PM	1.84						0.24*	0.22*	0.42*	0.31*
	VO	1.89						0.09	−0.07	0.14	0.09
	SP	1.14						0.08	0.36*	0.27	0.13
	WS	1.86						−0.01	0.23	0.11	0.39
(IS)	WR	1.67							0.16	0.06	0.17
	PM	1.60							−0.02	0.18	0.07
	VO	1.80							−0.16	0.05	0.00
	SP	1.66							0.28	0.19	0.05
	WS	1.87							0.24	0.12	0.40
(GI)	WR	1.46								−0.10	0.01
	PM	1.62								0.20	0.09
	VO	1.96								0.21	0.16
	SP	1.38								−0.09	−0.23
	WS	1.63								−0.12	0.16
(AM)	WR	1.56									0.11
	PM	1.42									−0.11
	VO	1.75									−0.05
	SP	1.47									−0.14
	WS	1.75									0.28
(SC)	WR	1.45									
	PM	1.53									
	VO	1.80									
	SP	1.61									
	WS	1.47									

*Significant at .01 level. Positive differences favor program at left.
**Stanford Achievement Test Scores (Grade Equiv.)

Comments.   In evaluating this result, one might wonder if the individualized programs in the analytic group were contributing more than their share of the weaker performances. The data in table 14.2 clearly show that this is not the case. The next question of concern is whether there is any systematic biasing of the vocabulary used on the test. The answer to this is not known, but it seems highly unlikely in view of the way the SAT was built. However, a careful evaluation of the test validity in relation to each program was not considered. As the authors note, the results reflect one grade only and could change with later grades.

A Comparison of Conventional and Contemporary Math Programs

Design.   This study by Hungerman compared intact groups of sixth graders from two metropolitan Detroit school systems of similar size and of average to above average socioeconomic status.[9] The experimental group consisted of ten classes (N = 305) of pupils who had studied the School Mathematics Study Group program (new math) in grades 4, 5, and 6. The control group consisted of ten classes (N = 260) of pupils who had studied a conventional arithmetic progam in grades 4, 5, and 6.

Premeasures.   No premeasures were made. The study checked for group equivalence by giving the California Test of Mental Maturity in March of the sixth grade year, and using the Warner scale to assess occupational level of the family's main wage earner. Groups were also compared on student age. The differences in occupational level and IQ favored the control group. For this reason, the results were analyzed using covariance adjustment of criterion scores.

Process measures.   No process measures were taken. Therefore, we do not know if the students in the different programs spent equivalent amounts of time in instruction, and we do not know how much they were taught or how well they were taught. From the size of the N's (305 versus 260), it appears that there was an average of 30.5 students per class in the contemporary math programs and only 26 per class in the conventional programs. The absence of the monitoring data implies that some difference on outcome measures could be related to variables other than the different programs used.

Outcome measures.   The California Arithmetic Test was used as a measure of conventional mathematics and given to both groups in March. The California Contemporary Mathematics Test was used as the measure of contemporary mathematics and given to both groups in April. The Aiken-Dreger Mathematics Attitude Scale was also given in April.

Analysis.   The analysis focused on answering four questions:

1 Do students in contemporary mathematics keep up on basic computational skills with those in conventional programs?
2 Are the concepts taught in the new math equally suitable for students of different IQ levels and social status?
3 How does contemporary math effect attitudes toward mathematics?
4 Are mathematics achievement and attitude related?

The covariance-adjusted outcome data on the California Arithmetic test showed significant differences favoring conventional programs on the subtests for Signs and Symbols and for Subtraction. Differences (not significant) favoring the conventional program were found on all other subtests (Meanings, Problems, Addition, Multiplication, and Division). Significant differences favoring the conventional program were found on the summary scores for Part I (Reasoning) and Part II (Fundamentals), as well as on the Total Score. Except for Signs and Symbols, where the size of the difference was about one-half standard deviation, all other differences were less than one-quarter standard deviation. Thus, the magnitude of the differences is not particularly significant educationally. An item analysis showed that differences favoring each program corresponded closely to program emphasis.

The covariance-adjusted outcome data on the California Contemporary Mathematics Test showed significant differences favoring the new math group on subtests for Numeration (Base 10), Nonmetric Geometry, Number Systems and Properties, and Other (logic, modulo). On summary scores for New Symbolism and Vocabulary and for Conventional Symbolism and Vocabulary, the new math group was also superior. A significant difference on Total Score, close to one standard deviation in magnitude, favored the new math group. The only subtests on which no differences were found were Measurement and Graphs. The magnitude of the significant differences on subtests averaged more than one-half standard deviation. Thus, the differences on the contemporary math test clearly favored the new math group.

The study found no significant differences of attitude toward mathematics. Within the experimental group, those with higher IQ's had more favorable attitudes toward math. A low positive correlation between IQ and attitude toward mathematics was also found for the control group. The correlations between IQ and math achievement was on the order of .70 within each group when tested with the math test appropriate to the instruction in each group. Socioeconomic level showed little or no relations to higher math attitudes or achievement.

Thus, it appears that those in the new math program show some loss in basic computational skills, but this is relatively minor when compared to gains shown on new math concepts. Low IQ or social status provided no special handicap in learning new, versus old, math. Attitudinal differences were not particularly important.

Comments. In reporting this study, the author did not consider the magnitude of the differences in evaluating them. Thus, she gave more weight to the computational skill loss in drawing conclusions than we have. This study nicely illustrates an approach to the evaluation of programs with different objectives. The final judgment in the evaluation, however, must rest on how one values the different objectives.

summary

The planning of an outcome study needs to answer six questions: Who will be tested when? What initial assessments will be made? What final assessments will be made? What measures will be taken to show continuous student progress and/or the effectiveness of program implementation? How are the data to be summarized? How are the findings to be communicated to others?

The checklist which follows provides a summary of the measures to be considered in planning an outcome study.

Checklist of Measures to Consider

Premeasures

- *If random assignment* to groups, pre-assessment on outcome measures is desirable but not necessary.
- *With intact groups,* measure student IQ and indicators of parental social class (education of parents, income, and so on). Also make pre-assessments of outcome measures.
- *With norm-group design,* pre-assess on outcome measures. A measure of IQ is desirable for describing the group.
- *Individual-subject design.* Take series of baseline measures before instituting change.

Process measures

- Obtain measures of teacher performance in terms of program requirements.
- Record lessons taught or pages covered weekly by group.
- Use instruction-referenced tests to measure student skill development each two to six weeks.
- Record time spent on each subject area.
- Attempt to obtain measures of academic behavior involving generalized performance beyond program materials.

Outcome measures

- Use normative tests that logically fit common program objectives and formats.
- When programs have different objectives, try to find measures of these differences that can be used with both the treatment and control group.
- Use criterion-referenced tests of common and not-common objectives. Measure time devoted to each objective.
- Obtain measures of program acceptance by students, teachers, and parents.
- Assess cost in terms of time and materials on a per-pupil basis.

Data analysis should begin by identifying the students on whom there is both pretest and posttest data. Plot the frequency distributions and compute means and SDs. Check to see that students on whom there are only pretest scores are not different from the rest. Check the distributions for floor and ceiling effects, and for changes in SDs from pretest to posttest. Compute tests of statistical significance using standard scores. Gain measures are not needed if treatment and comparison groups are equivalent at pretest. Use just a comparison of posttest scores. Where groups differ at pretest, use a covariance adjustment of posttest scores rather than a gain measure in forming conclusions. Remember to consider the educational significance of a difference, not just the statistical significance.

In reporting the results, state the purpose of the study, who was involved, and the overall outcome. Then back up the conclusion with specifics using grade norm or percentile scores and anecdotal information on student, parent, and teacher reactions. End the report with a recommendation.

Two studies were presented and critiqued to illustrate fairly comprehensive studies of educational program outcomes. These may be helpful as models.

self-test

1 differ;
  Random

2 norm-
  referenced

3 random

4 necessary

5 implemented;
  effect

6 interpretation

7 distributions

8 comparable

1 The key design consideration is that the groups _____ only in their programs of instruction. _____ assignment helps to insure this.

2 When a control group is not available, consider a _____-_____ comparison.

3 Premeasures are not essential when there is _____ assignment of students to conditions.

4 When using a norm-group-referenced design, pre-assessment on outcome measures is _____, and a measure of IQ is useful.

5 There are two kinds of process measures which are of central importance. The first assesses *teacher behavior* and is aimed at showing the degree to which an instructional program is _____. The second assesses student behavior and is aimed at demonstrating the _____ of instruction on the student.

6 The goal of a data analysis is to summarize the data in a way that facilitates _____.

7 A beginning step in analysis is to plot the _____ of pretest and post-test scores for the students who have both scores.

8 When scores are missing at pretest or posttest, the use of the partial data available will make the pretest and posttest means not _____, since they would be based on different students.

NUMBER RIGHT _____

exercise 1 programed practice

1 educational

2 group;
   procedures

3 differ;
   Random

4 premeasures

5 norm-
   referenced;
   objectives

6 Standard

7 norms

8 same time

9 random

10 social-class

11 outcome

12 necessary

1 Outcome evaluations can serve a political function within a system by providing a rational basis for accepting something new; they can also serve an _____ function by providing a basis for program selection and improvement.

2 Usually, a _____ design will be needed for an outcome study. Individual-subject designs are more likely to be helpful in studying the effects of possible variations in _____.

3 The key design consideration is that the groups _____ only in their programs of instruction. _____ assignment helps to insure this.

4 Where random assignment of students is not possible and intact groups are used, select groups that are comparable and obtain _____ to support their comparability.

5 When a control group is not available, consider a _____-_____ comparison. The key here is to find tests which will fairly measure the _____ of the programs to be compared.

6 _____ scores should be used for computing all summary statistics, rather than grade equivalents or percentiles.

7 A potential problem for norm-referenced comparisons arises because the _____ are often based on data obtained at only one or two times during the year.

8 This problem can be avoided by designing the study to test students at the _____ _____ as the norm group was tested.

9 Premeasures are not essential when there is _____ assignment of students to conditions.

10 When intact groups are used, premeasures should include an assessment of _____-_____-related variables.

11 With intact groups, pre-assessment on each _____ measure should also be made.

12 When using a norm-group referenced design, pre-assessment on outcome measures is _____, and a measure of IQ is useful.

13 In selecting outcome measures, it is important to analyze the _____ and format fit between tests and program before deciding to use a given test.

14 When programs being compared have different objectives, outcome measures can first be selected to reflect the _____ objectives which the school system expects to be met. Then, we can test for the _____ contribution of the different programs.

15 To avoid ceiling and floor effects, select test levels according to _____ achievement rather than grade level. However, this can create problems in interpretation if different students are evaluated with different _____ of a test.

16 An alternative is to choose the most reasonable test level for a _____, rather than for the individual, and adjust the interpretation of the results for possible ceiling and floor effects.

17 There are two kinds of process measures which are of central importance. The first assesses *teacher behavior* and is aimed at showing the degree to which an instructional program is _____. The second assesses student behavior and is aimed at demonstrating the _____ of instruction on the student.

18 Another kind of student monitoring measure involves samples of _____ student behavior that can be tested on a regular basis to show development of skills which extend beyond the examples used in instruction.

19 The goal of a data analysis is to summarize the information in a way that facilitates _____.

20 A beginning step in analysis is to plot the _____ of pretest and posttest scores for the students who have both scores.

21 Pretest and posttest _____ and standard deviations are then computed for students with _____ scores.

22 The data should be checked for irregularities such as ceiling effects or large changes in _____ _____.

23 Beyond this, tests of statistical _____ can be made appropriate to the design.

13 content

14 common; unique

15 student; levels

16 group

17 implemented; effect

18 generalizable

19 interpretation

20 distributions

21 means; both

22 standard deviations

23 significance

24 Two common mistakes in project analysis involve the use of _____ scores and the inclusion of students on whom there is _____ information.

25 If there is no difference between groups on pretest, then all that is needed is a simple comparison of groups at _____ rather than a comparison of gains. If the groups do differ at pretest, then the gain score method will exaggerate the effect for the group that was initially _____.

26 When scores are missing at pretest or posttest, the use of the partial data available will make the pretest and posttest means not _____, since they would be based on different students.

27 This problem can be overcome by basing the comparisons on only those students for whom there are _____ pretest and posttest scores.

28 Adapt your report to the technical sophistication of the _____.

29 Begin by stating the _____ of the study. Describe the students and teachers in the study, and the special program. Give an overall evaluation of the _____. Then back this up with a statement of the nature of the differences on key _____.

30 Describe the nature of the differences in percentages for criterion-referenced scores, and use _____ or grade norms for norm-referenced scores.

31 End the report with a _____ appropriate to the findings.

24 gain; partial

25 posttest;
   lower

26 comparable

27 both

28 audience

29 purpose;
   outcome;
   measures

30 percentiles

31 recommen-
   dation

discussion questions

1 Why should the classroom teacher need to know the procedures for evaluating programs?
2 What should be considered in selecting a design?
3 What problems can occur in using a norm-referenced design and how might they be overcome?
4 Explain the logic of a norm-referenced design.
5 Describe an individual-subject design that might be used in assessing a program aimed at some basic skills.

6   What premeasures are desirable for random-group designs, intact-group designs, norm-group-referenced designs, and individual-subject designs?

7   How can programs with different objectives be evaluated?

8   What problems can arise in selecting test levels and how might these be overcome?

9   Why might one be interested in gaining attitude measures in evaluating a program?

10 Describe the general procedure for assessing program cost.

11 Give two kinds of process measures that are important in evaluating an outcome study and explain why they are important.

12 What three steps do Horst et al. recommend in analyzing data for students with both pretests and posttests?

13 What irregularities do Horst et al. recommend be looked for in examining the data?

14 Give two common problems in measuring gains.

15 Give an outline for a report on a study to be given to a parent group.

16 Summarize the main procedures and findings in the study of reading programs by Bliesmer and Yarborough.

17 Summarize the main procedures and findings in the study of old and new math programs by Hungerman.

unit 15

Who Can Be Taught?

objectives

When you complete this unit you should be able to—

1 Explain why the question *Who can be taught?* involves a social issue of vital importance to the teacher.

2 Discuss the pros and cons of the belief that intelligence is fixed by heredity.

3 Discuss the pros and cons of the belief that intelligence determines what can be learned.

4 Distinguish between level measures of achievement and gain measures.

5 Answer the question: "What determines who can be taught?"

lesson

In unit 12 and 14 of *Teaching 2* we looked at the question *Who can be taught?* and concluded that much more can be done for the "retarded" and "disadvantaged" than has been assumed in the past. With good instruction it is not just the bright who can learn. With a background in research methods and statistical concepts, it is now possible to look more closely at some of the issues and evidence relating a person's background to the question, "Who can be taught?" For the teacher, an examination of this question is extremely important in determining how tests are used to make instructional decisions. What we believe can lead to a self-fulfilling prophecy. If we believe that students who score low on achievement tests in elementary school can never make it in college, we will place them in vocational training schools. This denies them the needed preskills, and they will not succeed in college. If we believe that students with lower IQ's need special classes because they are slower learners, and if these special classes are designed to teach less than the average class does, the prophecy will be confirmed: they will learn less. If the teacher uses IQ scores to group students for instruction in reading, and

294

provides only "readiness" tasks to the lower IQ students until they are "mentally mature," the teacher will find that those with lower IQ's are behind in reading.

Who can be taught? involves a vital social issue which has been with us in many forms throughout history. To those concerned with human development, it is known as the nature-nurture issue or the heredity-environment issue. To those concerned with the measurement of individual differences, it is known as the aptitude-achievement issue. It is in the context of the distinction between aptitude and achievement that the issue has had its most direct impact on educational practice.

Genetics, Intelligence, and Achievement

In 1869 Sir Francis Galton published *Hereditary Genius*, wherein he described an association between family membership and outstanding intellectual achievement.[1] These investigations had their root in the work of Galton's cousin Charles Darwin. Galton generally accepted the notion that adult characteristics are determined by heredity. The notion of a genetically fixed intelligence was transmitted to early leaders in American psychology by G. Stanley Hall,[2] whose student Lewis Terman constructed the first American intelligence test following the procedures used in France by a physician named Alfred Binet. With a measure of intelligence, experimental evidence began to be collected showing IQ's to be quite stable over time, supporting the notion of a fixed ability. In addition, studies of identical twins, fraternal twins, siblings, and unrelated persons produced correlations supporting a strong influence for heredity on the scores. With modern estimation procedures, Jensen summarizes the data to show that 80 percent of the variance in intelligence can be attributed to heredity.[3] Jensen goes so far as to suggest that early intervention studies for the disadvantaged could raise IQ no more than a few points because increasing IQ is probably not an attainable goal.[4]

The belief in a genetically-fixed intelligence takes on additional implications for education when coupled with data showing correlations in the .80 to .90 range between measures of intelligence and measures of school achievement.[5] The teacher is faced with conceptions (supported by research findings) which suggest that children with poorer genes learn less in school. The obvious solution for the teacher is to expend less energy on the (inferior) children who are doing poorly. One might also be inclined not to search for instructional methods that will work with all children. Fortunately for children and education, the basis for these conclusions can be challenged on many grounds.

Is Intelligence Inherited?

In unit 12 of *Teaching 2* we showed that IQ tests, such as the Stanford-Binet, measure learned behavior (operant behavior). Geneticists recognize this fact when they treat intelligence as a *phenotype* (a visible characteristic which includes effects of environmental influences) and not a *genotype* (characteristics which can be traced to specific genes, such as blood type). Jensen and others have attempted to deal with this fact by using an index (heritability index) which attempts to proportion variance in a phenotype to effects of environment and heredity, using empirical evidence and genetic theory. The geneticist Cavalli-Sforza[6] points out that four types of environmental differences can occur.

1 Within families: age, birth order, etc.
2 Between families (same social class): teaching methods, number of children, etc.
3 Between social classes: income, educational opportunities, nutrition, etc.
4 Between cultures: educational institutions, health practices, and a host of major sources of differences

The usual heritability index using twins is sensitive only to environmental variations of type 1 above; and these are variations as they exist now, not as they might be. When twins are reared apart, there is a chance to estimate environmental variation due to sources 2 and 3, but these kinds of data are very rare and likely to be biased. No studies have included level 4 environmental variations. The point to note is that the relative contribution of heredity to variation in IQ, as reflected in a heritability index, is an estimation based on data which probably *grossly underestimate* the role of environment. One could easily consider a 50-50 contribution of heredity and environment under existing conditions when cross-cultural variations are considered.

Beyond this, there is a more serious consideration for the teacher. Given that intelligence *is behavior* which is learned, within the constraints imposed by a partially genetically controlled physical structure, the question of the relative contribution of heredity and environment is not the real question for the teacher. The real question is, "How much can be done through instruction to improve intellectual functioning?"

The study of stature offers some information of interest to the teacher. Stature, like intelligence, is based on many different genetic contributions. It is not the effect of a single gene. In the last 70 to 100 years, average stature has shown an increase *on the order of one standard deviation.*[7] There is clear evidence that this effect cannot be attributed to genetic factors. In fact, there is evidence that socioeconomic factors are involved. For example, family size is negatively related to stature. Very likely, better nutrition is behind the increase in height.

In an analogous way, better education has likely produced a general rise in IQ of a similar magnitude during the past 70 years. As J. McV. Hunt[8] and others[9] have documented, environmental experiences can have profound influences in promoting and retarding intellectual development. In *Teaching 2*, unit 12, studies by Heber[10] and Engelmann[11] were reviewed; they suggest that the order of magnitude of the improvement in IQ which can be obtained with present technology is close to *two standard deviations* (30 IQ points). That is a difference between the current conception of average intelligence and bright, or between educable retarded and average. The difference is a very significant one.

Finally, it should be noted that the data on the consistency of measures of intelligence over time leave much room for alternative interpretations. For example, Bayley[12] found a correlation of .70 between the Stanford-Binet given at age 4 and age 16. This implies a predictable variance of 49 percent from one testing to the other. Conservatively correcting for unreliability of the measures, true predictable variance would not exceed 60 percent. This leaves much room for environmental influences.

Is Achievement Different from Intelligence?

In 1927, Truman Kelley pointed out that "the correlation between a good battery achievement test and an intelligence test is found to be very high."[13] About 90 percent of the reliable variance is common, leaving a scant 10 percent that is different. Kelley believed that, for practical purposes, two measures of the same behavior were given different names and then one was used to "explain" the other. If this is the case, then to say that intelligence is a *cause* of good performance on an achievement test is circular reasoning. One measure of achievement is called intelligence and then used to explain another measure of achievement. Thus, achievement causes achievement.

But is there a difference between an IQ test and an achievement test? Lloyd Humphreys suggests that there is a difference in the way the tests are built. While both are measures of learned behavior, achievement tests tend to focus on more recent learning, while intelligence tests tend to focus on older learning.[14]

If we were to summarize the implication of the two questions we have asked so far, we would conclude that:

1 Some proportion of the variation in the behavior called intelligence can be attributed to a contribution of heredity, but there is much room for environmental influences to make people smarter or duller.
2 The high correlations between measures of intelligence and achievement batteries do not imply that intelligence causes achievement. They only show that a measure of *past achievement* is related to *current achievement*.

Can Past Achievement Really Predict Current Achievement?

If we discard the hereditary issue and concern ourselves with whether or not future achievement (learning) can be predicted from past achievement (intelligence), we still have a problem. As early as 1939, John Anderson[15] reported that mental age correlated with the general *level* of achievement, but not with year-to-year *gains* in learning. Those who started higher in achievement ended higher in achievement, but did not gain more. It is our opinion that the failure to distinguish between measures of levels and of gains is a source of much confusion in the intelligence-achievement issue.

Figure 15.1 shows a hypothetical correlation between a grade-equivalent measure of achievement (expanded standard scores could be used with no change in the argument) and mental age.* The posttest X's, which are circled, show a high positive correlation between the two measures. The pretest achievement measures also correlate highly with mental age, but the gain measures show no relationship to mental age (see figure 15.2).

———

*Traditionally IQ was computed as this ratio: $IQ = \dfrac{\text{Mental Age (MA)}}{\text{Chronological Age (CA)}}$. Now most IQ tests determine IQ as a standard score and compute mental age as an age-equivalence score.

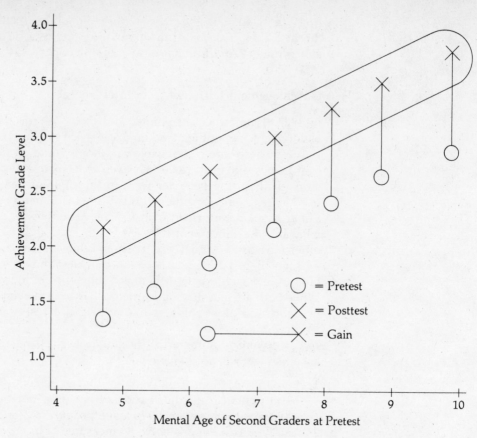

Figure 15.1 Hypothetical Correlation Between Mental Age, and Achievement for Grade-Level Measures

To understand this better, consider the following:

(1) Mental Age is a measure of past achievement (PA)

PA

(2) The achievement pretest is a measure of past achievement (PA)

PA

(3) The achievement gain is a measure of new learning (NL)

NL

(4) The achievement posttest is a measure of past achievement plus new learning

PA + NL

Mental Age (1) and achievement pretest (2) will correlate highly because they are largely measures of the same thing (past achievement). Mental Age (1) and the gain measure (3) are measuring largely different things and should not correlate highly. However, mental age (1) and the posttest achievement scores (4) still have in common a big hunk of past achievement and therefore correlate highly. *Correlations reflect what two measures have in common.* Achievement *level* measures are likely to have much more in common with mental age measures than are achievement *gain* measures.

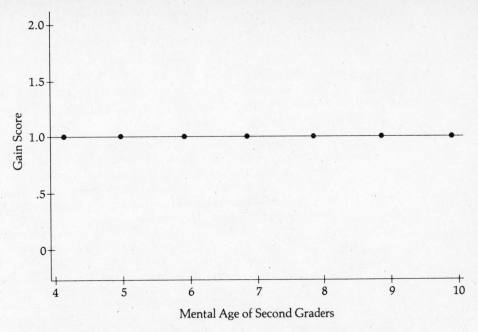

Figure 15.2 Scatter-Plot Between Mental Age and Achievement Gain Scores for the Data from Figure 15.1

The evidence showing correlations of .80 to .90 between intelligence test scores and achievement test scores have been based on level-type measures rather than gain measures. Because of this, they cannot have much relevance for making judgments on the effects of past achievements on *current instructional progress*. A fresh approach to the problem is needed to understand how prior learning can influence new learning. Our own data[16] show that within-grade-level correlations of entry IQ with criterion-referenced achievement test gains in reading are about .55 for the Distar I program and .20 for Distar II. In arithmetic, the correlations of entry IQ with achievement gains are about .30 at both levels 1 and 2.* Since age is relatively constant in these analyses, the correlations with IQ are equivalent to correlations with mental age in the examples given above.

---

*These correlations are corrected for unreliability of the measures. It should be noted that one reason that correlations between IQ and gain measures may be lower than those with level measures is because the gain measures are likely to be less reliable than level measures. Gain measures tend to reduce the total variance relative to error variance and thus tend to be less reliable. The higher the correlation between pretest and posttest, the more likely the gain measure will be unreliable. The reliability of a gain from X to Y can be expressed as follows:

$$\text{Reliability of the gain (Y-X)} = \frac{r_{XX} + r_{YY} - 2\,r_{XY}}{2\,(1 - r_{XY})}$$

where Y-X is the gain score, r_{XX} is the reliability of the pretest, r_{YY} is the reliability of the posttest, and r_{XY} is the pretest-posttest correlation. By reporting correlations corrected for the effects of unreliability, this problem can be dealt with. The formula used to correct a correlation for unreliability is this:

$$\text{True } r_{XY} = \frac{r_{XY}}{\sqrt{r_{XX}}\ \sqrt{r_{YY}}}$$

Does IQ Measure Ability to Learn?

The correlation between intelligence and achievement has been interpreted to suggest that intelligence be defined as the *ability to learn*. This leads to another kind of examination of the relation of measures of past learning to new learning. The interpretation of IQ as a measure of ability to learn is not well supported by the data. The following quote is from Cronbach's summary of the issues:

> The belief that intelligence tests measure ability to learn has been sharply challenged, notably in papers by Woodrow (1946) and J. Anderson (1939). Anderson contended that children with high mental ages do not gain more from year to year than duller children—they finish higher, but they also started higher. Woodrow found negligible correlations between mental tests and gains in laboratory learning. Such conclusions are open to question on technical grounds, but they posed a challenge worth taking seriously. Ability to learn rapidly is an important intellectual power; it should be measured if possible. Anderson and Woodrow considered the mental test a summary only of past learning. Crystallized ability [learned skill] helps where new knowledge builds on old. But what helps one to master lessons so novel that everyone starts even?
>
> Only recently have there been substantial studies of the relation between conventional tests and rate of learning. The work of Stevenson & Odom (1965) is illustrative. They gave CTMM [California Test of Mental Maturity] to fourth- and sixth-graders, and also put them through a number of learning tasks. One type required the child to learn, from trials-with-correction, a series of arbitrary responses. For example, sets of three drawings were presented repeatedly, one set at a time, in scrambled order; in each set, one drawing was designated as the desired response. On the first appearance of the set the child could only guess, but on later appearances the successful learner would recall the right answer. Two tasks of this sort called for rote discrimination learning; a third called for concept attainment. The learning scores intercorrelated 0.40 or better. (For our purposes, we give a single correlation; the authors gave data for separate grade and sex groups.) Correlations of learning scores with MA [Mental Age] were essentially zero. The learning measures are not very reliable, but even so, if the mental test were appreciably related to learning, the correlations for MA should be 0.25 or better. There was a fourth learning task, uncorrelated with the three tasks just described. This was a paired-associates task requiring the child to recall which word had been paired, a few trials earlier, with a certain nonsense syllable. *This* learning score correlated about 0.45 with MA. (The correlations with Language and Nonlanguage MAs were nearly identical.) This is puzzling. MA correlates with one learning task as highly as the reliability of the learning-score permits, but does not correlate with three other measures of learning. The rest of the studies on this problem give equally variable results (see Gulliksen, 1968, and G. Olson *et al.*, 1968).
>
> We conclude that "learning rate" or "ability to learn" is not a satisfactory construct. Learning *of what?* And *from what instruction?* There are many kinds of learning tasks, and often a person who is excellent in one is poor in another. Brighter children seem to have an advantage in a task in which one can use mediation. For example, they do better at paired-associates learning where one can make up a meaningful sentence to connect the stimulus and response words. Older and brighter children are more likely to have acquired this technique. Jensen and Rohwer (1965) indicate that one can teach this trick to children of school age, and when this is done the learning of the test-dull child very nearly matches that of the test-bright child. Additional evidence comes from studies

by Flavell and his associates (see Moely *et al.*, 1969); many children who score poorly on a test can do very much better when they are given enough experience and guidance to proceed efficiently. It is becoming increasingly clear that what we measure when we expose a child to a task for the first time is quite different from what we measure when he has learned how to play the game. Too many studies of individual differences have employed very short tests or very short learning periods. To obtain information relevant to school situations, we need to test how well the child can do after he has spent several periods on a certain kind of task, and has been given the sort of coaching a teacher can provide. There is a suspicion afoot that education calls for analytic ability just because the materials are capable of being put into meaningful relationships *and* the instructor has either failed to so display the relationships or has given an explanation that is hard to follow. Then one has to use his brains![17]

In these last few sentences, Cronbach is suggesting that high level analytical ability as measured by IQ tests may be important for learning in situations where the *teaching is bad!* Under poor teaching conditions, only the smart kid has a chance to "psyche out" what the teacher is trying to convey.

Another very critical point identified by Cronbach lies in his key questions, "Learning *of what?* And *from what instruction?*" These questions point to the fundamental difference in viewpoint between those concerned with the measurement of aptitude and achievement through norm-referenced tests and those concerned with effective instruction. *Measurement people* are oriented to the statistical study of individual differences using *summary* scores which are further summarized by statistical computations. The specific behaviors involved are never looked at and are of little interest. *Learning-process people* are concerned with specific performances which can be demonstrated to be a function of the teaching process for individual students. When we get down to this more specific level, the critical concern is, "Does the student have the *preskills* assumed by this instructional program or not?" The question of prior achievements (intelligence) adds nothing more.

The behavioral psychologist also has trouble with the concept of *learning rate* on empirical grounds. When working with instructional programs the critical variables controlling learning rate are not individual differences in intelligence, but the degree of presence of preskills, the way in which reinforcers are used, the size of the program steps, the sequence of program steps, and the adequacy of the teaching demonstrations. *Learning rate can be widely manipulated by changing these variables in the teaching situation.* It is our suspicion that much of what goes under the label of an "individual's rate of learning," where instruction is not systematic, is related to *motivational conditions* (the individual's reinforcement history and the reinforcers operating in the classroom at the time).

Cronbach continues his discussion of learning rate with the following:

Despite the perplexities that arise when we try to explain low correlations of mental tests with learning, two general statements account for a great many findings. First, it is true that in instruction that presents connected materials— whether by a programmed text, a live teacher, or some more exotic method—the pupils high in mental age learn more than those low in mental age. Hence MA does represent one kind of ability to learn. When, however, the material is rote in nature, and no meaning can be supplied by the learner (as in many laboratory tasks), good general ability gives little or no advantage. There is some reason to think that rote memory is a separate ability. Good performance on a truly rote task may occur as often among those we call "dull" as among the bright.[18]

In *Teaching 2* we attempted to show that the teaching of *any* task involves tying some stimulus event(s) to some response events through reinforcement. The learning of tasks in isolation is what is meant by rote learning. Smart learning (the learning of a general case, as is involved in learning concepts and operations) requires an appropriate *sequence* of tasks so that only certain stimulus events are responded to and only certain response effects are produced and reinforced. This analysis says there are not different *kinds of learning*. All learning involves tasks. The difference is whether what was learned from some tasks contributes to being able to respond correctly to other tasks. Within this framework, what Cronbach is saying can be converted to this statement: *Meaningful learning is learning that uses prior teaching (or learning) to advantage.* The student who has learned more (has a higher mental age) can do better on tasks where what has been learned aids performance. When learning tasks are devised so as to *control for the effects of prior learning,* there seems to be no difference in the performance of "bright" and "dull" kids. This conclusion goes so strongly against the grain of our experience that it cannot possibly be true. However, consider the following experiment.

A Comparison of Two Extreme Groups

Linda Meyers[19] did a study in which the children had to learn to discriminate and name a set of five related concepts. In this study, five children with Down's Syndrome who had IQ's in the 30's were compared with five children with IQ's in the 130's. All children were five years old. The Down's Syndrome children had been in a special training program during much of the prior year where they had been taught to respond to simple instructions and to value tokens as rewards for learning. The "normal" children could already follow instructions and quickly learned to value the tokens which could be exchanged for a prize. Usually, in the comparison of learning rates of normal and retarded children, the ability to follow the directions used in the learning tasks and the motivation in the situation are not controlled. In this study they were both controlled. In addition, prior learning experiences relating to the task itself were controlled by devising a set of novel figures which were given nonsense names. The tasks were like these:

Task		Response
"This is a spreel. What is this?"	‿/\‿	"A spreel."
"This spreel is lack. What kind of spreel is this?"	‿/\‿/\‿	"Lack."
"This spreel is sote. What kind of spreel is this?"	‿/\‿	"Sote."

Five tasks were used. The first task was taught to criterion and then a new one was added. These two were brought to criterion and then a new one was added. *Cumulative programing* was used (see unit 9, *Teaching 2*) until all five were mastered to criterion.

The results showed that it took an average of 22 minutes for *each group* to learn the five concepts. A retention measure one week later showed approximately 75 percent retention by both groups, although there was more variability in retention for the Down's Syndrome children than the normals. While based on a small sample, the outcome is entirely consistent with the findings reported by Cronbach. The difference between our position and Cronbach's is that we believe the only difference between meaningful learning and rote learning is that "meaningful learning" can *take advantage of prior learning and so-called rote learning does not*. This being the case, the conclusion that IQ tests do not measure learning rate, or learning ability, but only the effects of past learning becomes a *strong statement* with *strong implications*.

Who Can Be Taught What?

This wandering trip through the world of research and nonsense leads to a very simple conclusion. What any person can be taught depends on what he or she has already learned, as well as the methods used in instruction. If the method of instruction is lecture and the same assignments are given thirty students of highly different backgrounds, it is very likely that some will fail because they lack the preskills assumed by the teacher. In this situation, an IQ test could, in part, predict who would succeed or fail. If the method of instruction systematically builds upon the skills each individual brings to the educational setting as discussed in *Teaching 2*, and uses good motivating procedures as discussed in *Teaching 1*, each student will learn to the degree he or she is effectively taught.

The fact that we are products of our genetic histories does not limit what we can learn *or* guarantee that *we will be taught*. Our genetic histories probably do have some influence on how well we learn, but since we have no measure of or control over the variables involved, the potential influences currently have no practical implications for the teacher.

The net effect of the arguments considered in this unit is this conclusion: *The potential power of instruction in increasing intellectual behavior has no known limit*. If we can imagine and even support with data a two-standard-deviation increase today, it seems entirely probable that, in another decade or two, we will have the skills and technology to consider another two standard deviations. Through better teaching, there is the promise of a smarter world tomorrow. It is our hope that these three volumes will make a small contribution in that direction.

summary

For the teacher, an examination of the question *Who can be taught*? is important in determining how tests are used to make instructional decisions. What the teacher believes can lead to a self-fulfilling prophecy. Two important beliefs have dominated thinking for over a century: that intelligence is largely fixed by heredity and that school achievement is largely determined by one's intelligence.

In current data on the inheritance of intelligence, effects of environment are probably grossly underestimated. As with the increase in physical stature during the past 70 years, environmental influences can markedly improve the behaviors we call intelligence. A two-standard-deviation increase is well within the range of current technology.

The presumed causative role of intelligence in school achievement is open to question on several grounds. First, as Kelley did, one can interpret the high correlation between IQ test scores and scores on achievement test batteries as simply two measures of achievement; or with Humphreys, we can note that IQ test items tend to focus on past achievements and achievement test items on more recent achievements. But to say that one measure of achievement *causes* the other is poor logic. We can only say that some measures of achievement are *related* to other measures of achievement.

When we distinguish between measures of *level* of achievement (such as mental age, grade level) and measures of *gain* in achievement (which are a function of current instruction), we find the relation between IQ and achievement gain becomes much smaller or disappears. A level measure combines past learning *and* current learning and, not surprisingly, is related to past learning. A gain measure reflects *only current learning* and shows at best low positive correlations with past learning. Cronbach's review of the relation of IQ to measures of learning (gain) implies that IQ relates to learning gain only when prior learning can be used to advantage in the new learning. Several studies reviewed by Cronbach and one by Linda Meyers show that when the effects of prior learning (including motivation) are controlled, the average rate of learning does not differ for bright and dull students. This conclusion is a far cry from popular belief.

For the present, we must conclude that the potential power of instruction in increasing intelligent behavior has *no known limit*. Through better teaching, people can be smarter. People learn what they are taught.

self-test

1 80

2 school
  achievement

3 genetics

---

1 With modern estimation procedures, Jensen summarizes the data to show that _____ percent of the variance in intelligence can be attributed to heredity.

2 The belief in a genetically fixed intelligence takes on additional implications for education when coupled with data showing correlations in the .80 to .90 range between measures of intelligence and measures of _____ _____.

3 The teacher is faced with conceptions (supported by research findings) which suggest that children with poorer _____ learn less in school.

4 Current experimental evidence suggests that an increase of _____ standard deviations in IQ can be obtained with current technology.

5 The high correlations between measures of intelligence and achievement batteries do not imply that intelligence _____ achievement. They only show that a measure of past achievement is _____ to current achievement.

6 The evidence showing correlations of .80 to .90 between intelligence test scores and achievement test scores have been based on _____- _____ measures rather than _____ measures. Because of this, they cannot have much relevance for making judgments on the effects of past achievements on _____ instructional progress.

7 The review by Cronbach implies that IQ scores relate to learning gains only when _____ _____ can be used to advantage in the new instruction.

NUMBER RIGHT _____

4 two

5 causes;
   related

6 level-type;
   gain; current

7 prior
   learning

exercise 1 programed practice

1 The answer to the question *Who can be taught?* is important for the teacher in determining how _____ are used to make instructional decisions.

2 What the teacher believes can lead to a _____-_____ prophecy.

3 The modern belief in a hereditarily fixed intelligence can be traced to _____, a cousin of Darwin.

4 With the construction of the first American _____ test by Terman, evidence was gathered supporting the notion of _____ ability.

5 In addition, studies of identical twins, fraternal twins, siblings, and unrelated persons produced correlations supporting a strong influence of _____ on the scores. With modern estimation procedures, Jensen summarizes the data to show that _____ percent of the variance in intelligence can be attributed to heredity.

1 tests

2 self-fulfilling

3 Galton

4 IQ; fixed

5 heredity; 80

6 school
  achievement

7 genetics

8 challenged

9 estimation;
  underestimate;
  50-50

10 instruction

11 one

12 IQ

13 two

14 same

15 older; new

6 The belief in a genetically fixed intelligence takes on additional implications for education when coupled with data showing correlations in the .80 to .90 range between measures of intelligence and measures of _____ _____.

7 The teacher is faced with conceptions (supported by research findings) which suggest that children with poorer _____ learn less in school.

8 Fortunately for children and education, the basis for these conclusions can be _____ on many grounds.

9 The first point to note is that the relative contribution of heredity to variation in IQ, as reflected in a heritability index, is an _____ based on data which probably grossly _____ the role of environment. One could easily consider a _____-_____ contribution of heredity and environment under existing conditions when cross-cultural variations are considered.

10 Beyond this, the real question for the teacher is, "How much can be done through _____ to improve intellectual functioning?"

11 In the last 70 to 100 years, average stature has shown an increase on the order of _____ standard deviation.

12 In an analogous way, better education has likely produced a general rise in _____ of a similar magnitude during the past 70 years.

13 Current experimental evidence suggests that an increase of _____ standard deviations in IQ can be obtained with current technology.

14 The high correlation between IQ test scores and achievement battery scores was interpreted by Kelley as implying that two measures of the _____ thing had been given different names.

15 Humphreys and others have suggested the IQ tests and achievement tests both measure achievements, but the IQ test focuses on _____ learning while the achievement test focuses on _____ learning.

16 It is possible to conclude that some proportion of the variation in the behavior called intelligence can be attributed to the contribution of _____, but there is a lot of room for _____ influences to make people smarter or duller.

17 Furthermore, the high correlations between measures of intelligence and achievement batteries do not imply that intelligence _____ achievement. They only show that a measure of past achievement is _____ to current achievement.

18 If we discard the hereditary issue as not really being central to the process of education and we concern ourselves with the issue of whether future achievement (learning) can be predicted from _____ achievement (intelligence), we still have a problem.

19 The evidence showing correlations of .80 to .90 between intelligence test scores and achievement test scores have been based on _____-_____measures rather than _____ measures. Because of this, they cannot have much relevance for making judgments on the effects of past achievements on _____ instructional progress.

20 The level measure is a measure of past achievement and current gain in learning. Thus it has much in _____ with other measures of past achievement (IQ). However, simple gain measures do not show a high relationship to _____.

21 The review by Cronbach implies that IQ scores relate to learning gains only when _____ _____ can be used to advantage in the new instruction.

22 Several studies reviewed by Cronbach and a study by Linda Meyers show that when the effects of prior learning (including motivation) are controlled, the average rate of learning does not _____ for bright and dull students.

23 It would seem that in terms of what we know now, the power of instruction in increasing intelligent behavior does not have a _____ _____.

---

16 heredity;
  environmental

17 causes;
  related

18 past

19 level-type;
  gain; current

20 common; IQ

21 prior
  learning

22 differ

23 known limit

discussion questions

1. Why should the teacher be interested in knowing how a person's background affects what he or she can be taught?
2. Why do you suppose the author's state that the question "Who can be taught?" involves a vital social issue?
3. What is the basis of the belief in a genetically fixed intelligence?
4. On what bases can the notion of a genetically fixed intelligence be challenged?
5. What is the basis for the belief that intelligence determines what you can learn?
6. On what bases can the belief that intelligence determines what can be learned be questioned?
7. How does a person's background affect what he or she can be taught?

unit 16

Review 2

objectives

This review unit is designed to remind you of some of the material covered earlier in the course. This unit is *not* designed to teach you new material, except for the overview of stimulus and response functions. If any terms or concepts are mentioned that you do not understand, you should go back to the original material and study it carefully. In addition, you should go back through the exercises you did for each unit and make sure that you know the correct answer for each item.

review

Unit 9. Norm-Referenced Achievement Tests

Norm-referenced achievement tests attempt to test the "common core" of what is happening in elementary and secondary education today. The most popular tests have been revised in the past five to eight years. Most of the achievement tests are constructed by starting with a group of general objectives defined by a group of curriculum experts on the basis of texts and programs in use in the schools. Test items are then written, tried out, and edited for logical consistency, difficulty level, ambiguity, and item information relating to reliability and validity. Finally, a representative sample of students is tested to provide a basis for constructing test norms. In contrast to criterion-referenced tests, the objectives of norm-referenced tests are usually broader and not specific to particular instructional programs. Items are preferred which discriminate between the persons taking the test, and scores are interpreted according to their placement in the distribution of scores obtained by the norm group.

Three types of tests were discussed. *Diagnostic tests* in reading and arithmetic have been used in planning remedial programs. We have suggested that the reading tests be used primarily to obtain norm-referenced measures (although crude) of oral reading rate and accuracy. The diagnostic arithmetic tests, which are essentially criterion-referenced tests, are also useful in remedial work when tied to appropriate corrective procedures. *Single-subject tests* can be found for almost any subject area. The most common tests used in elementary schools are measures of reading readiness. In discussing their use we have suggested that such tests might best be thought of as tests of preskills assumed by basal reading programs. Keep in mind that with proper analysis and procedures, these preskills can be taught.

Four of the most commonly used *achievement batteries* were illustrated and discussed in more detail. Each of the tests is technically quite sophisticated. They enjoy a wide spread use in the evaluation of educational programs today. Such tests are sometimes useful in making gross decisions about student placement, but they are not designed for use in making precise placements in a particular curriculum. Similarly, they are not sensitive enough nor program-specific enough for use in evaluating the process of instruction. These tests may be useful in the "norm-referenced evaluation" of a single program or in the experimental comparison of two or more programs. The major problem in such use is one of forming a careful judgment of the degree to which the tests measure program objectives. Test builders could do much to aid this judgment by giving more precise specifications of the objectives being measured by the tests. Norm-referenced tests are not useful in teacher evaluation, but may have many uses in student selection for special programs and in guidance. There are some tough ethical issues to be considered when tests are proposed for use in the selection of students for special programs.

Unit 10. Interpreting Norm-Referenced Test Scores

The normal curve or normal distribution is useful in interpreting norm-referenced test scores because it provides a practical basis for converting standard scores to statements about the percentage of persons likely to have scores higher or lower than a given score. The area under the curve can be divided into portions which sum to one. The proportion of area between any two points gives the relative frequency of persons likely to fall between those two points. By multiplying the proportion by 100, the percentage of persons falling under a section of the curve can be obtained. A table based on the normal distribution (appendix B) can be used to convert any standard score (in z-score form) to a statement of the percentage of persons having higher or lower scores. It can also be used to find the percentage of persons likely to fall between any two z-scores. The following are important examples:

Normal Curve Section	Percent of Cases Included	Bases
Mean to 1 SD	34%	
1 SD to 2 SDs	14%	
2 SDs to 3 SDs	2%	
Mean to 2 SDs	48%	(34% + 14%)
Mean to 3 SDs	50%	(34% + 14% + 2%)
−1 SD to +1 SD	68%	(34% + 34%)
−2 SDs to +2 SDs	96%	(48% + 48%)
−3 SDs to +3 SDs	100%	(50% + 50%)

Transformed standard scores are desirable because they eliminate negative scores and decimal parts. To transform a set of z-scores, multiply the z-scores by the desired standard deviation for the transformed distribution and then add the desired mean for the transformed distributions. T-scores are transformed standard scores with a mean of 50 and a standard deviation of 10. IQ scores are transformed standard scores with a mean of 100 and a standard deviation of 15 (or 16). Graduate Record Examination scores are transformed standard scores with a mean of 500 and a standard deviation of 100. Stanines are transformed standard scores with a mean of 5 and a standard deviation of 2 which can only take on the whole numbers 1 to 9.

Appendix B can also be used to help interpret any transformed standard score. Simply convert it back to a z-score using the following:

$$z = \frac{X - M}{SD}$$

where X is the transformed standard score, M is the mean of the transformed distribution and SD is the standard deviation of the transformed distribution.

Most popular achievement test batteries use an *expanded standard score* to interrelate different levels of tests. The standard deviation is kept at approximately 10 for any given level, and the means are allowed to progress from level to level.

Ranks assign 1 to the best score, 2 to the next best, and so on. A percentile rank specifies the percentage of scores which are lower than a given score. Percentiles allow for a direct statement of the percent of persons in the norm group who score lower than a given score. This feature makes percentiles useful in presenting test data to parents, However, percentiles can be misinterpreted when used to evaluate gains or compare different sudents. Percentiles tend to exaggerate differences near the mean and undervalue differences near the ends of a disribution.

Grade-equivalent scores assign scale scores on the basis of the average raw score earned by a group at a given grade. A similar procedure is followed to develop age-equivalent scores. Interpreting *changes* in grade-equivalent scores can be deceptive. Some skills may develop rapidly in the early grades and then level off, so that a change in grade-norm from fourth to eighth grade might represent very little learning. Knowledge of the relation of grade-equivalents and expanded standard scores can alert one to the problem areas. There is also a problem in the meaning of grade-equivalence. A second grader with a grade-equivalent score of 6.0 cannot necessarily do sixth-grade work. He doesn't even take the sixth-grade test. He can do second-grade work as well as the average sixth grader is estimated to do second-grade work.

Norm-referenced scores are based on the performance of some norm group on the test. The norm group provides a frame of reference for score interpretation. An obtained score is high or low *in relation to* a specified norm group, such as, all *second graders in the United States*. The major achievement batteries provide norms based on a representative national sample. Tests using norms from different samples are not likely to produce the same result because of norm sample differences and test differences. However, the Anchor Test Study suggests that for reading at grades 4, 5, and 6, these differences are not very great. The study also provides a basis for comparing groups tested with different achievement tests.

Local norms and norms based on students "like yours" are desirable when using norm-referenced tests to evaluate program effectiveness.

In the last section of this unit, practice was provided in using norm tables to convert raw scores to norm-referenced scores.

Unit 11. Interpreting Correlation Coefficients

The concept of correlation is important for understanding how norm-referenced tests are constructed and evaluated. In a four-fold table, a high positive correlation exists when most of the cases fall in the $++$ and $--$ quadrants. A high negative correlation exists when most of the cases fall in the $-+$ and $+-$ quadrants. No correlation exists when the cases are equally distributed throughout the four quadrants.

When there is a range of scores for two different measures we can plot these scores on a joint-frequency distribution or scatter diagram. It is possible to judge the nature of the correlation from the shape of the scatter diagram. In a high correlation, the data points tend to fall along a line. If the correlation is positive, this line slopes from the bottom left to the top right quadrant. If the correlation is negative, this line slopes from the bottom right to the top left quadrant. Low or zero correlations have scatter plots where the data points spread all over.

The most important index of the degree of relation between two variables is the Pearson correlation coefficient or r. Starting with z-scores, the Pearson r is obtained by multiplying each z_X by its pairmate z_Y, summing these products, and taking the average by dividing by N.

$$r = \frac{\text{Sum } z_X \cdot z_Y}{N}$$

When computing r from raw scores the formula is:

$$r = \frac{N\Sigma XY - (\Sigma X) \cdot (\Sigma Y)}{\sqrt{N\Sigma X^2 - (\Sigma X)^2} \ \sqrt{N\Sigma Y^2 - (\Sigma Y)^2}}$$

The symbol Σ in this formula stands for *sum* of the cases.

When the properties of r are examined in z-score form, it is easier to see what it means when r takes on positive and negative values. The Pearson r is positive when more cases fall in the quadrants which produce positive products (++ and − −), and r is negative when more of the cases fall in the quadrants which produce negative products (−+ and + −). The Pearson r can take on values from +1 to −1. A correlation of +1 is a perfect positive correlation. A correlation of −1 is a perfect negative correlation. A zero correlation indicates that two measures are unrelated.

Measures of association can also be computed with dichotomous variables, although the details of how it is done are not important here.

Unit 12. Test Theory as it Applies to Achievement Tests

The reliability of a test is concerned with the contribution of errors of measurement to test scores. If there is no error, the reliability is 1. As the proportion of error variance to total variance increases, reliability decreases. The contribution of error to test scores is determined by correlating two measures (or the average of all possible measures) of the same thing. This can be done with parallel form measures, dividing a test into odd-item and even-item halves, or by computing an alpha coefficient, which gives the average of all possible split halves. A reliability coefficient, when multiplied by 100, gives the percent of the variance in a set of test scores that can be attributed to true scores.

The standard error of measurement is found by taking the square root of 1 minus the reliability coefficient and multiplying this by the standard deviation of a test. In evaluating an individual test score, plus or minus 2 times the standard error of measurement will give the interval within which the true mean should fall with a 95 percent confidence. With standardized achievement tests, 2 times the standard error of measurement is most typically about six-tenths of a grade level. Reliabilities under .90 are not very tolerable when the test scores are used for decisions about individuals. One way to improve the reliability of a test is to make it longer.

A test can have different validities for different uses. With norm-referenced achievement tests, the question of validity for program evaluation rests largely on the appropriateness of the test content and a criterion of sensitivity of the test to instruction. The criterion for sensitivity to instruction used for most achievement tests is that more students in higher grades pass the item than do students in lower grades. Predictive validity of a test depends on its correlation with some future performance, such as success in college. When validity is expressed as a correlation between a test and some criterion, the correlation is best interpreted by squaring this validity coefficient. This will give the proportion of variance (or *percent*, if multiplied by 100) in the criterion that is predictable from the test. Unreliability in tests or criteria will reduce validity coefficients in a predictable way.

Item analysis of the tryout form of a test is used to build a final test form with maximum reliability and validity. This is accomplished by eliminating items that most persons pass and fail, by keeping items that best discriminate between high and low scorers on the test (item reliability index), and by keeping items students in higher grades pass but those in lower grades fail (validity index). While the use of these procedures will generally lead to good measures of individual differences, they have potential problems when used to build measures to evaluate the effects of *school instruction*. The use of the criterion of higher percent passing with increasing grade level biases item selection away from measures sensitive to school instruction and toward other characteristics that change with age such as mental age and/or nonschool instruction. Selecting items that discriminate high and low test scorers can serve to accentuate this bias away from measures of the effects of school instruction. If language development at home or home-directed instruction contributes to test performance, and such instruction is associated with parental education, then the achievement test measures will come to reflect social class-related variables.

In our judgment the test area most biased by these factors is that of *reading comprehension*. This bias may occur because of a failure to control the choice of vocabulary words used in tests after third grade. Logical aspects of comprehension should be tested mainly with words whose meaning all students have been taught. Vocabulary can be tested separately. These problems could be overcome by using a more direct measure of sensitivity to instruction (pretest, instruction, posttest), and by the control of admissible vocabulary used so that it is appropriate to vocabulary actually taught in school.

Unit 13. Research Design and Evaluation of Research Studies

There are two kinds of research concerned with relating causes and effects—correlational research and experimental research. In correlational research, relations between variables as they now exist are studied. The difficulty with correlational research is that knowledge of a relation is not sufficient evidence to make an inference about a cause. The relations *might* be pointing to a cause, but we don't know if that is really so. In general, we should be very skeptical about drawing causal conclusions from correlational studies.

Experimental research requires the changing of an independent variable, making at least two measurements on some dependent variable, and comparing the measures to draw a conclusion. In group design, the measurements are taken on two (or more) groups which are treated differently. In individual subject designs, the measurements are taken from different treatment conditions on the same subjects.

To permit unambiguous interpretations of an experimental study, use a design that will control for alternative interpretations of the results. In research on teaching, this usually involves other events which change with time which might account for an outcome, such as:

1 *Other experiences* that involve learning
2 *Maturation*
3 *Test practice*
4 *Changes in group membership*
5 *Changes in tests*
6 *Score changes due to unreliability of tests*
7 *Extreme-group selection effects* (statistical regression)

In group designs, control of these potential influences is best achieved by the use of a control group. However, the use of a control group raises a question of comparability of control group and treatment group in terms of important background characteristics. Random assignment of persons to treatment and control groups is the most effective means of coping with this problem. Where random assignment is not possible, caution must be exercised in interpreting results.

In individual-subject designs, control is achieved over differences in personal history by using the same persons under baseline and various treatment conditions. A significant treatment effect has to produce an effect on the dependent variable that is in addition to that shown during baseline measurements. To rule out other interpretations of effects associated with time, reversal designs, multiple-baseline designs, and simple replications are used.

Some of the more important group designs are:

1 Random assignment to groups, pretest and posttest.
2 Random assignment to groups, posttest only.
3 No random assignment (intact groups), pretest and posttest. Check for initial differences on critical variables. Adjust outcomes for pretest differences.
4 Simple replication.
5 Norm-referenced comparison. Use the norm group of a standardized test as the comparison group. The goal is to show a significant improvement in standings on the norms (pretest to posttest) for the experimental group.

The two main individual-subject designs are:
1 Reversal designs, where baseline and experimental conditions are alternated.
2 Multiple-baseline designs, where for the same subject, different behaviors are changed at different times; or where the same behavior is changed at different times for different subjects.

Group and individual designs can be combined to make both within-group and between-group comparisons. When a baseline shows systematic changes over time, this may be especially helpful. Multiple control groups are sometimes useful in isolating different possible interpretations of an outcome. Monitoring of the experimental and control conditions is necessary to insure that unplanned happenings do not influence the outcomes.

Three questions need to be answered in drawing conclusions. First, is there a difference? Second, if there is, to what can it be attributed? Third, how general is the finding?

In answering the first question for group designs, the answer focuses on the question of statistical significance. Is the difference obtained large enough, relative to the standard error of the difference, to justify a conclusion of statistical significance? The critical ratio provides one basis for making this decision when two means are involved. When more than two means are being compared, analysis of variance can be used. If a difference is statistically significant, it is still necessary to decide if the difference is educationally significant. With a large enough N, almost any difference could be found to be statistically significant. A difference of one-fourth to one-half standard deviation on most achievement tests is likely to have educational significance. In answering the question, "Is there a difference?" for individual-subject designs, the basic procedure for building confidence that an effect is real is to use *replication* within the same study or in the new study.

In answering the second question, "To what is the difference attributable?" it is necessary to determine the degree to which the design controls for alternative interpretations. Is a control group used which is *comparable* to the treatment group? Is there monitoring evidence to show that the difference was actually produced by the experimental treatment? In individual subject designs, are procedures used to rule out other things that change with time? Was the change called the experimental treatment the only change made?

In answering the third question, "How general are the findings?" it is necessary to find out what was sampled in building the experimental procedures or groups. When replication of an effect is shown across a sample of similar things, a basis for a generalization is provided.

Unit 14. Outcome Evaluation Revisited

The planning of an outcome study needs to answer six questions: Who will be tested when? What initial assessments will be made? What final assessments will be made? What measures will be taken to show continuous student progress and/or the effectiveness of program implementation? How are the data to be summarized? How are the findings to be communicated to others?

The checklist which follows provides a summary of the measures to be considered in planning an outcome study.

Checklist of Measures to Consider

Premeasures
- *If random assignment* to groups, pre-assessment on outcome measures is desirable but not necessary.
- *With intact groups,* measure student IQ and indicators of parental social class (education of parents, income, etc.). Also make pre-assessments of outcome measures.
- *With norm-group design,* pre-assess on outcome measures. A measure of IQ is desirable for describing the group.
- *Individual-subject design.* Take series of baseline measures before instituting change.

Process measures
- Obtain measures of teacher performance in terms of program requirements.
- Record lessons taught or pages covered weekly by groups.
- Use instruction-referenced tests to measure student skill development each two or six weeks.
- Record time spent on each subject area.
- Attempt to obtain measures of academic behavior involving generalized performance beyond program materials.

Outcome measures

- Use normative tests that logically fit common program objectives and formats.
- When programs have different objectives, try to find measures of these differences that can be used with both the treatment and control group.
- Use criterion-referenced tests of common and not-common objectives. Measure time devoted to each objective.
- Obtain measures of program acceptance by students, teachers, and parents.
- Assess cost in terms of time and materials on a pre-pupil basis.

Data analysis should begin by identifying the students on whom there is both pretest and posttest data. Plot the frequency distributions and compute means and SDs. Check to see that students on whom there are only pretest scores are not different from the rest. Check the distributions for floor and ceiling effects, and for changes in SDs from pretest to posttest. Compute tests of statistical significance using standard scores. Gain measures are not needed if treatment and comparison groups are equivalent at pretest. Use just a comparison of posttest scores. Where groups differ at pretest, use a covariance adjustment of posttest scores rather than a gain measure in forming conclusions. Remember to consider the educational significance of a difference, not just the statistical significance.

In reporting the results, state the purpose of the study, who was involved, and the overall outcome. Then back up the conclusion with specifics using grade norm or percentile scores and anecdotal information on student, parent, and teacher reactions. End the report with a recommendation.

Unit 15. Who Can Be Taught?

For the teacher, an examination of the question *Who can be taught?* is important in determining how tests are used to make instructional decisons. What the teacher believes can lead to a self-fulfilling prophecy. Two important beliefs have dominated thinking for over a century: that intelligence is largely fixed by heredity and that school achievement is largely determined by one's intelligence.

In current data on the inheritance of intelligence, effects of environment are probably grossly underestimated. As with the increase in physical stature during the past 70 years, environmental influences can markedly improve the behaviors we call intelligence. A two-standard-deviation increase is well within the range of current technology.

The presumed causative role of intelligence in school achievement is open to question on several grounds. First, as Kelley did, one can interpret the high correlation between IQ test scores and scores on achievement test batteries as simply two measures of achievement; or with Humphreys, we can note that IQ test items tend to focus on past achievements and achievement test items on more recent achievements. But to say that one measure of achievement *causes* the other is poor logic. We can only say that some measures of achievement are *related* to other measures of achievement.

When we distinguish between measures of *level* of achievement (such as mental age, grade level) and measures of *gain* in achievement (which are a function of current instruction), we find the relation between IQ and achievement gain becomes much smaller or disappears. A level measure combines past learning *and* current learning and, not surprisingly, is related to past learning. A gain measure reflects *only current learning* and shows at best low positive correlations with past learning. Cronbach's review of the relation of IQ to measures of learning (gain) implies that IQ relates to learning gain only when prior learning can be used to advantage in the new learning. Several studies reviewed by Cronbach and one by Linda Meyers show that when the effects of prior learning (including motivation) are controlled, the average rate of learning does not differ for bright and dull students. This conclusion is a far cry from popular belief.

For the present, we must conclude that the potential power of instruction in increasing intelligent behavior has no *known* limit. Through better teaching, people can be smarter. People learn what they are taught.

review exercises

Unit 9.

1 What are the key steps in building a norm-referenced test?

2 What are four ways in which the construction of norm-referenced and criterion-referenced tests differ?

3 Name and give examples of three kinds of achievement tests.

4 Describe three kinds of response conventions used in the MAT, CAT, SAT, and SRA.

5 What is the Mental Measurement Yearbook series?

6 Discuss the uses of norm-referenced achievement tests in diagnostic-remedial work.

7 Discuss the use of norm-referenced tests in student placement.

8 What is a "norm-referenced evaluation"?

9 What two requirements must be met in making a "norm-referenced evaluation"?

10 What is the major problem in using norm-referenced tests to compare the effects of different programs?

11 Should norm-referenced test data be used in teacher evaluation? Why?

12 What value-issues arise in the use of tests in selection of students?

13 How might norm-referenced tests be used in guidance?

Unit 10.

1 Why is the normal distribution of use in interpreting norm-referenced test scores.

2 What percentage of the cases (approximately) falls between the following standard score units on the normal curve? 0 to 1 SD, 1 SD to 2 SDs, 2 SDs to 3 SDs, 0 to 2 SDs, 0 to 3 SDs.

3 What are z-scores?

4 What is a transformed standard score and how is the transformation accomplished?

5 Give three examples of transformed standard scores.

6 How wide is the band covered by a stanine unit in z-score units?

7 How is Appendix B used to interpret transformed standard scores?

8 What is an expanded standard score?

9 How can one interpret the fact that on the Metropolitan, for reading and math, the mean expanded standard score progresses less and less each year (table 10.2)?

10 How do you rank order a set of scores?

11 What are percentile ranks (percentiles, centiles)?

12 Why are percentiles useful?

13 What problems arise in interpreting gain scores, or difference scores when expressed as percentiles? Give an example.

14 How are age- and grade-equivalent scores determined?

15 Suppose a fifth grader obtains a grade-equivalent score of 9.3 grades. What does this mean?

16 On the MAT, would a grade-equivalent gain in reading going from 2.0 to 4.0 be as much of a gain as going from 6.0 to 8.0? Explain your answer.

17 What is a norm population?

18 How are norm populations determined in standardizing the major achievement test batteries?

19 What was found in the Anchor Test Study?

20 How do you interpret a grade-equivalent score of 5.6?

Unit 11.

1 Be prepared to fill in the headings and entries on three four-fold tables to show a positive correlation, a negative correlation, and a zero correlation. Label each quadrant as ++, − −, − +, + −.

2 What is a joint-frequency distribution?

3 What is another name for a joint-frequency distribution?

4 How can a scatter plot be related to a four-fold table?

5 Draw scatter plots to illustrate each of the following:
a. a high positive correlation.
b. a high negative correlation.

c. a medium positive correlation.

d. a medium negative correlation.

e. a zero correlation.

6 What do correlations have to do with predictability?

7 In looking at a scatter plot, how does the length of the best-fit prediction line, relative to the scatter from this line, relate to the size of a correlation?

8 When both variables are in z-score units, how does the slope of the best-fit prediction line relate to the size of the correlation?

9 State exactly what kind of an average a Pearson r is.

10 What values can r take on?

11 Explain why r must be positive if most of the data points fall in the lower-left and upper-right quadrants of a scatter plot.

12 In analyzing items for test construction, we often are dealing with a dichotomous (pass-fail) score rather than a continuous variable as is necessary to compute r. How is this problem handled?

Unit 12.

1 Explain the equation $X = T + E$.

2 Relate reliability and validity to the equation in 1.

3 What is a variance?

4 Why does test theory (and much of statistical theory) deal with variances rather than standard deviations?

5 What is the basic procedure for determining the reliability of a measure?

6 What are some implications of the fact that a reliability coefficient can be expressed as the ratio of true-score variance to total variance, or as one minus the ratio of error variance to total variance?

7 What is parallel-form reliability?

8 What is a split-half reliability?

9 What is an alpha coefficient?

10 Define the standard error of measurement and explain how it can be used to determine the confidence interval for a test score.

11 How would you determine the range for a 99 percent confidence interval?

12 Use table 12.2 and determine the 95% confidence interval for a reading grade-equivalent score of 2.5.

13 If a unit length test has a reliability of .20, what would be the reliability of a test four times as long? (use figure 12.1).

14 What are the two main criteria for evaluating the validity of a norm-referenced achievement test?

15 How is sensitivity to instruction usually examined in item analysis for achievement tests?

16 Name and define three types of validity.

17 Why is it that achievement tests cannot be claimed to be universally valid?

18 How does one judge the size of a criterion-oriented validity coefficient?

19 What is the explicit relation of reliability to the validity of a test?

20   What are three principles central to item analysis in constructing a test?

21   What is the trouble with the usual criterion of sensitivity in instruction?

22   What potential biases are introduced by the criterion of discriminability?

23   Why would Stake refer to norm-referenced achievement tests as measures of "correlates of learning"?

24   What can norm-referenced tests do well?

25   Why do the authors suspect these tests would be biased in the norm-referenced evaluation of instructional programs for the disadvantaged, especially in the art of reading comprehension?

26   What are the possible solutions to the potential biases in norm-referenced tests?

Unit 13.

1   Give an example of descriptive research.

2   Describe the essential differences between correlational and experimental research.

3   Give an example of a correlational study.

4   Why should we be concerned with experimental designs?

5   What are some of the common alternative explanations for outcomes in educational research which are related to changes with time?

6   Explain the concept of statistical regression.

7   How do group designs control for individual differences in subject history and for other variables that can change with time?

8   How do individual-subject designs control for individual differences in subject history and for other variables that can produce changes with time?

9   Describe how a norm-referenced comparison is made and the cautions to be exercised.

10   Give an example of a reversal design.

11   What are some advantages of combining group and individual-subject designs?

12   Give some examples to show why it is important to monitor the experimental conditions to see what actually is happening.

13   What are three important questions to ask in drawing a conclusion from a research study?

14   In group designs, how would you answer the question, "Is there a difference?"

15   What is meant by the concept of statistical significance?

16   What is a standard error of a difference?

17   What is a critical ratio?

18   Explain why a critical ratio can be interpreted as a standard score (z-score).

19   What questions should you ask in deciding to what to attribute a difference *for a group design, for an individual-subject design?*

20   How do you decide what generalizations can be made from a study?

21   Give an example describing sampling in a study which would permit generalization across a class of dependent behaviors, a class of people, and a class of independent stimulus events.

Unit 14.

1 Why should the classroom teacher need to know the procedures for evaluating programs?

2 What should be considered in selecting a design?

3 What problems can occur in using a norm-referenced design and how might they be overcome?

4 Explain the logic of a norm-referenced design.

5 Describe an individual-subject design that might be used in assessing a program aimed at some basic skills.

6 What premeasures are desirable for random-group designs, intact-group designs, norm-group-referenced designs, and individual-subject designs?

7 How can programs with different objectives be evaluated?

8 What problems can arise in selecting test levels and how might these be overcome?

9 Why might one be interested in getting attitude measures in evaluating a program?

10 Describe the general procedure for assessing program cost.

11 Give two kinds of process measures that are important in evaluating an outcome study and explain why they are important.

12 What three steps do Horst et al. recommend be followed in analyzing data for students with both pretests and posttests?

13 What irregularities do Horst et al. recommend be looked for in examining the data?

14 Give two common problems in measuring gains.

15 Give an outline for a report on a study to be given to a parent group.

16 Summarize the main procedures and findings in the study of reading programs by Bliesmer and Yarborough.

17 Summarize the main procedures and findings in the study of "old" and "new" math programs by Hungerman.

Unit 15.

1 Why should the teacher be interested in knowing how a person's background affects what he or she can be taught?

2 Why do you suppose the author's state that the question "Who can be taught?" involves a vital social issue?

3 What is the basis of the belief in a genetically fixed intelligence?

4 On what bases can the notion of a genetically fixed intelligence be challenged?

5 What is the basis for the belief that intelligence determines what you can learn?

6 On what bases can the belief that intelligence determines what can be learned be questioned?

7 How does a person's background affect what he or she can be taught?

appendix A

Squares and Square Roots (1-999)

n	n²	√n	n	n²	√n	n	n²	√n	n	n²	√n
0	0	0.000	46	2 116	6.782	92	8 464	9.592	138	19 044	11.747
1	1	1.000	47	2 209	6.856	93	8 649	9.644	139	19 321	11.790
2	4	1.414	48	2 304	6.928	94	8 836	9.695	140	19 600	11.832
3	9	1.732	49	2 401	7.000	95	9 025	9.747	141	19 881	11.874
4	16	2.000	50	2 500	7.071	96	9 216	9.798	142	20 164	11.916
5	25	2.236	51	2 601	7.141	97	9 409	9.849	143	20 449	11.958
6	36	2.449	52	2 704	7.211	98	9 604	9.899	144	20 736	12.000
7	49	2.646	53	2 809	7.280	99	9 801	9.950	145	21 025	12.042
8	64	2.828	54	2 916	7.348	100	10 000	10.000	146	21 316	12.083
9	81	3.000	55	3 025	7.416	101	10 201	10.050	147	21 609	12.124
10	100	3.162	56	3 136	7.483	102	10 404	10.100	148	21 904	12.166
11	121	3.317	57	3 249	7.550	103	10 609	10.149	149	22 201	12.207
12	144	3.464	58	3 364	7.616	104	10 816	10.198	150	22 500	12.247
13	169	3.606	59	3 481	7.681	105	11 025	10.247	151	22 801	12.288
14	196	3.742	60	3 600	7.746	106	11 236	10.295	152	23 104	12.329
15	225	3.873	61	3 721	7.810	107	11 449	10.344	153	23 409	12.369
16	256	4.000	62	3 844	7.874	108	11 664	10.392	154	23 716	12.410
17	289	4.123	63	3 969	7.937	109	11 881	10.440	155	24 025	12.450
18	324	4.243	64	4 096	8.000	110	12 100	10.488	156	24 336	12.490
19	361	4.359	65	4 225	8.062	111	12 321	10.536	157	24 649	12.530
20	400	4.472	66	4 356	8.124	112	12 544	10.583	158	24 964	12.570
21	441	4.583	67	4 489	8.185	113	12 769	10.630	159	25 281	12.610
22	484	4.690	68	4 624	8.246	114	12 996	10.677	160	25 600	12.649
23	529	4.796	69	4 761	8.307	115	13 225	10.724	161	25 921	12.689
24	576	4.899	70	4 900	8.367	116	13 456	10.770	162	26 244	12.728
25	625	5.000	71	5 041	8.426	117	13 689	10.817	163	26 569	12.767
26	676	5.099	72	5 184	8.485	118	13 924	10.863	164	26 896	12.806
27	729	5.196	73	5 329	8.544	119	14 161	10.909	165	27 225	12.845
28	784	5.292	74	5 476	8.602	120	14 400	10.954	166	27 556	12.884
29	841	5.385	75	5 625	8.660	121	14 641	11.000	167	27 889	12.923
30	900	5.477	76	5 776	8.718	122	14 884	11.045	168	28 224	12.961
31	961	5.568	77	5 929	8.775	123	15 129	11.091	169	28 561	13.000
32	1 024	5.657	78	6 084	8.832	124	15 376	11.136	170	28 900	13.038
33	1 089	5.745	79	6 241	8.888	125	15 625	11.180	171	29 241	13.077
34	1 156	5.831	80	6 400	8.944	126	15 876	11.225	172	29 584	13.115
35	1 225	5.916	81	6 561	9.000	127	16 129	11.269	173	29 929	13.153
36	1 296	6.000	82	6 724	9.055	128	16 384	11.314	174	30 276	13.191
37	1 369	6.083	83	6 889	9.110	129	16 641	11.358	175	30 625	13.229
38	1 444	6.164	84	7 056	9.165	130	16 900	11.402	176	30 976	13.267
39	1 521	6.245	85	7 225	9.220	131	17 161	11.446	177	31 329	13.304
40	1 600	6.325	86	7 396	9.274	132	17 424	11.489	178	31 684	13.342
41	1 681	6.403	87	7 569	9.327	133	17 689	11.533	179	32 041	13.379
42	1 764	6.481	88	7 744	9.381	134	17 956	11.576	180	32 400	13.416
43	1 849	6.557	89	7 921	9.434	135	18 225	11.619	181	32 761	13.454
44	1 936	6.633	90	8 100	9.487	136	18 496	11.662	182	33 124	13.491
45	2 025	6.708	91	8 281	9.539	137	18 769	11.705	183	33 489	13.528

n	n^2	$\sqrt{n}$	n	n^2	$\sqrt{n}$	n	n^2	$\sqrt{n}$	n	n^2	$\sqrt{n}$
184	33 856	13.565	235	55 225	15.330	286	81 796	16.912	337	113 569	18.358
185	34 225	13.601	236	55 696	15.362	287	82 369	16.941	338	114 244	18.386
186	34 596	13.638	237	56 169	15.395	288	82 944	16.971	339	114 921	18.412
187	34 969	13.675	238	56 644	15.427	289	83 521	17.000	340	115 600	18.439
188	35 344	13.711	239	57 121	15.460	290	84 100	17.029	341	116 281	18.466
189	35 721	13.748	240	57 600	15.492	291	84 681	17.059	342	116 964	18.493
190	36 100	13.784	241	58 081	15.524	292	85 264	17.088	343	117 649	18.520
191	36 481	13.820	242	58 564	15.556	293	85 849	17.117	344	118 336	18.547
192	36 864	13.856	243	59 049	15.588	294	86 436	17.146	345	119 025	18.574
193	37 249	13.892	244	59 536	15.621	295	87 025	17.176	346	119 716	18.601
194	37 636	13.928	245	60 025	15.652	296	87 616	17.205	347	120 409	18.628
195	38 025	13.964	246	60 516	15.684	297	88 209	17.234	348	121 104	18.655
196	38 416	14.000	247	61 009	15.716	298	88 804	17.263	349	121 801	18.682
197	38 809	14.036	248	61 504	15.748	299	89 401	17.292	350	122 500	18.708
198	39 204	14.071	249	62 001	15.780	300	90 000	17.321	351	123 201	18.735
199	39 601	14.107	250	62 500	15.811	301	90 601	17.349	352	123 904	18.762
200	40 000	14.142	251	63 001	15.843	302	91 204	17.378	353	124 609	18.788
201	40 401	14.177	252	63 504	15.875	303	91 809	17.407	354	125 316	18.815
202	40 804	14.213	253	64 009	15.906	304	92 416	17.436	355	126 025	18.841
203	41 209	14.248	254	64 516	15.937	305	93 025	17.464	356	126 736	18.868
204	41 616	14.283	255	65 025	15.969	306	93 636	17.493	357	127 449	18.894
205	42 025	14.318	256	65 536	16.000	307	94 249	17.521	358	128 164	18.921
206	42 436	14.353	257	66 049	16.031	308	94 864	17.550	359	128 881	18.947
207	42 849	14.387	258	66 564	16.063	309	95 481	17.578	360	129 600	18.974
208	43 264	14.422	259	67 081	16.093	310	96 100	17.607	361	130 321	19.000
209	43 681	14.457	260	67 600	16.125	311	96 721	17.635	362	131 044	19.026
210	44 100	14.491	261	68 121	16.155	312	97 344	17.664	363	131 769	19.053
211	44 521	14.526	262	68 644	16.186	313	97 969	17.692	364	132 496	19.079
212	44 944	14.560	263	69 169	16.217	314	98 596	17.720	365	133 225	19.105
213	45 369	14.596	264	69 696	16.248	315	99 225	17.748	366	133 956	19.131
214	45 796	14.629	265	70 225	16.279	316	99 856	17.776	367	134 689	19.157
215	46 225	14.663	266	70 756	16.310	317	100 489	17.804	368	135 424	19.183
216	46 656	14.697	267	71 289	16.340	318	101 124	17.833	369	136 161	19.209
217	47 089	14.731	268	71 824	16.371	319	101 761	17.861	370	136 900	19.235
218	47 524	14.765	269	72 361	16.401	320	102 400	17.889	371	137 641	19.261
219	47 961	14.799	270	72 900	16.432	321	103 041	17.916	372	138 384	19.287
220	48 400	14.832	271	73 441	16.462	322	103 684	17.944	373	139 129	19.313
221	48 841	14.866	272	73 984	16.492	323	104 329	17.972	374	139 876	19.339
222	49 284	14.900	273	74 529	16.523	324	104 976	18.000	375	140 625	19.365
223	49 729	14.933	274	75 076	16.553	325	105 625	18.028	376	141 376	19.391
224	50 176	14.967	275	75 625	16.583	326	106 276	18.055	377	142 129	19.419
225	50 625	15.000	276	76 176	16.613	327	106 929	18.083	378	142 884	19.442
226	51 076	15.033	277	76 729	16.643	328	107 584	18.111	379	143 641	19.468
227	51 529	15.067	278	77 284	16.673	329	108 241	18.138	380	144 400	19.494
228	51 984	15.100	279	77 841	16.703	330	108 900	18.166	381	145 161	19.519
229	52 441	15.133	280	78 400	16.733	331	109 561	18.193	382	145 924	19.545
230	52 900	15.166	281	78 961	16.763	332	110 224	18.221	383	146 689	19.570
231	53 361	15.199	282	79 524	16.793	333	110 889	18.248	384	147 456	19.596
232	53 824	15.232	283	80 089	16.823	334	111 556	18.276	385	148 225	19.621
233	54 289	15.264	284	80 656	16.852	335	112 225	18.303	386	148 996	19.647
234	54 756	15.297	285	81 225	16.882	336	112 896	18.330	387	149 769	19.672

n	n²	√n	n	n²	√n	n	n²	√n	n	n²	√n
388	150 544	19.698	439	192 721	20.952	490	240 100	22.136	541	292 681	23.259
389	151 321	19.723	440	193 600	20.976	491	241 081	22.159	542	293 764	23.281
390	152 100	19.748	441	194 481	21.000	492	242 064	22.181	543	294 849	23.302
391	152 881	19.774	442	195 364	21.024	493	243 049	22.204	544	295 936	23.324
392	153 664	19.799	443	196 249	21.048	494	244 036	22.226	545	297 025	23.345
393	154 449	19.824	444	197 136	21.071	495	245 025	22.249	546	298 116	23.367
394	155 236	19.849	445	198 025	21.095	496	246 016	22.271	547	299 209	23.388
395	156 025	19.875	446	198 916	21.119	497	247 009	22.294	548	300 304	23.409
396	156 816	19.900	447	199 809	21.142	498	248 004	22.316	549	301 401	23.431
397	157 609	19.925	448	200 704	21.166	499	249 001	22.338	550	302 500	23.452
398	158 404	19.950	449	201 601	21.190	500	250 000	22.361	551	303 601	23.473
399	159 201	19.975	450	202 500	21.213	501	251 001	22.383	552	304 704	23.495
400	160 000	20.000	451	203 401	21.237	502	252 004	22.405	553	305 809	23.516
401	160 801	20.025	452	204 304	21.260	503	253 009	22.428	554	306 916	23.537
402	161 604	20.050	453	205 209	21.284	504	254 016	22.450	555	308 025	23.558
403	162 409	20.075	454	206 116	21.307	505	255 025	22.472	556	309 136	23.580
404	163 216	20.100	455	207 025	21.331	506	256 036	22.494	557	310 249	23.601
405	164 025	20.125	456	207 936	21.354	507	257 049	22.517	558	311 364	23.622
406	164 836	20.149	457	208 849	21.378	508	258 064	22.539	559	312 481	23.643
407	165 649	20.174	458	209 764	21.401	509	259 081	22.561	560	313 600	23.664
408	166 464	20.199	459	210 681	21.424	510	260 100	22.583	561	314 721	23.685
409	167 281	20.224	460	211 600	21.448	511	261 121	22.605	562	315 844	23.707
410	168 100	20.248	461	212 521	21.471	512	262 144	22.627	563	316 969	23.728
411	168 921	20.273	462	213 444	21.494	513	263 169	22.650	564	318 096	23.749
412	169 744	20.298	463	214 369	21.517	514	264 196	22.672	565	319 225	23.770
413	170 569	20.322	464	215 296	21.541	515	265 225	22.694	566	320 356	23.791
414	171 396	20.347	465	216 225	21.564	516	266 256	22.716	567	321 489	23.812
415	172 225	20.372	466	217 156	21.587	517	267 289	22.738	568	322 624	23.833
416	173 056	20.396	467	218 089	21.610	518	268 324	22.760	569	323 761	23.854
417	173 889	20.421	468	219 024	21.633	519	269 361	22.782	570	324 900	23.875
418	174 724	20.445	469	219 961	21.656	520	270 400	22.804	571	326 041	23.896
419	175 561	20.469	470	220 900	21.679	521	271 441	22.825	572	327 184	23.917
420	176 400	20.493	471	221 841	21.703	522	272 484	22.847	573	328 329	23.937
421	177 241	20.518	472	222 784	21.726	523	273 529	22.869	574	329 476	23.958
422	178 084	20.543	473	223 729	21.749	524	274 576	22.891	575	330 625	23.979
423	178 929	20.567	474	224 676	21.772	525	275 625	22.913	576	331 776	24.000
424	179 776	20.591	475	225 625	21.794	526	276 676	22.935	577	332 929	24.021
425	180 625	20.616	476	226 576	21.817	527	277 729	22.956	578	334 084	24.042
426	181 476	20.640	477	227 529	21.840	528	278 784	22.978	579	335 241	24.062
427	182 329	20.664	478	228 484	21.863	529	279 841	23.000	580	336 400	24.083
428	183 184	20.688	479	229 441	21.886	530	280 900	23.022	581	337 561	24.104
429	184 041	20.712	480	230 400	21.909	531	281 961	23.043	582	338 724	24.125
430	184 900	20.736	481	231 361	21.932	532	283 024	23.065	583	339 889	24.145
431	185 761	20.761	482	232 324	21.955	533	284 089	23.087	584	341 056	24.166
432	186 624	20.785	483	233 289	21.977	534	285 156	23.108	585	342 225	24.187
433	187 489	20.809	484	234 256	22.000	535	286 225	23.130	586	343 396	24.207
434	188 356	20.833	485	235 225	22.023	536	287 296	23.152	587	344 569	24.228
435	189 225	20.857	486	236 196	22.045	537	288 369	23.173	588	345 744	24.249
436	190 096	20.881	487	237 169	22.068	538	289 444	23.195	589	346 921	24.269
437	190 969	20.905	488	238 144	22.091	539	290 521	23.216	590	348 100	24.290
438	191 844	20.928	489	239 121	22.113	540	291 600	23.239	591	349 281	24.310

n	n²	√n	n	n²	√n	n	n²	√n	n	n²	√n
592	350 464	23.331	643	413 449	25.357	694	481 636	26.344	745	555 025	27.295
593	351 649	24.352	644	414 736	25.377	695	483 025	26.363	746	556 516	27.313
594	352 836	24.372	645	416 025	25.397	696	484 416	26.382	747	558 009	27.331
595	354 025	24.393	646	417 316	25.417	697	485 809	26.401	748	559 504	27.350
596	355 216	24.413	647	418 609	25.436	698	487 204	26.420	749	561 001	27.368
597	356 409	24.434	648	419 904	25.456	699	488 601	26.439	750	562 500	27.386
598	357 604	24.454	649	421 201	25.475	700	490 000	26.458	751	564 001	27.404
599	358 801	24.747	650	422 500	25.495	701	491 401	26.476	752	565 504	27.423
600	360 000	24.495	651	423 801	25.515	702	492 804	26.495	753	567 009	27.441
601	361 201	24.515	652	425 104	25.534	703	494 209	26.514	754	568 516	27.459
602	362 404	24.536	653	426 409	25.554	704	495 616	26.533	755	570 025	27.477
603	363 609	24.556	654	427 716	25.573	705	497 025	26.552	756	571 536	27.495
604	364 816	24.576	655	429 025	25.593	706	498 436	26.571	757	573 049	27.514
605	366 025	24.597	656	403 336	25.613	707	499 849	26.589	758	574 564	27.532
606	367 236	24.617	657	431 649	25.632	708	501 264	26.608	759	576 081	27.550
607	368 449	24.637	658	432 964	25.652	709	502 681	26.627	760	577 600	27.568
608	369 664	23.658	659	434 281	25.671	710	504 100	26.646	761	579 121	27.586
609	370 881	24.678	660	435 600	25.690	711	505 521	26.665	762	580 644	27.604
610	372 100	24.698	661	436 921	25.710	712	506 944	26.683	763	582 169	27.622
611	373 321	24.718	662	438 244	25.729	713	508 369	26.702	764	583 696	27.641
612	374 544	24.739	663	439 569	25.749	714	509 796	26.721	765	585 225	27.659
613	375 769	24.759	664	440 896	25.768	715	511 225	26.739	766	586 756	27.676
614	376 996	24.779	665	442 225	25.788	716	512 656	26.758	767	588 289	27.695
615	378 225	24.799	666	443 556	25.807	717	514 089	26.777	768	589 824	27.713
616	379 456	24.819	667	444 889	25.826	718	515 524	26.796	769	591 361	27.731
617	380 689	24.839	668	446 224	25.846	719	516 961	26.814	770	592 900	27.749
618	381 924	24.860	669	447 561	25.865	720	518 400	26.833	771	594 441	27.767
619	383 161	24.880	670	448 900	25.884	721	519 841	26.851	772	595 984	27.785
620	384 400	24.900	671	450 241	25.904	722	521 284	26.870	773	597 529	27.803
621	385 641	24.920	672	451 584	25.923	723	522 729	26.889	774	599 076	27.821
622	386 884	24.940	673	452 929	25.942	724	524 176	26.907	775	600 625	27.839
623	388 129	24.960	674	454 276	25.962	725	525 625	26.926	776	602 176	27.857
624	389 376	24.980	675	455 625	25.981	726	527 076	26.944	777	603 729	27.875
625	390 625	25.000	676	456 976	26.000	727	528 529	26.963	778	605 284	27.893
626	391 876	25.020	677	458 329	26.019	728	529 984	26.981	779	606 841	27.911
627	393 129	25.040	678	459 684	26.038	729	531 441	27.000	780	608 400	27.928
628	394 384	25.060	679	461 041	26.058	730	532 900	27.019	781	609 961	27.946
629	395 641	25.080	680	462 400	26.077	731	534 361	27.037	782	611 524	27.964
630	396 900	25.100	681	463 761	26.096	732	535 824	27.056	783	613 089	27.982
631	398 161	25.120	682	465 124	26.115	733	537 289	27.074	784	614 656	28.000
632	399 424	25.140	683	466 489	26.134	734	538 756	27.092	785	616 225	28.018
633	400 689	25.159	684	467 856	26.153	735	540 225	27.111	786	617 796	28.036
634	401 956	25.179	685	469 225	26.173	736	541 696	27.129	787	619 369	28.054
635	403 225	25.199	686	470 596	26.192	737	543 169	27.148	788	620 944	28.071
636	404 496	25.219	687	471 969	26.211	738	544 644	27.166	789	622 521	28.089
637	405 769	25.239	688	473 344	26.230	739	546 121	27.185	790	624 100	28.107
638	407 044	25.259	689	474 721	26.249	740	547 600	27.203	791	625 681	28.125
639	408 321	25.278	690	476 100	26.268	741	549 081	27.221	792	627 264	28.142
640	409 600	25.298	691	477 481	26.287	742	550 564	27.240	793	628 849	28.160
641	410 881	25.318	692	478 864	26.306	743	552 049	27.258	794	630 436	28.178
642	412 164	25.338	693	480 249	26.325	744	553 536	27.276	795	632 025	28.196

n	n²	√n	n	n²	√n	n	n²	√n	n	n²	√n
796	633 616	28.213	847	717 409	29.108	898	806 404	29.967	949	900 601	30.806
797	635 209	28.231	848	719 104	29.120	899	808 201	29.983	950	902 500	30.822
798	636 804	28.249	849	720 801	29.138	900	810 000	30.000	951	904 401	30.838
799	638 401	28.267	850	722 500	29.155	901	811 801	30.017	952	906 304	30.855
800	640 000	28.284	851	724 201	29.172	902	813 604	30.033	953	908 209	30.871
801	641 601	28.302	852	725 904	29.189	903	815 409	30.050	954	910 116	30.887
802	643 204	28.320	853	727 609	29.206	904	817 216	30.067	955	910 025	30.903
803	644 809	28.337	854	729 316	29.223	905	819 025	30.083	956	913 936	30.919
804	646 416	28.355	855	731 025	29.240	906	820 836	30.100	957	915 849	30.935
805	648 025	28.373	856	732 736	29.257	907	822 649	30.116	958	917 764	30.952
806	649 636	28.390	857	734 449	29.275	908	824 464	30.133	959	919 681	30.968
807	651 249	28.408	858	736 164	29.292	909	826 281	30.150	960	921 600	30.984
808	652 864	28.425	859	737 881	29.309	910	828 100	30.166	961	923 521	31.000
809	654 481	28.443	860	739 600	29.326	911	829 921	30.183	962	925 444	31.016
810	656 100	28.461	861	741 321	29.343	912	831 744	30.199	963	927 369	31.032
811	657 721	28.478	862	743 044	29.360	913	833 569	30.216	964	929 296	31.048
812	659 344	28.496	863	744 769	29.377	914	835 396	30.232	965	931 225	31.064
813	660 969	28.513	864	746 496	29.394	915	837 225	30.249	966	933 156	31.081
814	662 596	28.531	865	748 225	29.411	916	839 056	30.265	967	935 089	31.097
815	664 225	28.548	866	749 956	29.428	917	840 889	30.282	968	937 024	31.113
816	665 856	28.566	867	751 689	29.445	918	842 724	30.299	969	938 961	31.129
817	667 489	28.583	868	753 424	29.462	919	844 561	30.315	970	940 900	31.145
818	669 124	28.601	869	755 161	29.479	920	846 400	30.332	971	942 841	31.161
819	670 761	28.618	870	756 900	29.496	921	848 241	30.348	972	944 784	31.177
820	672 400	28.636	871	758 641	29.513	922	850 084	30.364	973	946 729	31.193
821	674 041	28.653	872	760 384	29.530	923	851 929	30.381	974	948 676	31.209
822	675 684	28.671	873	762 129	29.547	924	853 776	30.397	975	950 625	31.225
823	677 329	28.688	874	763 876	29.563	925	855 625	30.414	976	952 576	31.241
824	678 976	28.705	875	765 625	29.580	926	857 476	30.430	977	954 529	31.257
825	680 625	28.723	876	767 376	29.597	927	859 329	30.447	978	956 484	31.273
826	682 276	28.740	877	769 129	29.614	928	861 184	30.463	979	958 441	31.289
827	683 929	28.758	878	770 884	29.631	929	863 041	30.480	980	960 400	31.305
828	685 584	28.775	879	772 641	29.647	930	864 900	30.496	981	962 361	31.321
829	687 241	28.792	880	774 400	29.665	931	866 761	30.512	982	964 324	31.337
830	688 900	28.810	881	776 161	29.682	932	868 624	30.529	983	966 289	31.353
831	690 561	28.827	882	777 924	29.698	933	870 489	30.545	984	968 256	31.369
832	692 224	28.844	883	779 689	29.715	934	872 356	30.561	985	970 225	31.385
833	693 889	28.862	884	781 456	29.732	935	874 225	30.578	986	972 196	31.401
834	695 556	28.879	885	783 225	29.749	936	876 096	30.594	987	974 169	31.417
835	697 225	28.896	886	784 996	29.766	937	877 969	30.610	988	976 144	31.432
836	698 896	28.914	887	786 769	29.783	938	879 844	30.627	989	978 121	31.448
837	700 569	28.931	888	788 544	29.799	939	881 721	30.643	990	980 100	31.464
838	702 244	28.948	889	790 321	29.816	940	883 600	30.659	991	982 081	31.480
839	703 921	28.966	890	792 100	29.833	941	885 481	30.676	992	984 064	31.496
840	705 600	28.983	891	793 881	29.850	942	887 364	30.692	993	986 049	31.512
841	707 281	29.000	892	795 664	29.866	943	889 249	30.708	994	988 036	31.528
842	708 964	29.017	893	797 449	29.883	944	891 136	30.725	995	990 025	31.544
843	710 649	29.034	894	799 236	29.900	945	893 025	30.741	996	992 016	31.559
844	712 336	29.052	895	801 025	29.917	946	894 916	30.757	997	994 009	31.575
845	714 025	29.069	896	802 816	29.933	947	896 809	30.773	998	996 004	31.591
846	715 716	29.086	897	804 609	29.950	948	898 704	30.790	999	998 001	31.607

appendix B

Percent of Cases Falling Below and Above a Given Standard Score (z) for a Normal Distribution

Note: When z is *negative*, just reverse the tables for the percent values. That is, treat *above* as *below*, and *below* as *above*.

z	Percent Below	Percent Above	z	Percent Below	Percent Above	z	Percent Below	Percent Above
.00	50.00	50.00	.38	64.80	35.20	.76	77.64	22.36
.01	50.40	49.60	.39	65.17	34.83	.77	77.94	22.06
.02	50.80	49.20	.40	65.54	34.46	.78	78.23	21.77
.03	51.20	48.80	.41	65.91	34.09	.79	78.52	21.48
.04	51.60	48.40	.42	66.28	33.72	.80	78.81	21.19
.05	51.99	48.01	.43	66.64	33.36	.81	79.10	20.90
.06	52.39	47.61	.44	67.00	33.00	.82	79.39	20.61
.07	52.79	47.21	.45	67.36	32.64	.83	79.67	20.33
.08	53.19	46.81	.46	67.72	32.28	.84	79.95	20.05
.09	53.59	46.41	.47	68.08	31.92	.85	80.23	19.77
.10	53.98	46.02	.48	68.44	31.56	.86	80.51	19.49
.11	54.38	45.62	.49	68.79	31.21	.87	80.78	19.22
.12	54.78	45.22	.50	69.15	30.85	.88	81.06	18.94
.13	55.17	44.83	.51	69.50	30.50	.89	81.33	18.67
.14	55.57	44.43	.52	69.85	30.15	.90	81.59	18.41
.15	55.96	44.04	.53	70.19	29.81	.91	81.86	18.14
.16	56.36	43.64	.54	70.54	29.46	.92	82.12	17.88
.17	56.75	43.25	.55	70.88	29.12	.93	82.38	17.62
.18	57.14	42.86	.56	71.23	28.77	.94	82.64	17.36
.19	57.53	42.47	.57	71.57	28.43	.95	82.89	17.11
.20	57.93	42.07	.58	71.90	28.10	.96	83.15	16.85
.21	58.32	41.68	.59	72.24	27.76	.97	83.40	16.60
.22	58.71	41.29	.60	72.57	27.43	.98	83.65	16.35
.23	59.10	40.90	.61	72.91	27.09	.99	83.89	16.11
.24	59.48	40.52	.62	73.24	26.76	1.00	84.13	15.87
.25	59.87	40.13	.63	73.57	26.43	1.01	84.38	15.62
.26	60.26	39.74	.64	73.89	26.11	1.02	84.61	15.39
.27	60.64	39.36	.65	74.22	25.78	1.03	84.85	15.15
.28	61.03	38.97	.66	74.54	25.46	1.04	85.08	14.92
.29	61.41	38.59	.67	74.86	25.14	1.05	85.31	14.69
.30	61.79	38.21	.68	75.17	24.83	1.06	85.54	14.46
.31	62.17	37.83	.69	75.49	24.51	1.07	85.77	14.23
.32	62.55	37.45	.70	75.80	24.20	1.08	85.99	14.01
.33	62.93	37.07	.71	76.11	23.89	1.09	86.21	13.79
.34	63.31	36.69	.72	76.42	23.58	1.10	86.43	13.57
.35	63.68	36.32	.73	76.73	23.27	1.11	86.65	13.35
.36	64.06	35.94	.74	77.04	22.96	1.12	86.86	13.14
.37	64.43	35.57	.75	77.34	22.66	1.13	87.08	12.92

z	Percent Below	Percent Above	z	Percent Below	Percent Above	z	Percent Below	Percent Above
1.14	87.29	12.71	1.61	94.63	05.37	2.08	98.12	01.88
			1.62	94.74	05.26	2.09	98.17	01.83
1.15	87.49	12.51	1.63	94.84	05.16			
1.16	87.70	12.30	1.64	94.95	05.05	2.10	98.21	01.79
1.17	87.90	12.10				2.11	98.26	01.74
1.18	88.10	11.90	1.65	95.05	04.95	2.12	98.30	01.70
1.19	88.30	11.70	1.66	95.15	04.85	2.13	98.34	01.66
			1.67	95.25	04.75	2.14	98.38	01.62
1.20	88.49	11.51	1.68	95.35	04.65			
1.21	88.69	11.31	1.69	95.45	04.55	2.15	98.42	01.58
1.22	88.88	11.12				2.16	98.46	01.54
1.23	89.07	10.93	1.70	95.54	04.46	2.17	98.50	01.50
1.24	89.25	10.75	1.71	95.64	04.36	2.18	98.54	01.46
			1.72	95.73	04.27	2.19	98.57	01.43
1.25	89.44	10.56	1.73	95.82	04.18			
1.26	89.62	10.38	1.74	95.91	04.09	2.20	98.61	01.39
1.27	89.80	10.20				2.21	98.64	01.36
1.28	89.97	10.03	1.75	95.99	04.01	2.22	98.68	01.32
1.29	90.15	09.85	1.76	96.08	03.92	2.23	98.71	01.29
			1.77	96.16	03.84	2.24	98.75	01.25
1.30	90.32	09.68	1.78	96.25	03.75			
1.31	90.49	09.51	1.79	96.33	03.67	2.25	98.78	01.22
1.32	90.66	09.34				2.26	98.81	01.19
1.33	90.82	09.18	1.80	96.41	03.59	2.27	98.84	01.16
1.34	90.99	09.01	1.81	96.49	03.51	2.28	98.87	01.13
			1.82	96.56	03.44	2.29	98.90	01.10
1.35	91.15	08.85	1.83	96.64	03.36			
1.36	91.31	08.69	1.84	96.71	03.29	2.30	98.93	01.07
1.37	91.47	08.53				2.31	98.96	01.04
1.38	91.62	08.38	1.85	96.78	03.22	2.32	98.98	01.02
1.39	91.77	08.23	1.86	96.86	03.14	2.33	99.01	00.99
			1.87	96.93	03.07	2.34	99.04	00.96
1.40	91.92	08.08	1.88	96.99	03.01			
1.41	92.07	07.93	1.89	97.06	02.94	2.35	99.06	00.94
1.42	92.22	07.78				2.36	99.09	00.91
1.43	92.36	07.64	1.90	97.13	02.87	2.37	99.11	00.89
1.44	92.51	07.49	1.91	97.19	02.81	2.38	99.13	00.87
			1.92	97.26	02.74	2.39	99.16	00.84
1.45	92.65	07.35	1.93	97.32	02.68			
1.46	92.79	07.21	1.94	97.38	02.62	2.40	99.18	00.82
1.47	92.92	07.08				2.41	99.20	00.80
1.48	93.06	06.94	1.95	97.44	02.56	2.42	99.22	00.78
1.49	93.19	06.81	1.96	97.50	02.50	2.43	99.25	00.75
			1.97	97.56	02.44	2.44	99.27	00.73
1.50	93.32	06.68	1.98	97.61	02.39			
1.51	93.45	06.55	1.99	97.67	02.33	2.45	99.29	00.71
1.52	93.57	06.43				2.46	99.31	00.69
1.53	93.70	06.30	2.00	97.72	02.28	2.47	99.32	00.68
1.54	93.82	06.18	2.01	97.78	02.22	2.48	99.34	00.66
			2.02	97.83	02.17	2.49	99.36	00.64
1.55	93.94	06.06	2.03	97.88	02.12			
1.56	94.06	05.94	2.04	97.93	02.07	2.50	99.38	00.62
1.57	94.18	05.82				2.51	99.40	00.60
1.58	94.29	05.71	2.05	97.98	02.02	2.52	99.41	00.59
1.59	94.41	05.59	2.06	98.03	01.97	2.53	99.43	00.57
1.60	94.52	05.48	2.07	98.08	01.92	2.54	99.45	00.55

z	Percent Below	Percent Above	z	Percent Below	Percent Above	z	Percent Below	Percent Above
2.55	99.46	00.54	2.77	99.72	00.28	2.99	99.86	00.14
2.56	99.48	00.52	2.78	99.73	00.27	3.00	99.87	00.13
2.57	99.49	00.51	2.79	99.74	00.26	3.05	99.89	00.11
2.58	99.51	00.49	2.80	99.74	00.26	3.10	99.90	00.10
2.59	99.52	00.48	2.81	99.75	00.25	3.15	99.92	00.08
2.60	99.53	00.47	2.82	99.76	00.24	3.20	99.93	00.07
2.61	99.55	00.45	2.83	99.77	00.23	3.25	99.94	00.06
2.62	99.56	00.44	2.84	99.77	00.23	3.30	99.95	00.05
2.63	99.57	00.43	2.85	99.78	00.22	3.35	99.96	00.04
2.64	99.59	00.41	2.86	99.79	00.21	3.40	99.97	00.03
2.65	99.60	00.40	2.87	99.79	00.21	3.45	99.97	00.03
2.66	99.61	00.39	2.88	99.80	00.20	3.50	99.98	00.02
2.67	99.62	00.38	2.89	99.81	00.19	3.55	99.98	00.02
2.68	99.63	00.37	2.90	99.81	00.19	3.60	99.98	00.02
2.69	99.64	00.36	2.91	99.82	00.18	3.65	99.99	00.01
2.70	99.65	00.35	2.92	99.82	00.18	3.70	99.99	00.01
2.71	99.66	00.34	2.93	99.83	00.17	3.75	99.99	00.01
2.72	99.67	00.33	2.94	99.84	00.16	3.80	99.99	00.01
2.73	99.68	00.32	2.95	99.84	00.16	3.85	99.99	00.01
2.74	99.69	00.31	2.96	99.85	00.15	3.90	100.00	00.00
2.75	99.70	00.30	2.97	99.85	00.15	3.95	100.00	00.00
2.76	99.71	00.29	2.98	99.86	00.14	4.00	100.00	00.00

appendix C

Test Publishers

American College Testing Program, P. O. Box 168, Iowa City, Iowa 52240

American Guidance Service, Inc., Publishers' Building, Circle Pines, Minnesota 55014

California Test Bureau, Del Monte Research Park, Monterey, California 93940

Committee on Diagnostic Reading Tests, Inc., Mountain Home, North Carolina 28758

Consulting Psychologists Press, Inc., 577 College Avenue, Palo Alto, California 94306

Cooperative Test Division, Educational Testing Service, Princeton, New Jersey 08540

E-B Press, Box 10459, Eugene, Oregon 97401

Harcourt, Brace & World, Inc., 757 Third Avenue, New York, New York 10017

Houghton Mifflin Company, 1 Beacon Street, Boston, Massachusetts 02107

Institute for Personality and Ability Testing, 1602 Coronado Drive, Champaign, Illinois 61822

Personnel Press, Inc., 20 Nassau Street, Princeton, New Jersey 08540

The Psychological Corporation, 304 East 45th Street, New York, New York 10017

Psychological Test Specialists, Box 1441, Missoula, Montana 59804

Research Psychologists Press, Goshen, New York 10924

Scholastic Testing Service, Inc., 480 Meyer Road, Bensenville, Illinois 60106

Science Research Associates, Inc., 259 East Erie Street, Chicago, Illinois 60611

Scott, Foresman and Company, 433 East Erie Street, Chicago, Illinois 60611

Sheridan Supply Co., P. O. Box 837, Beverly Hills, California 90213

C. H. Stoelting Co., 424 North Homan Avenue, Chicago, Illinois 60624

Teachers College Press, Teachers College, Columbia University, New York, New York 10027

United States Government Printing Office, Washington, D. C. 20402

Western Psychological Services, Box 775, Beverly Hills, California 90213

references

Unit 1

1 R. Glaser, "Instructional Technology and the Measurement of Learning Outcomes," *American Psychologist,* 1963, *18,* pp. 510-522.

2 R. F. Mager, *Preparing Instructional Objectives* (Belmont, Calif.: Fearon Publishers, 1962).

3 W. J. Popham, *Criterion-Referenced Instruction* (Belmont, Calif.: Fearon Publishers, 1973).

4 ——, *The Uses of Instructional Objectives* (Belmont, Calif.: Fearon Publishers, 1973).

5 ——, "Instructional Objectives Exchange," (Post Office Box E, Reseda, Calif.).

6 B. S. Bloom (ed.), *Taxonomy of Educational Objectives, Handbook I: Cognitive Domain* (New York: David McKay, 1956).

7 J. C. Flanagan, W. M. Shanner, and R. F. Mager, *Behavioral Objectives: Science, Social Studies, Mathematics, Language Arts* (Palo Alto, Calif.: Westinghouse Learning Press, 1971).

8 ——, *Prescriptive Reading Inventory* (Monterey, Calif.: CTB/McGraw-Hill, 1972).

9 J. Gessel, *Diagnostic Mathematics Inventory* (Formerl: *Prescriptive Mathematics Inventory)* (Monterey, Calif.: CTB/McGraw-Hill, 1972).

10 H. A. Wilson, "A Judgmental Approach to Criterion-Referenced Testing." In C. W. Harris, M. C. Alkin, and W. J. Popham (eds.), *Problems in Criterion-Referenced Measurement* (Los Angeles: Center for the Study of Evaluation, UCLA, 1974, Monograph No. 3.), pp.26-36.

11 C. W. Harris, "Problems of Objectives-Based Measurement." (Los Angeles: Center for the Study of Evalsation, UCLA, 1974, Monograph No. 3.), pp. 83-91.

12 R. L. Baker, "Measurement Considerations in Instructional Product Development." (Los Angeles: Center for the Study of Evaluation, UCLA, 1974, Monograph No. 3.), p.38.

A. J. Nitko, "Problems in the Development of Criterion-Referenced Tests: the IPI Pittsburgh Experience." (Los Angeles: Center for the Study of Evalsation, UCLA, 1974, Monograph No. 3.), pp. 59-82.

13 S. Engelmann and E. Bruner, *Distar Reading I,* second edition, (Chicago: Science Research Associates, 1974), lesson 44.

Unit 3

1 W. C. Becker, S. Engelmann, and D. R. Thomas, *Teaching 2: Cognitive Learning and Instruction* (Palo Alto: Science Research Associates, 1975).

2 S. Engelmann and E. Bruner, *Teacher's Guide for Distar Reading I,* second edition, (Chicago: Science Research Associates, 1974), pp. 12, 32 and 33.

3 S. Engelmann and S. Hanner, *Survival Skills Reading Test* (Eugene, Or.: E-B Press, 1976).

Unit 4

1 G. R. Burket, "Empirical Criteria for Distinguishing and Validating Aptitude and Achievement Measures." In D. R. Green (ed.), *The Aptitude-Achievement Distinction* (Monterey, Calif.: CTB/McGraw-Hill, 1974), pp. 7-49.

2 H. A. Wilson, "A Judgmental Approach to Criterion-Referenced Testing," In C. W. Harris, M. C. Alkin, and W. J. PXOPHAM (eds.), *Problems in Criterion-Referenced Measurement* (Los Angeles: Center for the Study of Evaluation, UCLA, 1974, Monograph No. 3), p . 26-36.

3 N. E. Freeberg and E. Payne, "Parental Influence on Cognitive Development in Early Childhood: A Review," *Child Development,* 1967, *38,* pp. 65-87.

4 G. V. Glass, "Statistical and Measurement Problems in Implementing the Stull Act." In N. L. Gage (ed.), *Mandated Evaluation of Education: A Conference on California's Stull Act* (Stanford, Calif.: Stanford Center for Research and Development in Teaching, 1973. Distributed by Educational Resources Division, Capital Publications, Suite G-12, 2430 Pennsylvania Ave., N. W., Washington, D. C., 20037).

5 C. W. Harris, "Problems of Objectives-Based Measurement." In C. W. Harris, M. C. Alkin, and W. J. Popham (eds.), *Problems in Criterion-Referenced Measurement* (Los Angeles: Center for the Study of Evaluation, UCLA, 1974, Monograph No. 3.), pp. 83-91.

6 S. Engelmann, L. Carnine, W. C. Becker, *Reading I Continuous Progress Test* (From manuscript in preparation for publication by Science Research Associates; all rights reserved by authors).

Unit 5

1 D. Bushell, Jr., *Classroom Behavior* (Englewood Cliffs, N. J.: Prentice-Hall, 1973), pp. 64-65.

2 R. Jones, "Learning Activities Packages: An Approach to Individualized Instruction," *Journal of Secondary Education,* 1968, *43,* pp. 178-183.
R. L. Talbert, "A Learning Activity Package, What is it?" *Educational Screen and Audiovisual Guide,* 1968, *47,* pp. 20-21.
A. B. Wolfe and J. E. Smith, "At Nova, Education Comes in Small Packages," *Nation's Schools,* 1968, *81,* pp. 48-49.

3 H. C. Morrison, *The Practice of Teaching in the Secondary School* (Chicago: University of Chicago Press, 1926).

4 "Precision Teaching in Perspective: An Interview with Ogden R. Lindsey," *Teaching Exceptional Children,* 1971, *3,* pp. 114-119.
H. P. Kunzelmann (ed.), *Precision Teaching* (Seattle: Special Child Publications, 1970).

5 "Diagnostic Inventories, Math I, II, II," "Diagnostic Inventories, Reading," (Eugene, Or.: Regional Resource Center for Handicapped Children, Clinical Services Building, University of Oregon).

6 D. Bushell, Jr., op. cit., note 1, p. 44.

7 D. Bushell, Jr., ibid., pp. 40, 46.

8 W. C. Becker, "Early Indications of Positive Outcomes." Paper delivered at the Educational Staff Seminar, George Washington University, Washington, D. C., February 14, 1974.
Education as Experimentation—Evaluation of the Follow Through Planned Variation Model, vol. 1A, *Early Effects* (Cambridge, Mass.: Abt Associates, 1974).
Interim rpeort on the evaluation of Follow Through: An experimental program for early education of disadvantaged children (Washington, D. C.: HEW, Office of Education, Follow Through Evaluation Section, June, 1974).

9 R. T. Eichelberger, *Follow Through Grant Proposal to USOE, 1975-76* (Pittsburgh: University of Pittsburgh, Learning Research and Development Center, 1975).

10 A. M. Hofmeister, *A Task Analysis Approach to Learning Difficulties* (Text in preparation. Logan, Utah: Utah State University, Department of Special Education), chapter 5.

Unit 6

1 The University of Oregon Direct-Instruction Follow Through Model was supported by grant OEG-0-70-4257 (286) from the U. S. Office of Education. The views expressed in this unit, however, are solely those of the authors.

Unit 7

1 A. M. Hofmeister, "Diagnostic Test: Capitol Letters and Punctuation," in *A Task Analysis Approach to Learning Difficulties* (Text in preparation. Logan, Utah: Utah State University, Department of Special Education), chapter 3.

2 Ibid., chapter 2.

3 S. Engelmann and S. Hanner, *Survival Skills Reading Test* (Eugene, Or.: E-B Press, 1976).

4 S. Engelmann, W. Becker, L. Carnine, L. Meyers, J. Becker, and G. Johnson, *Corrective Reading Program* (Chicago: Science Research Associates, 1974).

5 *Vermont ESEA Title I Final Evaluation Report 1973-74,* (Prepared for: Vermont State Department of Education, Montpelier, Vermont, by CTB/McGraw-Hill Department of Programs and Services, Monterey, Calif.).

6 *Prescriptive Reading Inventory* (Monterey, Calif.: CTB/McGraw-Hill, 1972).

7 *Prescriptive Reading Inventory, Interpretive Handbook* (Monterey, Calif.: CTB/McGraw-Hill, 1972), p. 30.
Prescriptive Reading Inventory, Orange Book (Monterey, Calif.: CTB/McGraw-Hill, 1972), pp. 13, 15.

Unit 9

1 J. V. Gilmore and E. C. Gilmore, *Gilmore Oral Reading Test,* Form A, (New York: World Boook, 1952). Forms C and D are now published by Harcourt Brace Jovanovich.

2 J. Gessel, *Diagnostic Mathematics Inventory* (Monterey, Calif.: CTB/McGraw-Hill, 1972).

3 O. Buros, *The Seventh Mental Measurement Yearbook* (Highland Park: Gryphon Press, 1972).

4 *California Achievement Test* (Monterey, Calif.: CTB/McGraw-Hill, 1970). Examples are from *Level I,* Form A.

5 *Metropolitan Achievement Test* (New York: Harcourt Brace Jovanovich, 1970). Examples are from *Primary II,* Form F.

6 *Stanford Achievement Test* (New York: Harcourt Brace Jovanovich, 1968). Examples are from *Intermediate I,* Form Y.

7 *SRA Achievement Series* (Chicago: Science Research

Associates, 1969). Examples are from *Multilevel Edition (Grades 4-9)*, Form D.

8 O. Buros, op. cit., note 3.

9 *Cooperative Primary Tests* (Princeton, N. J.: Cooperative Test Division, Educational Testing Service, 1965).

10 *Comprehensive Tests of Basic Skills* (Monterey, Calif.: CTB/McGraw-Hill, 1968-70).

11 *Iowa Test of Basic Skills* (New York: Houghton Mifflin, 1971).

12 *Wide Range Achievement Test* (Wilmington, Del.: Guidance Associates, 1965).

13 *Gates-MacGinitie Reading Tests* (New York: Teacher's College Press, 1965, 1969).

14 A. M. Hofmeister, *A Task Analysis Approach to Learning Difficulties* (Text in preparation. Logan, Utah: Utah State University, Department of Special Education).

Unit 10

1 P. G. Loret, A. Seder, J. C. Bianchini and C. A. Vale, *Anchor Test Study: Equivalence and Norms Tables for Selected Reading Achievement Tests (Grades 4, 5, 6)*, Office of Education Report No. 74-305 (Washington, D.C.: U. S. Government Printing Office, 1974).

2 *California Achievement Test, Examiner's Manual, Form A, Level 1*, (Monterey, Calif.: CTB/McGraw-Hill, 1970). p. 74.

3 *Ibid.*, pp. *78-79*.

4 *Metropolitan Achievement Test, Teacher's Handbook, Primary II*, (New York: Harcourt Brace Jovanovich, 1971). p. 6.

Unit 12

1 H. Gulliksen, *Theory of Mental Tests* (New York: Wiley, 1950).

2 L. J. Cronbach, *Essentials of Psychological Testing*, third edition, (New York: Harper & Row, 1970), pp. 160-161.

3 *Ibid*, pp. 163-164.

4 *Metropolitan Achievement Test, Teacher's Handbook, Primary II Battery* (New York: Harcourt Brace Jovanovich, 1970), p. 16.

5 H. Gulliksen, op. cit., note 1, p. 81.

6 *Metropolitan Achievement Test, Teacher's Handbook, Primary II Battery*, p. 16.

7 L. J. Cronbach, op. cit., note 2, p. 164.

8 R. E. Stake, *Measuring What Learners Learn (with a Special Look at Performance Contracting)* (Urbana, Ill.: Center for Instructional Research and Curriculum Evaluation, University of Illinois, 1972, mimeo).

9 N. E. Freeberg and E. Payne, "Parental Influence on Cognitive Development in Early Childhood: A Review," *Child Development*, 1967, *38*, pp. 65-87.

10 G. V. Glass, "Statistical and Measurement Problems in Implementing the Stull Act." In N. L. Gage (ed.), *Mandated Evaluation of Education: A Conference on California's Stull Act* (Stanford, Calif.: Stanford Center for Research and Development in Teaching, 1973. Distributed by Educational Resources Division, Capital Publications, Suite G-12, 2430 Pennsylvania Ave., N. W., Washington, D. C., 20037).

11 *The Rationale, Development, and Standardization of a Basic Word Vocabulary Test*, DHEW Publication No. (HRA) 74-1334 (Washington, D. C.: U.S. Government Printing Office, 1974).

12 G. V. Glass, op. cit., note 11.

Unit 13

1 We are indebted to Howard Sloane for the development of the analysis of experimental versus correlational research and for the "three questions" to consider in drawing conclusions about research.

2 D. T. Campbell and J. C. Stanley, "Experimental and Quasi-Experimental Designs for Research on Teaching." In N. Cage (ed.), *Handbook of Research on Teaching* (Chicago: Rand-McNally, 1963), pp. 171-246.

3 M. Sidman, *Tactics of Scientific Research* (New York: Basic Books, 1960).

4 C. E. Cass, "Psycholinguistic Disabilities of Children with Reading Problems," *Exceptional Children*, 1966, *32*, pp. 533-539.

5 B. D. Bateman (ed.), *Reading Performance and How to Achieve it* (Seattle: Bernie Straub Publishing Co. and Special Child Publications, 1973), p. 97.

6 H. E. Shimota, "Some Characteristics of Poor Readers," *Journal of Educational Research*, 1964, *58*, pp. 106-111.

7 C. H. Bishop, "Transfer of Effects of Word and Letter Training in Reading," *Journal of Verbal Learning and Verbal Behavior*, 1964, *3*, pp. 215-221.

8 E. J. Gibson, "Learning to Read." In B. D. Bateman (ed.) op. cit., note 5, p. 291.

9 B. D. Bateman, "The Efficacy of an Auditory and a Visual Method of First-grade Reading Instruction With Auditory and Visual Learners," *College of Education Curriculum Bulletin*, 1967, 23:278, (Eugene, Or.: University of Oregon, 1967), pp. 6-14.

Unit 14

1 D. P. Horst, G. K. Tallmadge, and C. T. Wood, *A Practical Guide to Measuring Project Impact on Student Achievement*, Monograph No. 1 on Evaluation in Education (Washington, D. C.: U. S. Government Printing Office, 1975).

2 Ibid., page 54-58.

3 L. J. Cronbach, *Behavior Today*, February 10, 1975, vol. 6, no. 6, p. 383.

4 Gary Horton, personal communication.

5 D. P. Horst, et. al., op. cit., note 1, pp. 85-87.

6 Ibid., p. 47.

7 E. P. Bliesmer and B. H. Yarborough, "A Comparison of Ten Different Beginning Reading Programs in First Grade," *Phi Delta Kappan*, 1965, 46, pp. 500-504.

8 Ibid., p. 503.

9 A. D. Hungerman, "Achievement and Attitude of Sixth-Grade Pupils in Conventional and Contemporary Mathematics Programs," *The Arithmetic Teacher*, 1967, 14, pp. 30-39.

Unit 15

1 F. Galton, *Hereditary Genius* (New York: MacMillan, 1869).

2 J. McV. Hunt, *Intelligence and Experience* (New York: Ronald Press, 1961).

3 A. R. Jensen, "Another Look at Culture-Fair Testing." In J. Hellmuth (ed.), *Disadvantaged Child*, vol. 3, (New York: Brunner/Mazel, 1970), pp. 53-101.

4 A. R. Jensen, "How Much Can We Boost IQ and Scholastic Achievement?" *Harvard Educational Review*, 1969, 39, pp. 1-123.

5 T. L. Kelley, *The Interpretation of Educational Measurements* (Yonkers-on-Hudson, N. Y.: World Book, 1927).

6 L. L. Cavalli-Sforza, "Problems and Prospects of Genetic Analysis of Intelligence at the Intra- and Interrracial Level." In J. Hellmuth (ed.), *Disadvantaged Child*, vol. 3, (New York: Brunner/Mazel, 1970), pp, 111-123.

7 Ibid.

8 J. McV. Hunt, op. cit., note 2.

9 R. D. Hess and V. C. Shipman, "Early Experience and the Socialization of Cognitive Modes in Children," *Child Development*, 1965, *36*, pp. 869-886.
F. L. Strodtbeck, "The Hidden Curriculum in the Middle-Class Home." In J. D. Krumboltz (ed.), *Learning and the Educational Process* (Chicago: Rand-McNally, 1965), pp. 91-111.

10 R. Heber, H. Garber, S. Harrington, C. Hoffman, and D. Falender, *Rehabilitation of Families at Risk for Mental Retardation*, Progress Report, December, 1972 (Madison, Wisc.: Rehabilitation Research and Training Center in Mental Retardation, 1972).

11 S. Engelmann, "The Effectiveness of Direct Instruction on IQ Performance and Achievement in Reading and Arithmetic." In J. Hellmuth (ed.), *Disadvantaged Child*, vol. 3, (New York: Bruner/Mazel, 1971), pp. 339-361.

12 N. Bayley, Consistency and Variability in the Growth of Intelligence from Birth to Eighteen." *Journal of Genetic Psychology*, 1949, *75*, pp. 165-196.

13 T. L. Kelley, op. cit., note 5, p. 18.

14 L. G. Humphreys, "The Misleading Distinction Between Aptitude and Achievement Tests." In D. R. Green (ed.), *The Aptitude-Achievement Distinction* (Monterey, Calif.: CTB/McGraw-Hill, 1974), pp. 262-274.

15 J. E. Anderson, "The Limitations of Infant and Preschool Tests in the Measurement of Intelligence." *Journal of Psychology*, 1939, *8*, pp. 351-379.

16 W. C. Becker, "Some Necessary Conditions for the Controlled Study of Achievement and Aptitude." In D. R. Green (ed.), *The Aptitude-Achievement Distinction* (Monterey, Calif.: CTB/McGraw-Hill, 1974), p. 213.

17 L. J. Cronbach, *Essentials of Psychological Testing*, third edition, (New York: Harper & Row, 1970), pp. 292-293.

18 Ibid., pp. 293-294.

19 L. Meyers, "Comparison of Learning Rate and Retention Between a Mongoloid and Normal Population." (Urbana, Ill.: Thesis submitted in partial fulfillment of the degree of Masters of Arts, University of Illinois, College of Education, 1968).

glossary

age-equivalent score The mean chronological age (usually estimated) of individuals obtaining a given raw score or other score.

alpha reliability coefficient A type of internal consistency reliability coefficient. The value that would be obtained if the average of all possible split-half coefficients were computed. Same as Kuder-Richardson formula 20.

anchor test study A study which provides tables for converting scores on a variety of reading tests at grades 4, 5, and 6 to Metropolitan Achievement Test equivalents. See references.

battery A group of tests standardized on the same norm group so that scores on the different tests may be compared.

biserial correlation A coefficient of correlation computed from one continuous variable and one dichotomized variable (e.g., pass-fail). Both variables are assumed to be normally distributed.

common objectives Objectives common to two or more instructional programs. It is important to identify common objectives in designing outcome evaluations since programs are most readily compared on their common objectives.

confidence interval The interval defined by a given score ±2 standard errors of measurement is called the 95 percent confidence interval.

construct validity A measure of hypothetical construct such as anxiety, is said to have construct validity to the degree that predictions from theory relating that construct to other measures are confirmed.

content validity This is determined by seeing if the tests items are members of the set defined by the objectives of a test, and by determining the adequacy of sampling of the items used to measure objectives.

continuous-progress tests As used in the University of Oregon Follow Through Program, these are instructional-program-based tests given each six weeks to check adequacy of student mastery of what was taught.

control group A group not subject to the experimental treatment against which the effects of treatment are compared. A control group is sought which is like the experimental group in every important way prior to treatment. This may be accomplished by random assignment, matching, or selection of intact groups and checking for equivalence.

correlation A relation between two measures. See *Pearson correlation coefficient*.

correlational research Research where the relations between variables are studied, but where no variable is manipulated. Correlational research may point to causal variables as a "maybe." However, such research cannot prove causality.

criterion-referenced test A test on which performance is compared to some specified standard of performance in making an interpretation.

criterion validity A validity coefecient based on the correlation of a test with some standard used to judge the goodness of a test. A test of college aptitude might be validated against the criterion *grade-point average*.

critical ratio The difference between two means is divided by the standard error of the difference. The resulting ratio leads to a z-score. The probability of getting a z-score that large by chance can be determined from a table showing normal curve functions.

descriptive research Research where facts are described but no variable is manipulated to see its effect on another variable.

directions Any learning task must use directions to tell the student what to do. These directions must be considered in building a test of instruction.

Distar Acronym for *Direct Instructional System for Teaching and Remediation*. These programs were developed by S. Engelmann and others and are published by SRA.

error Any factor affecting a test score that reduces its validity. See standard error of measurement.

error variance The variance component in a set of obtained scores attributable to measurement errors.

expanded standard score Expanded standard scores are used to place different levels of the same test on the same scale. The goal is to keep the standard deviation of the test constant but allow the mean score on the tests to grow from grade to grade. These properties make expanded standard scores especially useful in measuring gains.

experimental research Research where an independent variable is manipulated and the effects of this manipulation on some dependent variable is measured.

four-fold point correlation A measure of association between two dichotomous variables (e.g., a measure of correlation between two pass-fail items).

four-fold table A table showing the joint frequency distribution for two dichotomous variables.

frequency distribution A graphing of scores arranged from high to low showing the number of persons obtaining each score (or falling in each score interval).

gain measures Gain measures are based on the difference between a pretest score and a posttest score. They are to be contrasted with measures of achievement level expressed as a grade-level or age-level.

geneotype A characteristic which can be traced to the action of a specific gene.

general-case set A term used in defining skills for testing. With a general-case set, after some members are taught, the student should be able to perform any member of the set. In defining such a set, it is sufficient to describe the characteristics of the set (the essential features of the concept, operation, or problem solving procedure).

generalizable findings Research findings can be generalized to the extent that some group of persons, behaviors, or procedures has been sampled from in setting up the design. If a study used a sample of second-grade teachers, we should be able to generalize to the group of second-grade teachers from which the sample was drawn.

grade-equivalent scores The mean grade level (usually estimated) of individuals obtaining a given raw score or some other score.

group design A design where different groups of subjects are treated differently. Each group goes through a different treatment and the effects are examined.

hereditability index An index for estimating the proportion of variance in a phenotype which can be attributed to the effects of heredity rather than environment.

individual-subject design A design where the subject serves as his/her own control. Data are taken on the same subject under different conditions.

Individually Prescribed Instruction (IPI) An instructional program involving systematic monitoring of progress through testing and individual prescriptions for learning activities based on past accomplishments and the next steps in a continuum of learning objectives. IPI was developed at the University of Pittsburgh Learning Research and Development Center and is distributed by Research for Better Schools (Philadelphia).

instructional-program based test A criterion-referenced test which is built around a specified instructional sequence and tests what is being taught.

internal consistency An approach to estimating the reliability of a test based on the degree to which the parts of the test lead to the same conclusion. Internal consistency measures include: *percent agreement index, alpha coefficient, split-half reliability coefficient,* and the correlation of a test item with a total test score.

item cluster Items are grouped so as to permit an isolation of component skills. If an important objective involves skills A+B+C, then test items would be built to measure this skill and the components A, B, and C, so that deficient skills can be pinpointed.

item difficulty Defined by the percent passing an item. More "difficult items" are passed by fewer people.

item reliability (discriminability) Usually the biserial correlation of an item with the total score.

joint-frequency distribution A graphic display of the scores on two measures at once. The presence of a correlation can usually be determined by inspecting a joint-frequency distribution.

learning activity packages A self-instructional teaching unit which provides for pretests, goal statements, instructional procedures, productive activities, posttests and progress guides.

level measure Level measures place students on a grade- or age-level continuum. They do not show how much students learned this year, but how much in all of their years. Only gain measures can cleanly reflect the effects of instruction.

linear-additive set A term used in defining skills for testing. With a linear-additive set, each member must be explicitly taught. Therefore, it is necessary to list each member in the set to define the set.

logical validity See *content validity*.

mean (M) The sum of the scores divided by the number of scores.

$$M = \frac{Sum\ X}{N}$$

median The middle score in a distribution. The 50th percentile. Half of the scores fall below and half above the median.

middle difficulty level In test construction theory, it is the point midway between a chance level of performance and a performance where every one gets the item right. If there are four response options, the chance level is 25 percent right and a perfect performance is 100 percent right. The middle difficulty level is 62.5 percent.

mode The score in a distribution which occurs most frequently.

multiple-baseline design A design where baselines are taken on two or more behaviors, for the same subject, or on two or more subjects for the same behavior. Then the experimental treatment is introduced at different points in time for the different behaviors or the different subjects. This procedure allows for a control of factors that might produce changes with time other than the treatment variable.

norm population The group from which a sample is taken in constructing norms for a test, such as all second graders in the United States.

norm-referenced design A program evaluation design which uses the improvement on norm-group based scores as the measure of program effectiveness. For example, a group might score at the 16th percentile on pretest and the 50th percentile on posttest. This improvement amounts to a full standard deviation and would be considered important.

norm-referenced test A test on which performance is compared to the scores received by some comparison group called the norm group. A given person's score is defined by its location in the frequency distribution of scores obtained by the norm group.

normal distribution A bell-shaped symmetrical distribution which is useful in interpreting standard scores. Nearly all scores in a normal distribution fall within plus or minus three standard deviations.

not-common objectives Objectives that two instructional programs do not have in common. These are objectives taught by only some of the programs being compared.

objectives Objectives define the goals of instruction. An objective defines a class of behaviors any one of which the student should be able to perform after instruction.

objectives-based test A criterion-referenced test that is built to measure a set of behavioral objectives without giving consideration to how the objectives will be taught.

one-tailed test In testing for statistical significance between two means, a one-tailed test gives the probability of getting a difference in a predicted direction.

outcome evaluation Procedures to evaluate the end result of an instructional program (by term, by year, etc.).

outcome measures In evaluating educational programs, outcome measures may consist of norm-referenced tests, criterion-referenced tests, measures of attitude, and/or program acceptance.

parallel-form reliability A method of estimating reliability by correlating the scores (on the same persons) from two parallel forms of the same test.

Pearson correlation coefficient (r) The most commonly used coefficient of correlation developed by Karl Pearson. Given two measures in z-score form, r is equal to the average of the z-score products of the two scores for each person.

percent agreement index A method for determining the response consistency (reliability) produced by different items on a criterion-referenced test scored pass (+) or fail (−). The agreements in pattern for individuals (++ and −−) are divided by the agreements plus disagreements (N). The agreement indexes for pairs of items can then be averaged to obtain an overall measure of consistency.

percent right score The number of items a person gets right, divided by the total number of items on the test.

percentile rank (percentile, centile) A point in a distribution below which fall the percent of cases specified by the rank. If a score has a percentile rank of 90, it means that 90 percent of the scores in the distribution fall below that score.

phenotype A visable characteristic that is the function of both heredity and environment.

population A total group as opposed to some part of it or a sample from it.

precision teaching An approach to individualizing instruction based on defining student performances and gaining progress measures of these performances on a regular basis. The measures of progress are usually graphed to show the progress visually.

predictable variance (common variance) In interpreting a correlation, the square of the correlation coefficient (r) gives the proportion of one variable which can be predicted from the other. It is the variance common to the two measures.

prediction line On a scatter diagram relating X and Y, the prediction line for predicitng Y from X is determined by fitting a line to the mean Y values for any X value.

premeasures In evaluating educational programs, premeasures are needed for norm-referenced comparisons, when non-random assignment is used in forming groups, and for individual-subject designs (baseline). Premeasures are taken to allow a judgment of initial group equivalence, to adjust outcomes for initial differences, and/or to evaluate student gains as a function of a program.

process evaluation Procedures to evaluate the key steps of progress within an instructional program to insure effective instruction or correction of procedures before it is too late.

process measures In evaluating instruction, process measures can provide data on the degree to which an experimental program is being implemented. This can be useful information in evaluating the meaning of outcome measures.

progress units Any measure that can readily show student progress through an instructional program, such as pages read, units completed, lessons mastered.

random assignment A procedure for assigning individuals to experimental and control groups such that each person has an equal probability of being assigned to each group.

random sample Any sample selected from a population in such a way that each member of the population has an equal chance of being included in the sample.

range The difference between the highest and lowest score on a test obtained by some group.

rank The position of persons in a group based on their test scores going from high to low. The top score is assigned rank 1, the next, 2, etc. When several persons have the same score, they each are given the average of the ranks for the positions involved.

raw score The first summary score on a test, usually the number of correct responses.

reliability The degree to which a test is consistent in measuring whatever it measures. This is shown by the consistency in results produced by parts of a test, *or* by the consistency of result produced by different forms of the same test, or by the consistency of result produced by using the same test at different points in time.

reliability of a gain score The reliability of a gain score can be expressed as a function of the reliability of the pretest (X) posttest (Y) and the correlation between them (r_{XY}).

$$\text{Rel. } Y - X = \frac{r_{XX} + r_{YY} - 2r_{XY}}{2(1 - r_{XY})}$$

representative sample A sample that matches the population being sampled on important variables for the purposes under study. In norming achievement tests, samples may be representative in terms of number of students from each region, from urban and rural areas, from socioeconomic classes, etc.

response consistency See *percent agreement index.*

response requirements Any learning task must require some form of student response. The response requirements taught in a program must be considered in building a test of instruction.

reversal design An individual-subjects design where a baseline condition (A) is followed by a treatment condition (B) and then a return to the baseline condition (A).

sample See *random sample.*

scatter diagram See *joint frequency distribution.*

sensitivity to instruction Test items are sensitive to instruction when they are failed prior to the instruction and passed after the instruction.

significant difference Any difference that can be attributed to factors other than chance variations.

split-half reliability A reliability estimate obtained by correlating scores based on odd-numbered items with even-number items and correcting for the length of the test.

standard deviation (SD) A measure of the spread of scores in a distribution from the mean.

$$SD = \sqrt{\frac{\text{Sum } (X - M_X)^2}{N}}$$

standard error of measurement (SD_E) An estimate of the standard deviation of the measurement errors on a test.

$$SD_E = SD_X \sqrt{1 - r_{XX}}$$

If a student's score is 45 and the standard error of measurement is 3, we would expect his score to fall between 39 and 51 about 95 percent of the time.

standard error of the difference between means

$$= \sqrt{\frac{SD_e{}^2}{Ne} + \frac{SD_c{}^2}{Nc}}$$

where e is one group and c another.

standard score (SS) A score expressed as the number of standard deviations it falls above or below the mean. z is the most common standard score and equals

$$\frac{X - M_X}{SD_X}$$

See also *transformed standard scores.*

stanines Standard scores with a mean of 5 and a standard deviation of 2 which can take on only the unit values from 1 to 9.

statistical regression If a group is selected for extreme scores on a test (e.g., IQ's under 80), on retest their average scores will be closer to the test mean (for IQ, the mean is 100). This regression toward the mean occurs because of a biased effect of measurement errors produced by the selection of extreme scores. For example, the below 80 IQ group would include persons whose true scores were abovoe 80 but scored below 80 by chance, and exclude those persons whose true scores were below 80, but scored above 80 by chance.

statistical significance A statistic is said to be significant when the probability that the result is not due to chance factors exceeds a specified level. At the .05 level, the result would occur by chance less than 5 times in 100. At the .01 level, the result would occur by chance less than 1 time in 100.

subskills These are skills which are taught in a program and then consolidated into other more complex skills.

T-scores A transformed standard score with a mean of 50 and a standard deviation of 10.

t-test A test for the significance of the difference between two means used with small samples (N less than 30).

terminal skills These are the skills the student is expected to perform at the end of a given program.

test-retest reliability A reliability estimate based on giving the same test at two different times to the same persons.

tracks In building instructional-program-based tests, tracks may be defined by a set of skills taught with a common format (e.g., sounds), or by a sequence of skills using different formats but building to a more complex terminal objective (e.g., addition).

transofrmed-standard score Most norm-referenced tests use transformed-standard scores rather than z-scores to eliminate negatives and decimals. A desired mean and standard deviation are selected and the transformed scores equal $(z \cdot SD) + M$. An IQ test uses a mean of 100 and a standard deviation of 15.

true score A theoretical score entirely free of errors of measurement. Also defined as the mean that would be obtained from a large series of measurements of the same thing assuming only random errors.

true-score variance The variance component in a set of obtained scores not due to errors of measurement. An obtained test variance can be divided into true-score variance and error variance.

two-tailed test In testing for statistical significance between two means, the two-tailed test gives the probability of getting a difference favoring either mean. A one-tailed test gives the probability of getting a difference in a predicted direction.

validity The degree to which a test measures what it purports to measure. For achievement tests this is usually based on an evaluation of the content of the test.

validity index For criterion-referenced tests, the gain in the percent passing items after instruction over the percent passing the same items before instruction (sensitivity to instruction). For norm-referenced tests, validity indexes are based on the correlation of an item with some criterion.

variance (SD²) The variance of a distribution is the square of the standard deviation. Variances can be added while standard deviation cannot. This property makes them useful in test construction theory.

z-score

$$z = \frac{X - M_X}{SD_X}$$

author index

Alkin, M. C., 4, 64
Anderson, J. E., 297, 300
Anderson, R. C., 268

Baker, R. L., 6
Bateman, B. D., 261, 264, 265, 266, 268
Bayley, N., 296
Becker, J., 129
Becker, W. C., 41, 66, 92, 110, 129, 268, 299
Bianchini, J. C., 185
Bishop, C. H., 263
Bliesmer, E. P., 267, 283, 284
Bloom, B. S., 4
Bolvin, J., 6
Bruner, E., 7, 42
Burket, G. R., 64
Buros, O., 156, 164, 225
Bushell, D., Jr., 82, 89, 90, 91

Campbell, D. T., 244
Carnine, L., 66, 129
Cass, C. E., 261
Cavelli-Sforza, L. L., 296
Chall, J., 268
Cronback, L. J., 224, 225, 226, 280, 300–1, 302, 303

Darwin, C., 295

Ebel, R. L., 268
Eichelberger, R. T., 93, 94
Engelmann, S., 7, 41, 42, 50, 66, 110, 127, 128, 296

Falender, D., 296
Flanagan, J. C., 4
Flavell, J., 300
Freeberg, N. E., 64, 232

Gage, N. L., 64, 232
Galton, F., 295
Garber, H., 296
Gessel, J., 4, 155
Gibson, E. J., 264
Gilmore, E. C., 154
Gilmore, J. V., 154
Glaser, R., 2, 6, 133
Glass, G. V., 64, 232
Green, D. R., 64, 297, 299
Gulliksen, H., 223, 226, 300

Hall, G. S., 295
Hanner, S., 50, 128, 129
Harrington, S., 296
Harris, C. W., 4, 64
Heber, R., 296
Hess, R. D., 296
Hoffman, C., 296
Hofmeister, A. M., 94–95, 124, 127, 165
Horst, D. P., 275–76, 277, 281, 282
Horton, G., 280
Humphreys, L. G., 297
Hungerman, A. D., 286

Hunt, J. McV., 295, 296

Jensen, A. R., 295, 300
Johnson, G., 129
Jones, R., 183

Keller, F. S., 83
Kelley, T. L., 295, 297
Krumboltz, J. D., 296
Kunzelmann, H. P., 84

Lindsey, R., 84
Lindvall, C. M., 6
Loret, P. G., 185

Mabry, J., 268
Mager, R. F., 4
Meyers, L., 129, 302
Moely, B. E., 300
Morrison, H. C., 83

Nitko, A. J., 6

O'Leary, K. D., 268
O'Leary, S. G., 268
Odom, R. D., 300
Olson, G., 300

Parker, R. K., 268
Payne, E., 64, 232
Popham, W. J., 4, 6, 7, 64, 153
Ramp, G., 89
Resnick, L., 93
Rohwer, W. D., Jr., 300

Seder, A., 185
Shanner, W. M., 4
Shepler, W., 93
Shimota, H. E., 262
Shipman, V. C., 296
Sidman, M., 247
Sloane, H., 243
Smith, J. E., 83
Stachnik, T., 268
Stake, R. E., 232
Stanley, J. C., 244
Stevenson, H. W., 300
Strodtbeck, F. L., 296

Talbert, R. L., 83
Tallmadge, G. K., 275–76, 277, 281, 282
Terman, L., 295
Thomas, D. R., 41

Ulrich, R., 268

Vale, C. A., 185

Wilson, H. A., 4, 64
Wolfe, A. B., 83
Wood, C. T., 275–76, 277, 281, 282
Woodrow, H., 300

Yarborough, B. H., 267, 283, 284

subject index

Achievement and intelligence, 297–303
Achievement Series. *See* SRA Achievement Series
Age-equivalent scores, 182–83
Alpha reliability coefficient, 224
Alternative explanations (in research), 244–45
Anchor Test Study, 275–76
Attitudes, measure of, 279

Behavior Analysis, Follow Through Model, 82, 89–92
Behavioral objectives, 3–6
Biserial correlation, 213, 230
Bootstrap approach, 133–34

California Achievement Tests, 156, 157, 159, 186–89, 275
CAT. *See* California Achievement Tests
Ceiling effects, 278, 281
Checkout procedures, 81
Common objectives, 123–26, 128, 166, 277–78
Comparison standard, 18
Comparisons of programs. *See* Common objectives
Confidence interval, 224–25
Construct validity, 226, 228
Content validity, 63–64, 226–27, 277
Control groups, 245–47, 249, 250, 273
Correlation, 201–13
Correlational research, 243–44
Criterion-referenced tests, 2–11, 18, 28, 40–50, 279
Criterion validity, 226–28
Critical ratio, 251–53
Cumulative programming, 48–49

Descriptive research, 243
Diagnostic Mathematics Inventory, 155
Diagnostic testing, 66–67, 153–55, 164–65
Direct Instruction Follow Through Model, 9, 110–18
Directions, 5, 45, 50, 64, 126
DISTAR, 6, 7, 8, 41, 42–45, 47, 49, 66, 110, 165, 277
Durrell Listening-Reading Series, 154

Educational significance of a difference, 253
Engelmann-Becker Follow Through Model. *See* Direct Instruction Follow Through Model
Error, 58, 223
Error variance, 223
Expanded standard scores, 179–80, 190–91, 225
Experimental designs, 244–50
Experimental research, 244–54

Four-fold point correlation, 213
Frequency distributions, 19, 20, 175

Gain measures, 282, 297–99
General-case set, 6, 41–42, 48, 58–60
Genetics and intelligence, 295–96
Gilmore Oral Reading Test, 154–55
Grade-equivalent scores, 182–83, 186
Gray Oral Reading Test, 154
Group designs, 244–47, 250

Individual-subject designs, 244, 247–48, 253
Individually Prescribed Instruction (IPI), 6–7, 93
Instructional-program based tests, 6–11, 40–50
Instructions. *See* Directions
Internal consistency, 224
Item analysis, 153, 229–32
Item clusters, 128
Item difficulty, 229
Item reliability, 230, 232

Joint-frequency distributions, 203–5

Kuder-Richardson formula, 20, 224

Learning activity packages, 83–84
Linear-additive set, 41–42, 48, 58, 62, 126, 232

MAT. *See* Metropolitan Achievement Test
Mean, 19, 20–21
Median, 30
Mental Measurement Yearbook, 156, 225
Metropolitan Achievement Test, 156, 157, 160, 179–80, 190–91, 225–26, 275
Middle difficulty level, 229
Mode, 29–30
Monitoring student progress, 79–95, 111–18
Multiple-baseline designs, 248
Multiple control groups, 249

Norm population, 183–85
Norm-referenced designs, 166, 247, 273, 277
Norm-referenced tests, 2–3, 28, 152–67, 277
   construction of, 153
   types of, 153–64
   uses of, 164–67
Norm tables, 185–91
Normal curve. *See* Normal distribution
Normal distribution, 174–76
Norms for criterion-referenced tests, 133–34
Not-common objectives, 126–27

Objective-based tests, 4–6, 10
Objectives, 58, 153
One-tailed tests, 252
Outcome evaluations, 123–34, 272–87
   analysis of data, 281–82
Outcome measures, 277–80

Parallel-form reliability, 224
Pearson correlation coefficient (r), 209–13
Percent agreement index, 59–62
Percent right scores, 19, 27
Percentile ranks (percentiles, centiles), 181–82, 186, 188–90
Pittsburg LRDC Follow Through Model, 93–94
Placement testing, 80, 111–12, 165–66
Precision teaching, 84–89
Prediction line, 208–9
Premeasures, 273, 276–77

Teaching 3 is set in ten-point Palatino,
a typeface designed in 1950 by Hermann Zapf.
Typesetting is by Chapman's Phototypesetting, Fullerton, California,
and printing by The Segerdahl Corp., Wheeling, Illinois.

Sponsoring Editor: Michael Zamczyk
Project Editor: Carol Harris
Designer: Paula Tuerk

6789/4321